Pro iOS5 Tools

Xcode Instruments and Build Tools

Brandon Alexander
Brad Dillion
Kevin Y. Kim

Apress®

Pro iOS5 Tools: Xcode Instruments and Build Tools

ISBN-13 (pbk): 978-1-4302-3608-5

ISBN-13 (electronic): 978-1-4302-3609-2

Trademarked names, logos, and images may appear in this book. Rather than use a trademark symbol with every occurrence of a trademarked name, logo, or image we use the names, logos, and images only in an editorial fashion and to the benefit of the trademark owner, with no intention of infringement of the trademark.

The use in this publication of trade names, trademarks, service marks, and similar terms, even if they are not identified as such, is not to be taken as an expression of opinion as to whether or not they are subject to proprietary rights.

President and Publisher: Paul Manning
Lead Editor: Steve Anglin and Michelle Lowman
Technical Reviewer: Anselm Bradford
Editorial Board: Steve Anglin, Mark Beckner, Ewan Buckingham, Gary Cornell, Morgan Ertel, Jonathan Gennick, Jonathan Hassell, Robert Hutchinson, Michelle Lowman, James Markham, Matthew Moodie, Jeff Olson, Jeffrey Pepper, Douglas Pundick, Ben Renow-Clarke, Dominic Shakeshaft, Gwenan Spearing, Matt Wade, Tom Welsh
Coordinating Editor: Anita Castro
Copy Editor: Heather Lang and Mary Behr
Compositor: MacPS, LLC
Indexer: SPI Global
Artist: SPI Global
Cover Designer: Anna Ishchenko

Distributed to the book trade worldwide by Springer Science+Business Media, LLC., 233 Spring Street, 6th Floor, New York, NY 10013. Phone 1-800-SPRINGER, fax (201) 348-4505, e-mail orders-ny@springer-sbm.com, or visit www.springeronline.com.

For information on translations, please e-mail rights@apress.com, or visit www.apress.com.

Apress and friends of ED books may be purchased in bulk for academic, corporate, or promotional use. eBook versions and licenses are also available for most titles. For more information, reference our Special Bulk Sales–eBook Licensing web page at www.apress.com/bulk-sales.

The information in this book is distributed on an "as is" basis, without warranty. Although every precaution has been taken in the preparation of this work, neither the author(s) nor Apress shall have any liability to any person or entity with respect to any loss or damage caused or alleged to be caused directly or indirectly by the information contained in this work.

Any source code or other supplementary materials referenced by the author in this text is available to readers at www.apress.com. For detailed information about how to locate your book's source code, go to http://www.apress.com/source-code/.

Contents at a Glance

Contents

About the Authors

 **Brandon Alexander** is an iOS developer, writer and conference speaker living in Decatur, Georgia with his wife and daughter. Brandon began iOS development in 2008 and has spoken at several conferences. As a developer, Brandon enjoys making technology transparent to users and elegantly useful; as a speaker and writer, he loves teaching others about technology so that they can do the same. When he's not coding, writing or speaking at conferences, Brandon enjoys magic and photography. He can be found on twitter at @whilethis and via email at brandon.alexander@gmail.com.

 Coming from an autodidactic background, **Brad Dillon** taught himself the technologies of his trade, working his way through web development, animation, and other desktop-based interactive platforms, finally finding his home in touchscreen interface development. Since the iPhone SDK launched, Brad has been building apps for iOS devices full time. With a passion for user experience and a deep understanding of the technologies at play, Brad has helped to build solutions that bridge the gap between the devices, users, and global brands. He can be found online at http://jbradforddillon.com, and followed on Twitter at @jbradforddillon.

 **Kevin Y. Kim** is a founder and partner of AppOrchard LLC, a Tipping Point Partners company focused on sustainable iOS development. A graduate of Carnegie Mellon University, he was first exposed to the NeXTStep computer (the ancestor of today's iPhone) while a programmer at the Pittsburgh Supercomputing Center and has been hooked ever since. His career has spanned finance, government, biotech and technology, including Apple where he managed the Apple Enterprise Services team for the New York metro area. He resides in the Alphabet City section of New York City with his wife and a clowder of rescued cats.

About the Technical Reviewer

 **Anselm Bradford** is a lecturer in digital media at the Auckland University of Technology (AUT) in New Zealand, where he researches interactive media, web media, and visual communication. His experience with Internet-related development stretches back to 1996, when he hand-coded his first web site. He may be found @anselmbradford on Twitter and occasionally blogs at AnselmBradford.com.

Acknowledgments

They say writing a book is a lot of work. This book wasn't any different. Documentation was read and many dead ends were found when looking for the best way to do something. But the end product is something we are all proud of. This book isn't just the product of the three of us; there were many people involved.

The first person I want to thank is Steve Anglin who approached me at 360|iDev and simply asked me if I wanted to write a book. Without knowing how much effort was involved, I reached out to Dave Mark who gave me some sound advice and introduced me to Scott Penberthy who wrote the GDB section and authored our back end.

The next person who deserves a great deal of credit is Anita Castro. Anita kept us in line and pushed us to get all the needed components done and as close to the schedule as possible.

The next set of thank yous goes to our wonderful editors: Ralph Moore, who made sure the text made plenty of sense from a developer's perspective, Anselm Bradford, who followed all of the instructions in the book and made sure everything worked as we explained them, Heather Lang and Mary Behr who helped us all look like great authors, Christine Ricketts who was responsible for the final pieces and production on this book. Without these people, this book would still exist in some files sitting on a server somewhere.

I also want to thank my coauthors, Brad and Kevin. They really stepped up when I was in a pinch and needed help getting this book over the final hump to get it to completion. I know they sacrificed a great deal during the process. Writing a book on a set of tools while they are in beta is not an easy task, so thank you guys!

I also want to thank my wife, Erin, who endured through many hours of me in my office working on this project while waiting on our wonderful daughter, Sage, to enter the world. She kept me focused when I was having writer's block. And I want to thank my wonderful daughter Sage for giving me the motivation to see this project to completion. I couldn't have finished this without the two of you!

Brandon Alexander

Thanks to all of the misfits who publish ideas and share experiences, be it in 140 characters, or hundreds of pages. Thanks to my parents, for teaching me how to teach myself. Most of all, thank you to my wife Jennifer for always supporting me and my work, however geeky she may find it, and to our kids Nevaeh and Jack, for keeping the hours between code sprints both fun and challenging.

J. Bradford Dillon

Thanks to my friends and colleagues at AppOrchard for their patience through the last several months of curmudgeonly behavior and for helping me make this project successful. Thanks to my wife, Annie, for making sure I worked on this book when I would have rather been watching baseball. Thanks to my cats, PK, Manny, Leela and Kit-en, for always walking across the keyboard when I needed a break. KTHXBAI.

Kevin Y. Kim

Introduction

The iOS platform has exploded in popularity over the past few years and is showing no signs of slowing down. The app marketplace has become highly competitive and the users are becoming accustomed to great experiences. This makes our jobs as app developers very difficult. What sets a great application apart from other applications? We're going to attempt to answer that question through the course of this book.

Why Write a Book on Tools?

They say, "An artisan is only as good as his/her tools." This is generally true for most professions. As developers, we usually only need a text editor and a compiler. While that setup can get the job done, a great set of tools starting with the IDE (Integrated Development Environment) and moving to performance analysis and debugging tools can greatly improve a developer's efficiency during the development and debugging process. The main problem a developer faces, especially with new versions of these tools being released, is how does one effectively use these tools? This is the space where this book fits. This book is all about using the amazing developer tools that Apple has provided and how to use them to make our apps great.

How This Book Is Organized

This book is all about process. As you'll read in Chapter 1, no matter what stage you are in, this book will help you on your journey to being a better developer. The first few chapters of this book are all about debugging and performance tuning. We're going to take a project from a state that needs a lot of work to ready for beta testing. Then we take a look at how to improve our efficiency as developers and let the tools do most of our work for us. We will even automate a lot of the process to let us focus on more important issues. The final part of the book is how to share our application with testers, respond to feedback and finally start sharing code between our applications. The last chapter is all about navigating and customizing Xcode to fit our own workflow.

Support and Contributions

If you run into any issues or find a great tip to help those reading this book, head over to http://proiostools.com/forum/ and participate in the discussion! The goal here is to get a great community going that will intersect with the great iOS development community that already exists. We're here to help and would love to see what kind of tips and tricks you discover while going through the book.

Chapter 1

Wax On, Wax Off

By now, you have written an iOS application or two. You have also learned that making a great app is hard work. From spontaneous crashes to memory leaks and bugs that create other bugs, the simplest of apps can quickly become a nightmare. Fortunately, these issues are easy to diagnose with the tools at our disposal.

That is what this book is mostly about. We have a toolbox available to us as iOS developers. Ultimately, the question quickly becomes: Which tool is best for the task at hand? This book will answer that question for most of your cases. For the cases where there is no obvious answer, you will be equipped with some approaches and techniques that will point you in the right direction.

Who Is This Book For?

In most crafts, the transition from being a complete beginner to being capable is usually swift. The goal during this transition is simply to become functional with the tools and understand the language the craftsmen speak. This transition also builds confidence in the new practitioner. At the end of this transition, practitioners are fully capable of accomplishing most tasks and solving most problems thrown at them.

Most stop at proficient, however. As a magician, I progressed from a newcomer to the art to a proficient amateur relatively quickly. As I learned a new technique or a new effect, I was very excited to practice. As my skill improved, that desire to practice lessened, and I even became bored with rehearsing the same effect or technique over and over. My skill had reached a plateau. I know what I must do to get to the next level, but I don't want to go there right now. That is OK with me.

How is this relevant to software development? First, like any craft, a certain set of programming skills is rapidly acquired, including learning the syntax of a language, understanding flow control, using basic software design patterns, and debugging by writing to standard out and basic use of the provided debugger. The next phase of a developer's path to mastery is learning more about how a language and platform work, more design patterns and their appropriate uses, and more about the debugger. The final, never-ending, phase is simply fine-tuning all of these skills and finding better solutions to existing problems, as well as learning how to reuse code more. This learning path is not the same for every developer. Sometimes, different parts of development are easier to grasp than others.

The point here is that I don't want you to get frustrated when you don't progress as fast as you'd like. Software development is hard. The thing that separates a hobbyist from a professional is the level of commitment. The commitment to go from a proficient hobbyist to a professional generally takes you into career mode. This level of dedication takes more than just hours of practice. You have to start looking at how other software is made. Surrounding yourself with others that develop for the same platform, especially those who are better than you, is key to growing. By purchasing this book, you are also acknowledging that you want to be a better developer. My goal is to help you learn at least one new skill. If you do that, my job is done, and if you do more, even better!

So who is this book for? This book is for those who are ready to reach the next level. Whatever skill level you are at, this book has something for you. Perhaps you are a master at object-oriented programming, and performance tuning is something you want to learn. Or maybe you want to know the best way to create a universal application for iOS without rewriting half your application. The only prerequisite is that you have some exposure to iOS development and Objective-C.

What This Book Is

This book is a guide that will take you from an alpha quality application to a feature-complete and tested application ready for submission to the App Store. This book contains many tricks of the trade, from diagnosing memory issues to tweaking scroll views to squeeze the last bit of performance out of the device. In the end, you'll want to have this book on your desk with pages marked for quick reference on how to solve common problems.

Will this book solve all of your problems? Probably not, but you will walk away with some techniques for solving problems in a very systematic way. Deep down, we're scientists, and following the scientific method for solving problems in software will, in the end, help us learn how to prevent the problem next time.

This book also follows a realistic software life cycle. We'll pick up a project at the end of development, and we'll take it through beta testing and finish with a shippable product. We'll hit some common roadblocks and look at how iOS works; we'll even work around some interesting issues. We'll also find some useful libraries written by people who cared enough to share their solutions to particular problems.

What You Need to Get Started

To get the most out of this book, you'll need a paid developer account in the iOS Dev Center. This will give you the ability to test on an iOS device as well as run the performance tools against the iOS device. We will do several things on the device itself, and your best bet is to go ahead and sign up for the paid developer account if you don't have one already. At the time of this writing, the cost is $99 USD for a one-year subscription to the iOS developer program.

If creating an account is not an option for you, you can download Xcode 4 from the Mac App Store. This will give you the Xcode IDE as well as Instruments. You'll have the ability to develop and debug your applications in the iOS Simulator, and you can run some of the performance tools against that simulator. However, you won't be able to do some of the debugging and performance testing that we'll cover later on in this book.

To get set up with the iOS Dev Center, go to http://developer.apple.com/ios/. Figure 1–1 shows what the home page looks like. Click the Register link at the top to get started. If you want to deploy your applications to iOS devices, this is your best bet. If you are an enterprise developer, check out the enterprise developer program.

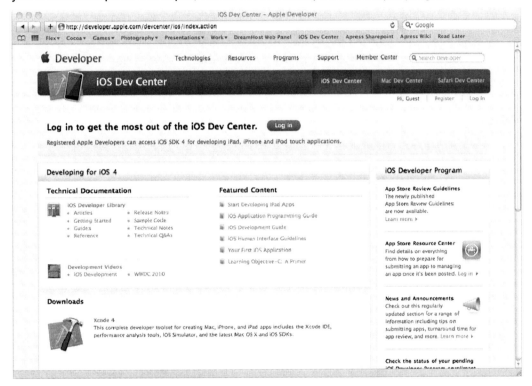

Figure 1–1. *The iOS Dev Center home page*

After you download and install the latest development tools, fire up Xcode, and take a look around. If you are used to Xcode 3, you'll notice Xcode 4 looks completely different. Don't worry; we'll step through the features as we make it through the chapters in this book. If you're new to the platform, say hello to Xcode. I'm sure you'll be friends in no time (don't worry; friends have fights from time to time). Either way, we're in for quite the journey as you learn how to get the most out of the toolbox Apple provides, as well as some great third-party tools.

What's in This Book

This book follows one single project. We're going to pick up this project from an initial alpha state and prepare it for beta testing. Then, we'll walk through the beta testing phase and get some useful feedback from the testers in the form of bug reports and feature requests. You'll learn how to optimize your workflow with automation and migrate to a universal application. The final part is figuring out a great way to share some code with the developer community and finally talk about getting the most out of Xcode 4 and some other useful tools.

Here is a quick overview of each chapter:

- *Chapter 2, First Class Tools (Xcode, Interface Builder and Instruments)*: In this chapter, you'll meet Xcode 4, and the other tools included with the developer tools package for iOS development. Here, we'll talk about new layout of Xcode and what the integration of Interface Builder gives us. We'll also open Instruments, and you'll get acquainted with a tool we'll be using for some of our performance testing and debugging.

- *Chapter 3, Three Screens and. . .Well, It Runs*: Here, we'll dive right into checking out an existing project and take a look at how to use Git and GitHub directly from Xcode. We'll also walk through the first build of our project for this book: Super Checkout.

- *Chapter 4, Memory Management and Diagnostics*: In this chapter, we'll diagnose and solve the number one reason for application crashes. We'll talk about memory management in Objective-C and some best practices. We'll also dive into our first use of Instruments to help diagnose some of these pesky memory issues.

- *Chapter 5, Core Animation and Smooth Scrolling*: Now that we've fixed the memory issues, we'll dive into tuning Core Animation and make our tables scroll like butter. You'll learn your second instrument and some interesting quirks about the rendering model on iOS.

- *Chapter 6, Networking, Cache, and Power Management*: In this chapter, you'll learn all about networking and how the built-in iOS networking APIs work. We'll take a look at a popular networking library and replace the existing networking layer to enhance the application. We'll also talk about caches; we'll explore some caching techniques and why caching might or might not be a good idea. The final part of this chapter will be all about power management. You'll learn about the different radios on an iOS device and how they affect battery drain and how to detect problems.

- *Chapter 7, Prepare the Beta!*: Now that we've addressed some of the big problems in Super Checkout, we'll prepare the application for beta testing. We'll take a look at some beta distribution techniques and some ideas for managing beta testing.

- *Chapter 8, Why are things Breaking?*: We're getting bug reports, the server API changes and all sorts of things are going wrong. In this chapter, we'll take a look at a way to break down our application into testable components to reduce the number of bugs in our code. You'll also learn how to have Instruments automatically drive the application and report any errors. We'll end with a suite of tests to ensure our application is stable and stays that way if we need to make changes.

- *Chapter 9, Can we Automate Some of This?*: We're one step away from a fully automated build system that runs our tests for each new push to source control. We'll meet our trusty build management tool of choice and how to push new builds out to testers automatically.

- *Chapter 10, Now They Want an iPad Version*: Now that feature requests are slowing down, we find that we need an iPad-compatible version of Super Checkout. In this chapter, you'll learn how to migrate Super Checkout to a universal binary and the different techniques for sharing code among the different sizes of iOS devices.

- *Chapter 11, How do I Share Some of This?*: Our application is ready to ship, but we've created some great stuff that we want to break out into a static library so we can share the code among multiple projects and even with the development community as a whole. We'll take a look at how to share the code on GitHub and have a brief discussion over open source licenses.

- *Chapter 12, One More Thing*: By now, we've taken an application from being crash prone and buggy to being something that is ready to ship. Here, we'll look at some other pieces of Xcode and how to speed up our workflow. We'll also look at some great third-party tools that will speed up development and reduce the amount of boilerplate code you have to write.

Here We Go!

Are you ready to get started? Good! A quick note before you turn the page and dive into the project. We're going to cover a lot of information. Trying to take in all of this information in one sitting is probably not a good idea. Take it one chapter at a time, and repeat sections as necessary. Trust me; some of these topics had to be revisited several times before they were put down in this book.

If you get stuck or find yourself getting sleepy, step away for a moment or even grab some shut-eye. This will help you clear your head, and your brain will work on the material while you are doing other things. You'll come back, something will click, and you'll notice that you understand the topic better. Learning is an active process, and as Aaron Hillegass says in *Cocoa Programming for Mac OS X*, "Caffeine is not a substitute for sleep."

Now, fire up Xcode 4, open your notebook, and turn the page to get started. We're going to have some fun.

Chapter 2

First-Class Tools

Xcode has undergone another major revision. This time around, Xcode has one giant window with tabs. A ton of new features with this release make the developer's job easier. Some of these new features include

- A single, unified window that brings everything together.

- The Jump Bar brings quicker navigation through a project as well as a single source file without taking up too much space.

- Interface Builder is fully integrated into Xcode allowing for even tighter integration between the nib and source.

- The Xcode Assistant is a two-pane editor that, when enabled, will pick an appropriate file to view next to the editor in which you are editing.

- LLVM 3.0 is fully integrated into the Xcode which means better syntax highlighting, code completion and many other features that LLVM has.

- Fix-it uses some features of LLVM to not only display compile errors but suggest quick fixes.

- Xcode has better integration with some common version control systems: Git and Subversion (SVN).

- A brand new debugger: LLDB is to GDB as LLVM is to GCC.

- Instruments has a new interface featuring a Jump Bar and other features borrowed from the Xcode interface.

With these new features and enhanced workflows, finding your way around when you are used to Xcode 3 can be a tad frustrating. The plan for this chapter is to take a look at some of the new features of Xcode and see where some of the more common features have moved.

Taking a Look Around

Let's start by creating a simple project and putting some of these things into practice. We're not going to be creating anything meaningful yet; the cool stuff will start in the next chapter. We will be taking a look at where some of the more common tasks can be completed in Xcode 4 as well as some of the new user interface enhancements.

To get started, launch Xcode 4. We're going to create a new project, so click the Create a new Xcode project button shown in Figure 2–1.

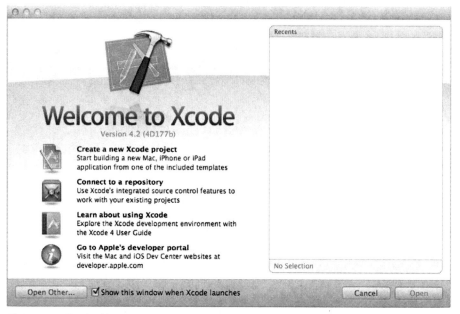

Figure 2–1. *The familiar screen that greets us when we launch Xcode*

For this chapter, we're going to create a Navigation-based Application. Select that option, and click Next. In the next screen, we name our project, declare our company identifier, and select any other project preferences. Go ahead and name the project **Super Hello World**, and fill in the company identifier in reverse DNS form. For this exercise, we will use **com.example**. Also check Use Core Data and Include Unit Tests for this project. Your screen should look similar to the one shown in Figure 2–2.

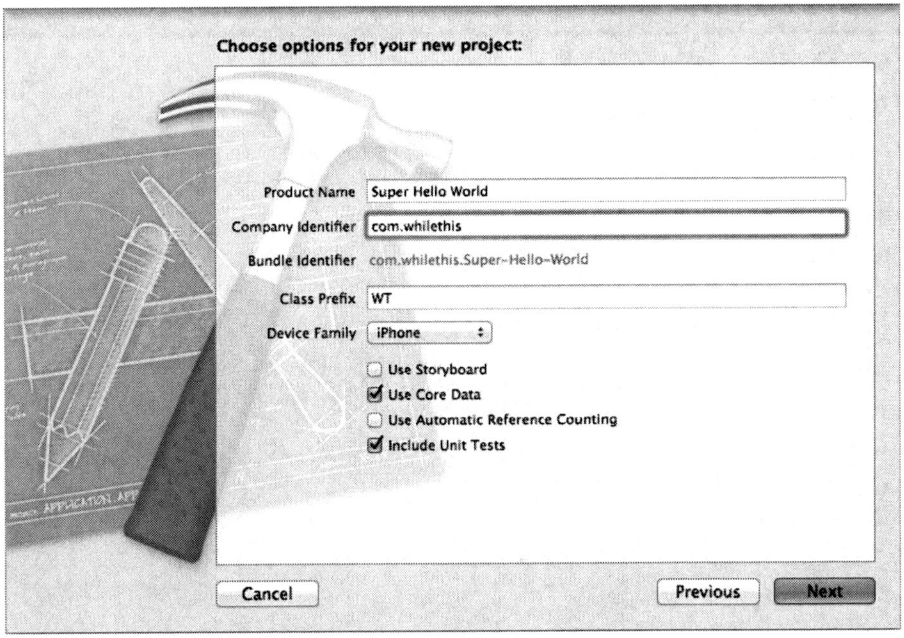

Figure 2–2. *The project naming screen now includes the creation of a unit test target.*

Clicking Next will bring up a sheet asking us where to save the project. Go ahead and choose a location for the project, and select the check box for creating a local Git repository. Clicking Create creates the project and takes you directly into the project settings for Super Hello World.

The first things shown are the project details (see Figure 2–3). The item selected in the middle column is the default target for the project. You will also notice the unit testing target is placed below it. If you want to make any changes to the way the project is compiled and packaged, modify the particular target. If you are used to the way this was done in Xcode 3, you'll notice that modifying targets is now consolidated into this one area; you no longer have to go to the Info pane for modifying the target as you did in Xcode 3.

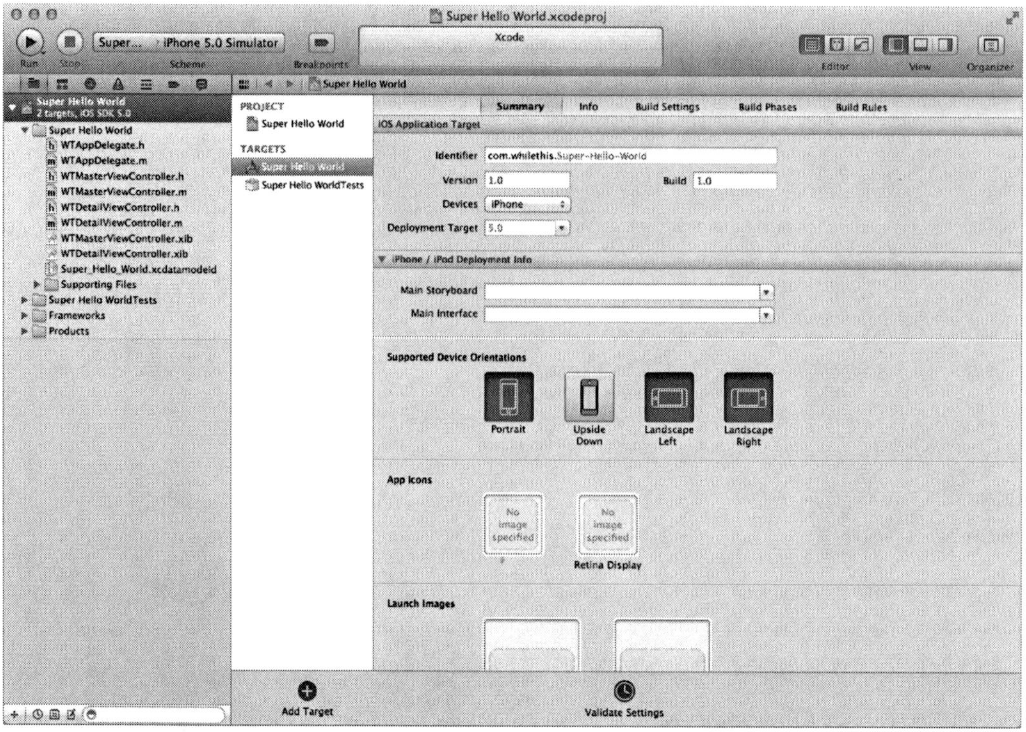

Figure 2–3. *Xcode now had a default editor modifying project metadata and targets.*

Now that our project is created, you can see a somewhat familiar view that you are used to in Xcode 3—except there are some new items there.

Figure 2–4 shows the following main sections of the application:

- On the top, the toolbar
- On the left, the Navigator area
- On the bottom, the Debugger area
- On the right, the Utilities area
- In the middle, the Editor area

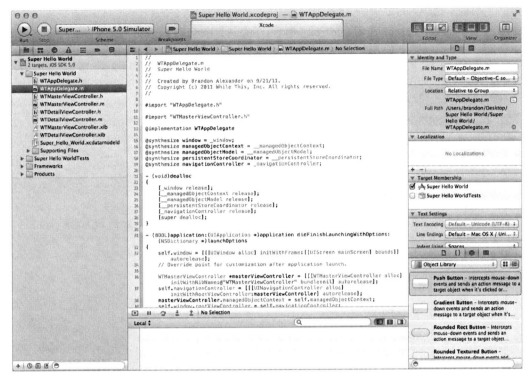

Figure 2–4. *The Xcode workspace window with every pane open*

So Many Panes!

The first thing you probably noticed is how easy it is to lose precious editor space. The good news is we can close all the panes and focus on code alone. Before we get too far ahead of ourselves, shall we take a look at each section of Xcode and see what it brings us?

At the top is the toolbar. In the toolbar, you can select the active deployment target and run your application. You can also select the appropriate editor for you as well as open and close panes. The button on the far right launches the Organizer window that allows you to manage iOS devices and all of your projects.

The pane on the left is the Navigator area. In this pane, you can choose one of many navigators to interact with. The navigators available to you are Project, Symbol, Search, Issue, Debug, Breakpoint, and Log. The Project navigator is the default navigator that allows you to navigate the files within your project. The Symbol navigator shows you the symbols in the project in a hierarchical or flat view. The Search navigator lets you search your project for text and shows the results below. The Issue navigator shows you any compiler errors or warnings in near-real time with the new compiler technologies built into Xcode.

The next two navigators are for debugging. The Debug navigator is only active during a debug session. You can view information based on threads or queues. Viewing by queues lets you see into the different dispatch queues and shows what kind of queue you're looking at. The Breakpoint pane is where you manage the breakpoints in your application. As with Xcode 3, you can create new breakpoints, move them around, disable them, and remove them.

The final navigator is the Log navigator. Any action you perform that is normally recorded will be placed in here, including builds, static analysis, source control operations, and debug sessions.

Editors and the Utilities That Follow Them

The area you'll spend most of your time in will be the Editor area. Xcode has several file editors available for you to access:

- Source code
- Project and build settings
- Property list (plist) files
- Rich text files
- Core data models
- Core data mapping models
- XIB (XML nib) files
- AppleScript
- Scripting dictionary files

There are also file viewers that include graphics, videos, and several other file viewers.

There are also three different types of editors to choose from. You can access these editor types from the toolbar. The Standard Editor is your basic editor that lets you edit files as you would normally. The Assistant Editor (see Figure 2–5) is a new type of editor that lets you edit your source files with an assistant showing you a related file next to it. For example, when you are editing a source file and you select the Assistant Editor, the header file is displayed next to it. If you were to open a nib file, the assistant allows you to view the associated header (from the File's Owner property of the nib) and interact with it. From here, you can actually control-drag elements from the nib into the source editor, and Xcode will place the appropriate property in the code where you put it.

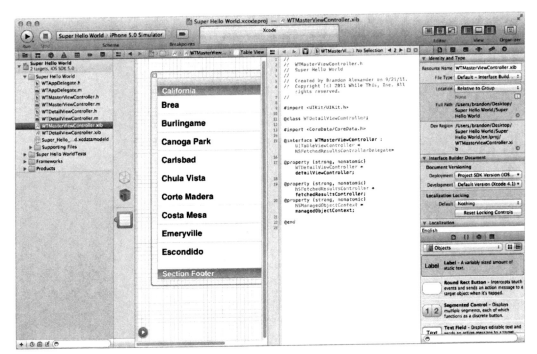

Figure 2–5. *The Assistant Editor shows you a nib with the File's Owner header next to it.*

Some file types will not have any counterparts that you can open with the assistant. If this is the case, you can manually select which editor you want next to the selected file. In order to do this, you'll use the Jump Bar in the Assistant Editor to select the file that is shown. You can edit the location of the assistant editor by going to **View ➤ Assistant Editor** and indicating whether the Assistant editor goes on the right or underneath the Standard Editor.

The other editor option is the Version Editor. This editor will show you the changes you've made to the selected file if you have source control turned on. At the time of this writing, Xcode 4 only supports Git and Subversion for source control. From the Version Editor, you can view the history of the file by clicking the time button at the bottom of the space between the diff viewer. From the same screen, you can also view the blame history as well as a log-annotated view of the file's history (see Figure 2–6).

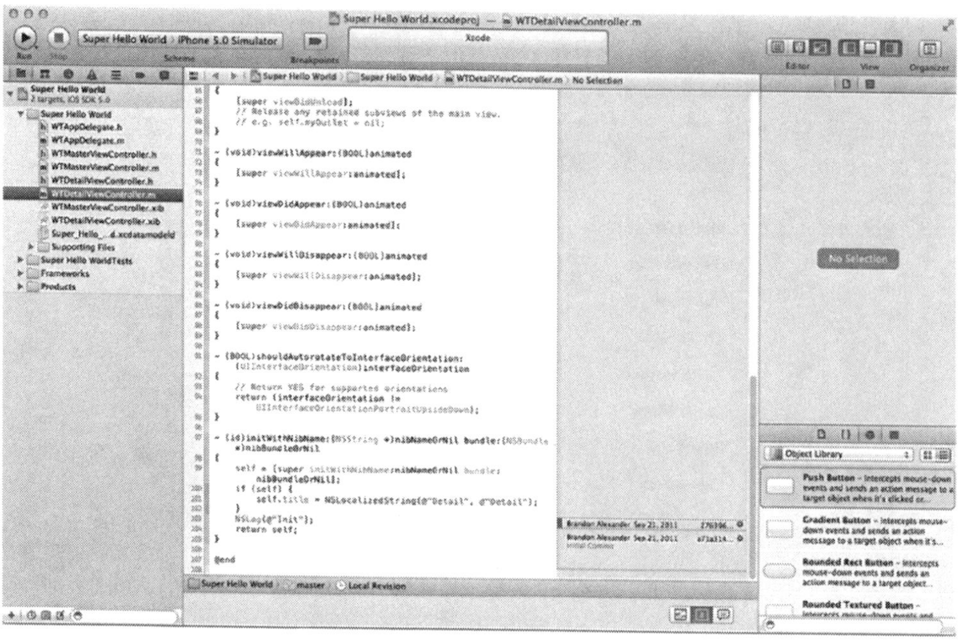

Figure 2–6. *The Version Editor gives you the ability to view the file's history as well as version annotations, affectionately known as the blame view.*

In Figure 2–6, you can also see the Utilities area to the right of the editors. This pane shows contextual information based on your selection. In Figure 2–5, we have the `RootViewController` nib selected, and you can see that the Utilities area looks similar to the Inspector window from Interface Builder in the previous version of Xcode. If you select a source file, you'll see the same information you would see when clicking Get Info in Xcode 3. From there, you can select which target the source file belongs to as well as numerous other tidbits about the file.

As you navigate through the source file, you can click the Show Quick Help button of the Utilities area to see brief information about any symbols the cursor is in. From there, you can click any blue item, which may open the headers file, other documentation, or sample code depending on the context of what was clicked. Take a moment to play around with the different editors and get familiar with the new interface. Don't worry; I'll be here when you get back.

Jump Bars

While you were getting acquainted to the editor, did you notice the bar at the top? It is called the Jump Bar, which allows you to navigate quickly through your file. Figure 2–7 shows the Jump Bar for the `RootViewController` in the project we have created.

Figure 2–7. *The Jump Bar is a navigation tool that is always available to the editor it is above. It is also available in Instruments to perform the same types of tasks.*

Using the Jump Bar is a quick way to navigate through your project without having to find the file using the Project navigator. The Related Files button (the one that looks like an equal sign) pops up a list that allows you to see recent files, unsaved files, and numerous other lists that pertain to the file currently being viewed.

The back and forward buttons allow you to navigate through your history of files in the editor that is open. Swiping left and right with two fingers will allow you to quickly navigate through the files, as you can within Safari on Lion.

Everything else to the right is a breadcrumb trail showing how to get to the method you are editing, starting with the project. In Figure 2–7, you see we started with the project and in the Super Hello World group is the file `RootViewController.m`, and we are looking at the `fetchedResultsController` selector. Clicking any of the items displays a list of siblings and allows you to drill down into each successive level.

The Organizer

Xcode 4 brings a new organizer that does pretty much what the name implies: it organizes your development workspace. You can open it by clicking the Organizer button on the toolbar or by pressing ⇧⌘2. Figure 2–8 shows the Organizer open to the Projects tab. The Organizer has five main purposes:

- Manage development devices
- Manage source control repositories
- Manage recent projects
- Manage archived builds
- Show documentation

Take a look at the Devices section. If you are a registered developer, you can manage all of your developer profile, provisioning profiles, old iOS software images, device logs, and screenshots from this section. You can also see specific device information that Xcode collects on each device when you plug it in. When you plug in a device, you can take screenshots (for App Store submissions) and even save a screenshot as the launch image.

The next tab to look at is the Repositories tab. It shows the repositories for recent projects that have been set up with source control. You can set up repository links and check out new working copies of repositories if there is an existing project you are checking out. As was mentioned previously, Xcode only supports Git and Subversion. Any other source control will have to be managed from an external tool.

Figure 2–8 shows the Projects tab. This tab shows you the projects that Xcode knows about. It shows you which projects are currently open and other basic information about the project. This view also lets you manage project snapshots.

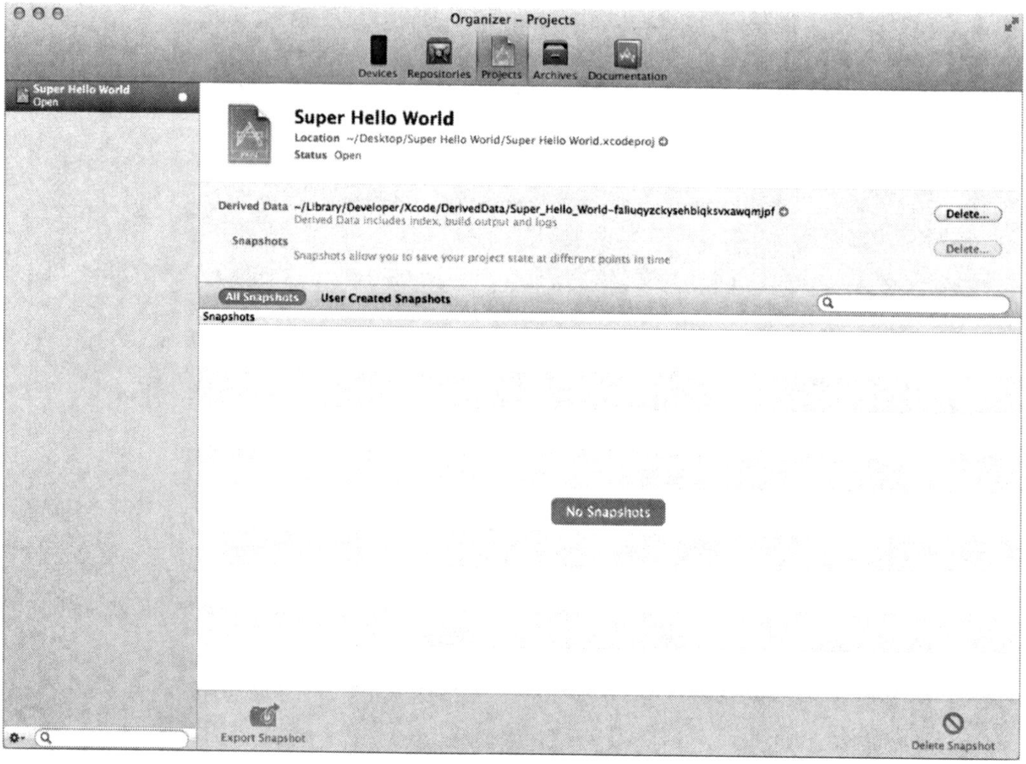

Figure 2–8. *The Organizer with the list of projects you've worked with*

The next tab lets you manage archived applications. Application archiving was brought to Xcode in version 3 to allow iOS developers an easy way to submit applications for approval. After archiving the application, you can validate the binary to check for commonly missed items before you submit the application to the store, share an ad hoc build with beta testers, or submit the application to the store.

The final tab in the organizer is the documentation tab. This is your gateway to the documentation for iOS, Mac OS, and Xcode 4. While looking at any documentation, you'll find a Jump Bar at the top, which acts just like the Jump Bar in your source editors.

Tabs, Tabs, and More Tabs

Let's look at one last item before we head back to our project: tabs. Xcode has tabs that allow you to have multiple editors open at once in the same window. Figure 2–9 shows Xcode with three tabs open.

Figure 2–9. *Multiple tabs within Xcode*

These tabs bring more than just multiple editors. You can pull the tabs out of the window and open a brand new window with that configuration. This means you can have one window open for editing source code and another for editing a nib file. Each tab can be configured and has its own history management. If there is only one tab open, you can show or hide the tab bar by going to **View ➤ Show/Hide Tab bar**.

Why don't you go ahead and navigate through the different views within Xcode? I'll still be here when you get back.

Getting Back to the Code

Now that we've taken a more in-depth look at Xcode, let's do some basic modifications to our project and start checking in changes to our local Git repository. In this chapter, we're going to build a very simple data collection application. We're going to modify the core data model, add a new view controller, and then check all of the changes into source control.

Before we begin, build the application to make sure it compiles. Go to **Product ➤ Build** or press ⌘B. The project should compile with no errors. Clean the project to purge any build artifacts by going to **Product ➤ Clean** or pressing ⌘⇧K.

Updating the Core Data Model

The first thing we're going to do is modify the core data model. Begin by opening the data model (click Super_Hello_World.xcdatamodeld in the Project Manager pane) in Xcode, and update the model as shown in Figure 2–10.

Figure 2–10. *Our very simple model for Super Hello World*

As you can see, we replaced the Event entity with the Person entity with two properties: firstName and lastName. Once that is complete, we're going to create an NSManagedObject subclass by selecting the Person entity and in the menu bar going to **Editor ➤ Create NSManagedObject Subclass....** A sheet will appear asking you where to save the model class, click Create, and you'll see a brand new Person header and implementation in your Project navigator.

Our sample application is going to display a list of names, so let's modify our Person class to have the following header:

```
#import <Foundation/Foundation.h>
#import <CoreData/CoreData.h>
@interface Person : NSManagedObject {
@private
}
@property (nonatomic, retain) NSString * firstName;
@property (nonatomic, retain) NSString * lastName;

-(NSString *) fullName;

@end
```

And this is our implementation:

```
#import "Person.h"

@implementation Person
@dynamic firstName;
@dynamic lastName;

-(NSString *) fullName {
    return [NSString stringWithFormat:@"%@ %@", [self firstName], [self lastName]];
}

@end
```

All we're doing here is adding a fullName method to calculate the person's full name.

Now that we have modified the model, we need to update the RootViewController with these changes and update what is displayed in the table. We only need to update the class in a few places; Listing 2–1 shows the affected methods.

Listing 2–1. *Modifying the RootViewController to Reflect the New Model*

```
- (void)configureCell:(UITableViewCell *)cell atIndexPath:(NSIndexPath *)indexPath
{
    Person *person = (Person *)[self.fetchedResultsController
objectAtIndexPath:indexPath];
    cell.textLabel.text = [person fullName];
}
- (void)insertNewObject
{
    // Create a new instance of the entity managed by the fetched results controller.
    NSManagedObjectContext *context = [self.fetchedResultsController
managedObjectContext];
    NSEntityDescription *entity = [[self.fetchedResultsController fetchRequest] entity];
    Person *newManagedObject = (Person *)[NSEntityDescription
insertNewObjectForEntityForName:
    [entity name] inManagedObjectContext:context];

    // If appropriate, configure the new managed object.
    // Normally you should use accessor methods, but using KVC here avoids the need to
add a custom class to the template.
    [newManagedObject setFirstName:@"Jonny"];
        [newManagedObject setLastName:@"Appleseed"];

    // Save the context.
    NSError *error = nil;
    if (![context save:&error])
    {
        /*
        Replace this implementation with code to handle the error appropriately.

        abort() causes the application to generate a crash log and terminate. You
should not use this function in a shipping application, although it may be useful during
development. If it is not possible to recover from the error, display an alert panel
that instructs the user to quit the application by pressing the Home button.
        */
        NSLog(@"Unresolved error %@, %@", error, [error userInfo]);
        abort();
    }
}

- (NSFetchedResultsController *)fetchedResultsController
{
    if (__fetchedResultsController != nil)
    {
        return __fetchedResultsController;
    }

    /*
     Set up the fetched results controller.
    */
    // Create the fetch request for the entity.
```

```
    NSFetchRequest *fetchRequest = [[NSFetchRequest alloc] init];
    // Edit the entity name as appropriate.
    NSEntityDescription *entity = [NSEntityDescription entityForName:@"Person"
        inManagedObjectContext:self.managedObjectContext];

    [fetchRequest setEntity:entity];

    // Set the batch size to a suitable number.
    [fetchRequest setFetchBatchSize:20];

    // Edit the sort key as appropriate.
    NSSortDescriptor *sortDescriptor = [[NSSortDescriptor alloc] initWithKey:@"lastName"
ascending:YES];
    NSArray *sortDescriptors = [[NSArray alloc] initWithObjects:sortDescriptor, nil];

    [fetchRequest setSortDescriptors:sortDescriptors];

    // Edit the section name key path and cache name if appropriate.
    // nil for section name key path means "no sections".
    NSFetchedResultsController *aFetchedResultsController = [[NSFetchedResultsController
alloc]
        initWithFetchRequest:fetchRequest
  managedObjectContext:self.managedObjectContext
        sectionNameKeyPath:nil
                        cacheName:@"Root"];
    aFetchedResultsController.delegate = self;
    self.fetchedResultsController = aFetchedResultsController;

    [aFetchedResultsController release];
    [fetchRequest release];
    [sortDescriptor release];
    [sortDescriptors release];

        NSError *error = nil;
        if (![self.fetchedResultsController performFetch:&error])
        {
            /*
            Replace this implementation with code to handle the error appropriately.

                abort() causes the application to generate a crash log and terminate. You
    should not use this function in a shipping application, although it may be useful during
    development. If it is not possible to recover from the error, display an alert panel
    that instructs the user to quit the application by pressing the Home button.
            */
            NSLog(@"Unresolved error %@, %@", error, [error userInfo]);
            abort();
        }

    return __fetchedResultsController;
}
```

One last thing to do is to add #import "Person.h" under the header import. All we've done so far is update the RootViewController to display each person's full name. We've also updated it to input a dummy name when the Add button is clicked. Now that we have made some updates and added a feature, let's check these changes into the Git repository.

First, take a look at the Project navigator. You should see something similar to Figure 2–11.

Figure 2–11. *The Project navigator uses your source control system to track your files and shows you what files are modified and what files are new.*

Now, we'll check in all of the modified files as a part of one Git commit. There are multiple ways to accomplish this: select **File ➤ Source Control ➤ Commit** or select the modified files you want to add to the commit, right-click, and select **Source Control ➤ Commit Selected Files…**. Either way, you'll be presented with the view shown in Figure 2–12.

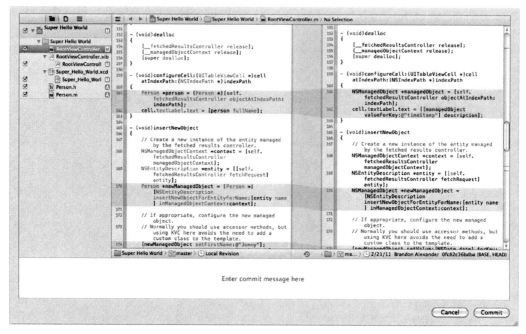

Figure 2–12. *The commit sheet allows you to inspect outgoing changes and enter a commit message.*

Since we want all of our changes to go into this commit, we won't deselect any of the files in the Project view. Take a moment to look at the different views for the outgoing changes: Project view, File view, and Flat view. The Project view shows your changes in the context of how the project is structured in terms of the groups. The File view shows the files as they exist on the file system. The Flat view takes any structure out of the listing and lets you see a raw listing of files. Now take a look at the built-in diff viewer, which shows the changes that will be committed. You can copy the source changes by right-clicking either editor view. Doing so puts a patch-formatted diff in your pasteboard.

Since we're good developers, we're going to put something meaningful in our commit message like: "changes" or "Continued development". Go ahead and enter a commit message and click commit.

Adding a New View Controller

Now that our application has a modified model and we're able to add some managed objects, let's create a modal view controller to insert new objects that come from user input. Before we add the files, create a new group called NewPersonViewController under the Super Hello World group (by right-clicking Super Hello World and selecting **New Group**). Next, add a new file to this group by right-clicking the group and selecting **New File**. Select the UIViewController subclass, and click Next. Make it a subclass of UITableViewController, and check "With XIB for user interface." Click Next, name the file NewPersonViewController.m, and click Save.

Let's add some custom cells. Open the NewPersonViewController.xib file, turn on Assistant editor mode, and make sure the header file is open to the right of the .xib file. We're going to add some custom table cells to our XIB and plug them into our new view controller. The library of user interface (UI) elements to drag into the XIB is located at the bottom of the Utilities pane. Click "Show the Object library", and drag in two UITableViewCell items (shown as Table View Cell in the list). Drag a UITextField (Text Field in the list) inside each of those cells, and modify the border style to be invisible (by clicking the "Show the Attributes inspector" button in the Utilities pane and selecting the first button in the Border Style tab bar). Set the placeholder text to be **First Name** and **Last Name** respectively. Close the Utilities pane, and control-drag the First Name cell (UITableViewCell, not UITextField) to the header file (open in the right editor pane), putting the cursor where you would place properties—under the closing curly bracket of the interface declaration. Name the property firstName. Do the same with the last name cell, naming it lastName.

You have created the outlet properties for the cells; now, we're going to create outlet properties for the text fields. Control-drag the text fields themselves and name them: firstNameInput and lastNameInput. Figure 2–13 shows the final product.

So far, we've created a new view controller, modified the XIB to include some new interface elements, and tied the XIB to the class. Now, let's fill in the details. Listing 2–2 shows the updates we're making to the header for the new person view controller.

Listing 2–2. *The modifications for NewPersonViewController.h*

```
#import <UIKit/UIKit.h>

#define kSectionCount      1
#define kRowCount          2

@class Person;

@class NewPersonViewController;

@protocol NewPersonViewControllerDelegate <NSObject>

@required
-(void) viewController:(NewPersonViewController *)vc didSaveWithPerson:(Person *)p;
-(void) viewControllerDidCancel:(NewPersonViewController *)vc;

@end

@interface NewPersonViewController : UITableViewController {
    id<NewPersonViewControllerDelegate> delegate;
    UITableViewCell *firstNameCell;
    UITableViewCell *lastNameCell;
    UITextField *firstNameInput;
    UITextField *lastNameInput;

    NSManagedObjectContext *managedObjectContext;
}
@property (nonatomic, assign) id<NewPersonViewControllerDelegate> delegate;
@property (nonatomic, retain) IBOutlet UITableViewCell *firstNameCell;
@property (nonatomic, retain) IBOutlet UITableViewCell *lastNameCell;
```

```
@property (nonatomic, retain) IBOutlet UITextField *firstNameInput;
@property (nonatomic, retain) IBOutlet UITextField *lastNameInput;
@property (nonatomic, retain) NSManagedObjectContext *managedObjectContext;

@end
```

Listing 2–3 shows the modified version of the implementation of the NewPersonViewController class.

Listing 2–3. *The updated NewPersonViewController.m*

```
#import "NewPersonViewController.h"
#import "Person.h"

@implementation NewPersonViewController
@synthesize delegate;
@synthesize firstNameCell;
@synthesize lastNameCell;
@synthesize firstNameInput;
@synthesize lastNameInput;
@synthesize managedObjectContext;

- (void)dealloc
{
        delegate = nil;
        [firstNameCell release], firstNameCell = nil;
        [lastNameCell release], lastNameCell = nil;
        [firstNameInput release], firstNameInput = nil;
        [lastNameInput release], lastNameInput = nil;
        [managedObjectContext release], managedObjectContext = nil;
        [super dealloc];
}

- (void)didReceiveMemoryWarning
{
    // Releases the view if it doesn't have a superview.
    [super didReceiveMemoryWarning];

    // Release any cached data, images, etc that aren't in use.
}

#pragma mark - View lifecycle

- (void)viewDidLoad
{
    [super viewDidLoad];

    // Uncomment the following line to preserve selection between presentations.
    // self.clearsSelectionOnViewWillAppear = NO;

    // Uncomment the following line to display an Edit button in the navigation bar for
this view controller.
    UIBarButtonItem *saveButton = [[UIBarButtonItem alloc]
        initWithBarButtonSystemItem:UIBarButtonSystemItemSave target:self
action:@selector(savePressed:)];
    self.navigationItem.rightBarButtonItem = saveButton;
    [saveButton release];
```

```
        UIBarButtonItem *cancelButton = [[UIBarButtonItem alloc]
            initWithBarButtonSystemItem:UIBarButtonSystemItemCancel target:self
            action:@selector(cancelPressed:)];
        self.navigationItem.leftBarButtonItem = cancelButton;
        [cancelButton release];
}

- (void)viewDidUnload
{
    [self setFirstNameCell:nil];
    [self setLastNameCell:nil];
    [self setFirstNameInput:nil];
    [self setLastNameInput:nil];
    [super viewDidUnload];
    // Release any retained subviews of the main view.
    // e.g. self.myOutlet = nil;
}

- (void)viewWillAppear:(BOOL)animated
{
    [super viewWillAppear:animated];
}

- (void)viewDidAppear:(BOOL)animated
{
    [super viewDidAppear:animated];
}

- (void)viewWillDisappear:(BOOL)animated
{
    [super viewWillDisappear:animated];
}

- (void)viewDidDisappear:(BOOL)animated
{
    [super viewDidDisappear:animated];
}

-
(BOOL)shouldAutorotateToInterfaceOrientation:(UIInterfaceOrientation)interfaceOrientatio
n
{
    // Return YES for supported orientations
    return (interfaceOrientation == UIInterfaceOrientationPortrait);
}

#pragma mark - Table view data source

- (NSInteger)numberOfSectionsInTableView:(UITableView *)tableView
{
    // Return the number of sections.
    return kSectionCount;
}

- (NSInteger)tableView:(UITableView *)tableView numberOfRowsInSection:(NSInteger)section
{
    // Return the number of rows in the section.
```

```
    return kRowCount;
}

- (UITableViewCell *)tableView:(UITableView *)tableView
cellForRowAtIndexPath:(NSIndexPath *)indexPath
{
        if([indexPath row] == 0) {
                return firstNameCell;
        } else {
                return lastNameCell;
        }
}

#pragma mark - Table view delegate

- (void)tableView:(UITableView *)tableView didSelectRowAtIndexPath:(NSIndexPath
*)indexPath
{
    //Nothing to see here, move along
}

#pragma mark - Actions received

-(void) savePressed:(id)sender {
    NSManagedObjectContext *context = [self managedObjectContext];

    Person *newPerson = (Person *)[NSEntityDescription
insertNewObjectForEntityForName:@"Person"
        inManagedObjectContext:context];

    [newPerson setFirstName:[firstNameInput text]];
    [newPerson setLastName:[lastNameInput text]];

        NSError *error = nil;
    if (![context save:&error])
    {
        /*
        Replace this implementation with code to handle the error appropriately.

        abort() causes the application to generate a crash log and terminate. You
should not use this function in a shipping application, although it may be useful during
development. If it is not possible to recover from the error, display an alert panel
that instructs the user to quit the application by pressing the Home button.
        */
        NSLog(@"Unresolved error %@, %@", error, [error userInfo]);
        abort();
    }

        [delegate viewController:self didSaveWithPerson:newPerson];
}

-(void) cancelPressed:(id)sender {
        [delegate viewControllerDidCancel:self];
}

@end
```

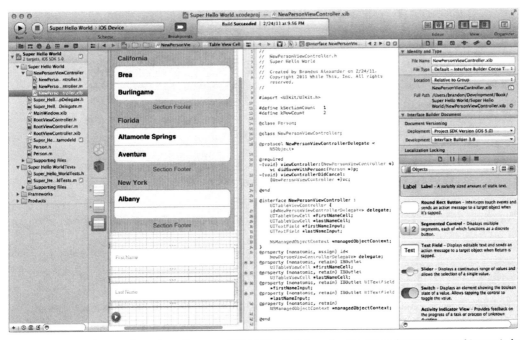

Figure 2–13. *The final product of creating some UITableViewCells in code. There's no longer any need to create in code and then wire up in Interface Builder—one step creates your user interfaces via Interface Builder now.*

Now we need to modify our `RootViewController` to launch our new view controller. If you'll notice in the header, we're declaring a protocol for a delegate. We'll also need to tell the `RootViewController` that it is complying with that protocol so it receives the appropriate messages when the modal view controller is finished.

Let's start by modifying the header file to conform to the protocol:

```
@interface RootViewController : UITableViewController
<NSFetchedResultsControllerDelegate, NewPersonViewControllerDelegate>
```

Now we'll update the `insertNewObject` method, shown in Listing 2–4, in the implementation to pop up our new view controller. We can't forget to import `NewPersonViewController.h`.

Listing 2–4. *The insertNewObject selector that handles presenting the newly created NewPersonViewController.*

```
- (void)insertNewObject
{
        NewPersonViewController *newPersonVC = [[NewPersonViewController alloc]
initWithNibName:@"NewPersonViewController" bundle:nil];
        [newPersonVC setDelegate:self];
        [newPersonVC setManagedObjectContext:[self.fetchedResultsController
managedObjectContext]];

        UINavigationController *navController = [[UINavigationController alloc]
initWithRootViewController:newPersonVC];

        [self presentModalViewController:navController animated:YES];
```

```
        [navController release];
        [newPersonVC release];
}
```

The final step is to implement the protocol methods, as shown in Listing 2–5.

Listing 2–5. *The NewPersonViewControllerDelegate protocol implementation*

```
#pragma mark - NewPersonViewControllerDelegate Methods
-(void) viewController:(NewPersonViewController *)vc didSaveWithPerson:(Person *)p {
        [self dismissModalViewControllerAnimated:YES];
}

-(void) viewControllerDidCancel:(NewPersonViewController *)vc {
        [self dismissModalViewControllerAnimated:YES];
}
```

We are finished adding a new view controller to this project. Check the changes into source control, and let's move on.

Considering Our Progress So Far

We have created a super simple app that adds data to a core data store and uses an interface built with Interface Builder. Quite a bit of the code was generated for us, and we didn't leave Xcode. Now that we have a working application and the source code managed by source control, let's take a moment to review what we've done.

We've taken a brief look at the new development tools, and you've seen some of the enhancements Apple has made to improve the development workflow. There are many other features we haven't touched yet, so spend more time navigating around and learn a few keyboard shortcuts.

The project we created in this chapter is a very simple project and didn't have a need for referencing any static libraries. Xcode 4 supports multiple projects within one workspace, and we only used one project within the workspace.

Now that our application works, let's take a look at how to launch our application for some profiling using Instruments.

Instruments Time

We're not going to go very far into Instruments; that topic is for the rest of this book. For this chapter, we'll take a look at how to launch Instruments from Xcode and the different instruments that are available.

You could go to Product ➤ Profile to launch Instruments, but we're going to look at build schemes and see what options we have for building our application. Figure 2–13 shows the left part of the toolbar in the Xcode window. In the middle, you'll see the active scheme for launching the application. If you click the drop-down, you'll see the available schemes and within each scheme, the deployment type. For now, we're using the iPhone Simulator to run everything.

First, a scheme is a collection of targets to build, a configuration to use, and a collection of tests to run. Schemes can be defined on a per-project basis, or you can define a workspacewide scheme. How you set these depends on your project. In our Super Hello World project, we have one scheme that can be run against three different destinations. We'll cover schemes in depth in a later chapter. A destination is the architecture in which the project is built against and run against, Figure 2–14 shows the Super Hello World target building on the iPhone 4.

Figure 2–14. *The scheme drop-down points you to the availble build schemes for your project.*

Go ahead and click **Edit Schemes…** in the drop-down menu, and take a look at the configuration options for running applications. There are six different activities to perform on your application: build, run, test, profile, analyze, and archive. The build activity is performed when you build your project. You can modify the targets that are built based on the scheme and choose which other activities can be run on a specified target. The run activity (see Figure 2–15) installs and runs the application on whichever destination you chose. The test action simply builds and executes the unit test target against the chosen destination. The profile activity will be explained later in this section. The analyze action runs the static analyzer against your code; we'll cover the static analyzer in a later chapter. The archive action builds the appropriate configuration and packages the artifacts for archiving and sends it to the Archives section of the Organizer for further action.

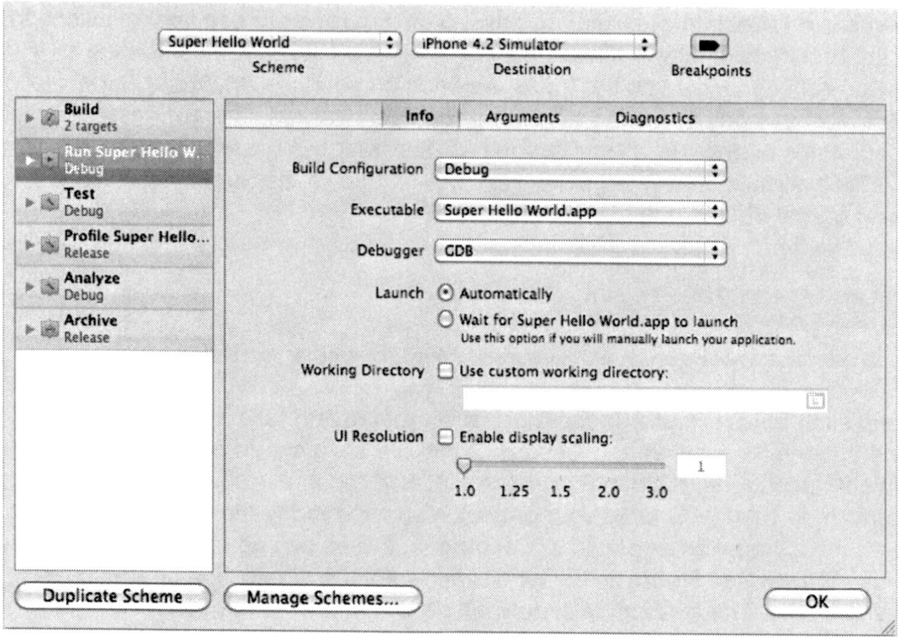

Figure 2–15. *The scheme editor sheet shows you the different options available for launching your application in different contexts.*

Now, let's work with the profile action. Figure 2–16 shows the scheme editor with the profile action expanded. As with all of the different actions, there are pre-actions and post-actions to perform; running a script or sending e-mail. Being able to execute actions before and after your profile action can be helpful when automating a build process.

Take a look at Figure 2–16, which shows the settings for building and running the application for profiling. In the Info tab, you can change the build configuration that is used, use a different executable, define a particular instrument that will be launched on a successful build, change the working directory for the application, and change the UI resolution while the application is being run. In the Arguments tab, you can choose to use the run action's arguments or define specific ones for profiling.

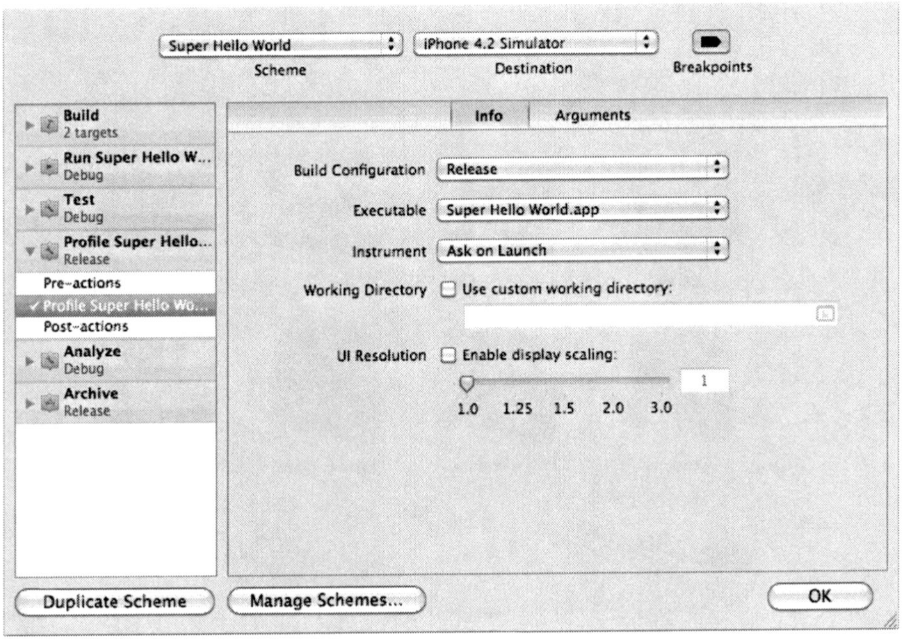

Figure 2–16. *The configuration sheet for the Profile action in the scheme editor.*

Get to Instruments Already

OK, I know, we're not in Instruments yet; we're getting there. If the scheme editor sheet is still open, click OK. Now, go ahead and launch Instruments by going to **Product ➤ Profile**, and Xcode will build the project and launch Instruments. After Instruments is launched, you will be presented with the launch screen shown in Figure 2–17.

If you are launching to an iOS device, you will see more instruments available to you. For this example, we're going to use the Leaks instrument against the simulator. Select Leaks in the dialog box, and click Profile.

Instruments will launch with the Leaks and Allocations instruments running. After the application launches, you'll see some spikes in the Allocations instrument as objects are allocated in memory. We won't go into what that means quite yet, but now you know how to launch instruments from Xcode.

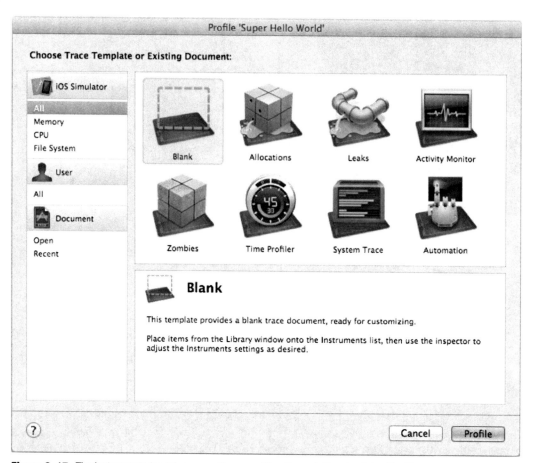

Figure 2–17. *The Instruments launch screen allows profiling through the simulator. Profiling against the device will show more instruments.*

So Many Instruments

Instruments is a great tool for diagnosing issues within your application. However, learning how to use its tools effectively is the key for tuning an application to make it hum. Before we dive into many of the instruments in the coming chapters, let's take a brief look into the Instruments UI and a brief overview of each of the different instruments available to you.

Figure 2–18 shows a run of our application for this chapter. The toolbar at the top lets you start or stop the collection of data, attach to different applications running on the system, and perform other high-level tasks to pare down the data you are collecting. The Instruments part shows different graphs of the data that each instrument is collecting. In our example, there are zero leaks detected and a spike of memory allocated near application launch.

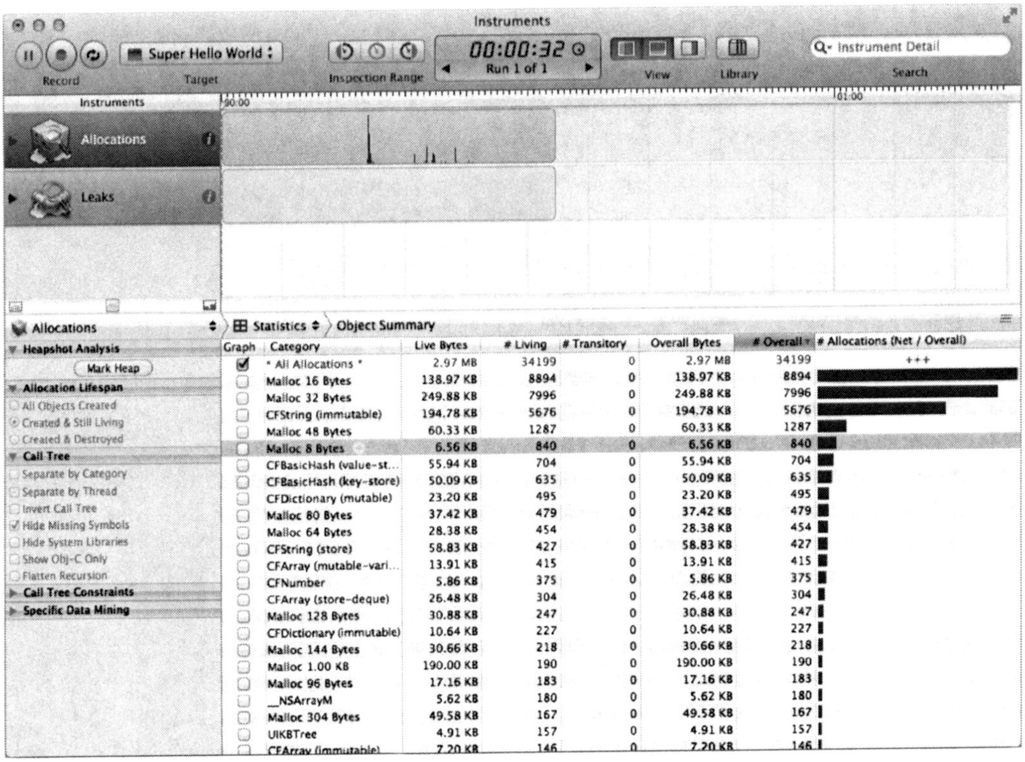

Figure 2–18. *Instruments running Allocations and Leaks against our Super Hello World application*

The area below the Instruments pane shows the active instrument with the Jump Bar to the right. The detailed information below the Jump Bar is specific data from the selected instrument. Clicking either the instrument in the Instruments pane or selecting it in the active instrument drop-down changes the view of data. Go ahead and check out what data the Leaks instrument would show if it had detected any leaks.

We've taken a look at the Allocations and Leak instruments. There are a number of other instruments to use:

- **Activity Monitor**: This instrument monitors overall system activity and statistics. These statistics include CPU, memory, disk, and network usage. It also monitors other processes to see how the entire system is performing under various conditions.

- **Time Profiler**: This instrument performs low-overhead time-based sampling of processes running on the system at any given time.

- **Automation**: This instrument executes a script that simulates user interaction on an iOS application launched from Instruments.

- **Energy Diagnostics**: This instrument monitors the on/off state of different components of the device and provides energy usage while the application is running.

- **System Usage**: This instrument records I/O system activity related to files, sockets, and shared memory for a single process.

- **Core Animation**: This instrument measures graphics performance of an application as well as CPU usage of a process.

- **OpenGL ES Driver**: This instrument measures OpenGL ES performance. This instrument will not be covered in this book.

- **OpenGL ES Analysis**: This instrument measures and analyzes OpenGL ES activity to detect correctness and performance issues. This instrument will not be covered in this book.

Tuning Performance

The rest of this book is going to use the routine outlined in this section when tracking down performance bottlenecks. When diagnosing a performance problem, the process is basically the same regardless of what the performance issue is. Following these principles will save headaches and reduce the number of errors you might introduce to the application.

Performance tuning is a very scientific process. First, come up with a part of the application that you think might need a tune-up and collect data around that part of the application. Your hypothesis might be correct, and you'll find where the bottleneck might be. However, the aspect of the application you are testing might not be the problem. Always be prepared for that to happen. Always be prepared to change the hypothesis and adapt to your data. If the data says something isn't running poorly, chances are it isn't.

When you find the bottleneck or poor performance, find one or two metrics to measure. The key to tuning is always metrics. Ensuring the changes you are making only tweak that one metric will make for a successful tuning session.

Another rule of thumb is to change one thing at a time. Changing multiple things simultaneously can cause problems because the two changes might cancel themselves out or introduce unknown errors. We're usually working with very complex systems with many moving parts, and introducing changes can introduce bugs. A good idea is to have unit tests in place to make sure you aren't changing the functionality while improving performance. I ran into that problem once when I was taking a course in high-performance computing. The task was to write an evolutionary algorithm to solve a complex, multivariate algebraic equation. I had a working algorithm, but I thought it was a bit slow so I started tweaking it. After I completed my tweaks, I tested it, and it worked only half the time, while the original version worked 100 percent of the time. I ultimately realized that I had changed too much and couldn't track down the change that broke the algorithm. I was truly thankful for version control after realizing that.

As you read the rest of this book, remember that we're truly interested in large improvements in performance (but still striving for zero leaks—users hate leaky applications). Do you think it would be worth spending hours on a tweak that could potentially improve the speed by less than one percent? Will your users notice that you squeezed two extra frames per second to top out at 80 frames per second? I don't think so. We're interested in large-scale changes that will be noticeable to the user.

Summary

We covered a lot of material in this chapter. We've taken a brand new project and added some new classes and user interfaces using Xcode's new built-in Interface Builder component. We've also modified the data model and generated model classes to create a slightly more complicated application.

At the end, we looked at the Scheme editor to understand where the build configurations are housed in Xcode. The final step was to launch Instruments and see the great integration between these great tools. Everything we covered in this chapter may seem overwhelming at first, but you'll get the hang of it. Apple has truly provided developers with some top-notch tools that get out of the way as we take some great ideas and turn them into wonderful experiences for our users.

It is time to dive into the project for the rest of this book. You know what the tools do; now let's use them.

Three Screens . . . and Well, It Runs

In the previous chapter, we covered some highlights of how to use the new iOS developer tools. The chapters that follow will build on that base and show you some great techniques for turning your application into something that will bring your users back time and time again. In order to do this, we are going to spend the next several chapters walking through an application that has, shall we say, a few problems. Some will be obvious, and others will take some digging to find. The application we're going to use is a virtual fruit stand. The requirements for the application are to display the product inventory including the product's image, view a product's details, add to a shopping cart, view the shopping cart, and check out. The application is in an alpha stage at this point; it has met the basic requirements but it needs some attention in regards to performance and has some crashing issues.

Working with GitHub

For this project, we're going to pull the source code from an existing repository. The project is hosted up on a social coding web site called GitHub. Head over to `www.github.com/signup/free` and create a free account. At the time of this writing, the registration form looks like the one shown in Figure 3–1.

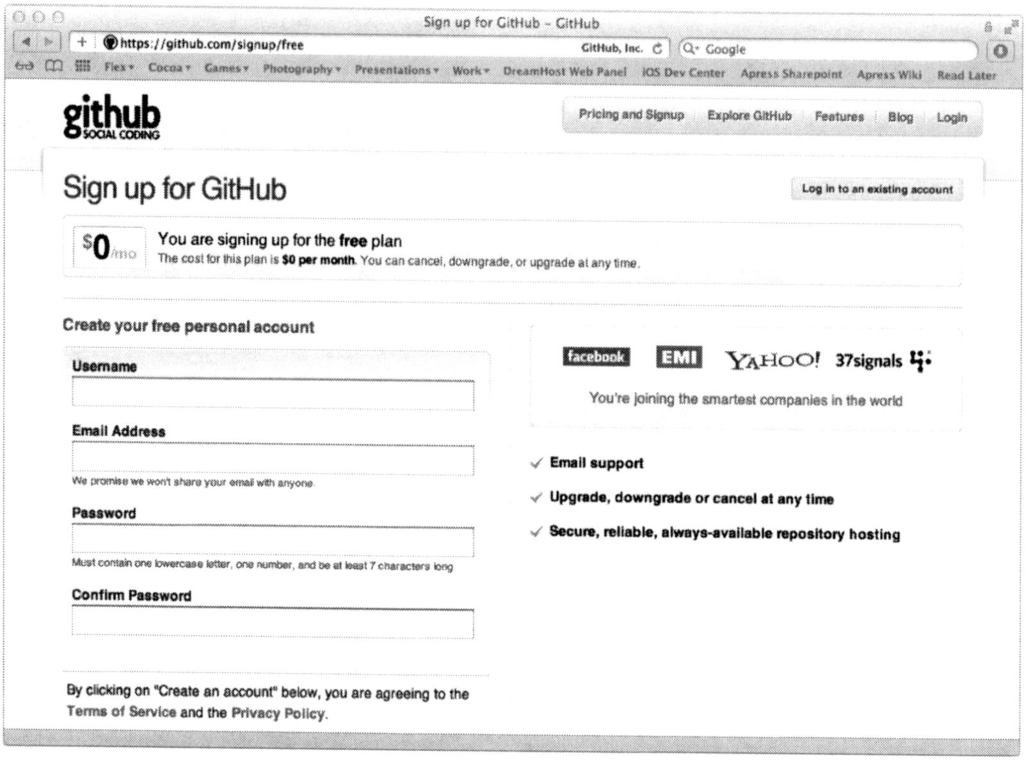

Figure 3–1. *The GitHub registration screen*

GitHub offers a free account that gives you the ability to create unlimited (at the time of this writing) public Git repositories. Paid accounts are available that will let you invite other developers to contribute to private repositories. The application we're going to follow throughout this book is hosted as a public repository.

> **NOTE:** Git is a distributed version control system. It is packaged with Xcode, so there isn't anything more to install. We're going to utilize Xcode's built-in Git support to track our changes throughout this book. Git has a very powerful command-line interface, so picking up a little bit of Git command line kung fu will increase your productivity as a developer.

The next step to getting code checked out from GitHub is setting up your SSH public keys. Head over to `https://github.com/account/ssh`, and click "Add another public key" (see Figure 3–2).

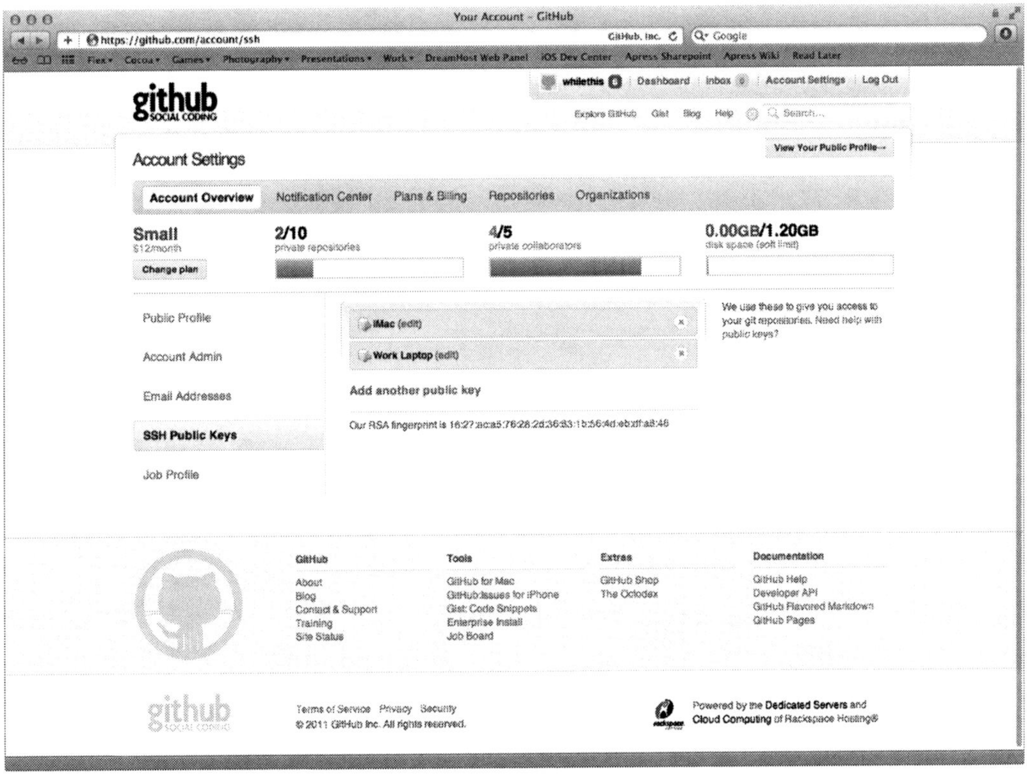

Figure 3–2. *We're about to add a public key, so we can check out our code securely over SSH.*

Setting up a public SSH key is super simple. In fact, the fine folks at GitHub have published instructions on how to set up your SSH keys here: http://help.github.com/mac-set-up-git/ (see Figure 3–3).

Figure 3–3. *Setting up SSH keys on OS X*

Once Git is set up on your machine and the SSH keys are configured, you're ready to move on to forking the project and navigating through the application.

Connecting to Super Checkout

Now, let's fork the project so you can pull it down and start making your changes. The main project can be found at `https://github.com/whilethis/Super-Checkout`. When you fork the project, you'll have your own personal copy of the repository to check out and push to or pull from. To create a fork, click the Fork button in the upper-right corner of the main project web page (see Figure 3–4).

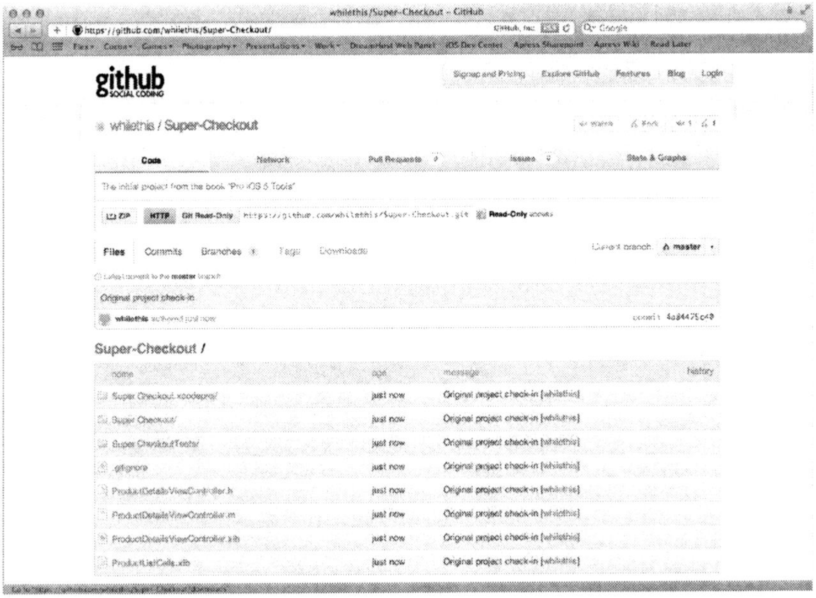

Figure 3–4. *On the original project's screen, clicking the Fork button will create your very own copy of the Git repository.*

From the forked project's site, copy the URL that looks like the one shown in Figure 3–5.

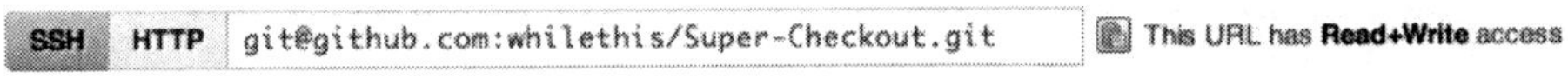

Figure 3–5. *Your project will have your github.com username instead of whilethis in the URL*

Now, fire up Xcode 4, and the Welcome to Xcode screen shown in Figure 3–6 comes up. In the previous chapter, we created a new project from scratch. This time, we're going to connect to a repository.

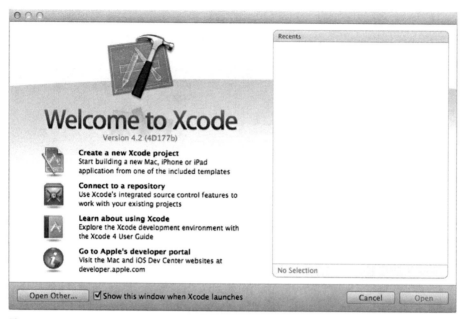

Figure 3–6. *The Welcome to Xcode screen lets you create a new project or connect to a source code repository.*

Click the "Connect to a repository" button. You are prompted to enter the repository's location, as shown in Figure 3–7. Enter the repository URL copied from GitHub, and Xcode will automatically check to see if the host is reachable and allow you to continue. Click Next, and we'll save the code on disk.

If, for some reason, you try to connect to GitHub before configuring your SSH keys, you'll be prompted to confirm the identity of the Git server and challenged for a username and password. The entire reason we set up the SSH keys is to prevent these issues from happening. If, however, you have set up the SSH keys and didn't issue the ssh –T command, you'll be presented with the identity confirmation screen shown in Figure 3–8.

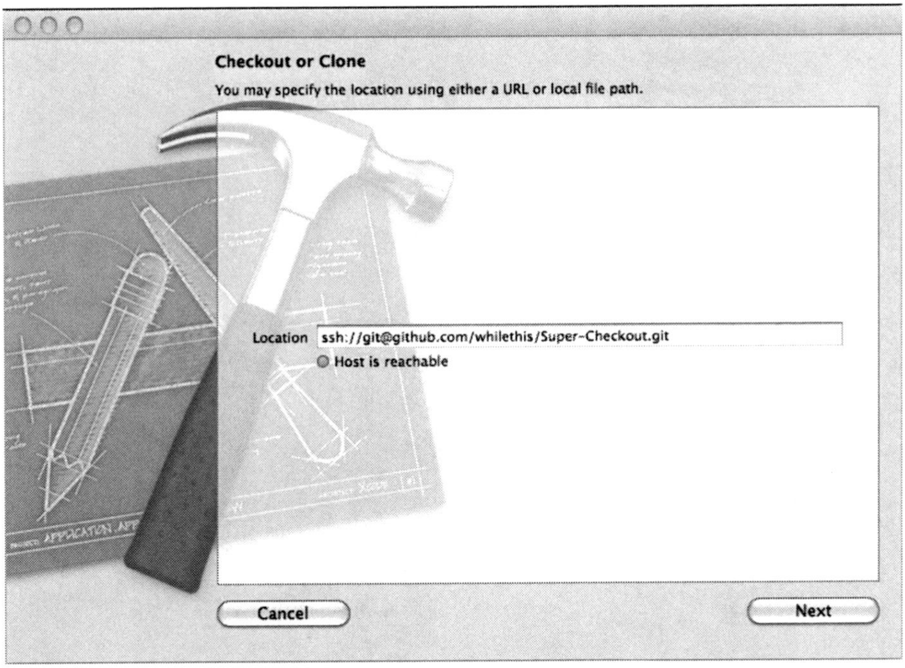

Figure 3–7. *Xcode 4 automatically detects the type of repository when checking out code from an existing repository.*

> **NOTE:** Make sure you choose the same repository type when connecting to a remote repository directly. Xcode will try to clone or check out the repository using the protocol of the type chosen in Figure 3–8.

Next, you tell Xcode the name of the project and what type of repository it is (see Figure 3–8). Name the project **Super Checkout**, and click Clone.

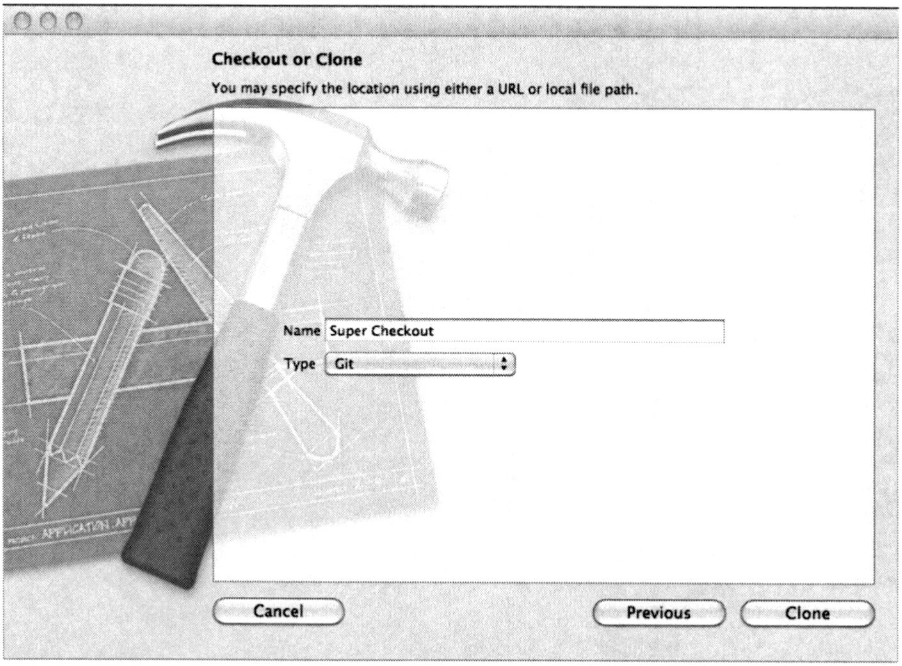

Figure 3–8. *Naming your project and choosing the repository type*

The next screen asks you where to put your working copy. Choose a location on disk, and click Clone. If the clone operation is complete, you'll be presented with the options Open Project and Don't Open (see Figure 3–9). Click Open Project, and we're off to the races. If you skip the public key creation we covered earlier, you will see some confirmation dialogue boxes and other authentication issues. If you run into any issues, head back to the public key creation step and try again.

Figure 3–9. *A successful clone of our Super Checkout project*

Taking a Look Around

The application is pretty simple. It consists of a navigation controller with a table view controller to display the product inventory, a product details view controller as a drill-down from the product inventory, a shopping cart controller that is presented as a flip-over modal view controller. The module that communicates with the service is a simple engine that uses the same approach that Matt Gemmell (http://instinctivecode.com/) took with his Twitter engine.

The API engine handles the communication with the server and invokes the parser to parse the data coming from the server. The server speaks in JSON (JavaScript Object Notation), and the project is using the SBJSON library (https://github.com/stig/json-framework/) to parse the data into native Cocoa Touch classes. Each view controller gets its own instance of the engine and uses delegation to ensure the server communication is asynchronous.

The user interface is mostly table views with some custom cells designed in Interface Builder.

Running Super Checkout

Run the application in the simulator or your test device. Your screen should match the ones shown in Figure 3–10. The first thing you should notice is a lag in loading images; we'll address that issue in a later chapter. Tapping a product takes you to the product details screen, and tapping the Add To Basket button adds the item to your order. The Cart button flips the view over and shows you your cart.

Figure 3–10. *The Super Checkout application in its alpha form*

As you navigate and become accustomed to the application, you'll notice that if you move from the product details back to the inventory quickly and in rapid succession, the application will likely crash. It is crashes like this and other such issues that make this application alpha quality and in need of some updating and tweaking.

Navigating the Project (and Xcode)

Managing the workflow within Xcode is key to being efficient in developing and enhancing any project. Knowing how to navigate the editors without leaving the keyboard can improve your speed of development and, well, is just plain cool. Xcode 4 has introduced some nice new features that take advantage of the new interface. It has also changed a number of common keyboard shortcuts from Xcode 3.

Quite possibly one of the most useful keyboard shortcuts in Xcode 4 is ⌘J. When pressed, the shortcut pops up the "Move focus to . . ." editor window (see Figure 3–11). The highlighted area is where the focus will move to if you press enter. Navigating between tabs is as easy as moving the selection with the arrow keys. Moving the selection to the side of the current editor (the area with a plus sign) creates a new assistant editor.

Move focus to SuperCheckoutAPIEngine.m

Figure 3–11. *The "Move focus to . . ." feature lets you move focus between tabs and create assistant editors.*

Switching between an implementation file and its header used to be accomplished by pressing command-option-up arrow. Xcode 4 has changed that shortcut to command-control-up arrow, or you can use a three-finger swipe up or down gesture on a trackpad if that gesture is not already mapped by the Operating System (Lion uses the three-finger swipe extensively).

Option-click a symbol to bring up a small popover that displays details about the symbol. From the popover, you can view the header of the class or view the documentation if it is a framework class.

Command-click a symbol to go to its declaration. If the symbol is a variable, the declaration of that variable will be highlighted. If the symbol is a class, the editor will show the header where the symbol is declared.

Option-command-click a symbol to open an assistant editor and perform the same operation as command-click.

Pressing command-shift-O will bring up an Open Quickly dialogue box. In this box, you can type the beginning of a filename, and the files that match that name will be displayed below it. This is a very handy way to quickly open files.

These keyboard shortcuts (and many others) can be quickly referenced in Chapter 12.

Summary

The idea behind the application in this chapter is to mimic an alpha-quality application to give us plenty of areas to improve performance. The final product will be an application that doesn't crash and performs on a level of a properly architected application. We're going to be profiling, refactoring, and rewriting different aspects of the application as we move forward with the tuning part of this book. We're in for quite the ride, so turn the page and let's get started!

Chapter 4

Memory Management and Diagnostics

In the previous chapter, we looked at an application that is basically feature complete but still needs a lot of work. We have our project set up with source control from Github, and we are ready to start fixing this application to make it ready for beta testing. The fun stuff starts in this chapter.

The likelihood of our application crashing is very high at this point. We know that one of the main reasons an application is rejected from the App Store is because it crashes. In this chapter, you are going to learn how to fix memory-related crashes and find memory leaks before they cause performance issues on the device. We're going to approach finding these issues in a very methodical way so that these steps can be followed for your future applications. Each step will be incrementally more technical as we will be getting closer and closer to the hardware. Fortunately, we have access to some very powerful tools and will be able to knock out a number of memory-related bugs.

This chapter's application was developed using manual reference counting. The latest tools introduce a new technology called automatic reference counting (ARC). The first thing we'll do is to create an ARC branch to convert the application to ARC. After that, we'll discuss issues that can arise with ARC and look at what Instruments gives us to fix those problems. The rest of the book will assume manual reference counting, however.

The rest of this chapter is going to be all about memory-related crashes and fixing memory leaks as they pertain to manual reference counting. The first thing we're going to cover is creating a branch in our local repository to localize our changes and make it easier to merge with the master branch at the end. Then, we'll talk about prevention techniques so issues won't come up. The rest of this chapter will start off pretty high level, and we'll tackle a memory-related crash in Super Checkout. As we go deeper into tackling crashing bugs, we'll be talking more in depth about how to diagnose these types of bugs.

The last part of this chapter will be spent talking about memory leaks. You'll learn how to use Instruments to detect and locate memory leaks. After we're done with that, you'll be armed with the tools and knowledge to combat memory related crashes and to plug leaking memory before the application reaches the App Store.

Branches Are Our Friends

"Commit early and often" is a mantra developers should live by. This mantra is aided by the use of distributed version control systems such as Git or Mercurial. The idea here is to create a local branch for a feature and roll that set of changes into the master branch when the feature is complete. In short, this allows us to have a feature branch so we could quickly switch back to the master branch to work on something else without losing any changes. Since we're using Git, we can leverage some of the basic integrations with Xcode and leave some of the more powerful features for the command line (or GUI tool of your choice). Gone are the days of a commit breaking the build, causing you to anger your team and buy them donuts.

> **NOTE:** We can also branch projects with Subversion. The difference is the branches are created on the server as well. The concept is the same as with Git, but the location of everything is slightly different.

Before we begin mucking around with the application, we're going to create a branch and merge it when we're finished fixing our iteration of updates to the application. To create the branch, open Xcode 4 and go to **File ➤ Source Control ➤ Repositories**, which will open up the Organizer window. Click the Repositories tab. Find Super Checkout in the list on the left, and click Branches to see one branch in the list. Click the Add Branch button at the bottom of the window. A sheet like the one shown in Figure 4–1 is displayed that lets you create the branch. Type **ARC_Transition** for the branch name and base it off the master branch by setting the starting point to "master." Check the option to automatically switch to the branch so we can begin making changes after the branch is complete.

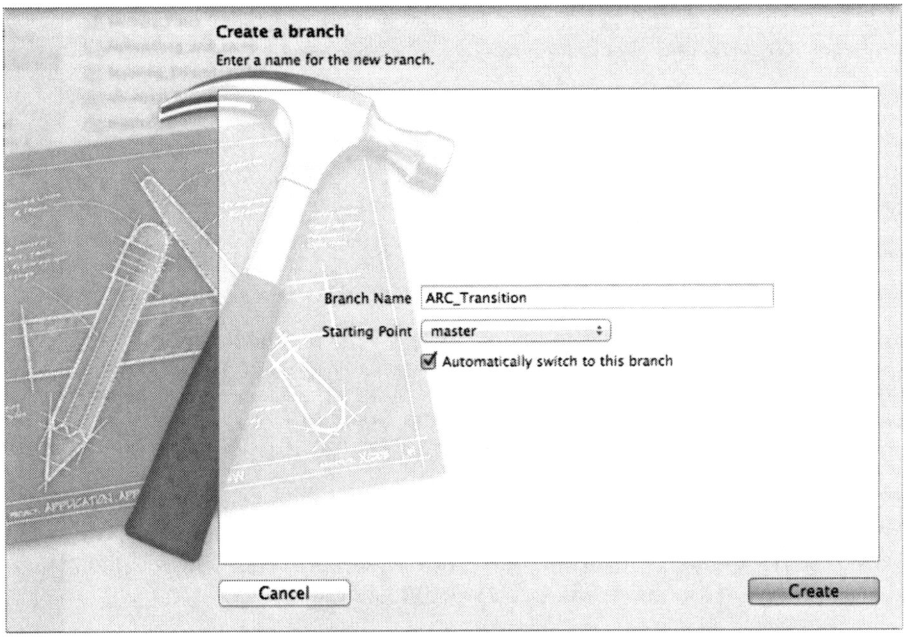

Figure 4–1. *Creating a new branch is easy via Xcode 4's new source control management GUI.*

Finally, click Create. Now that we have switched to the newly created branch, we can start performing major surgery on this branch without messing up anything, other than possibly the current branch. We're now ready to start transitioning Super Checkout to automatic reference counting. Each chapter will create one or more branches, so we can collect each set of updates to the repository. This doesn't follow what will happen in real life, but we're going to get as close to it as we can.

Automatic Reference Counting

Automatic reference counting, or ARC, is a brand new technology Apple has given us in the latest LLVM compiler. When the ARC flag is set on the compiler, all of the memory management code is generated for you. This means any type of memory management code can now get removed from the source. Put simply, any calls to release, copy, retain, or autorelease are simply removed.

Memory management isn't quite a simple as that though. Some new lifetime qualifiers must be implemented to give the compiler hints on what needs to be done from a memory management point of view. These qualifiers are

- __strong: In a strong (retained) reference, the balancing release or autorelease is generated by the compiler.

- __weak: In this reference, when the reference is released, the pointer is set to nil automatically.

- __unsafe_unretained: This is simply a reference. This qualifier is dangerous because you can still have a dangling pointer.

- __autoreleasing: This one tells the compiler that it will be passed by reference (id *) and will be autoreleased upon return.

When declaring properties, there are three new property attributes; two can be used in iOS 4 and above and one can be used only in iOS 5:

- strong: This is a strong reference; it works like the __strong qualifier and can be used in iOS 4 and above.

- weak: An automatically nilling reference, like the __weak qualifier, and it can only be used in iOS 5.

- unsafe_unretained: This is simply a reference, like the __unsafe_unretained qualifier, and can be used in iOS 4 and above.

This list is not exhaustive, and there are many other new things to keep in mind when developing with ARC enabled. One such thing is the autorelease pool. In short, with ARC, there is no such thing as an NSAutoreleasePool object. Instead, you will use the new @autorelease block. It looks like what you see in Listing 4–1.

Listing 4–1. *The New and Improved Autorelease Pool*

```
@autoreleasepool {
        //long loop with a lot of objects created and destroyed
}
```

The next important thing to remember when coding with ARC is to never invoke retain, release, or autorelease. Ever. The compiler will even complain about it when you do. ARC enforces several other rules, and the "Programming with ARC" article in Apple's developer documentation is a great place to start. When we convert our project to ARC, we might run into some of these rules during the conversion. If we do, we'll talk about them.

Converting to ARC

We're going to convert Super Checkout to ARC now. This conversion will require some major surgery on the code base, which is why we branched the code. So, without further ado, let's start the conversion. The first thing is open up the project and go to **Edit ➤ Refactor ➤ Convert** to Objective-C ARC. When you do this, a sheet (see Figure 4–2) is displayed. Check both of the boxes to convert the unit test and application targets. If any of the targets are currently using an older version of the compiler, the compiler version will be updated to LLVM 3.0.

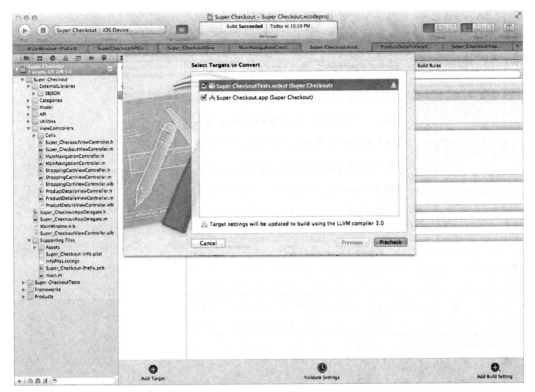

Figure 4–2. *The target selection sheet before the precheck is performed.*

Clicking the Precheck button will perform a compilation and inform you whether or not the project can be converted. As Figure 4–3 shows, Super Checkout is not quite ready for ARC yet. We will need to fix some errors first.

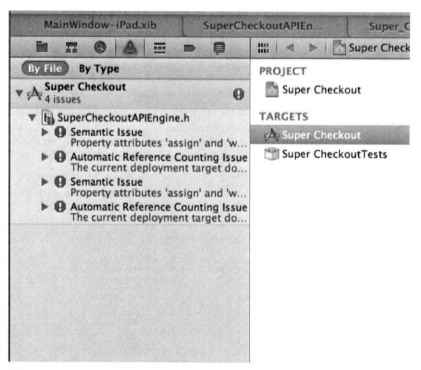

Figure 4–3. *The errors returned by the precheck run.*

Clicking the first item in the list will take us to SuperCheckoutAPIEngine.h and you'll find that the file was modified by adding __weak to the property declaration. To fix this, remove __weak and replace assign with unsafe_unretained. We are doing this because we're targeting iOS 4 and later. If we were targeting iOS 5, we would use the weak attribute. The line should now look like this:

```
@property (nonatomic, unsafe_unretained) NSObject<SuperCheckoutAPIEngineDelegate>
*delegate;
```

In this instance, there is also an ivar declared previously. Since the ivar is declared and the property attributes are set, we have two options. The first is to label the delegate ivar as __unsafe_unretained. The second is to remove the line altogether and let the compiler synthesize the ivar. Since we are adopting the modern way of doing things, remove the line altogether. This will make the ivar block of the class look like this:

```
@interface SuperCheckoutAPIEngine : NSObject<SCJSONParserDelegate> {
    NSMutableDictionary *connections;    // MGTwitterHTTPURLConnection objects
    NSString *APIDomain;
}
```

There are some ivars remaining. Since the default behavior for ARC is strong, we don't need to update them. Now, perform the transition again. This time, the error you run into is an NSString being cast as a CFStringRef. We know we can do this because NSString is toll-free bridged between the CF object and the Objective-C object. If you notice,

Xcode will recommend to place __bridge in front of the CFStringRef cast using the Fix-It feature. Go ahead and let Xcode do this.

Perform the conversion again. This should bring you a new set of errors. This set exists in some external library code. Since we're in a branch, let's go ahead and modify the code. None of the problems are particularly tricky. Either let Fix-It add the appropriate code or remove calls to memory management code. When you are done with these edits, run the conversion tool again and if all the problems have been removed, you'll be greeted with Figure 4–4. This sheet tells you that the conversion will be successful. Click Next to continue.

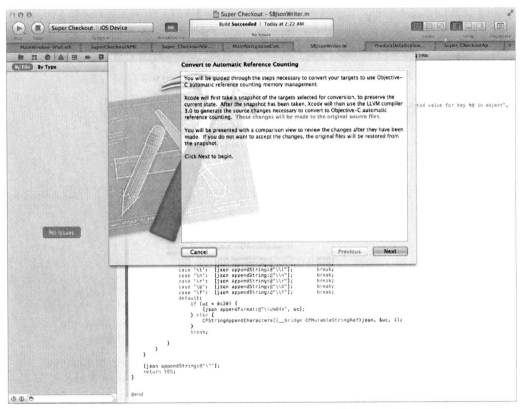

Figure 4–4. *The precheck has passed, and now, we're ready to make the final conversion to ARC.*

After clicking Next, Xcode will recommend creating a snapshot. Snapshots are great to take a quick snapshot of the current configuration just in case something goes wrong during the conversion process. Click Enable, and Xcode will continue with the conversion after creating a new snapshot.

When the conversion is complete, Xcode will give you a view as to what was changed and will give you the opportunity to back out if some of the changes look a bit extreme (see Figure 4–5). Click Continue, and then commit your code with a meaningful commit message.

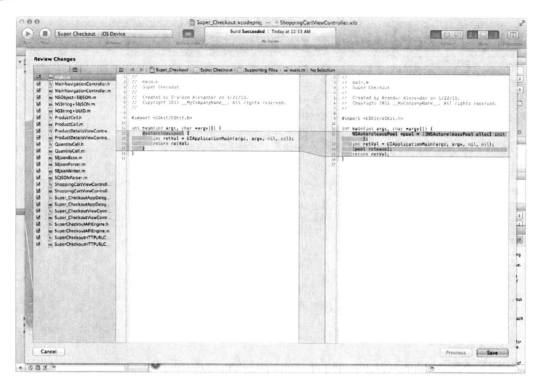

Figure 4–5. *The conversion to ARC is complete, and Xcode is showing you its handiwork.*

Recognizing Retain Cycles

As great as ARC is, we still have to be cognizant as to what is going on within our application. You may be saying, "It is 2011, and I still have to worry about memory leaks?" The answer is yes. No matter how sophisticated our tools get, they won't catch everything. The most likely error we'll run into with ARC is the retain cycle.

A retain cycle is defined as an object graph that contains a closed loop of retained references. Figure 4–6 shows a typical retain cycle. If we release objects A and B, ARC will think that the rest of the objects are still in use and will not insert the appropriate release statements.

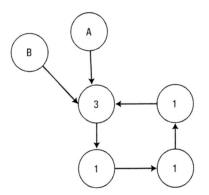

Figure 4–6. *In this common retain cycle, the numbers show the retain count before A and B are deallocated.*

So how do we fix retain cycles? Well, it depends. If we are targeting iOS 5 and above, make one of the references in the cycle a weak reference to break the cycle. Figure 4–7 shows what the object graph will look like if we make the appropriate reference weak.

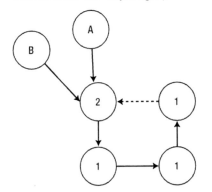

Figure 4–7. *Breaking the cycle requires making the correct reference.*

By making the reference to the parent node in the object graph, the graph is reclaimed when A and B go away.

How do we detect these cycles? Fortunately, Instruments has a new feature that detects retain cycles and visually shows you what the cycle looks like. When we cover using Instruments to detect leaks, we'll take a look at how Instruments will show you these cycles in a very simple example.

Getting Back to Manual Reference Counting

We're heading back to the land of release, retain, and autorelease. ARC is nice, but many things can be learned from manual reference counting. Since we created a branch for the ARC conversion, we can do the same thing to keep our fixes for the memory related issues we fix throughout this chapter. Give this new branch a name of Memory_Fixes, and base it off of the master branch and remember to switch to the new branch after creation!

Establishing Healthy Coding Practices

Benjamin Franklin once said, "An ounce of prevention is worth a pound of cure." So before we dive into modifying the code, let's take a moment to discuss some best practices for proper memory management and things you can do while developing an application to prevent memory-related bugs and crashes before they crop up. These practices range from how the language and runtime work to good coding practices and general guidelines.

The first thing about memory management, especially with iOS development, is the retain count. Since the iOS platform does not have garbage collection, we have to maintain our memory appropriately manually. Understanding the concepts of when to retain memory and when to release it is absolutely necessary to be a good citizen on an iOS device. We won't spend too much time talking about the nuances of retain counts and these things, but it is necessary to touch some of the highlights.

To Retain or Not to Retain, That Is the Question

A common mistake that is made when developing applications in Objective-C is not releasing retained memory. Most of the time, failing to release memory is a mistake, so picking up some good habits is always a good thing. Unreleased memory leaks, plain and simple. A good rule of thumb for knowing when to release memory is given by the acronym NARC:

- New
- Alloc
- Retain
- Copy

Anytime any of these messages is sent to an object, you now own that object, so you must release it when you are finished. However, there are always exceptions to this rule. When a method should return an object, sending autorelease to the object is always necessary. There are some performance considerations when using autorelease however. Since autorelease sends the object to live in the autorelease pool for the current scope block, sending thousands of objects to such a pool would be a bad idea, especially on an older iOS device. A good example of what we're talking about is creating a fast loop to create one million strings (Listing 4–2).

Listing 4–2. *One Million Autoreleased Strings!*

```
for(int i = 0; i < 1000000; i++) {
    string = [[[NSString alloc] initWithFormat:@"String %i", i] autorelease];
    //Process string and create other autoreleased objects….
}
```

The preceding code creates one million strings and autoreleases them. Running the Allocations instrument against this code gives you the graph shown in Figure 4–7.

The appropriate way to fix this issue can be found in Listing 4–3.

Listing 4–3. *One Million Autoreleased Strings in Their Very Own Autorelease Pools*

```
for(int i = 0; i < 1000000; i++) {
    NSAutoreleasePool *pool = [[NSAutoreleasePool alloc] init];
    string = [[[NSString alloc] initWithFormat:@"String %i", i] autorelease];
    //Process string and create other autoreleased objects….
    [pool release];
}
```

Compare the graph from Figure 4–8 to the graph in Figure 4–9. What these graphs don't show is the scale. Since we're creating one million strings, each string is allocated and autoreleased upon the next iteration of the run loop. By creating an autorelease pool, as Figure 4–8 shows, the system reclaims the memory more frequently and allows for better utilization of the resources available.

Figure 4–8. *The Allocation graph of one million strings autoreleased to the same pool*

Figure 4–9. *The Allocation graph of one million strings autoreleased in their own pool*

Since devices have a finite amount of memory, using autorelease pools is absolutely necessary to keep your application from triggering memory warnings and the operating system from terminating your application as well as keeping the application responsive. Manual releasing of objects during a tight loop is expensive.

Remembering and being disciplined when managing memory is the key to reducing memory leaks. Take a look at your approach and decide which memory management technique is best for you. If you are creating discrete objects and manipulating them, release them when you are finished. If you are creating a large number of objects, creating an autorelease pool and draining it when you are finished is the best idea. The best time to do the latter is when performing a large number of string operations, since most string operations return autoreleased string instances.

Overall, remembering when to release or autorelease an object isn't very difficult. As long as the memory management is done when the code is first written, memory leaks will be kept at a minimum and leave you free to track down other types of issues.

Connecting Properties and Polymorphic Dots

Next in our discussion of memory management, we need to talk about Objective-C 2.0 properties. This very popular feature comes with the new Objective-C runtime and brings a new concept to the Objective-C language—dot notation.

Let's take a quick look at what properties give us and how they fit in the scope of memory management. For the sake of this discussion, we're going to talk about an object defined in Listings 4–4 and 4–5.

Listing 4–4. *The Header for Foo*

```
@interface Foo : NSObject {
    NSDictionary *bar;
}

@property (retain, nonatomic) NSDictionary *bar;

@end
```

Listing 4–5. *The Implementation for Foo*

```
#import "Foo.h"
@implementation Foo
@synthesize bar;

- (id) init {
    self = [super init];

    if(self) {
        self.bar = [NSDictionary dictionary];
    }

    return self;
}


-(void) setBar:(NSDictionary *)newBar {
    NSDictionary *oldDictionary = self.bar;
    bar = [newBar retain];
    [oldDictionary release];

    NSNotification *note = [NSNotification notificationWithName:@"barUpdated"
object:self];
    [[NSNotificationCenter defaultCenter] postNotification:note];
}

-(void) dealloc {
    self.bar = nil;
    [super dealloc];
}

@end
```

The Foo object has one property, an NSDictionary called bar. We are synthesizing the accessor and providing our own mutator. The idea behind the mutator is to send a notification that the property has changed. In the `init` method, we are using the property to initialize `bar` to be nil. Also note that in our `dealloc` method, the property is being set to nil.

Now, let's look at what is really going on when this code is executed. When the code is compiled, the code that uses properties basically gets translated into method calls. The following translations occur:

`{symbol}.foo`

is turned into

`[{sybmol} foo]`

Similarly, the following line

`{symbol}.foo = {some new object}`

is turned into

`[{symbol} setFoo:{some new object}]`

It is very easy to forget that this conversion happens. So when `init` is called, the new instance is actually calling `[self setFoo:[NSDictionary dictionary]]`. This means a notification is getting sent out when the object is created. The `dealloc` method does the same thing, so a notification is getting sent out when the object is deallocated. The latter is likely to cause more problems than the former because the notification carries with it a pointer to newly released memory.

A simple way to address those issues is to use the ivar directly in the `init` and `dealloc` methods. This reduces the likelihood of introducing `EXEC_BAD_ACCESS` errors when `bar` is updated on an instance of `Foo`. This also frees up any subclasses of `Foo` to do what they wish if they were to override the `setBar` method.

A very subtle topic with regards to memory management and properties is understanding what is going on. In the init method above, the compiled code is `[self setBar:[NSDictionary dictionary]]` so the method is getting passed an autoreleased object that is then retained by the `setBar` method. If `[[NSDictionary alloc] init]` was passed in, the dictionary would leak when bar was assigned a new object or the instance of Foo was released. This probably just saved an hour of debugging one leak.

This brings up an interesting topic regarding the use of properties, mainly the use of dot notation. While not necessarily a memory management topic, this topic is about the use of dot notation and good coding practices. Properties are a great thing; they make the generation of accessors and mutators fast and easy, since most of them are the basic boilerplate code that is very tedious and time consuming to write. Being able to control the type of code that is generated (i.e., retained, assigned or copied, atomic or nonatomic, read-write or read-only) is a great help as well.

The problem comes when you start mixing in C structs with your Objective-C properties. The dot syntax gets confusing fast with the two. A good suggestion for making the intent of the source code clear is to not use dot syntax with your Objective-C code. This gives the polymorphic dot one meaning. Take the following example:

```
UIView *newView = [[UIView alloc] init];

CGRect viewRect;

viewRect.origin.x = 0;
viewRect.origin.y = 0;
viewRect.size.height = 100;
viewRect.size.width = 100;

newView.frame = viewRect;

UIColor *color = [[UIColor alloc] initWithPatternImage:{some image}];
newView.backgroundColor = color;
[color release];

[self.view addSubview:newView];
[newView release];
```

We're creating a new view, setting up its frame, and setting its background color before adding it to the current view. It's pretty straightforward, but someone new to the platform won't know the full intent of the code. Look at the code that sets the background color. It is very easy to forget to release the color being set after setting it on the new view because the intent isn't very clear. Taking the suggestion offered previously, we can rewrite the code to look like this:

```
UIView *newView = [[UIView alloc] init];

CGRect viewRect;

viewRect.origin.x = 0;
viewRect.origin.y = 0;
viewRect.size.height = 100;
viewRect.size.width = 100;

[newView setFrame:viewRect];

UIColor *color = [[UIColor alloc] initWithPatternImage:image];
[newView setBackgroundColor:color];
[color release];

[self.view addSubview:newView];
[newView release];
```

The full intent is more easily understood. The background color that is created and set on the created view is clearly owned by the created view and released after it's set. The code that is manipulating the view's frame is clearly manipulating a C struct, and the rest of the code is Objective-C.

> **NOTE**: Talking about code structure is always a touchy thing, so the thoughts behind not using the dot syntax are simply a suggestion. These are not hard and fast rules; think of them like the rules about the location of the curly brace and spaces over tabs. While the merits of using one over the other can be fun to argue over coffee, we're in this to develop applications. Users don't care what the source code looks like.

Performing Static Analysis

There are ways to find common coding errors before the application is run. The new LLVM compiler brings this capability to us. Running the static analyzer on the source often is always a good idea. It can outline problems with the code before the application is even run.

Xcode 4 has the static analyzer integrated and allows you to analyze your code and find problems before they come up. To run the static analyzer, go to **Product ➤ Analyze**. This builds the application and runs the build artifacts through the static analyzer and returns the results to you. Figure 4–10 shows the results of a static analysis run in the problems tab in the Navigator area.

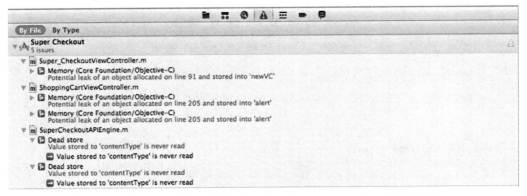

Figure 4–10. *Static analysis shows different kind of problems from dead code to memory leaks.*

Running the static analyzer often during development is a good idea to prevent the most common errors in your code. These results give you enough information to see what the problem is and a start on how to fix them. Some of these items can be very complicated. For example, an object that is declared at the top of a method and then a complicated set of loops and conditionals can leave the object in a state where it is leaking. Another example is overreleasing an object. An object that is instantiated and then told to autorelease and finally is released later in the method will trigger a static analysis error.

Let's take two of the cases from Figure 4–9.

The first item in the list from Figure 4–9 is in Super_CheckoutViewController.m on line 91. Let's take a look at the offending method:

```
- (void)tableView:(UITableView *)tableView didSelectRowAtIndexPath:(NSIndexPath
*)indexPath {
ProductDetailsViewController *newVC = [[ProductDetailsViewController alloc]
    initWithNibName:@"ProductDetailsViewController" bundle:nil];

    [newVC setSelectedProduct:[inventory objectAtIndex:[indexPath row]]];

    [self.navigationController pushViewController:newVC animated:YES];
}
```

The static analyzer tells us the method exits with an object having a "+1 retain count." Can you spot the offending code? Based on the NARC system, we have an allocated object and now balancing release. Adding [newVC release]; as the last line will resolve this problem.

The next example is using the static analyzer to find dead code. In SuperCheckoutAPIEngine.m, we can see the analyzer found a "Dead store" problem. Click on the problem and the editor will show you the error location in the code. Here is the offending method:

```
- (NSMutableURLRequest *)_baseRequestWithMethod:(NSString *)method
                                path:(NSString *)path
                         requestType:(SuperCheckoutRequestType)requestType
                         queryParameters:(NSDictionary *)params
{
    NSString *contentType = [params objectForKey:@"Content-Type"];
    if(contentType){
        params = [params MGTE_dictionaryByRemovingObjectForKey:@"Content-Type"];
    }else{
        contentType = @"application/x-www-form-urlencoded";
    }

    // Construct appropriate URL string.
    NSString *fullPath = [path
 stringByAddingPercentEscapesUsingEncoding:NSNonLossyASCIIStringEncoding];
        if (params && ![method isEqualToString:HTTP_POST_METHOD]) {
        fullPath = [self _queryStringWithBase:fullPath parameters:params prefixed:YES];
    }

    NSString *connectionType = @"http";
```

The static analyzer keyed in on the contentType object not being read. It appears the analyzer found an instance where some code later in the method was removed and some of its setup wasn't. Removing the block of code containing the contentType object will satisfy the static analyzer.

Why don't you go through the rest of the static analyzer results and fix the problems it found?

Aiming for removing all of the blue (the color of static analyzer warnings in the editor) should be the ultimate goal. There are always going to be instances where the static analyzer will show a false positive, but those are fairly rare. One instance where the analyzer will show a false positive is in a common `init` method form:

```
if(self = [super init]) {
    //Do something
}

return self;
```

The static analyzer will notice that you are doing an assignment inside the conditional. It doesn't really like this, yet the code is perfectly valid. I'd like to take a moment to bring up a topic we previously discussed. While this code is valid, is it clear? Sure, you could wrap the assignment in parentheses and satisfy the analyzer, but this doesn't necessarily make the code easier to read. I have adopted the following init style:

```
self = [super init];

if(self) {
    //Do stuff
}

return self;
```

Not only does this pass static analysis, it clearly shows what is going on. Going through and fixing an entire codebase to adopt this new style will take forever, so that isn't recommended. So the lesson here is to initially always ask yourself, "Is this code clear?" Clarity makes for better code and fewer problems, especially during maintenance and adding new features to an existing application.

With these techniques for being proactive against memory leaks, a majority of the common issues related to leaking memory will be prevented. Clarity of code is key to ensuring a codebase stays clean especially in a team environment. Building up technical debt by cutting corners can be fruitful in the short term, but in a maintenance cycle, it can be a huge detriment.

In the end, software has to ship, so learning how to balance technical debt versus doing things absolutely the right way is a career-long lesson. Hopefully, these techniques and the ones that follow will decrease the amount of time you spend debugging and tracking down these issues in your application.

Zombies—No Not Those Kind of Zombies

Since we've inherited a preexisting codebase, we have to go through and manually find the issues so we can remove any memory leaks and find any crashers that are directly related to memory management. To do this, we're going to fire up Instruments and enable `NSZombie` detection.

Zombies? No, we're not looking for "we want to eat your brain" zombies. That is an entirely different book. The kind of zombies we're looking for are pointers to junk memory. When an object is released for the final time and its retain count is zero, the object is deallocated, and the memory is quickly reclaimed by the system. But the pointer to that block of memory is still valid.

How do we detect zombies? First, we need to create an environment variable called NSZombieEnabled and set it to YES. We can do this by opening our scheme editor. Go to **Product ➤ Edit** Scheme or pressing ⌘ + <. With the scheme editor open, choose the Run Super Checkout option on the left, and select the Arguments tab. Add an environment variable with a name of NSZombieEnabled and a value of YES. Your scheme should look like the one shown in Figure 4–11.

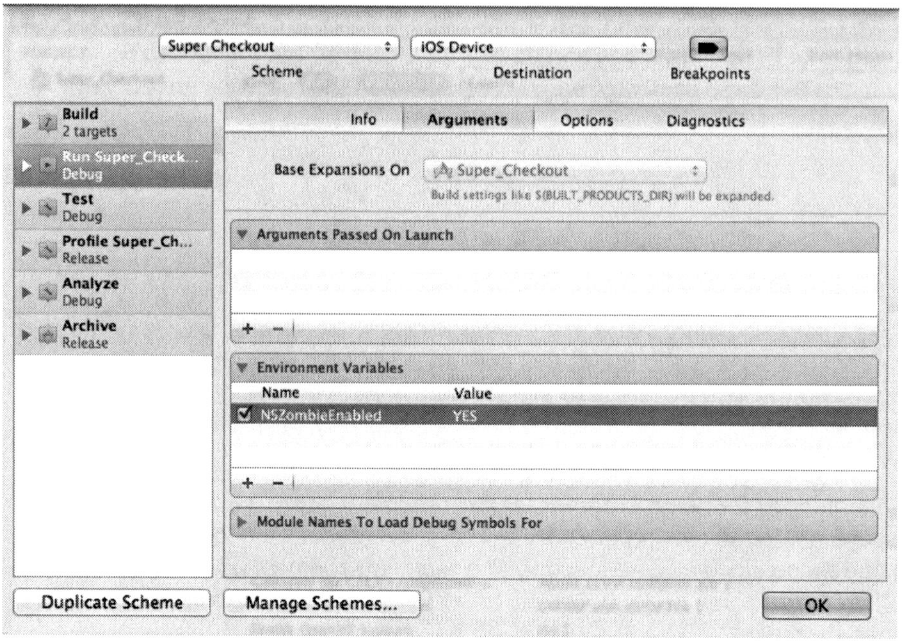

Figure 4–11. *Using the scheme editor to enable NSZombie detection*

We're about to run our application using the Profile action, so click Profile Super Checkout. Make sure the "Use the Run action's options" check box is checked under the Arguments tab. Now, you're ready to profile the application and find some zombies.

Make sure that the simulator is chosen for the destination target in the scheme chooser, click OK, and go to **Product ➤ Profile** to start the process. Instruments will start up with an option to select one of many templates. We're looking for zombies, so select the Zombies option, and click Profile (see Figure 4–12).

Figure 4–12. *The Instruments template screen before the iOS Simulator launches*

The iOS Simulator will launch the application, and you'll see Instruments in the background with the Allocations instrument watching memory allocations. This instrument is already configured to detect NSZombie objects, so all we need to do now is interact with the application. Let's go ahead and run through a test case to see if we can find an NSZombie.

The test case we're going to run through is adding a fruit to our cart and viewing our cart. Go ahead and select a fruit, configure the quantity, and click Add to Basket. After the item is added to the basket, the inventory list comes back into view. Click the Cart button at the top right, and you'll notice that the application crashes. As Figure 4–13 shows, Instruments has detected a message passed to an instance of NSZombie.

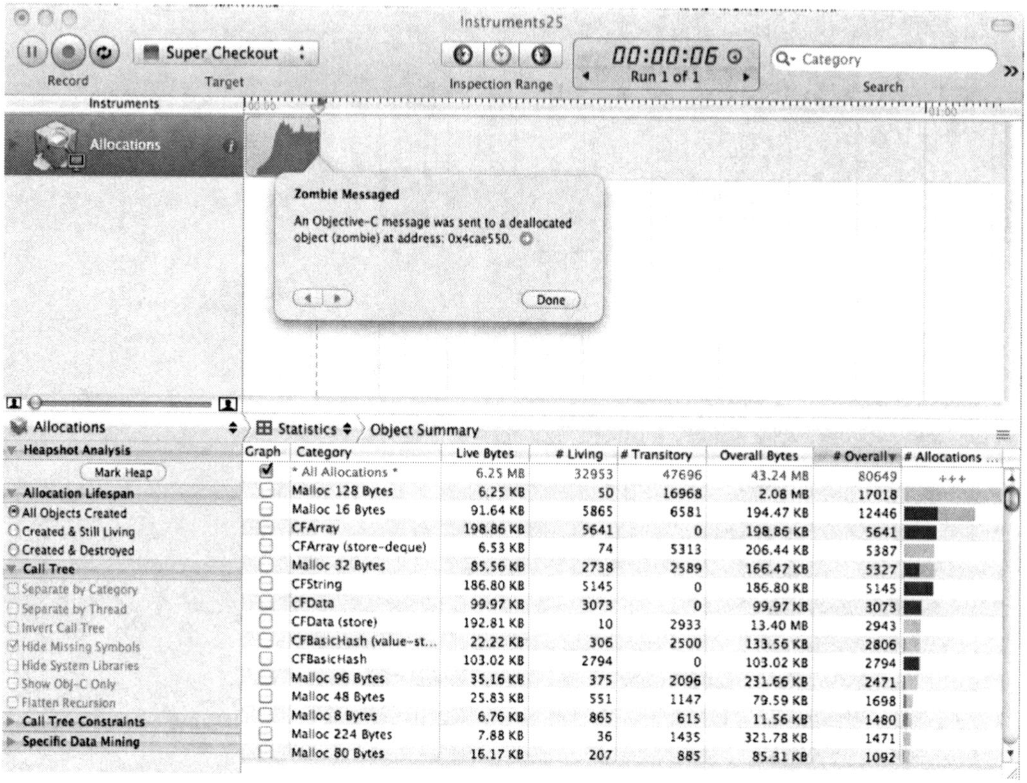

Figure 4–13. *Instruments has detected a message being passed to an instance of NSZombie.*

We know that we have a pretty serious bug on our hands, because the application crashes. We've used Instruments to detect it, and now, we need to fix it. Click the arrow next to the message that popped up, and the details of the changes to the retain count of the offending object come up. In these details, we can see the following events happen (see Figure 4–14):

1. The `malloc` method is run on the object.

2. The object is then added to the autorelease pool.

3. The object is retained.

4. The object is released, twice.

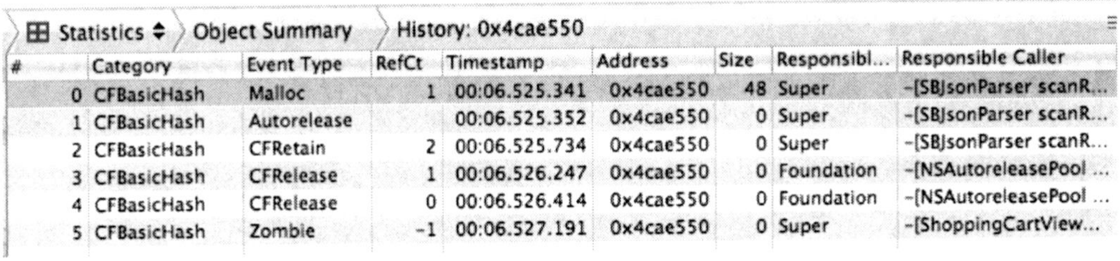

Statistics ◆ Object Summary History: 0x4cae550

#	Category	Event Type	RefCt	Timestamp	Address	Size	Responsibl...	Responsible Caller
0	CFBasicHash	Malloc	1	00:06.525.341	0x4cae550	48	Super	-[SBJsonParser scanR...
1	CFBasicHash	Autorelease		00:06.525.352	0x4cae550	0	Super	-[SBJsonParser scanR...
2	CFBasicHash	CFRetain	2	00:06.525.734	0x4cae550	0	Super	-[SBJsonParser scanR...
3	CFBasicHash	CFRelease	1	00:06.526.247	0x4cae550	0	Foundation	-[NSAutoreleasePool ...
4	CFBasicHash	CFRelease	0	00:06.526.414	0x4cae550	0	Foundation	-[NSAutoreleasePool ...
5	CFBasicHash	Zombie	-1	00:06.527.191	0x4cae550	0	Super	-[ShoppingCartView...

Figure 4–14. *The offending object's retain count history*

Figure 4–14 also shows when these items occurred, the responsible library, and the responsible caller. We're mostly interested in the responsible caller. Looking at the information Instruments gives us, we can see three calls into the `SBJsonParser` class, two `NSAutoreleasePool` drains, and the zombie call being made in `ShoppingCartViewController`. Look at the call stack for the call to the zombie object: open the right pane of the Instruments window (using the right button above View in the toolbar at the top of the window), and select the Zombie call in the event list.

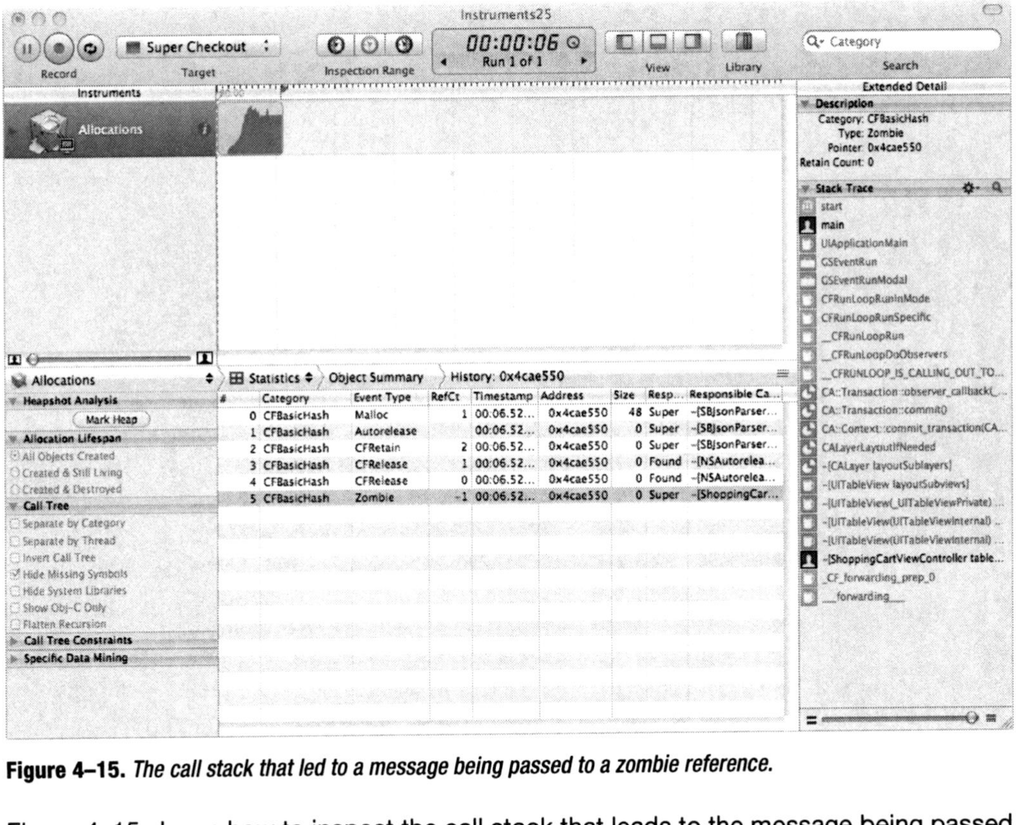

Figure 4–15. *The call stack that led to a message being passed to a zombie reference.*

Figure 4–15 shows how to inspect the call stack that leads to the message being passed to a zombie and the ultimate reason the application crashed. The call stack we're looking at shows some Objective-C runtime and framework calls being made. We're not too interested in those, so double-click the `ShoppingCartViewController` call in the call stack. This will take us to the offending code. The offending line is right here:

```
NSDictionary *cartItem = [[shoppingCart objectForKey:@"items"] objectAtIndex:[indexPath row]];
```

The code looks simple enough. We're grabbing an array from a dictionary and getting an item out of that array. Where is the zombie in this instance? The only object we're working with is the `shoppingCart`, so that must be it. But why is it a zombie reference? A clue lies in the history of this object. The object begins in the `SBJsonParser` and winds up in the `ShoppingCartViewController`. Why is the view controller not retaining it? Good question! Let's take a journey to one of the delegate callbacks, `cartContentsReceived:forRequest:` to be exact. Here is the method:

```
-(void) cartContentsReceived:(NSDictionary *)cart forRequest:(NSString *)connectionIdentifier {
    shoppingCart = cart;

    NSNotification *note = [NSNotification notificationWithName:@"CartUpdated" object:[NSNumber
numberWithInt:[[shoppingCart objectForKey:@"items"] count]]];

    [[NSNotificationCenter defaultCenter] postNotification:note];

    [self.tableView reloadData];

    if([[shoppingCart objectForKey:@"items"] count] == 0) {
        [self setEditing:NO];
    }
}
```

Can you spot the issue? Yes, the problem is the first line of the method. To fix it, all we need to do is update that line to be

```
shoppingCart = [cart retain];
```

Now, let's run the application and perform the same steps. Does the application crash when you go to the shopping cart screen? No? Good. Congratulations! We have fixed our first glaring bug in the application.

Zombies in Other Threads (Well Sort Of)

So far, we've fixed a number of issues ranging from simple memory leaks found by the static analyzer to finding `NSZombie` instances. There are still more issues in this application. Let's say, for this example, that the QA department has come back with a crashing bug with the following description: "Application crashes when the user views the detail screen and quickly navigates back to the product screen. Problem is more prevalent on an iPhone on a 3G connection than on a Wi-Fi connection."

The QA engineer sent a crash log with the bug report (the actual crash log is longer, but we're interested in the main thread since that is where the crash happened):

```
Thread 0 name:  Dispatch queue: com.apple.main-thread
Thread 0 Crashed:
0   libobjc.A.dylib             0x00002c9a objc_msgSend + 18
1   Foundation                  0x000122ee -
[NSURLConnection(NSURLConnectionReallyInternal)
 sendDidFinishLoading] + 62
2   Foundation                  0x00012270 _NSURLConnectionDidFinishLoading + 72
3   CFNetwork                   0x0000f40a
URLConnectionClient::_clientDidFinishLoading(URLConnectionClient::ClientConnectionEventQ
ueu
e*) + 130
4   CFNetwork                   0x00003f42
 URLConnectionClient::ClientConnectionEventQueue::processAllEventsAndConsumePayload(XCo
nnectionEventInfo<XClientEvent, XClientEventParams>*, long) + 94
5   CFNetwork                   0x00003e34 URLConnectionClient::processEvents() + 64
6   CFNetwork                   0x00003de6
 URLConnection::multiplexerClientPerform(RunLoopMultiplexer*) + 30
7   CFNetwork                   0x00003d58 MultiplexerSource::perform() + 120
8   CFNetwork                   0x00003cd6 MultiplexerSource::_perform(void*) + 2
9   CoreFoundation              0x00075a72
  __CFRUNLOOP_IS_CALLING_OUT_TO_A_SOURCE0_PERFORM_FUNCTION__ + 6
10  CoreFoundation              0x00077758 __CFRunLoopDoSources0 + 376
11  CoreFoundation              0x000784e4 __CFRunLoopRun + 224
12  CoreFoundation              0x00008ebc CFRunLoopRunSpecific + 224
13  CoreFoundation              0x00008dc4 CFRunLoopRunInMode + 52
14  GraphicsServices            0x00004418 GSEventRunModal + 108
15  GraphicsServices            0x000044c4 GSEventRun + 56
16  UIKit                       0x0002ed62 -[UIApplication _run] + 398
17  UIKit                       0x0002c800 UIApplicationMain + 664
18  Super Checkout              0x00002648 0x1000 + 5704
19  Super Checkout              0x00002608 0x1000 + 5640
```

Not very helpful is it? Looking at the crash log, we can determine that the objc_msgSend call failed. Hmm, a message send failed. That is a pretty big hint; the most likely cause seems to be a message getting sent to a zombie. So what we're going to do now is launch the application with the Zombie instrument. There's a problem though. Based on the bug report, the problem is intermittent and more prevalent on a 3G connection. There is a way to slow your Internet connection, but we'll get to that in a later chapter. For now, we'll bypass using Instruments and attach a device to let Xcode break on the code that breaks.

> **NOTE:** If you don't have a device to connect to your Mac, you can follow the steps for slowing down your connection found in Chapter 6. Since you are running in the simulator, you can run the app against the Zombies instrument and get the same result as we did with the shopping cart screen bug.

Is the device connected? Make sure the device isn't connected to a Wi-Fi connection (if it is an iPhone). Now, run the application on the device by selecting the device deployment target in the Scheme selector (see Figure 4–16). Now, run the application on the device by going to **Product** ➤ **Run**. As the application starts loading images in the cells, begin rapidly selecting a product and tapping back. At some point, the application is going to crash, and Xcode will take over and you'll be presented at a GDB prompt with the application halted at the location shown in Figure 4–1.

Figure 4–16. *Xcode presents your device as it is named in iTunes. In this case, the device is called Communicator.*

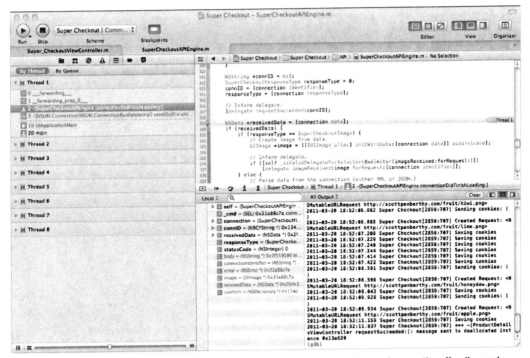

Figure 4–17. *Super Checkout has halted, and the debugger has taken control showing you the offending code.*

Take a look at the console, and you'll see the following text right before the GDB prompt:

```
2011-03-20 18:54:01.276 Super Checkout[2859:707] *** -[ProductDetailsViewController
 respondsToSelector:]: message sent to deallocated instance 0x13a620
```

Our suspicions were correct! We are sending a message to a deallocated object of type ProductDetailsViewController. The code that crashed is in SuperCheckoutAPIEngine.m and we can see the breakpoint stopped right after a call to the delegate of the class. To verify that the delegate is the culprit, expand the self pointer in the variables view next to the console as shown in Figure 4–18. If you don't see the variables view, click the button that shows both the Variables View and the console right above the console next to the Clear button.

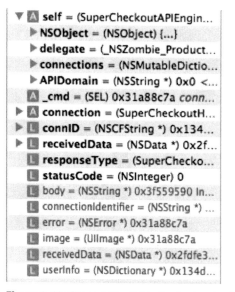

Figure 4–18. *The variables list in Xcode showing the delegate as an NSZombie*

By expanding the self variable, we can see that the delegate is an instance of an NSZombie. Now, let's look at what is going on behind the scenes. By rapidly selecting a product and going back to the product list, we're allocating a new view controller each time. Since the product details screen loads an image, it is using the API engine to get the image. Open the ProductDetailsViewController.m file to view the dealloc method:

```
- (void)dealloc {
    [apiEngine release];
    [selectedProduct release];
    [productDetailsHeader release];
    [productImage release];
    [productNameLabel release];
    [productPriceLabel release];
    [addToBasketCell release];
    [quantityCell release];
    [super dealloc];
}
```

Something is missing. We're not clearing out the delegate on the apiEngine before we release it. Go ahead and add [apiEngine setDelegate:nil]; before releasing apiEngine. Commit that change, and we've fixed another crashing bug.

This bug was a bit more difficult to find and reproduce, since it was sitting inside some asynchronous network code—it is easy to see how complicated these things become. This is the second line of defense against memory-related bugs.

Leaks

Now, assume QA has come back with a report that states the application grows more and more sluggish the longer it is being used. After several minutes of scrolling up and down, the application finally crashes. This problem sounds like a memory leak, so let's see what we can find.

Note that this problem arose after a deployment was made where some other code was updated and the following change was made to the imageReceived:forRequest: selector in Super_CheckoutViewController.m:

```
-(void) imageReceived:(UIImage *)image forRequest:(NSString *)connectionIdentifier {
    ProductCell *cell = (ProductCell *)[self.tableView
cellForRowAtIndexPath:[imageIndexPaths
 objectForKey:connectionIdentifier]];

    CGFloat target = 64;

    CGImageRef oldImage = [image CGImage];
    CGFloat imageWidth = (CGFloat)CGImageGetWidth(oldImage);
    CGFloat imageHeight = (CGFloat)CGImageGetHeight(oldImage);

    CGFloat widthFactor = target / imageWidth;
    CGFloat heightFactor = target / imageHeight;
    CGFloat factor = 1.0;

    if (widthFactor > 1.0 && heightFactor > 1.0) {
        factor = 1.0;
    } else {
        if (widthFactor >= heightFactor) {
            factor = widthFactor;
        } else {
            factor = heightFactor;
        }
    }

    CGColorSpaceRef colorSpace = CGColorSpaceCreateDeviceRGB();
    CGContextRef imageContext = CGBitmapContextCreate(NULL, imageWidth, imageHeight, 8,
4
 * imageWidth, colorSpace, kCGImageAlphaPremultipliedFirst);
    CGContextDrawImage(imageContext, CGRectMake(0, 0, imageWidth, imageHeight),
oldImage);
    CGContextScaleCTM(imageContext, imageWidth * factor, imageHeight * factor);
    CGImageRef newImage = CGBitmapContextCreateImage(imageContext);


    UIImage *resizedImage = [[UIImage alloc] initWithCGImage:newImage];

    [cell.productImage setImage:resizedImage];

    [imageIndexPaths removeObjectForKey:connectionIdentifier];
}
```

The requirements were to resize the image to match the dimensions of the image to be displayed. The new code has some pretty obvious issues, but we're going to run it through Instruments and locate the issues with the code.

We don't need to run the application on the device, so switch back to the simulator using the scheme selector. Profile the application, and this time, select Leaks when Instruments comes up and asks you which template to use (see Figure 4–19).

Figure 4–19. *Launching Instruments with the Leaks template*

When the application launches in the simulator, scroll up and down the table view several times, and you'll see a few leaks pop up in the Leaks instrument chart. Quit the iOS Simulator, and bring Instruments to the foreground to analyze the data. Click the Leaks chart to see a view like the one shown in Figure 4–20.

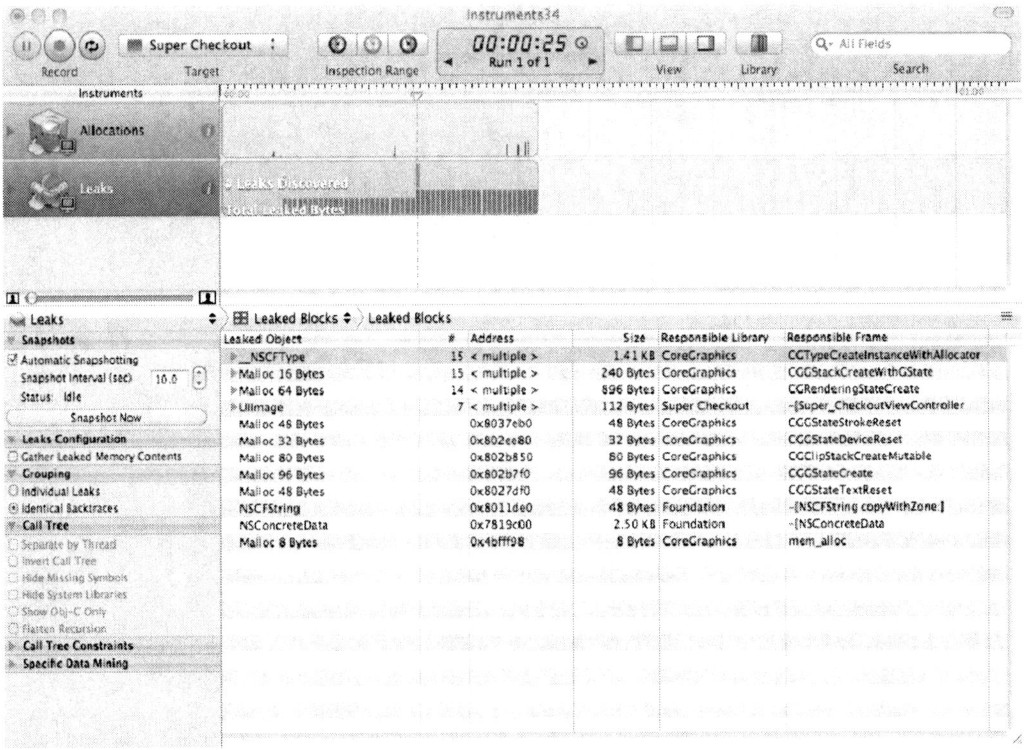

Figure 4–20. *Instruments showing a few leaks and the memory where the leak has been detected*

Let's take a moment to look at this data. Instruments is telling us there are several places where memory is leaking. The code that was introduced to the latest build has some Core Graphics code as well as some UIImage instances that appeared to be leaking. Instruments confirms the suspicions, but we don't know the details of the leaks. Expand the UIImage tree, and select the top UIImage instance. Now, click the arrow that is next to the memory address to display the details of the leak. This is like the allocations instrument when a zombie was sent a message. Figure 4–21 shows an example of this.

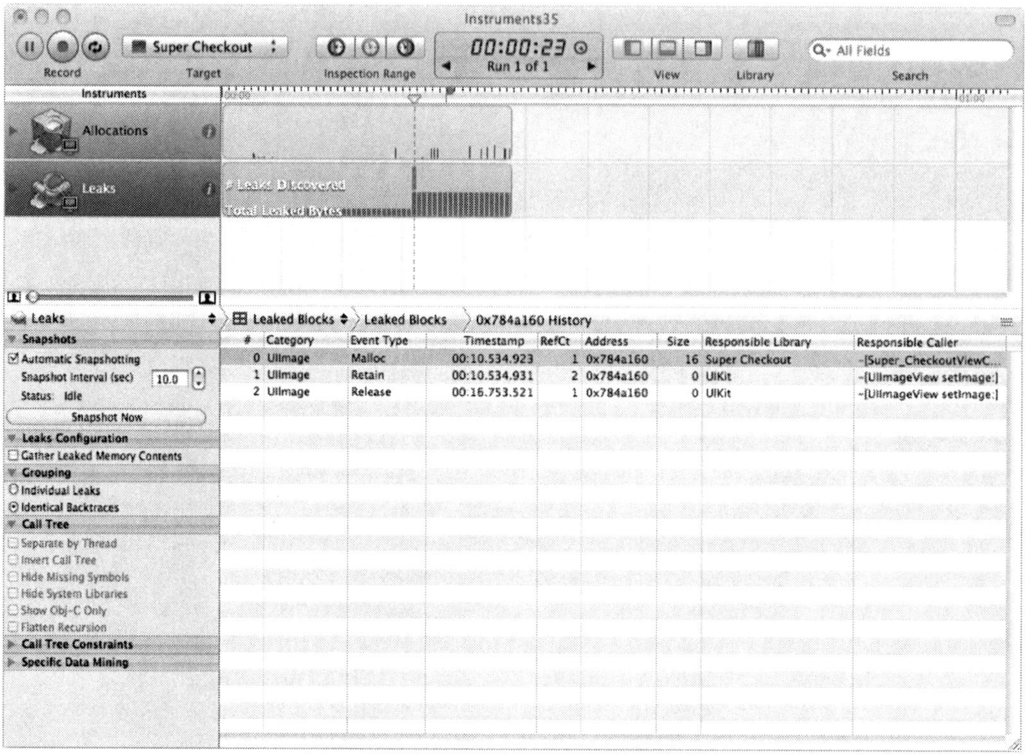

Figure 4–21. *In this Instruments detail view of a single leak, notice the reference count view and how it is left with a count of 1.*

Expand the Extended Detail pane (click the right main view button in the toolbar), and look at the call stack based on any of the items in the history of the leak. You've seen this view before, so double-click one of the call stack items that occur in our code. This brings up the source code for the offending file, and it has some annotations on it to let you know which variables are leaking and how much they are leaking. Figure 4–22 shows the same view.

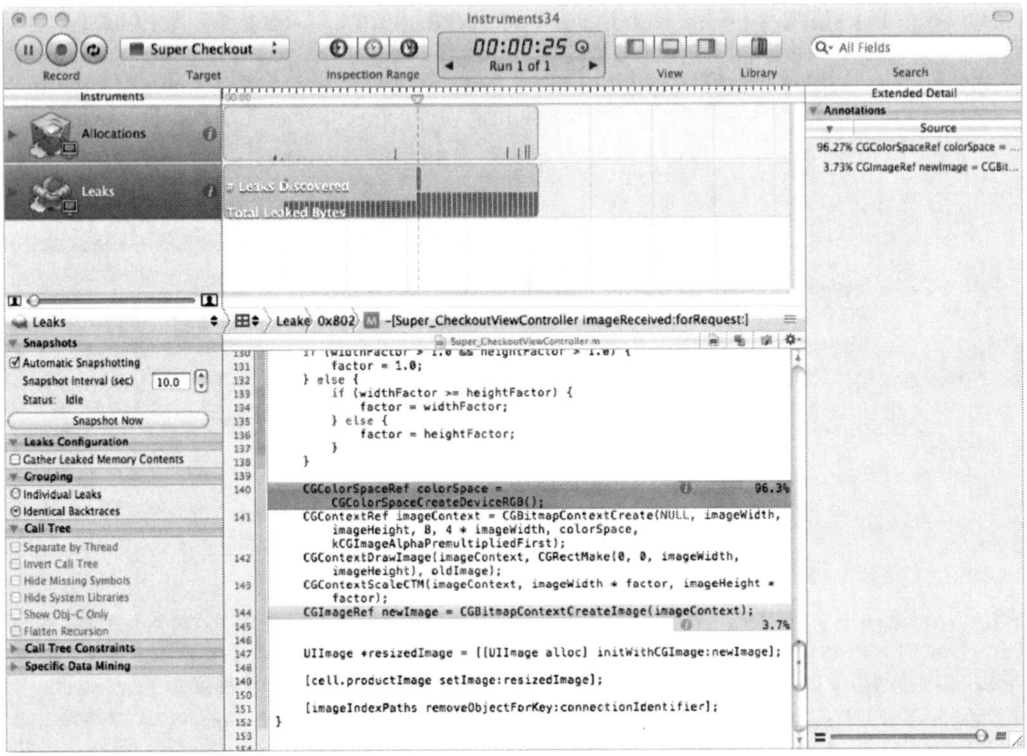

Figure 4–22. *Inspecting the source shows some likely culprits*

We've been able to track down which objects were leaked by the changes, so let's fix those leaks. Clicking the Xcode icon in the editor will bring up Xcode with the offending code in view. Since some of the code is using C APIs, we need to remember that pretty much any C function that has "create" in the name will create a new reference; we need to balance that with a release.

Open the file in Xcode, and modify the section under the `if` statement to match this:

```
CGColorSpaceRef colorSpace = CGColorSpaceCreateDeviceRGB();
CGContextRef imageContext = CGBitmapContextCreate(NULL, imageWidth, imageHeight, 8, 4
* imageWidth, colorSpace, kCGImageAlphaPremultipliedFirst);
CGContextDrawImage(imageContext, CGRectMake(0, 0, imageWidth, imageHeight),
oldImage);
CGContextScaleCTM(imageContext, imageWidth * factor, imageHeight * factor);
CGImageRef newImage = CGBitmapContextCreateImage(imageContext);

CGColorSpaceRelease(colorSpace);
CGContextRelease(imageContext);

UIImage *resizedImage = [[UIImage alloc] initWithCGImage:newImage];

[cell.productImage setImage:resizedImage];

CGImageRelease(newImage);
[resizedImage release];
```

Now, rerun the application through leaks, and scroll around a bunch. Did that fix the issue? A few leaks are still detected by Instruments. OK, we're going to dive in and look at these leaks. We've fixed the original issue, but I'm not happy until all leaks are taken care of. Figure 4–23 shows one of the items from Instruments that it thinks is leaking:

#	Category	Event Type	Timestamp	RefCt	Address	Size	Responsible Library	Responsible Caller
0	CFString	Malloc	00:04.012.019	1	0x163830	48	Foundation	-[NSCFString copyWithZ...
1	CFString	Autorelease	00:04.012.040		0x163830	0	Super Checkout	-[SuperCheckoutAPIEng...
2	CFString	CFRetain	00:04.012.732	2	0x163830	0	Foundation	-[NSCFString retain]
3	CFString	CFRelease	00:04.053.943	1	0x163830	0	Foundation	-[NSAutoreleasePool drain]

Figure 4–23. *An example of a leak found in an autorelease pool*

Figure 4–23 shows an example of a leak (the last in the list) that was detected in an autorelease pool. If we follow the memory history for this object, we see the following:

- *Malloc*: Retain count is 1

- *Autorelease*: Added to the current autorelease pool

- *Retain*: Retain count is 2

- *Release*: Retain count is 1

What we have is an object that is sitting in an autorelease pool ready to be released. Why hasn't it been released then? The answer lies in our main function. When the application starts up, an autorelease pool is created. If another autorelease pool isn't created, and the code is being executed on the main thread, those objects get added to the autorelease pool created for the application. This means the memory will stick around until the application is terminated, and the topmost autorelease pool is drained. For more information about autorelease pools, check out "Memory Management Programming Guide" in the Apple Developer Library.

Don't feel like you have license to create autorelease pools everywhere, however. Since we live in a memory-constrained world as iOS developers, we need to be good citizens and clean up after ourselves. Creating autorelease pools can cause unintended consequences, so use an autorelease pool only when absolutely necessary. A good time to create one is in a pretty tight loop that could very easily create a lot of quickly used temporary objects.

Revisiting Retain Cycles

Earlier in the chapter, we discussed detecting retain cycles with Instruments. Since Super Checkout doesn't have any retain cycles, we're going to have to manufacture one. Rather than walking you through building a brand new project and manufacturing a retain cycle, I've already done the hard work for you. This example fits within the same workflow as using the Leaks instrument in Instruments.

The new feature in Instruments that shows you retain cycles can be found in the Jump Bar for the Leaks instrument. Figure 4–24 shows the manufactured retain cycle with the appropriate item selected in the Jump Bar.

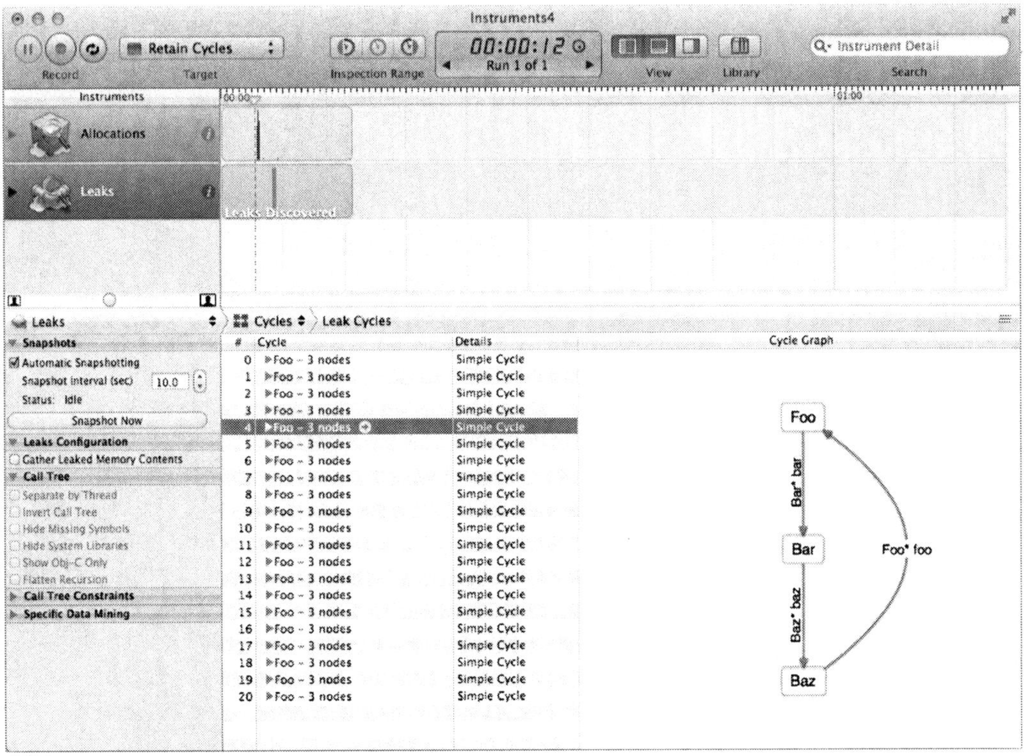

Figure 4–24. *Instruments showing a simple retain cycle*

The first thing to notice in Figure 4–17 is the graph to the right. This shows the exact cycle in memory and how the references relate to each other. The cycle in question shows a typical child retaining a parent. In the list to the left, you can see the various cycles from this run. They are all the same in this case, and the workflow for finding the stack trace to determine where the cycle was created.

In this example, clicking the arrow next to the cycle will bring up Figure 4–25 (the right area is expanded for extra detail). The resulting view is a better view of the retain cycle, and the stack trace that caused the cycle. Clicking each node will bring up a different stack trace, so you can determine where in the code the cycle was truly created and break it.

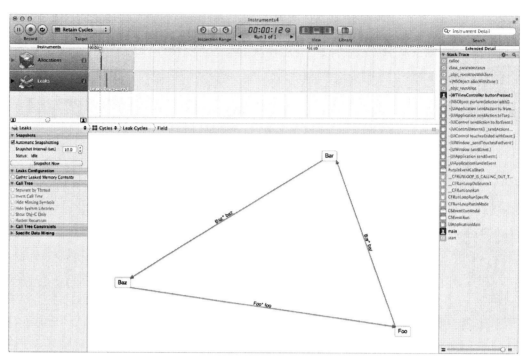

Figure 4–25. *The cycle details with the stack trace showing where the cycle started.*

With cycles out of the way, we are well on our way to fully using the tools at our disposal for finding and fixing memory related issues.

GDB Kung Fu

When all else fails, you have a very interesting bug. As you discovered in the previous example, asynchronous code is extremely hard to debug. Throw in multithreaded code that modifies the same objects, locking or not, and you can create some interesting problems to solve. There are entire branches of computer science to tackling some of these types of problems.

Super Checkout is a pretty simple application. The inputs and outputs are well defined, and the network communication is fairly trivial. Your application is likely not going to be as trivial. You might be running into deadlocks, an occurrence where two threads are waiting on each other to finish with a resource or race conditions. Those two problems are very hard to diagnose without stepping in with a very low level tool.

GDB, Don't Fail Me Now

One of my favorite songs growing up was Little Feat's, "Don't Fail Me Now." The song came out about the same time that Richard Stallman was starting his GNU's Not Unix push for free software. Back then, C was the de facto standard for any sort of Unix programming. His debugger was GDB, the Gnu Debugger.

GDB is the heart and soul of the Xcode and Instrument debugging tools. Many of the beautiful charts, histograms, and menus are Apple's delicious design and marketing prowess applied to GDB.

Sometimes, however, the GUI can get in the way. If you've reached at this stage of our chapter and still haven't found your bug, its truly time to crack your knuckles, shake your fingers a bit, and dive into the command-line GDB tool suite. You might hum to yourself, "GDB, don't fail me now."

Getting Started with GDB

To get yourself comfortable with GDB, place a visual breakpoint in the `viewDidLoad:` method of `Super_CheckoutViewController.m` (see Figure 4–26). To create a visual breakpoint, click anywhere in the gutter of the editor.

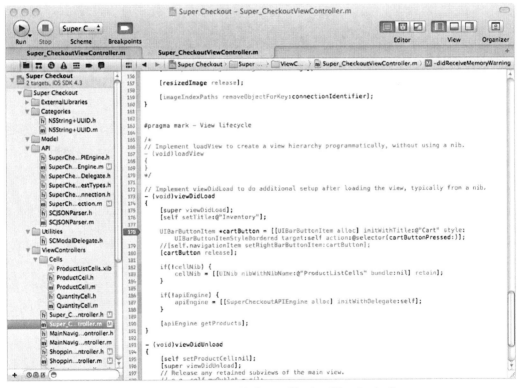

Figure 4–26. *A visual breakpoint on line 178 placed in* **Super_CheckoutViewController.m**

Run the application and when the app breaks, press ⌘ + shift + Y to pull up the debugging console if it is not already visible. Three unassuming blue letters will be waiting for you, ensconced in parentheses, as shown Figure 4–27.

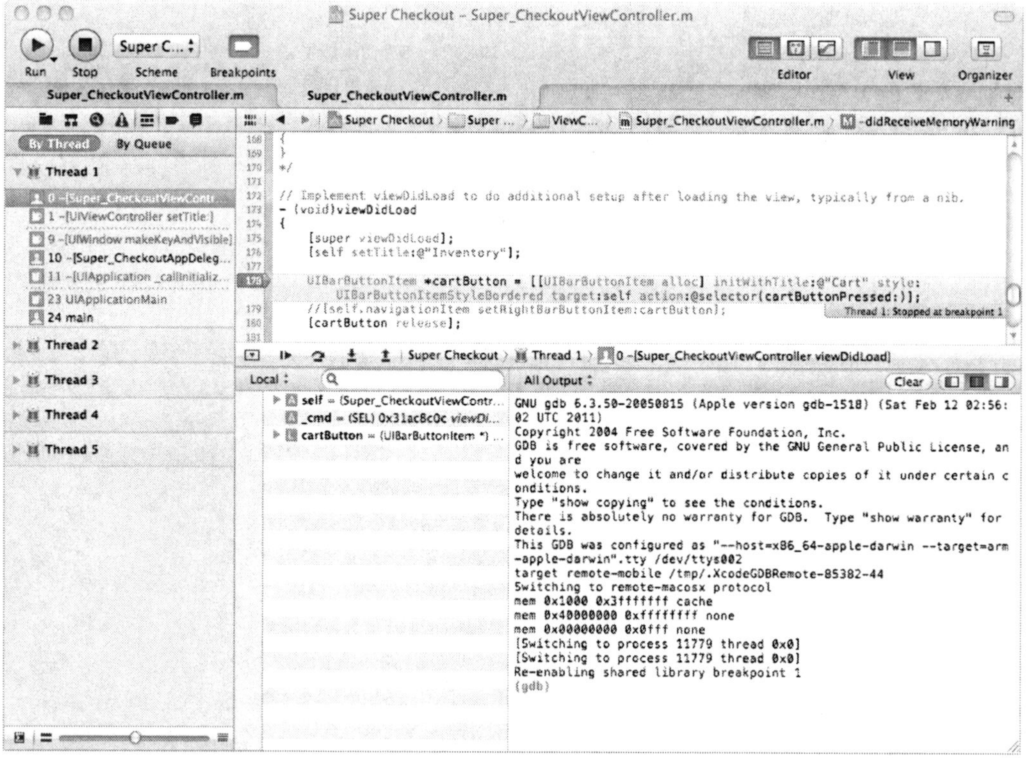

Figure 4–27. *GDB awaiting your command after breaking on a visual breakpoint*

Figure 4–27 shows the default prompt for the GDB debugger. Do not be afraid. It's friendly. It knows how to add, multiply, and perform any C expression. Click next to the (gdb) prompt. We often use the p command followed by an expression for quick evaluations. Try typing p 2+2 and pressing return. You should see the following output:

```
(gdb) p 2+2
$1 = 4
```

You can build on the result. GDB sets dollar sign variables for expressions you enter. Let's take our number and add 10:

```
(gdb) p $1+10
$2 = 14
```

Play with it a bit. Soon, you may get bored. The real value in GDB is the ability to dynamically evaluate expressions, inspect variables, set breakpoints, and adjust variables' values on the fly as you hunt down your memory bug.

Remove the visual breakpoint by dragging the breakpoint out of the gutter into some other space. The breakpoint will then go "poof," similar to the way an icon gets removed from the Dock in OS X. You can enable or disable breakpoints by selecting or deselecting the breakpoints button next to the scheme selector in the toolbar in Xcode.

Determining Context—Where Am I?

Now that you're comfortable with typing some basic commands, let's find a place where our application needs more debugging help. Run the application, and add a fruit to your cart. Move to the shopping cart view, and try to remove the item by touching the edit button or swiping the cell to delete it. The application blows up with an exception from the table view. This is a great place to dive into GDB, since this is a runtime exception and not a memory issue. The exception occurs on line 170, so place a visual breakpoint on line 168, where we invoke [tableView beginUpdates].

Stop the application, and rerun the application performing the same steps. This time the application halts at our breakpoint. Let's see where our breakpoint has occurred in code. Click in the console panel, and enter the l command, for "listing," and press return:

```
(gdb) l
163         // Delete the row from the data source
164         NSDictionary *item = [[shoppingCart objectForKey:@"items"]
objectAtIndex:[indexPath row]];
165
166         [apiEngine removeProductFromCart:[item objectForKey:@"id"] withQuantity:[item
objectForKey:@"quantity"]];
167
168         [tableView beginUpdates];
169         [tableView deleteRowsAtIndexPaths:[NSArray arrayWithObject:indexPath]
withRowAnimation:UITableViewRowAnimationRight];
170         [tableView endUpdates];
171
172     }
(gdb)
```

GDB shows a block of code that surrounds the current breakpoint. You can see more information about why GDB has stopped with the backtrace command, asking for the first item on the stack. That will be the most recent function call.

```
(gdb) bt 1
#0  -[ShoppingCartViewController tableView:commitEditingStyle:forRowAtIndexPath:]
(self=0x12e080, _cmd=0x31ab6e38, tableView=0x9c0c00,
editingStyle=UITableViewCellEditingStyleDelete, indexPath=0x1b6750) at
/Users/brandon/Development/iOS/Super Checkout/Super Checkout/../Super
Checkout/ShoppingCartViewController.m:168
(More stack frames follow...)
(gdb)
```

We see that the debugger has stopped at line 168 of our source code. The listing showed us a visual context, a few lines before and after where it stopped. That's the static part of your code. It gives you a sense of what your app is about to do. The debugger also shows the dynamic context, or the live stack of function calls that got you here in the first place.

Let's look a little deeper now. Type the command bt 5, which standards for "show me five function calls into the stack;" this command is called a backtrace:

```
(gdb) bt 5
#0  -[ShoppingCartViewController tableView:commitEditingStyle:forRowAtIndexPath:]
(self=0x12e080, _cmd=0x31ab6e38, tableView=0x9c0c00,
editingStyle=UITableViewCellEditingStyleDelete, indexPath=0x1b6750) at
/Users/brandon/Development/iOS/Super Checkout/Super Checkout/../Super
Checkout/ShoppingCartViewController.m:168
#1  -[ShoppingCartViewController tableView:commitEditingStyle:forRowAtIndexPath:]
(self=0x1b6750, _cmd=0x318bb84b, tableView=0x2fdfdcac, editingStyle=10226688,
indexPath=0x12e080) at /Users/brandon/Development/iOS/Super Checkout/Super
Checkout/../Super Checkout/ShoppingCartViewController.m:168
#2  0x3193dfb4 in -[UITableViewCell(UITableViewCellInternal)
deleteConfirmationControlWasClicked:] ()
#3  0x330da570 in -[NSObject(NSObject) performSelector:withObject:withObject:] ()
#4  0x31766ec8 in -[UIApplication sendAction:to:from:forEvent:] ()
(More stack frames follow...)
(gdb)
```

This is a manual way of showing the same information Xcode gives us in the Debug navigator, in the Navigator area. You can navigate the stack backtrace visually and see the code change from other source if the code is your own, or assembly if it is into framework code (see Figure 4–28).

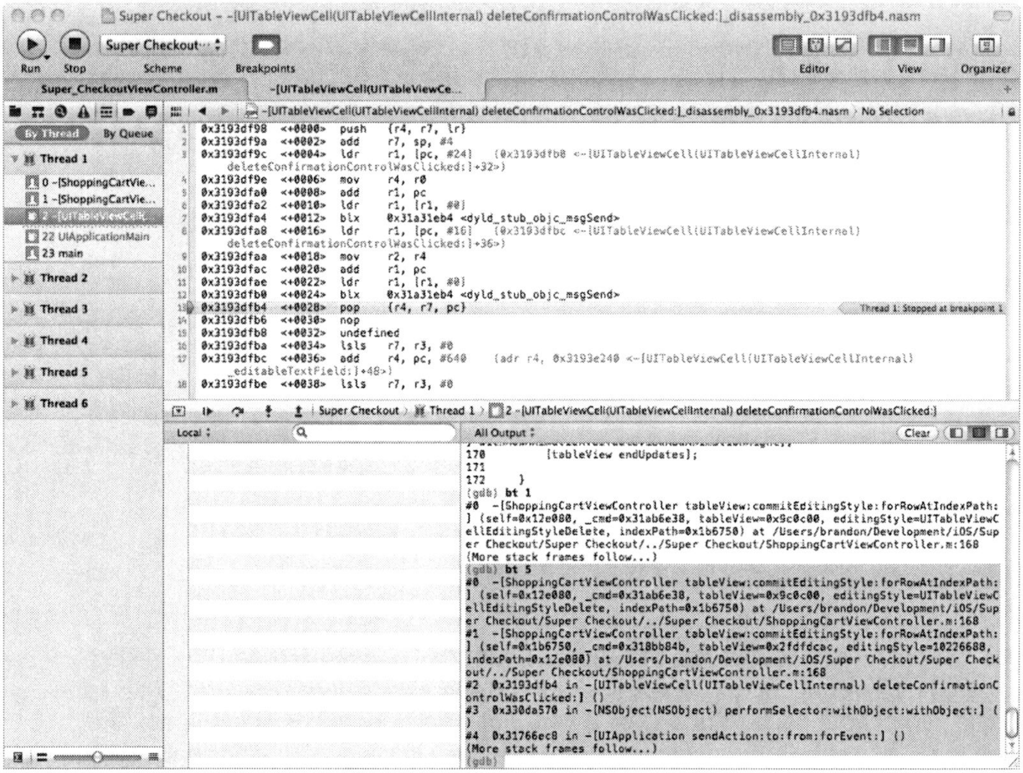

Figure 4–28. *Navigating the stack backtrace visually using the Debug Navigator*

Inspecting Data—What Have I Got?

We should also take a peek at the runtime values to understand what's been going on. GDB provides a wealth of tools for inspecting values. Check out the arguments to our method with info args. See all the local variables in your current stack frame with info locals:

```
(gdb) info args
self = (ShoppingCartViewController *) 0x12e080
_cmd = (SEL) 0x31ab6e38
tableView = (UITableView *) 0x9c0c00
editingStyle = UITableViewCellEditingStyleDelete
indexPath = (NSIndexPath *) 0x1b6750
(gdb) info locals
item = (NSDictionary *) 0x126f00
(gdb)
```

That's nice.

The command whatis inspects the runtime type of an argument and is quite useful for NSDictionary entries, delegates (of type id), and polymorphic arguments. Memory bugs can occur when you've got a type mismatch, that is, when performing operations you think are safe on the wrong type. Here we examine the type of item:

```
(gdb) whatis item
type = NSDictionary *
(gdb)
```

OK, that's what we expected. We can peek inside the structure. This is what Xcode uses when you ask to print an argument on your console. Type po followed by your variable name; po is short for "print object":

```
(gdb) po item
{
    id = 3;
    name = "Blood Orange";
    price = 110;
    quantity = 1;
    subtotal = 110;
}
(gdb)
```

Here, we can inspect that state of the application before it blows up. We haven't quite looked at the error we ran into earlier though. Type c at the GDB prompt to continue execution and allow the application to crash again. Let's inspect the problem a bit deeper. The console reads as follows:

```
(gdb) c
Continuing.
2011-03-21 01:00:28.681 Super Checkout[3550:707] *** Assertion failure in -[UITableView
_endCellAnimationsWithContext:], /SourceCache/UIKit/UIKit-1448.89/UITableView.m:995
2011-03-21 01:00:28.711 Super Checkout[3550:707] *** Terminating app due to uncaught
exception 'NSInternalInconsistencyException', reason: 'Invalid update: invalid number of
rows in
section 0.  The number of rows contained in an existing section after the update (1)
must be equal
```

to the number of rows contained in that section before the update (1), plus or minus the number of
rows inserted or deleted from that section (0 inserted, 1 deleted).'
*** Call stack at first throw:
(
    0   CoreFoundation   0x3316a64f __exceptionPreprocess + 114
    1   libobjc.A.dylib   0x32b60c5d objc_exception_throw + 24
    2   CoreFoundation   0x3316a491 +[NSException
raise:format:arguments:] + 68
    3   Foundation   0x338b7573 -[NSAssertionHandler
handleFailureInMethod:object:file:lineNumber:description:] + 62
    4   UIKit   0x31879379 -
[UITableView(_UITableViewPrivate)
_endCellAnimationsWithContext:] + 4500
    5   UIKit   0x318832f9 -[UITableView
endUpdatesWithContext:] + 28
    6   UIKit   0x318832d5 -[UITableView endUpdates] +
16
    7   Super Checkout   0x00004287 -[ShoppingCartViewController
tableView:commitEditingStyle:forRowAtIndexPath:] + 314
    8   UIKit   0x318bb84b -
[UITableView(UITableViewInternal)
animateDeletionOfRowWithCell:] + 58
    9   UIKit   0x3193dfb5 -
[UITableViewCell(UITableViewCellInternal) deleteConfirmationControlWasClicked:] + 28
   10 CoreFoundation   0x330da571 -[NSObject(NSObject)
performSelector:withObject:withObject:] + 24
   11 UIKit   0x31766ec9 -[UIApplication
sendAction:to:from:forEvent:] + 84
   12 UIKit   0x31766e69 -[UIApplication
sendAction:toTarget:fromSender:forEvent:] + 32
   13 UIKit   0x31766e3b -[UIControl
sendAction:to:forEvent:] + 38
   14 UIKit   0x31766b8d -[UIControl(Internal)
_sendActionsForEvents:withEvent:] + 356
   15 UIKit   0x31767423 -[UIControl
touchesEnded:withEvent:] + 342
   16 UIKit   0x31765bf5 -[UIWindow
_sendTouchesForEvent:] + 368
   17 UIKit   0x3176556f -[UIWindow sendEvent:] + 262
   18 UIKit   0x3174e313 -[UIApplication sendEvent:] +
298
   19 UIKit   0x3174dc53 _UIApplicationHandleEvent +
5090
   20 GraphicsServices   0x32861e77 PurpleEventCallback + 666
   21 CoreFoundation   0x33141a97
__CFRUNLOOP_IS_CALLING_OUT_TO_A_SOURCE1_PERFORM_FUNCTION__ + 26
   22 CoreFoundation   0x3314383f __CFRunLoopDoSource1 + 166
   23 CoreFoundation   0x3314460d __CFRunLoopRun + 520
   24 CoreFoundation   0x330d4ec3 CFRunLoopRunSpecific + 230
   25 CoreFoundation   0x330d4dcb CFRunLoopRunInMode + 58
   26 GraphicsServices   0x3286141f GSEventRunModal + 114
   27 GraphicsServices   0x328614cb GSEventRun + 62
   28 UIKit   0x31778d69 -[UIApplication _run] + 404
   29 UIKit   0x31776807 UIApplicationMain + 670
   30 Super Checkout   0x00002351 main + 92
   31 Super Checkout   0x000022f0 start + 40

```
)
terminate called after throwing an instance of 'NSException'

Program received signal SIGABRT, Aborted.
0x343e0a1c in __pthread_kill ()
(gdb)
```

At least the exception is descriptive. It appears that we're not updating the shopping cart appropriately. Let's implement that now.

We're going to implement a private method in the `ShoppingCartViewController` class, and since we don't like compiler warnings, we are going to create a category on the class. So at the top of `ShoppingCartViewController.m`, add the bold code:

```
#import "ShoppingCartViewController.h"
#import "ProductCell.h"

@interface ShoppingCartViewController (PrivateMethods)
-(void) removeItemFromCart:(NSDictionary *) item;
@end

@implementation ShoppingCartViewController
```

Now add the implementation of the method. At the bottom of the file, add this:

```
#pragma mark - Private Methods
-(void) removeItemFromCart:(NSDictionary *) itemToRemove {
    NSMutableArray *newItemsArray = [NSMutableArray array];

    for(NSDictionary *item in [shoppingCart objectForKey:@"items"]) {
        if([item valueForKey:@"id"] == [itemToRemove valueForKey:@"id"]) {
            continue;
        }

        [newItemsArray addObject:item];
    }
}
```

Let's test our code now. Disable the breakpoint by either removing it from the editor or turn it off using the toggle button (I recommend turning breakpoints off for now; don't remove the breakpoint because the code hasn't been tested yet). Run the application, add an item to the cart, and remove it from the cart.

That didn't go well, did it? Go ahead and turn breakpoints back on (see why we didn't remove them all?). Let's investigate the issue by stepping through code. But we're going to do it the smart way by making a conditional breakpoint.

A conditional breakpoint only stops when certain values occur in the runtime of your program. This is very useful for values that change a lot, such as the position of a touch, values in long loops, or intermittent failures that seem to occur when certain values become null or reach a critical point.

In this instance, we're going to add several items to our cart and set a breakpoint in the looping code and see if it stops.

Breaking Up Is Not Hard to Do

The first thing we want to do is add a breakpoint to the conditional in the loop we just created (line 247 in `ShoppingCartViewController.m`). Run the application again and this time add several items to your cart. Enter the cart screen and remove one of the items to trigger the first breakpoint. Enter the breakpoint or 'info break' command see the internal breakpoint number assigned by GDB.

```
(gdb) info break
Num Type           Disp Enb Address    What
1   breakpoint     keep y   0x00003fd2 in -[ShoppingCartViewController
tableView:commitEditingStyle:forRowAtIndexPath:] at /Users/brandon/Development/iOS/Super
Checkout/Super Checkout/../Super Checkout/ShoppingCartViewController.m:172
        breakpoint already hit 1 time
2   breakpoint     keep y   0x00004622 in -[ShoppingCartViewController
removeItemFromCart:] at
/Users/brandon/Development/iOS/Super Checkout/Super Checkout/../Super
Checkout/ShoppingCartViewController.m:247
(gdb)
```

You may see other breakpoints listed. Look for the breakpoint corresponding to the loop we want to break once in. I've excerpted it in the preceding code snippet. We want the number in the leftmost column, 2. We want to stop this routine only when the `id` value in a dictionary has reached a value of the `id` of the item to be removed. Since we have that variable in scope, lets ask GDB what the item variable looks like by typing `po item`. The output for this run follows:

```
(gdb) po item
{
    id = 3;
    name = "Blood Orange";
    price = 110;
    quantity = 1;
    subtotal = 110;
}
(gdb)
```

The `id` we're interested in is 3. The objective-c code for this would be

```
[[item objectForKey: @" id"] intValue] == 3
```

The compiler would normally parse this statement, figure out the type of values for each message we send, and compute the expression. GDB can help us evaluate this, too, on the fly. We have to help it out a bit, though. Every single message must be strongly typed. All ambiguities must be eliminated. We do this with typecasting.

Change every message passing call in the condition by casting its type. We do that here:

```
((int) [[item objectForKey: @"id"] intValue] == 3)
```

Let's tell GDB to make breakpoint 14 conditional, that is, GDB will stop only when this condition becomes true. The syntax is `condition NN code`:

```
(gdb) condition 2 ((int) [[item objectForKey: @"id"] intValue] == 3)
```

(gdb)

That's it! Continue with the execution of our program by using the command c, for "continue":

(gdb) c

Soon enough, your debugger will stop when this condition has been reached.

Is there a way to do this in Xcode? Of course there is! What you want to do is go to the Breakpoint Navigator in the Navigator area, or right click the breakpoint you want to edit and click Edit Breakpoint in the contextual menu. Figure 4–29 shows the edit directly from the editor. Since this is simply a GUI on top of GDB, the pickiness is still valid. Typecast everything!

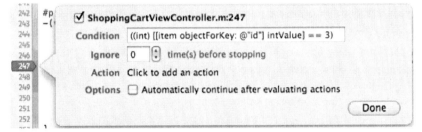

Figure 4–29. *Editing a breakpoint directly from Xcode*

Knowing both ways to make a breakpoint conditional is important. There are times where data can change rapidly and you will need to interact with GDB directly.

Putting It All Together

To finish our GDB training, we're going to step away from the bug for a moment and discuss one last thing with GDB.

The trick for evaluating expressions with typecasting is also useful for manipulating live data, in addition to evaluating conditional breakpoints. Let's combine what you've learned so far. Here, we append a string to a local argument, have GDB create a new string for us with a dollar-sign variable, and then inspect it with po:

```
(gdb) p (NSString *) [caption stringByAppendingString: @" foo"]
$6 = (NSString *) 0x3d9ef0
(gdb) po $6
Seen near Searching... foo
```

We can stuff these values into local variables, too. We change a value with the set <arg>=<value> command. Let's change the caption:

```
(gdb) set caption=$6
(gdb) po caption
Seen near Searching... foo
```

The best way to learn your way around GDB is to experiment. I keep a handy, though slightly ruffled, copy of the GDB quick reference guide next to us when I'm debugging particularly thorny problems; you can download it here:

```
http://refcards.com/docs/peschr/gdb/gdb-refcard-a4.pdf
```

Fixing Our Bug

Since you now have a white belt in GDB kung fu, let's try to solve this issue. We have the breakpoints set, and we are armed with the ability to modify live data and inspect memory. Let's tackle this bug and see what is going on.

Run the application, and add some items to the cart; make sure one of them is the same item that you have your conditional breakpoint set to break at. Try to remove that item from your cart, and let's step through the code.

Instead of typing c to continue, use n to step through and skip over function calls. Typing s steps into a function call and lets you follow the code through different function calls; it may take you into assembly code. When the application breaks, type n, and step over each line until we break on the line where we are skipping the item being removed.

When we break in the loop in question, before we continue, let's make sure the item gets skipped, and then we can compare the two arrays to make sure that item really was removed. To do that, keep stepping through until the method is about to return (or place a breakpoint at the closing curly brace and continue). Print out the contents of shoppingCart and newItemsArray. Here is an example:

```
(gdb) po shoppingCart
{
    items =     (
                {
            id = 1;
            name = Apple;
            price = 79;
            quantity = 1;
            subtotal = 79;
        },
                {
            id = 3;
            name = "Blood Orange";
            price = 110;
            quantity = 1;
            subtotal = 110;
        },
                {
            id = 2;
            name = Honeydew;
            price = 100;
            quantity = 1;
            subtotal = 100;
        }
    );
    total = 289;
```

```
}
(gdb) po newItemsArray
<__NSArrayM 0x4ce8260>(
{
    id = 1;
    name = Apple;
    price = 79;
    quantity = 1;
    subtotal = 79;
},
{
    id = 2;
    name = Honeydew;
    price = 100;
    quantity = 1;
    subtotal = 100;
}
)
```

The item is missing in the new array, but the shopping cart hasn't been updated. Wait! We're not modifying the shopping cart. Well, that was a silly mistake; let's fix this issue by adding the following lines after the end of the loop:

```
NSMutableDictionary *newCart = [NSMutableDictionary
dictionaryWithDictionary:shoppingCart];
[newCart setValue:newItemsArray forKey:@"items"];
shoppingCart = newCart;
```

Now, turn breakpoints off, and test the app. Works like a charm! Without GDB, we would have to resort to using NSLog statements everywhere.

When All Else Fails

If you have reached this point of debugging a problem, still have no solution, and a Google search on your issue is returning the same sites you've visited numerous times, it is time to punt. No, I don't mean punt your computer. That would hurt your foot, and you'd have to buy a new computer; hospital bills and a new computer won't fix the bug. Seriously, though, we've exhausted all options at this point because we've done the following:

- Ruled out messages going to deallocated memory
- Ruled out asynchronous code calling deallocated memory
- Prevented running out of memory and removed memory leaks
- Re-created the issue and stepped through the code using GDB

Wow, we've gone through a nice list of troubleshooting steps and gotten to the end. So what's next?

Heisenbugs

If the issue is a race condition, especially within multiple threads, you might be tempted to litter the code with NSLog statements to check state. Don't. Let me repeat that. Don't do it. By adding NSLog statements, you are changing the conditions of the race condition and could remove it altogether.

Wait, I bet you're asking, "Did he say not to remove the race condition?" Yes, I did say that. While that might be an acceptable solution in the short term, you could very well have a fundamental design issue in the application that will crop up later.

We call these types of bugs Heisenbugs, because they obey the Heisenberg uncertainty principle. The principle states that the simple act of measuring the occurrence of something changes the behavior altogether. For more information about this behavior, do some reading on the "double slit diffraction experiment," and you'll see what the big deal is.

Phone a Friend

Chances are, you're working within a team, so you can always ask a teammate. Having a fresh set of eyes on a problem can bring out the root cause of a bug, especially because of one question, "Why are you doing it this way?" That one question can bring a fresh perspective to the problem and bring about false assumptions when tackling a difficult issue.

The person you bring over to review the code will also have a different level of expertise with certain APIs. They will likely find a problem with the way you are using an API if that is the case. They might also have experience with that type of bug. Leveraging the expertise of your team is a great way to solve tricky issues and build trust within the team. Really, it's a win-win situation.

Start Over

Now, we've reached the end of our list. You've thrown everything at the issue, and it still crops up from time to time. If you've been at this for quite a while, take a break, or sleep on it. Sometimes, a good night's sleep can let your mind ponder on a problem, and you'll wake up with a possible solution.

If the issue is time critical, it might be time to throw up a white flag and redesign that section of code. Start by outlining how the system should behave with diagrams and other tangible things, and map out any edge cases that you think might cause the failure. Keep in mind that this isn't the time to redesign the entire system or module. Reassess your approach, and come up with a solution.

Starting over on the issue isn't really giving up; you've simply discovered one way that doesn't work. After this experience, you'll have a great story to share and experience with debugging that type of issue.

And We're Done . . . Almost

Wow, we've been on quite the journey through this chapter. We started off with an application that had some severe memory issues. It was crashing on some simple actions, and we've solved them. There are still some issues with the app, and we're going to continue with iterating through the application to march forward to releasing a beta version of Super Checkout.

What's left? We have to merge our branch back in with the master branch to continue development with master. Were you committing your changes incrementally as we modified the application? Yes? Good. If not, it's not a big deal for this application. I suggest committing early and often, especially since the Git repository is modified locally until you push to the remote repository.

If you haven't done so, perform a final commit of the project to the memory branch, and open up the Organizer to the Repositories tab. Select your working copy underneath the repository in the repository navigator. We want to switch back to the master branch, since it is going to be the destination of the merge. You can do this by clicking the Switch Branch button at the bottom of the working copy (see Figure 4–30).

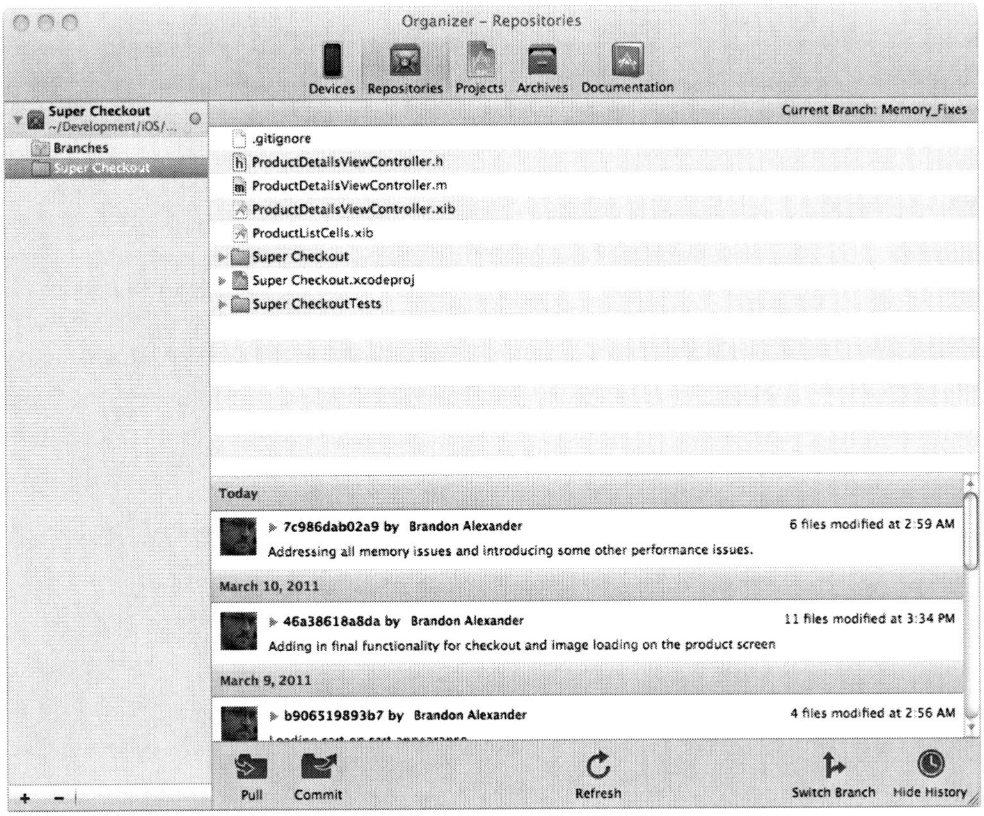

Figure 4–30. *Viewing the history of your working copy*

When you click the Switch Branch button, a sheet is brought up asking you to choose which branch to switch to (see Figure 4–31). Select the master branch, and click OK.

Figure 4–31. *The switch branch sheet*

Now, back in Xcode, we want to merge in the changes from the other branch, so you'll want to select **File ➤ Source Control ➤ Merge**. A sheet is displayed (see Figure 2-32) that asks you which branch to merge in; select Memory_Fixes, and click Choose.

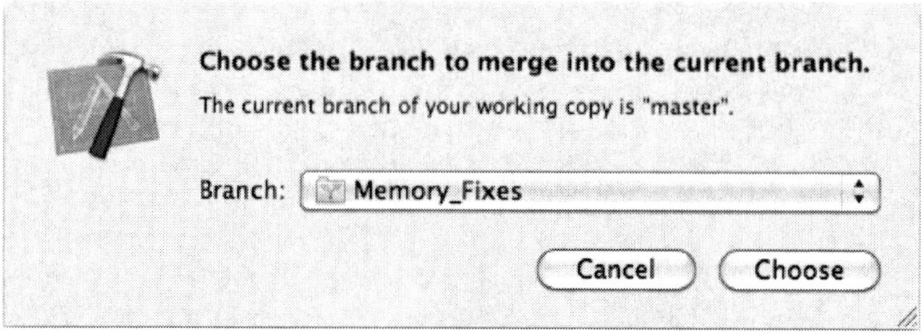

Figure 4–32. *Choosing the branch to merge from*

> **TIP:** Make sure your working copy is the branch you wish to merge to.

The next thing you will see is the final merge confirmation. This sheet allows you to decide which differences you want to include and shows you the preview of the local copy on the left. In the instance of a real conflict, the buttons at the bottom let you choose how you wish to merge the conflict in (see Figure 4–33).

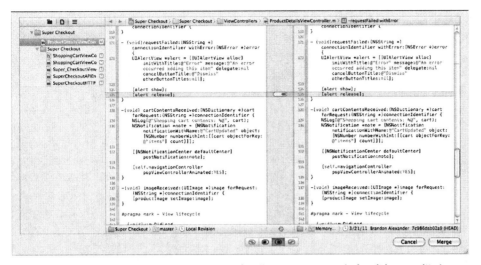

Figure 4–33. *The merge sheet is a handy way to visually see your merge before it is committed.*

Clicking Merge triggers Xcode to perform the merge exactly as you configured it and to commit the changes to the branch. The merge is complete, and switching back to the Organizer to view the revision history of your working copy will reflect the commits that were merged in (see Figure 4–34).

Figure 4–34. *Xcode automatically commits the merge to the repository.*

The merge is complete, and we're ready to move on with the rest of the polish.

Summary

We've covered a lot of ground in this chapter! We talked about the latest compiler technology and how to address memory relates issues. You can now consider yourself a zombie slayer and memory plumber. These accomplishments, however, are only the first steps in solving the problems with Super Checkout. Coming up next are addressing sluggish user interfaces and optimizing our application for creating fluid transitions and fast tables. It is time to learn how to use the next set of tools available to us. Are you ready? Good, turn the page, and let's go!

Chapter 5

Core Animation and Smooth Scrolling

There is nothing more annoying than a sluggish user interface. As developers, we have the job of ensuring applications are responsive and snappy. This is not always easy. Algorithms can become complicated and run for longer than expected. Designers design complicated views with heavy graphics. Combine the two, and you can easily run into a situation where a user interface becomes a bit choppy when scrolling. UITableViews are notorious for having this kind of issue.

In this chapter, you're going to learn how to design algorithms to run efficiently (or fake it) and design views to help the device calculate animations rather than the views themselves. By the end of this chapter, the product list screen of Super Checkout will scroll super fast, and you'll have some great techniques for designing views that will not choke the graphics processor when it is rendering those views to the screen.

You are in for quite the journey. We're going to cover some pretty complicated stuff, so grab some coffee and prepare for the ride.

Leveraging with the Main Thread

The most important part of your application is the main thread. It is the heartbeat of your application. Understanding how the main thread, also referred to as the event loop or run loop, works and its place in the life cycle of your application is key to designing a responsive application. To that end, let's take a look at how our application is launched and the run loop that our instance of UIApplication creates and manages.

The first thing we'll look at is the main.m file. In Listing 1-1, you'll see the main.m file as it exists in Super Checkout:

Listing 5–1. *Super Checkout's main.m File*

```
#import <UIKit/UIKit.h>

int main(int argc, char *argv[]) {
```

```
    NSAutoreleasePool *pool = [[NSAutoreleasePool alloc] init];
    int retVal = UIApplicationMain(argc, argv, nil, nil);
    [pool release];
    return retVal;
}
```

OK, you've seen this plenty of times. It is the default code created when Xcode creates a new project. What does it do though? Let's go line by line:

```
NSAutoreleasePool *pool = [[NSAutoreleasePool alloc] init];
```

creates an autorelease pool for the application.

```
int retVal = UIApplicationMain(argc, argv, nil, nil);
```

creates a single instance (a singleton) of UIApplication for the application, loads the MainWindow nib, and finally starts the main run loop. Loading the nib creates an instance of our implementation of the application delegate, so the application can receive the appropriate notifications during the application's life cycle.

```
 [pool release];
```

releases the autorelease pool to free up any leftover memory that was allocated and autoreleased. We discussed issues surrounding autorelease pools of this type in Chapter 4.

```
return retVal;
```

returns from the function and allows the application to exit and send the caller the return code.

This is all pretty simple stuff, but the beef of our concern lies within the invocation of UIApplicationMain(). This method, as mentioned previously, creates our instance of the UIApplication singleton and wires up everything so our application delegate gets called to set up the initial view and add it to the window for the application. After that happens, Cocoa Touch and UIKit take over and start the process for listening to inputs and drawing the user interface.

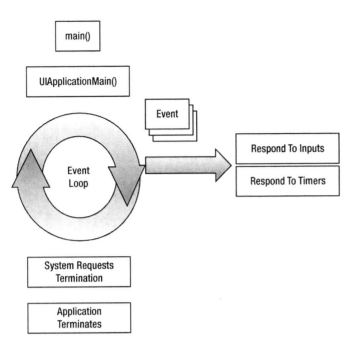

Figure 5–1. *The flow of an application outlining some important pieces of the application life cycle.*

Exploring the Event Loop

Before we get into finding badly performing code, let's take a detailed look at the event loop. When your application is launched, a process is created, and a single thread is created for that process. The event loop runs in this thread. As shown in Figure 5–1, the event loop performs two tasks: it responds to inputs and responds to timers. This concept is pretty simple, but in practice, things are complicated when you want to create an application that remains responsive. Timers are different from input sources in that they are triggered based on time-based calculation and are handled specially by the event loop. The second responsibility of the run loop is to respond to input sources. APIs like NSURLConnection run on the main thread and tie into the event loop when run in asynchronous mode.

When something happens, like the methods viewDidLoad: or touchesBegan:withEvent: are called, your code is executed on the main thread holding up the event loop. Generally, the code being executed is quick and control is returned back to where it belongs. Sometimes, however, that code can take quite some time to execute.

The mantra has always been, "Don't block the main thread." This is absolutely true when it comes to creating an application with a responsive user interface. The caveat to this mindset, however, is to avoid premature optimization. Donald Knuth once said, "We should forget about small efficiencies, say about 97% of the time: premature optimization is the root of all evil."

With that in mind, let's dive in and see what is broken with Super Checkout.

Optimizing Code Execution

For this part of the chapter, we're going to dive into some techniques for diagnosing (and hopefully fixing) code that is running too long. To do this, we need to spend a little time talking about how we can go about fixing this type of issue. Since we are looking at performance issues, we need to run the application in the environment it is meant to run in. This means running the application on whichever device is going to be the primary deployment target.

After that, we'll need to compile the application and prepare it to be run in a release configuration. Ideally, this would mean no NSLog statements and a full release-ready build. Getting this controlled environment is key to a good performance-tuning session.

So how do we set this up? I'm glad you asked! Fire up Xcode, follow the steps to create a new "Master-Detail application" project named Performance Tuning. You won't need all of the other options in the create project sheet; we're just using this project as a quick demonstration app.

Once your app is created, click the project name in the Project navigator panel to open the project settings in your editor. Next, click the project name in this new panel to show the project settings. In the Info tab, click the plus sign in the Configuration section and duplicate the release configuration. Name this configuration Profile (see Figure 5–2).

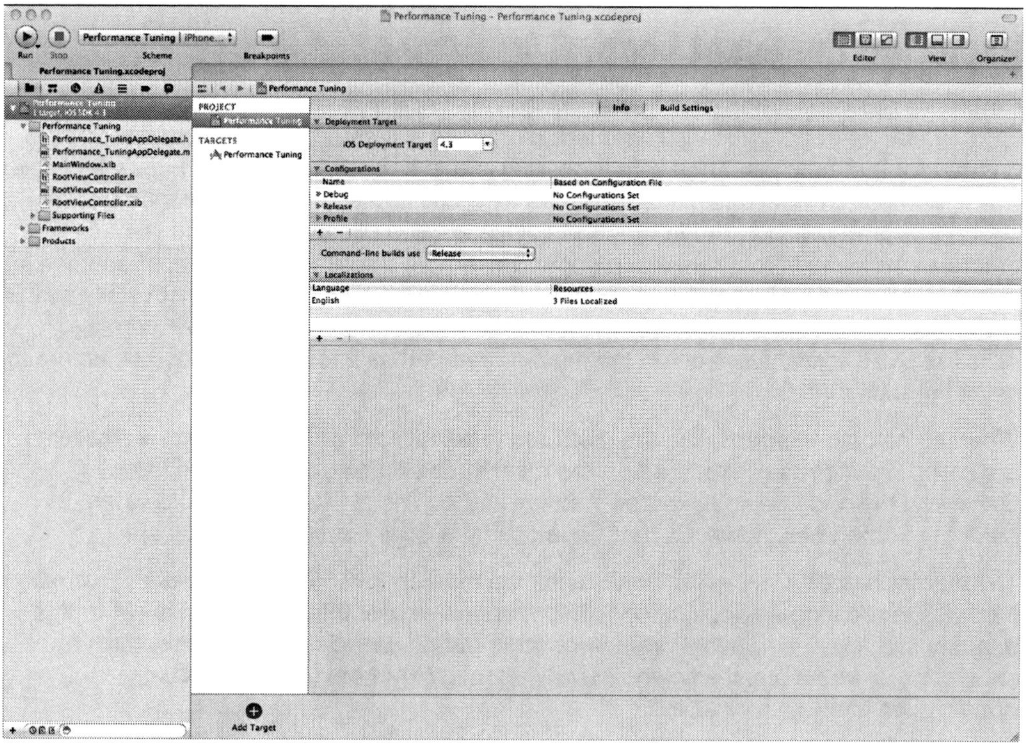

Figure 5–2. *Creating a Profile configuration*

The reason we're doing this is to separate the Release configuration, which is meant for distribution (ad hoc or to the App Store), and our profiling configuration, which is meant to run on a test device. Now click the Build Settings tab. In the Code Signing section, ensure the Profile entry has the iPhone Developer setting set. Notice in Figure 5–3, the All item is selected, as is Combined.

Figure 5–3. *Setting the code signing configuration for the new Profile configuration*

> **TIP:** Having different configurations for debugging, profiling, ad hoc releases, and distribution releases can really help with ensuring you're working with the appropriate build. The debug configuration may have some preprocessor macros defined that you might not need to use in your release configurations. Also, the release configurations will have some compiler optimization flags set that will create compiled code that runs faster. By duplicating the release configuration for the profile configuration, you ensure that the compiler optimization settings are duplicated, so you can see how your code will perform in real world situation.

Brief Tangent—All about Targets

While we're mucking about in Build Settings, let's talk briefly about the difference between the project settings, targets, and schemes. In the Build Settings shown in Figure 5–3, you selected the Combined option. This defines the build configuration for the project. You can override these settings in a target. The target is the configuration for a build. It inherits settings from the project-level Build Settings, and you can see it by clicking the Levels view in the Build Settings tab. So click the Performance Tuning target, and click the Build Settings tab. Now click Levels, and make sure All is selected. In Figure 5–4, you'll see the resulting screen and the inheritance of each build setting.

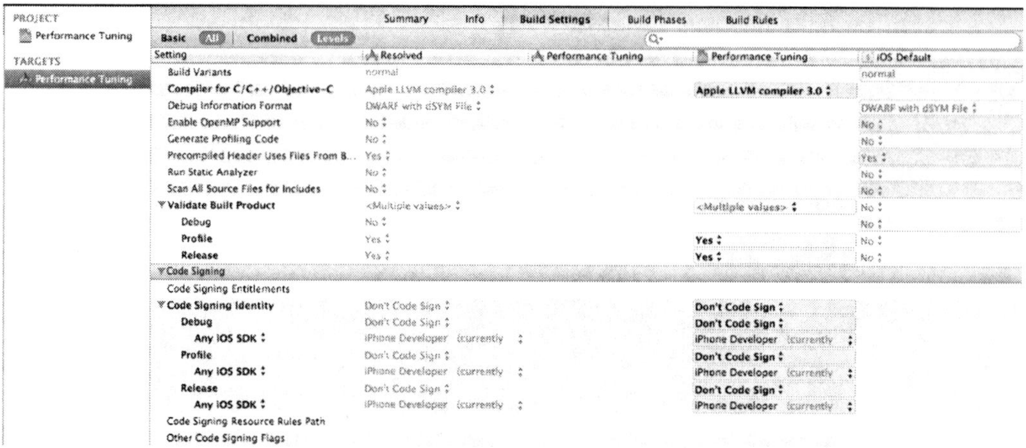

Figure 5–4. *The inheritance chain of the target all the way down to the resolved (final) setting*

What you are looking at is how each setting is finally resolved by Xcode. On the far right is the default setting. As you scan to the left, you see the project level setting and then the target setting with the final resolved value. The project and target settings are editable in this view.

As was mentioned previously, we'll talk briefly about schemes. We've opened the scheme editor before and are about to open it again. What we haven't defined is the scheme itself. The scheme is how a target, or targets, is put together to make a final build artifact. That's pretty much all there is to know about schemes at this level.

Getting Back to Profiling

Moving right along. Now, that the profile configuration is ready to go, we need to tell the profile scheme to use this configuration. Open the scheme editor like we did in Chapter 4 (by going to **Product ➤ Edit Scheme**). Click the Profile action, and modify the Build Configuration option in the Info tab to use the new configuration we just created (see Figure 5–5). Click OK, and we're ready to go.

> **NOTE:** In Chapter 4, we ran the application through Instruments and didn't go through the steps to create a new build configuration. We did so because we weren't running the application on a device. All the testing was through the simulator, so didn't have to worry about code signing issues. We're going to be running all of our tests on the device to get real-world performance so we need to worry about code signing issues that will come up when you prepare your app for release (ad hoc or to the App Store). This will reduce the number of headaches you will experience.

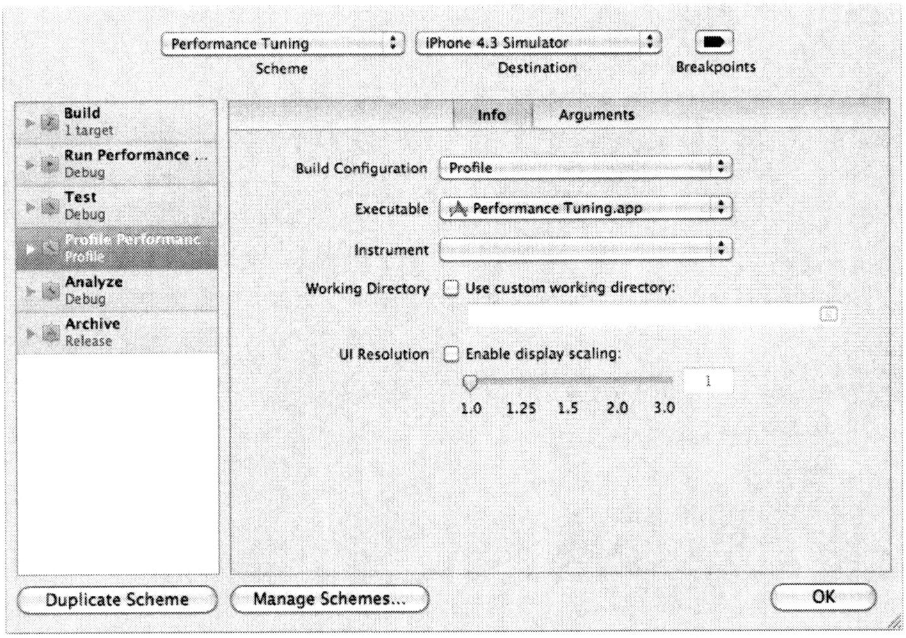

Figure 5–5. *Modifying the build configuration for running the application through the profiler*

Now that the configuration stuff is out of the way, let's implement some code to show an example of blocking the main thread. Open the `MasterViewController.m` file (the prefix may differ due to Xcode's automatic prefixing feature), and modify it to look like Listing 5–2.

Listing 5–2. *The Updated RootViewController (Substitute Your MasterViewController for RootViewController)*

```
#import "RootViewController.h"

@interface RootViewController()
-(NSInteger) fibonacci:(NSInteger) term;
@end

@implementation RootViewController

- (void)viewDidLoad
{
    [super viewDidLoad];
}

- (void)viewWillAppear:(BOOL)animated
{
    [super viewWillAppear:animated];
}

- (void)viewDidAppear:(BOOL)animated
{
    [super viewDidAppear:animated];
}
```

```objc
- (void)viewWillDisappear:(BOOL)animated
{
        [super viewWillDisappear:animated];
}

- (void)viewDidDisappear:(BOOL)animated
{
        [super viewDidDisappear:animated];
}

// Customize the number of sections in the table view.
- (NSInteger)numberOfSectionsInTableView:(UITableView *)tableView
{
    return 1;
}

- (NSInteger)tableView:(UITableView *)tableView numberOfRowsInSection:(NSInteger)section
{
    return 35;
}

// Customize the appearance of table view cells.
- (UITableViewCell *)tableView:(UITableView *)tableView
              cellForRowAtIndexPath:(NSIndexPath *)indexPath
{
    static NSString *CellIdentifier = @"Cell";

    UITableViewCell *cell = [tableView
dequeueReusableCellWithIdentifier:CellIdentifier];
    if (cell == nil) {
        cell = [[[UITableViewCell alloc] initWithStyle:UITableViewCellStyleDefault

reuseIdentifier:CellIdentifier] autorelease];
    }

    [[cell textLabel] setText:[NSString stringWithFormat:@"%i", [self
fibonacci:[indexPath row]]]];

    // Configure the cell.
    return cell;
}

- (void)tableView:(UITableView *)tableView didSelectRowAtIndexPath:(NSIndexPath
*)indexPath
{
}

- (void)didReceiveMemoryWarning
{
    // Releases the view if it doesn't have a superview.
    [super didReceiveMemoryWarning];

    // Relinquish ownership any cached data, images, etc that aren't in use.
}

- (void)viewDidUnload
{
```

```
    [super viewDidUnload];

    // Relinquish ownership of anything that can be recreated in viewDidLoad or on
demand.
    // For example: self.myOutlet = nil;
}

- (void)dealloc
{
    [super dealloc];
}

#pragma mark - Private
-(NSInteger) fibonacci:(NSInteger) term {
    if(term == 0) {
        return 0;
    } else if(term == 1) {
        return 1;
    } else {
        return [self fibonacci:term - 1] + [self fibonacci:term - 2];
    }
}

@end
```

Before we run the app, let's take a brief look at what is going on. In short, we're displaying the first 35 terms of the Fibonacci sequence. I chose the Fibonacci sequence mainly because the first terms can be calculated relatively quickly. As the terms get higher, the recursive nature of the algorithm makes the table a bit sluggish. If your device isn't selected as the deployment target, choose it in the scheme selector. Go ahead and run the app on your device, and check out the performance toward the bottom of the table view.

Performance is pretty bad toward the bottom, right? We know what the problem is, so let's consider how to use Instruments to diagnose the issue. With the device selected, run the application, and attach Instruments like we did in Chapter 4 by going to **Product** ➤ **Profile** or pressing ⌘I. Another way to run the application is by clicking and holding the run button at the top of the window and selecting Profile, as shown in Figure 5–6.

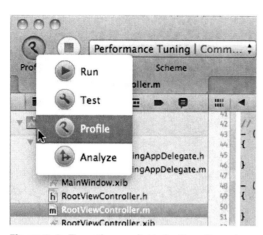

Figure 5–6. *The actions available for the active scheme.*

This will launch Instruments before the application is launched, and you will see the welcome screen. Select the Time Profiler template, and click Profile. After the application launches on your device, scroll down and watch the Instruments window display a nice chart showing what is going on. Check out Figure 5–7 to see the chart that was generated for me.

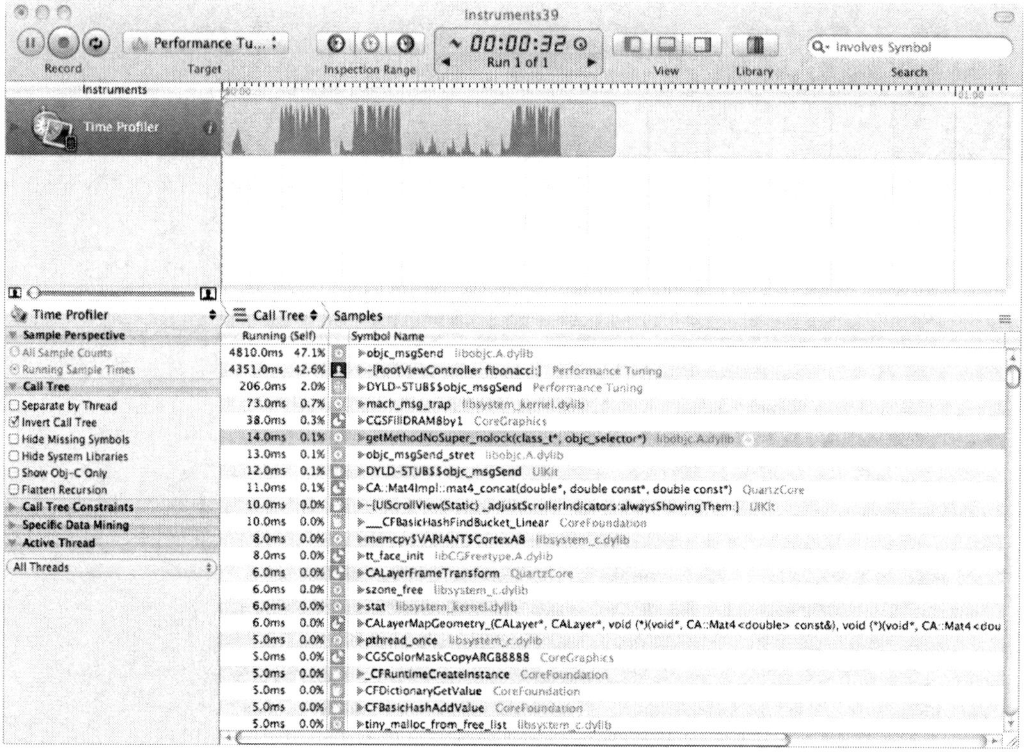

Figure 5–7. *The Time Profiler showing the amount of time in each method.*

Now that we have a pretty chart, what are we looking at? The Time Profiler Instrument stops your application on an interval to record stack trace information for each thread. This collected information gives you insight into what your application is spending most of its time doing, so you can determine bottlenecks in performance. Knowing that, let's take another look at the information presented in Figure 5–7. The table shows two main columns of information (note that right-clicking the headers will allow you to turn on other columns). The left-most column shows the running time of the methods on the right-most column. Looking at the second item from the top, we can see that we are spending quite a bit of time in the fibonacci: method.

We thought this would happen, and the data we collected confirms that hypothesis. If the data didn't suggest that, we would be able to interpret the data to figure out what is going on.

So why is the fibonacci: method taking so much time? Option-click the disclosure indicator to the left of [RootViewController fibonacci:], and check out how deeply the recursion goes. Pretty surprising, isn't it? This gives us insight as to how bad this algorithm performs in this scenario. So how do we fix it?

> **TIP:** Option-clicking a disclosure triangle will disclose all children of the triangle. This is an operating-system-wide feature.

There are a number of ways to approach this kind of problem. The problem could be purely algorithmic, and a tweak to improve running time or space could solve the issue. It could also be an approach issue. If the algorithm can't be improved and the running time really is quite bad, break the long running code off of the main thread (or pass it off to Grand Central Dispatch), and display a loading indicator. Your users will thank you.

This isn't a book on algorithms and computer science, so we're going to skip all of the theoretical stuff and go straight to the answer with a small explanation as to why it works. First, return to Xcode, and update the fibonacci: method to look like Listing 5–3.

Listing 5–3. *An Iterative Fibonacci Implementation Doesn't Create the Stack Issues You'll See with the Recursive Implementation*

```
#pragma mark - Private
-(NSInteger) fibonacci:(NSInteger) term {
    NSInteger first = 0;
    NSInteger second = 1;

    if(term == 0) {
        return first;
    } else if(term == 1) {
        return second;
    } else {
        NSInteger actualTerm = 0;
        for(int t = 1; t < term; t++) {
            actualTerm = first + second;

            first = second;
            second = actualTerm;
```

```
        }

        return actualTerm;
    }
}
```

What we've done here is transform the recursive algorithm to an iterative algorithm. This was a purely algorithmic approach to solving this problem. Now that we have a potential solution to the problem, profile the application again through the Time Profiler. If you still have the old Instruments session open and if the Time Profiler icon is toggled, open in the Instruments panel to see the old run below the current run. That way, you can perform the same test and see what the final results are. Check out Figure 5–8 to see the second run.

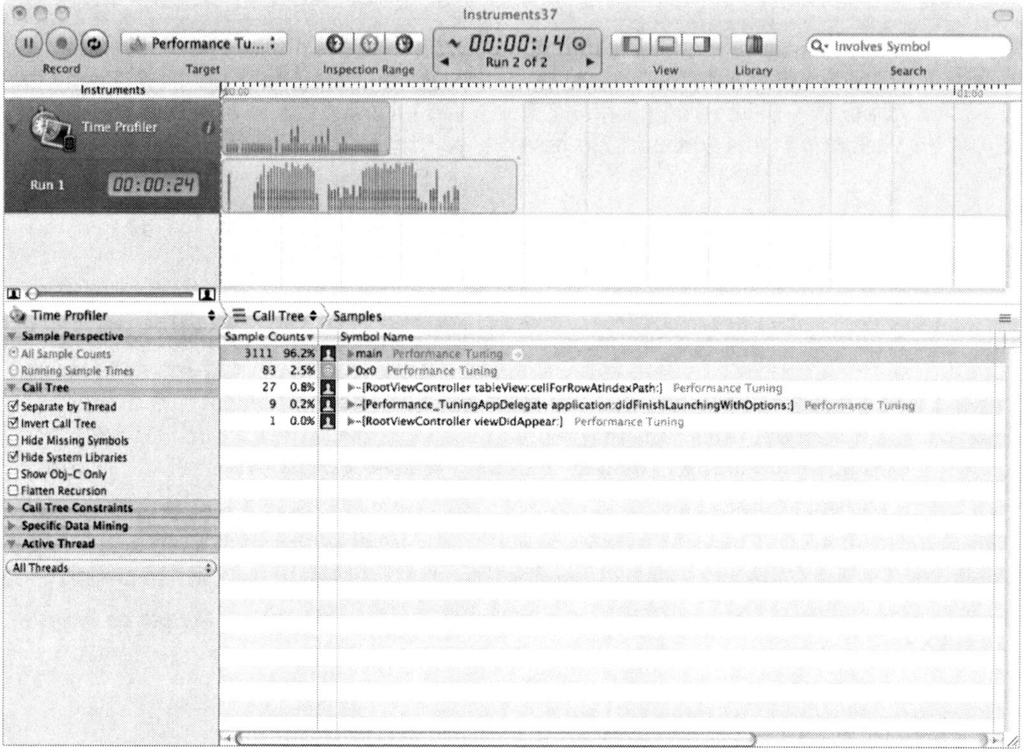

Figure 5–8. *This run looks much better.*

Looking at Figure 5–8, we can see clearly that the fibonacci: method isn't blocking the main thread at all. This verifies our solution, and now, we can move on to other issues in our code.

Improving the Product Screen

The product screen in Super Checkout does not scroll very well. Since you learned how to diagnose a similar problem previously, let's give the Time Profiler a run through to see if we can find out what is going on in the application.

Before we do this, we need to create a new branch off of the Memory_Fixes branch and call it Scrolling_Enhancements. Follow the same procedure that we followed in Chapter 4, and make sure your working copy is the newly created branch. After Xcode is finished making the branch and you are able to edit the code, ensure your device is connected and is selected as the deployment target in the scheme selector. Run the application using the Profile action, and select the Time Profiler instrument in Instruments.

The results you see in Instruments of scrolling up and down the product list several times is a bit confusing (see Figure 5–9).

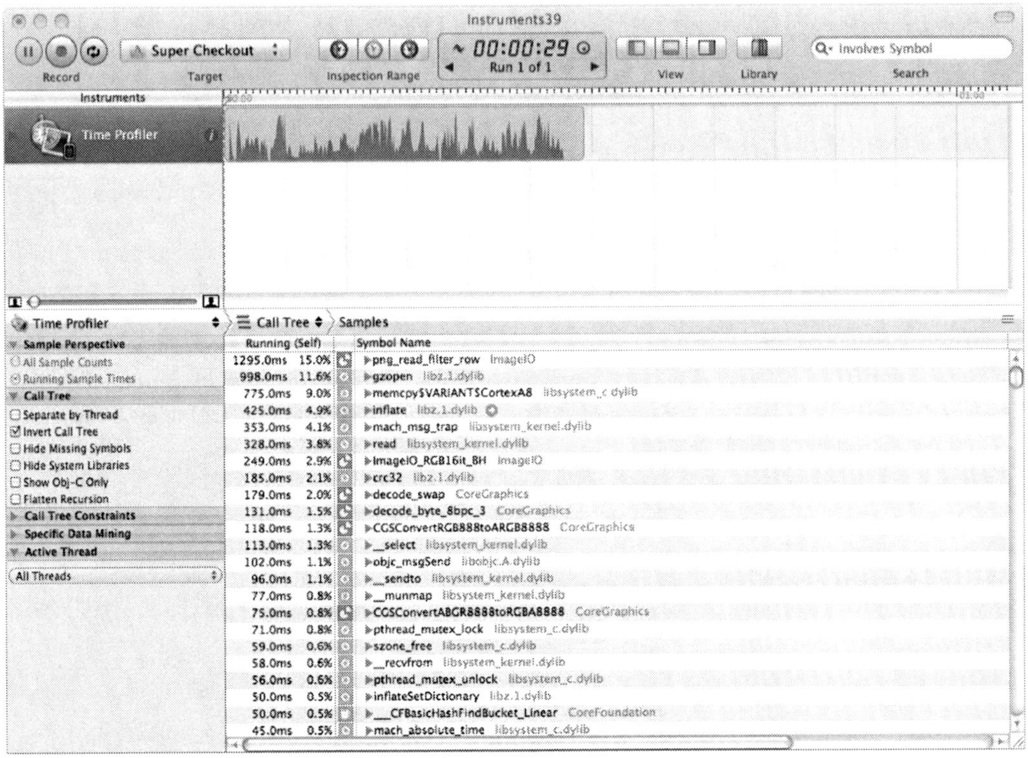

Figure 5–9. *Where is my code getting executed?*

In the Fibonacci example, it was pretty obvious where our code was misbehaving. In Figure 5–9, we can't see where our code is being executed. To weed out all of the stuff going on behind the scenes, click the Hide System Libraries check box on the left in the Call Tree section. This will give you a view that looks similar to the one shown in Figure 5–10.

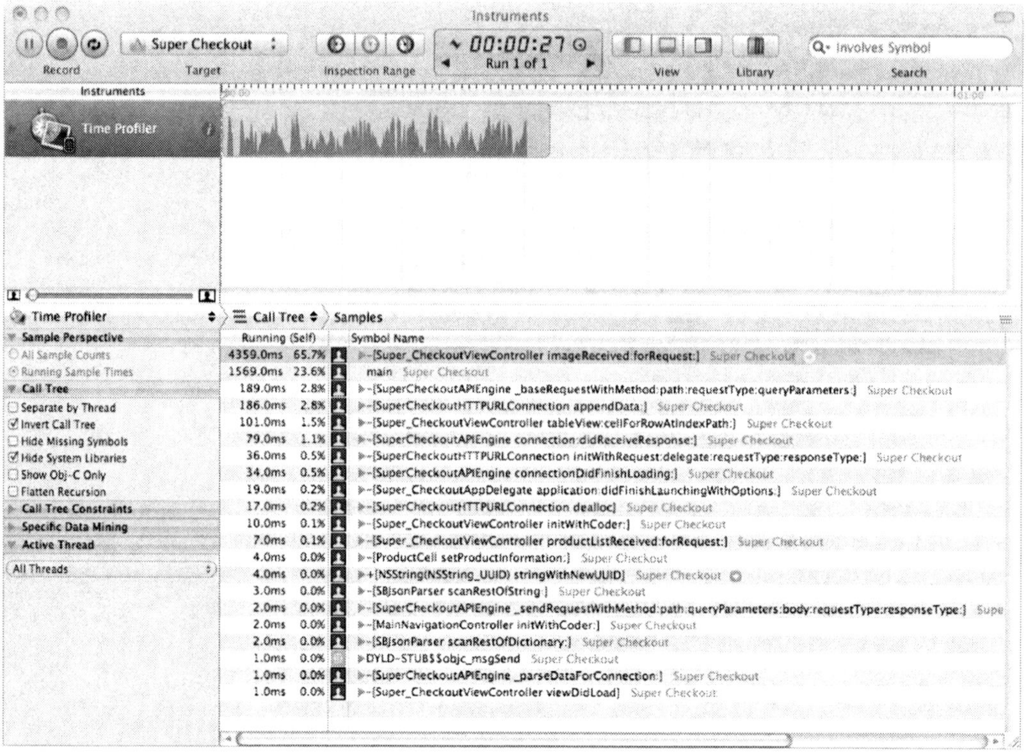

Figure 5–10. *The offending code is highlighted.*

By selecting the Hide System Libraries check box, we filter out all of the noise, so we can spot which line of our code is behaving badly. As Figure 5–10 shows, the imageReceived:forRequest: selector is misbehaving. Let's go ahead and take a look at Listing 5–4 to analyze that method.

Listing 5–4. *Can You Spot the Bottleneck in This Offending Method?*

```
-(void) imageReceived:(UIImage *)image forRequest:(NSString *)connectionIdentifier {
    ProductCell *cell =
        (ProductCell *)[self.tableView
cellForRowAtIndexPath:[imageIndexPathsobjectForKey:connectionIdentifier]];

    CGFloat target = 64;

    CGImageRef oldImage = [image CGImage];
    CGFloat imageWidth = (CGFloat)CGImageGetWidth(oldImage);
    CGFloat imageHeight = (CGFloat)CGImageGetHeight(oldImage);

    CGFloat widthFactor = target / imageWidth;
    CGFloat heightFactor = target / imageHeight;
    CGFloat factor = 1.0;

    if (widthFactor > 1.0 && heightFactor > 1.0) {
        factor = 1.0;
    } else {
```

```
        if (widthFactor >= heightFactor) {
            factor = widthFactor;
        } else {
            factor = heightFactor;
        }
    }

    CGColorSpaceRef colorSpace = CGColorSpaceCreateDeviceRGB();
    CGContextRef imageContext = CGBitmapContextCreate(NULL,

imageWidth,

imageHeight,

8,

4 * imageWidth,

colorSpace,

kCGImageAlphaPremultipliedFirst);
    CGContextDrawImage(imageContext, CGRectMake(0, 0, imageWidth, imageHeight),
oldImage);
    CGContextScaleCTM(imageContext, imageWidth * factor, imageHeight * factor);
    CGImageRef newImage = CGBitmapContextCreateImage(imageContext);

    CGColorSpaceRelease(colorSpace);
    CGContextRelease(imageContext);

    UIImage *resizedImage = [[UIImage alloc] initWithCGImage:newImage];

    CGImageRelease(newImage);
    [cell.productImage setImage:resizedImage];

    [resizedImage release];

    [imageIndexPaths removeObjectForKey:connectionIdentifier];
}
```

This is the code that was added in Chapter 4. It is doing quite a bit and is executed for each image returned. Furthermore, an image for a product is loaded each time a cell is created. Since this is a complicated issue with two possible causes, let's pick one of the issues. Doing network requests is the most expensive (and time consuming operation, we'll talk more about that in Chapter 6) so we're going to change how our images are loaded. Before we do so, we'll need to look a bit deeper at how UITableView and UIScrollView instances work. So before we implement a fix, let's talk about what the Cocoa Touch framework does while the user is scrolling a table view.

Looking Behind the Scenes of a Scroll View

When a scroll view is scrolling, it puts the current run loop in a special mode. This mode blocks pretty much everything from executing except for the pieces that draw the scroll view that is in motion. NSURLConnection is a great example of something that gets blocked while a scroll view is scrolling. While the view is scrolling, any data that comes back from the open socket gets queued up until the run loop is switched from UITrackingRunLoopMode to the default mode.

Knowing this will help you design a solution that will make sure requests aren't being made while the view is scrolling. Ideally, when scrolling is finished, the data that was queued up by any NSURLConnections that were open won't flood the app, and multiple calls to the delegate method are accomplished at once. This is going to require a pretty hefty update. Are you ready?

Lazily Loading Images

The following update will initiate the appropriate image requests when scrolling has stopped. To do this, we are going to have to create an actual model object and parse the products and to hold on to the image that is downloaded. Create a new NSObject subclass, and call it Product.

Open Product.h, and give it the interface in Listing 5–5.

Listing 5–5. *The Interface for a Product*

```
#import <Foundation/Foundation.h>
@interface Product : NSObject {
    NSString *productId;
    NSString *name;
    NSNumber *price;
    NSString *description;
    NSString *image;
    NSString *thumb;

    UIImage *productImage;
}

@property (nonatomic, retain) NSString *productId;
@property (nonatomic, retain) NSString *name;
@property (nonatomic, retain) NSNumber *price;
@property (nonatomic, retain) NSString *description;
@property (nonatomic, retain) NSString *image;
@property (nonatomic, retain) NSString *thumb;
@property (nonatomic, retain) UIImage *productImage;

- (id) initWithDictionary:(NSDictionary *)data;

@end
```

The implementation file looks like Listing 5–6.

Listing 5–6. *The Implementation for a Product*

```
#import "Product.h"


@implementation Product
@synthesize productId;
@synthesize name;
```

```
@synthesize price;
@synthesize description;
@synthesize image;
@synthesize thumb;
@synthesize productImage;

- (void)dealloc {
    [productId release], productId = nil;
    [name release], name = nil;
    [price release], price = nil;
    [description release], description = nil;
    [image release], image = nil;
    [thumb release], thumb = nil;
    [productImage release], productImage = nil;

    [super dealloc];
}

- (id) initWithDictionary:(NSDictionary *)data {
    self = [super init];
    if(self) {
        productId = [[data objectForKey:@"id"] copy];
        name = [[data objectForKey:@"name"] copy];
        price = [[data objectForKey:@"price"] copy];
        description = [[data objectForKey:@"description"] copy];
        image = [[data objectForKey:@"image"] copy];
        thumb = [[data objectForKey:@"thumb"] copy];
    }

    return self;
}

@end
```

Now that we have the Product model defined, we need to update quite a few files starting with the parsing code and the presentation of the data.

Open SuperCheckoutAPIEngine.m; look for the parsingSucceededForRequest:ofResponseType:parsedObjects: selector, and update it to look like Listing 5–7. Don't forget to import the Product header at the top of the file!

Listing 5–7. *Time to Speed Up This Baby!*

```
-(void)parsingSucceededForRequest:(NSString *)identifier

ofResponseType:(SuperCheckoutResponseType)responseType
                                  parsedObjects:(NSDictionary *)parsedObject {
    switch (responseType) {
        case SuperCheckoutProductList:
            if([self
_isValidDelegateForSelector:@selector(productListReceived:forRequest:)]) {
                NSArray *result = [parsedObject objectForKey:@"result"];
                NSMutableArray *newResult = [NSMutableArray arrayWithCapacity:[result
count]];

                for(NSDictionary *obj in result) {
                    Product *prod = [[Product alloc] initWithDictionary:obj];
```

```
                        [newResult addObject:prod];

                        [prod release];
                }


                [delegate productListReceived:[NSArray arrayWithArray:newResult]
        forRequest:identifier];
                }
                break;
            case SuperCheckoutCartContents:
                if([self
        _isValidDelegateForSelector:@selector(cartContentsReceived:forRequest:)]) {
                    [delegate cartContentsReceived:[parsedObject objectForKey:@"result"]
        forRequest:identifier];
                }

            default:
                break;
        }
    }
}
```

Next, update `ProductCell.h`, and import `Product.h` at the top of the file. Replace

```
@property (nonatomic, retain) NSDictionary *productInformation;
```

with the following line

```
@property (nonatomic, retain) Product *productInformation;
```

In `ProductCell.m`, replace the `setProductInformation:` selector with

```
-(void) setProductInformation:(Product *)newProductInformation {
        Product *oldInfo = productInformation;
    [oldInfo removeObserver:self forKeyPath:@"productImage"];

        productInformation = [newProductInformation retain];
    [productInformation addObserver:self forKeyPath:@"productImage"
options:NSKeyValueObservingOptionNew context:NULL];

        [productNameLabel setText:[productInformation name]];

        [productPriceLabel setText:[NSString stringWithFormat:@"$%1.2f",

[[productInformation price] floatValue]]];

        [oldInfo release];
}
```

Also, add the following key value observing method:

```
- (void)observeValueForKeyPath:(NSString *)keyPath
                              ofObject:(id)object
                                change:(NSDictionary *)change
                               context:(void *)context {
    if ([keyPath isEqual:@"productImage"]) {
        [productImage setImage:[change objectForKey:NSKeyValueChangeNewKey]];
    }
}
```

The next update is in Super_CheckoutViewController.h. For this one, make the file look
like this:

```
#import <UIKit/UIKit.h>
#import "SuperCheckoutAPIEngineDelegate.h"
@class SuperCheckoutAPIEngine;
@class ProductCell;

@interface Super_CheckoutViewController :
UITableViewController<SuperCheckoutAPIEngineDelegate, UIScrollViewDelegate> {
        NSArray *inventory;
        SuperCheckoutAPIEngine *apiEngine;

        UINib *cellNib;
        ProductCell *productCell;

        NSMutableDictionary *imageIndexes;
    NSMutableDictionary *imageDownloadsInProgress;
}

@property (nonatomic, retain) IBOutlet ProductCell *productCell;

@end
```

For Super_CheckoutViewController.m, update the file to look like this:

```
#import "Super_CheckoutViewController.h"
#import "SuperCheckoutAPIEngine.h"
#import "ProductCell.h"
#import "ProductDetailsViewController.h"
#import "Product.h"
@interface Super_CheckoutViewController(Private)
- (void)loadImagesForOnscreenRows;
@end

@implementation Super_CheckoutViewController
@synthesize productCell;
- (id)initWithNibName:(NSString *)nibNameOrNil bundle:(NSBundle *)nibBundleOrNil {
    self = [super initWithNibName:nibNameOrNil bundle:nibBundleOrNil];
    if (self) {
        // Custom initialization
    }
    return self;
}

//We are loading from a nib, so initWithCoder: is used
- (id) initWithCoder:(NSCoder *)aDecoder {
    self = [super initWithCoder:aDecoder];

    if(self) {
        imageIndexes = [[NSMutableDictionary alloc] init];
    }
    return self;
}

- (void)dealloc {
    [productCell release];
    [imageIndexes release];
```

```objc
        [super dealloc];
}

- (void)didReceiveMemoryWarning {
    // Releases the view if it doesn't have a superview.
    [super didReceiveMemoryWarning];
}

#pragma mark - UITableViewDataSource Methods
- (NSInteger)numberOfSectionsInTableView:(UITableView *)tableView {
    return 1;
}

- (NSInteger)tableView:(UITableView *)tableView numberOfRowsInSection:(NSInteger)section
{
    return [inventory count];
}

// Customize the appearance of table view cells.
- (UITableViewCell *)tableView:(UITableView *)tableView
cellForRowAtIndexPath:(NSIndexPath *)indexPath {
    ProductCell *cell = (ProductCell *)[tableView dequeueReusableCellWithIdentifier:

[ProductCell reuseIdentifier]];

    if(cell == nil) {
        [cellNib instantiateWithOwner:self options:nil];
        cell = productCell;
    }
    Product *item = (Product *)[inventory objectAtIndex:[indexPath row]];
    [cell setProductInformation:item];
    [self setProductCell:nil];

    //Fetch image for the cell
    if([item productImage] == nil) {
        if (self.tableView.dragging == NO && self.tableView.decelerating == NO) {
            NSString *requestId = [apiEngine getImageForProduct:[item thumb]];

            [imageIndexes setObject:[NSNumber numberWithInt:[indexPath row]]

forKey:requestId];
        }
    }

    return cell;
}


#pragma mark - UITableViewDelegate
- (void)tableView:(UITableView *)tableView didSelectRowAtIndexPath:(NSIndexPath
*)indexPath {
    ProductDetailsViewController *newVC =
        [[ProductDetailsViewController alloc]
initWithNibName:@"ProductDetailsViewController"

bundle:nil];
```

```objectivec
    [newVC setSelectedProduct:[inventory objectAtIndex:[indexPath row]]];

    [self.navigationController pushViewController:newVC animated:YES];
    [newVC release];
}

- (CGFloat)tableView:(UITableView *)tableView
        heightForRowAtIndexPath:(NSIndexPath *)indexPath{
    return 76.0;
}

#pragma mark - SuperCheckoutAPIEngineDelegate Methods
- (void)requestSucceeded:(NSString *)connectionIdentifier {
}

- (void)requestFailed:(NSString *)connectionIdentifier withError:(NSError *)error {
}

-(void) productListReceived:(NSArray *)products
                            forRequest:(NSString *)connectionIdentifier {
    NSLog(@"Products list: %@", [products description]);
    inventory = [products retain];
    [self.tableView reloadData];
}

-(void) imageReceived:(UIImage *)image forRequest:(NSString *)connectionIdentifier {
    Product *prod = (Product *)[inventory objectAtIndex:[[imageIndexes

objectForKey:connectionIdentifier] intValue]];

    CGFloat target = 64;

    CGImageRef oldImage = [image CGImage];
    CGFloat imageWidth = (CGFloat)CGImageGetWidth(oldImage);
    CGFloat imageHeight = (CGFloat)CGImageGetHeight(oldImage);

    CGFloat widthFactor = target / imageWidth;
    CGFloat heightFactor = target / imageHeight;
    CGFloat factor = 1.0;

    if (widthFactor > 1.0 && heightFactor > 1.0) {
        factor = 1.0;
    } else {
        if (widthFactor >= heightFactor) {
            factor = widthFactor;
        } else {
            factor = heightFactor;
        }
    }

    CGColorSpaceRef colorSpace = CGColorSpaceCreateDeviceRGB();
    CGContextRef imageContext = CGBitmapContextCreate(NULL,

imageWidth,

imageHeight,
```

```
8,

4 * imageWidth,

colorSpace,

kCGImageAlphaPremultipliedFirst);

    CGContextDrawImage(imageContext, CGRectMake(0, 0, imageWidth, imageHeight),
oldImage);
    CGContextScaleCTM(imageContext, imageWidth * factor, imageHeight * factor);
    CGImageRef newImage = CGBitmapContextCreateImage(imageContext);

    CGColorSpaceRelease(colorSpace);
    CGContextRelease(imageContext);
    UIImage *resizedImage = [[UIImage alloc] initWithCGImage:newImage];

    CGImageRelease(newImage);
    [prod setProductImage:resizedImage];

    [resizedImage release];

    [imageIndexes removeObjectForKey:connectionIdentifier];
}

// this method is used in case the user scrolled into a set of cells that don't have
//their app icons yet
- (void)loadImagesForOnscreenRows {
    if ([inventory count] > 0) {
        NSArray *visiblePaths = [self.tableView indexPathsForVisibleRows];
        for (NSIndexPath *indexPath in visiblePaths) {
            Product *product = [inventory objectAtIndex:indexPath.row];

            if([product productImage] == nil) {
                NSString *requestId = [apiEngine getImageForProduct:[product thumb]];

                [imageIndexes setObject:[NSNumber numberWithInt:[indexPath row]]
                                                  forKey:requestId];
            }
        }
    }
}

#pragma mark -
#pragma mark Deferred image loading (UIScrollViewDelegate)

// Load images for all onscreen rows when scrolling is finished
- (void)scrollViewDidEndDragging:(UIScrollView *)scrollView
                                      willDecelerate:(BOOL)decelerate {
    if (!decelerate) {
        [self loadImagesForOnscreenRows];
    }
}

- (void)scrollViewDidEndDecelerating:(UIScrollView *)scrollView {
    [self loadImagesForOnscreenRows];
```

```
}
#pragma mark - View lifecycle
// Implement viewDidLoad to do additional setup after loading the view, typically from a
//nib.
- (void)viewDidLoad {
    [super viewDidLoad];
    [self setTitle:@"Inventory"];
    UIBarButtonItem *cartButton =
                        [[UIBarButtonItem alloc] initWithTitle:@"Cart"

style:UIBarButtonItemStyleBordered

target:self

action:@selector(cartButtonPressed:)];
    //[self.navigationItem setRightBarButtonItem:cartButton];
    [cartButton release];

    if(!cellNib) {
        cellNib = [[UINib nibWithNibName:@"ProductListCells" bundle:nil] retain];
    }
    if(!apiEngine) {
        apiEngine = [[SuperCheckoutAPIEngine alloc] initWithDelegate:self];
    }

    [apiEngine getProducts];
}

- (void)viewDidUnload {
    [self setProductCell:nil];
    [super viewDidUnload];
    // Release any retained subviews of the main view.
    // e.g. self.myOutlet = nil;
}

- (BOOL)shouldAutorotateToInterfaceOrientation:

(UIInterfaceOrientation)interfaceOrientation {
    // Return YES for supported orientations
    return (interfaceOrientation == UIInterfaceOrientationPortrait);
}
@end
```

Quite a bit of code, huh? What we've accomplished with this major update is creating a
new model object, telling the API engine to return a list of these new model objects, and
updating the product list to handle these new objects. The performance piece of the
update was completed in Super_CheckoutViewController.m. Let's take a moment to
look what we are doing in greater detail, and then we'll see how it stacks up against our
last run.

In tableView:cellForRowAtIndexPath:, we updated it to use the product model, but the
performance enhancement comes here:

```
    if([item productImage] == nil) {
        if (self.tableView.dragging == NO && self.tableView.decelerating == NO) {
            NSString *requestId = [apiEngine getImageForProduct:[item thumb]];
```

```
            [imageIndexes setObject:[NSNumber numberWithInt:[indexPath row]]
  forKey:requestId];
        }
    } else {
        [cell.productImage setImage:[item productImage]];
    }
```

Here, we're checking to see if the image has been downloaded. Previously, we were downloading a new image each time a cell was requested. We're going to reduce the number of times the image is requested to reduce the number of times the problem method gets invoked. We're also reducing the number of times the images are being loaded by detecting if the table view is scrolling and not decelerating. Basically, we're only loading the images when the table is stationary and asking for cells.

What about when the table is animating and then stops? Good question! We updated the Super_CheckoutViewController to conform to the UIScrollViewDelegate protocol and we added these methods:

```
- (void)scrollViewDidEndDragging:(UIScrollView *)scrollView
                                      willDecelerate:(BOOL)decelerate {
    if (!decelerate) {
        [self loadImagesForOnscreenRows];
    }
}

- (void)scrollViewDidEndDecelerating:(UIScrollView *)scrollView {
    [self loadImagesForOnscreenRows];
}
```

These methods tell us when the table view is finished scrolling and finished decelerating. When that occurs, we are loading the images for the onscreen rows. This reduces the number of times we make a request to the number of products that are stationary on the screen.

Now that we have looked at the potential fix, let's take a look at how it performs in Instruments. I've run the new version in the same session as the last run to illustrate the difference in terms of the graph. Figure 5–11 shows the comparison, and we can tell the difference after the images are loaded in memory. We can see that imageReceived:forRequest: is still taking quite a bit of processing power though. Perhaps, the resizing code is a bit heavy for what we need.

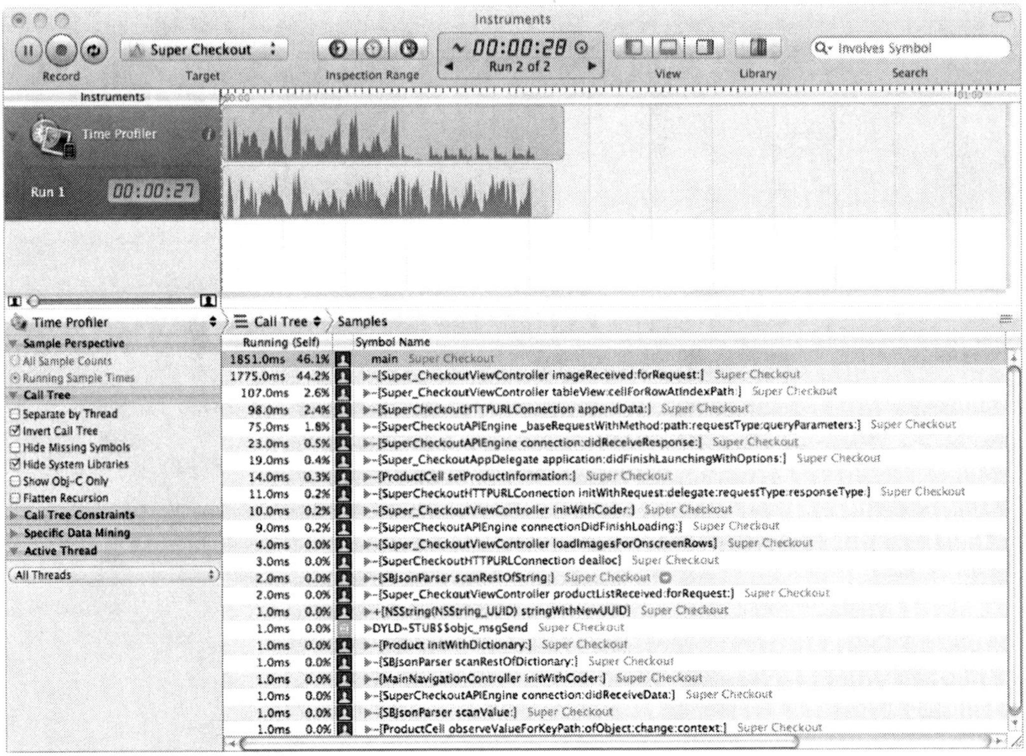

Figure 5–11. *Once the images are loaded, things looked a lot better.*

I'm still not happy with the way it is performing, so let's remove the image resizing code.
Update the `imageReceived:forRequest:` method in `Super_CheckoutViewController` to
look like this:

```
-(void) imageReceived:(UIImage *)image forRequest:(NSString *)connectionIdentifier {
    Product *prod = (Product *)[inventory objectAtIndex:[[imageIndexes

objectForKey:connectionIdentifier] intValue]];
    [prod setProductImage:image];
    [imageIndexes removeObjectForKey:connectionIdentifier];
}
```

Now, let's compare how it performs without the resize. I've run the two in the same
instruments session, so we can compare them (see Figure 5–12). As you can see,
removing the resizing code didn't really change the graph, but we did remove the poorly
performing code. The problem is that scrolling is still not how I'd like it.

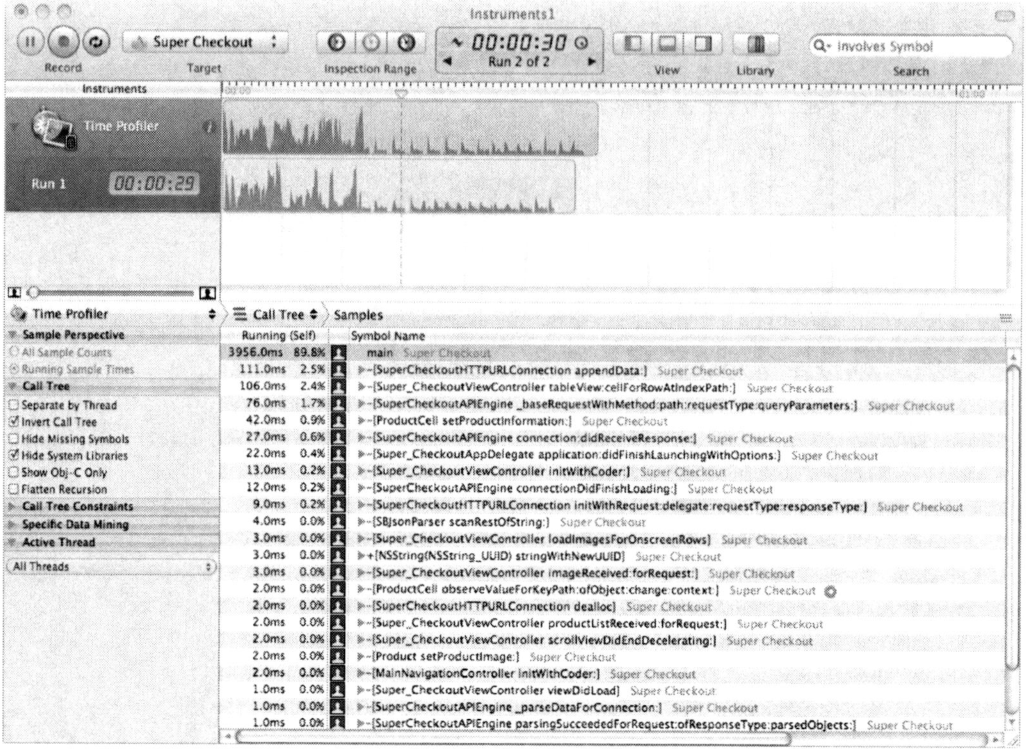

Figure 5–12. *Successfully removed some poorly performing code, but scrolling is still sluggish*

Bad Scrolling No More

We've hit the end of what the Time Profiler can give us, so it is time to pull out the big guns. We're going to get down to measuring the frame rate and see what kind of bottlenecks we're running into based on how Core Animation is performing. Before we get into using the Core Animation instrument, let's spend a few moments talking about how rendering happens in iOS.

A Brief look at Core Graphics

Each `UIView` subclass has mechanisms for drawing itself and controlling its own layout. These methods are called on demand by Cocoa Touch and usually follow calls to either `setNeedsDisplay` or `setNeedsLayout`. Since we have those methods, `drawRect:` and `layoutSubviews` should never be called directly. If you want to trigger `drawRect:`, call `setNeedsDisplay`, and Cocoa will figure out the best time to call call to `drawRect:`. The same can be said for `setNeedsLayout` and `layoutSubviews`. This ensures that all updates to the view get made at once, and a render is scheduled at the most convenient time for Cocoa to efficiently draw the views in question.

So what happens after you schedule a rendering of your view? Well, if you look at Figure 5–13, you can get a good overview of what goes on when Cocoa is rendering your view. This occurs on each and every UIView in your application, and this consistency becomes very important later.

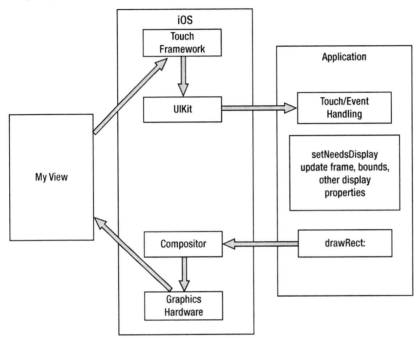

Figure 5–13. *An overview of the view drawing cycle*

Now that the basics are covered, let's dive into what goes on behind the scenes. The core element for each rendered view is the layer property on the view. This is the layer that is rendered by Core Animation. Core Animation resides in the media layer of the iOS architecture, directly underneath Cocoa Touch, where UIKit resides (see Figure 5–14). Core Animation is a part of the Core Graphics framework. Core Graphics is also referred to as Quartz 2D and does all of the heavy lifting in terms of drawing.

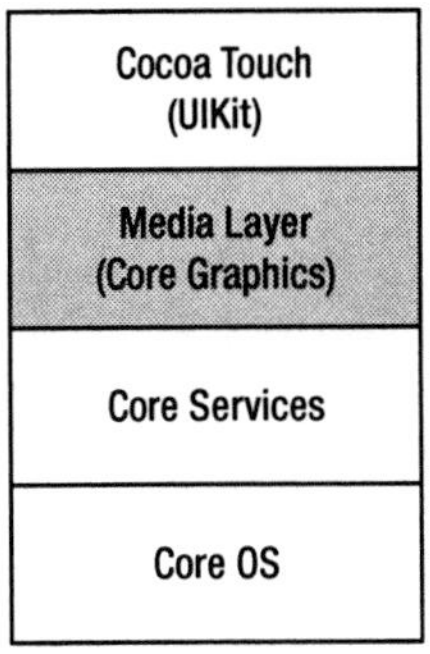

| Cocoa Touch (UIKit) |
| Media Layer (Core Graphics) |
| Core Services |
| Core OS |

Figure 5–14. *This is the basic architecture of iOS with the media layer highlighted; the media layer is where we'll spend most of our time.*

It is Core Graphics's job to render the entire screen of the application. It is also responsible for animating the transitions between different views. A great example of these kinds of animations is pushing a view controller on a `UINavigationController`'s view stack. `UIScrollView` instances also use Core Graphics to animate the scrolling of views as the user interacts with it. `UITableView` is a `UIScrollView`, so it needs to animate all of the table cells as the user scrolls up and down.

Getting Back to Instruments

Now, Super Checkout comes in the picture. The view that we are tuning is a table view, and our cells could be causing some of these performance issues based on how they are designed. To diagnose this, we need to profile Super Checkout with the Core Animation instrument.

Figure 5–15. *The Core Animation instrument*

The Core Animation instrument gives us a template for viewing a raw measurement of rendered frames per second as well as a CPU usage graph. This instrument also allows us to modify the way the application is rendered so we can get clues as to how Core Graphics is really rendering each view. Figure 5–16 gives you an idea of what options you can turn on; each one has its particular use. We're only interested in seeing the how the layers are blended right now.

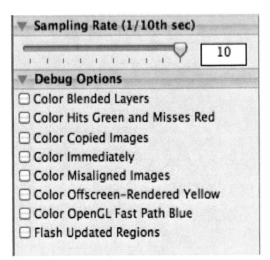

Figure 5–16. *The Debug options for getting some insight on how Core Graphics is rendering your application*

Go ahead and profile the application with the Core Animation instrument. After Instruments has launched and the application is going, turn on Color Blended Layers in the debug options. If you don't see those options, click the graph for the Core Animation instrument, and it will activate them. When you turn on blended layers, your screen will look very funky. Check out Figure 5–17, and we'll discuss what this information tells us.

In Figure 5–17, we're looking at a view of how Core Graphics sees our application. Remember how I mentioned that the compositor would be important later? This is the part I was referring to. This view shows us how Core Graphics draws and what kind of compositing it has to do.

> **NOTE:** Compositing is a fancy way of combining layered pieces on top of each other. There are some very sophisticated algorithms to composite multiple layers and create one image. Fortunately, the engineers behind Core Graphics have done all of the heavy lifting for us, so we don't have to worry about rendering each and every screen.

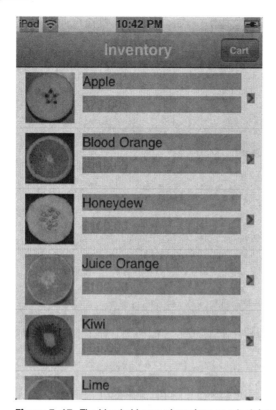

Figure 5–17. *The blended layers view gives us a look into how Core Graphics renders each screen.*

Take another look at Figure 5–16. Each different shade is its own layer. In fact, every time a new UIView (or a subclass of UIView) is created a new layer is created. These layers are of type CALayer and are actually the medium in which the view is drawn on. These layers are then composited to create the final image that is rendered on screen.

Compositing is expensive, so this is where the bottleneck can happen. Take a look at each UILabel for each cell. Quite a bit of empty space has to be rendered. If the view is marked as opaque, the compositor doesn't have to calculate what the view underneath the opaque view looks like with whatever might be on top of it. Imagine having three or four views with differing levels of alpha sitting on top of an image. The compositor has to work overtime to render the view. Throw animation at the picture and you get something that looks very stuttery because the compositor has to take a bit longer to render each intermediate frame.

There is a good way to fix this issue, however. Instead of managing numerous subviews in our table cell, we can draw our items directly in the view itself and render only one layer. Figure 5–18 gives you a view of what this looks like with blended layers turned on.

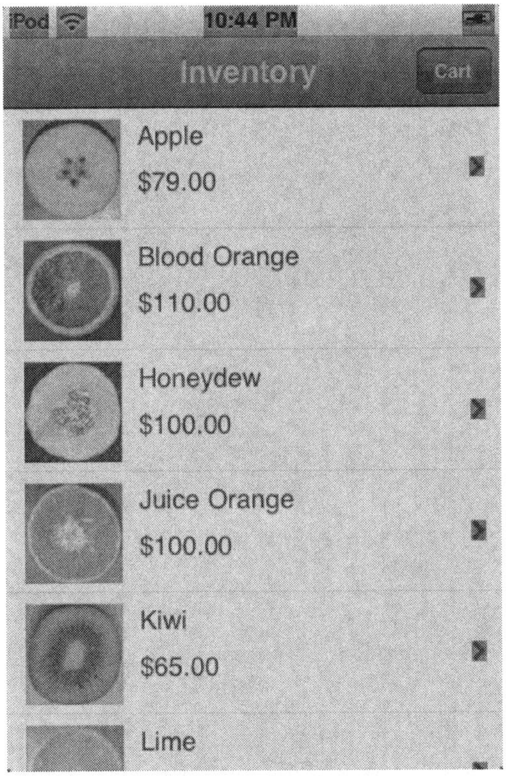

Figure 5–18. *Our newly designed cell with only one blended layer*

To update our cell to draw on one layer, we're going to use the same technique Loren Bricther used on Tweetie for iPhone and Twitter for iPhone. This technique involves creating an opaque UIView that covers the entire cell and creating a method for drawing on that view in a subclass. In order to do this, we need to create a new UITableViewCell subclass called SuperFastCell. Go ahead and create a new UITableViewCell subclass, and call it SuperFastCell.

Open SuperFastCell.h, and modify it to look like this:

```
#import <UIKit/UIKit.h>

@interface SuperFastCell : UITableViewCell {
    UIView *contentView;
}

-(void) drawCellView:(CGRect)rect;
@end
```

Now, open SuperFastCell.m, and modify it to look like this:

```
#import "SuperFastCell.h"

@class SuperFastCell;
```

```objc
@interface SuperFastCellView : UIView
@end

@implementation SuperFastCellView

- (void)drawRect:(CGRect)r {
       [(SuperFastCell *)[self superview] drawCellView:r];
}

@end

@implementation SuperFastCell

- (id)initWithStyle:(UITableViewCellStyle)style
       reuseIdentifier:(NSString *)reuseIdentifier {
    self = [super initWithStyle:style reuseIdentifier:reuseIdentifier];
    if (self) {
        contentView = [[SuperFastCellView alloc] initWithFrame:CGRectZero];
        contentView.opaque = YES;
        contentView.backgroundColor = [UIColor whiteColor];
        [self addSubview:contentView];
        [contentView release];
    }
    return self;
}

- (void) setFrame:(CGRect)frame {
    [super setFrame:frame];
    CGRect myBounds = [self bounds];
    myBounds.size.height -= 1;
    [contentView setFrame:myBounds];
}

- (void) setNeedsDisplay {
    [super setNeedsDisplay];
    [contentView setNeedsDisplay];
}

-(void) drawCellView:(CGRect)rect {
    //Subclasses will implement this
}

- (void)dealloc {
    [super dealloc];
}

@end
```

Now that we have our base class defined, we need to update our `ProductCell` class to use this new technique. Open `ProductCell.h`, and modify it to look like this:

```objc
#import <UIKit/UIKit.h>
#import "SuperFastCell.h"
@class Product;

@interface ProductCell : SuperFastCell {
}
```

```
+(NSString *) reuseIdentifier;

@property (nonatomic, retain) Product *productInformation;

@end
```

Now, open ProductCell.m, and modify it to look like this:

```objc
#import "ProductCell.h"
#import "Product.h"

@implementation ProductCell
@synthesize productInformation;

+(NSString *)reuseIdentifier {
    return @"ProductCell";
}

-(NSString *)reuseIdentifier {
    return [[self class] reuseIdentifier];
}

- (id)initWithStyle:(UITableViewCellStyle)style
        reuseIdentifier:(NSString *)reuseIdentifier
{
    self = [super initWithStyle:style reuseIdentifier:reuseIdentifier];
    if (self) {
        // Initialization code
    }
    return self;
}

-(void) setProductInformation:(Product *)newProductInformation {
    Product *oldInfo = productInformation;
    [oldInfo removeObserver:self forKeyPath:@"productImage"];

    productInformation = [newProductInformation retain];
    [productInformation addObserver:self
                                          forKeyPath:@"productImage"

options:NSKeyValueObservingOptionNew
                                          context:NULL];

    [oldInfo release];

    [self setNeedsDisplay];
}

- (void)setHighlighted:(BOOL)lit {
    // If highlighted state changes, need to redisplay.
    if([self isHighlighted] != lit) {
        [super setHighlighted:lit];
        [self setNeedsDisplay];
    }
}

-(void) drawCellView:(CGRect)rect {
```

```
    UIFont *font = [UIFont fontWithName:@"Helvetica" size:17.0];
    CGContextRef context = UIGraphicsGetCurrentContext();
    CGContextSaveGState(context);

    CGImageRef prodImage = [[productInformation productImage] CGImage];
    CGContextDrawImage(context, CGRectMake(12, 6, 64, 64), prodImage);
    //86, 6
    //Helvetica 17 black
    CGSize textSize;
    textSize = [[productInformation name] sizeWithFont:font];

    if([self isHighlighted]) {
        CGContextSetStrokeColorWithColor(context, [[UIColor whiteColor] CGColor]);
        CGContextSetFillColorWithColor(context, [[UIColor whiteColor] CGColor]);
    } else {
        CGContextSetStrokeColorWithColor(context, [[UIColor blackColor] CGColor]);
        CGContextSetFillColorWithColor(context, [[UIColor blackColor] CGColor]);
    }

    [[productInformation name] drawInRect:CGRectMake(86, 6, textSize.width,
textSize.height)
                                                            withFont:font];


    //Helvetica 17 light gray
    NSString *priceString = [NSString stringWithFormat:@"$%1.2f",

[[productInformation price] floatValue]];
    textSize = [priceString sizeWithFont:font];

    if([self isHighlighted]) {
        CGContextSetStrokeColorWithColor(context, [[UIColor whiteColor] CGColor]);
        CGContextSetFillColorWithColor(context, [[UIColor whiteColor] CGColor]);
    } else {
        CGContextSetStrokeColorWithColor(context, [[UIColor lightGrayColor] CGColor]);
        CGContextSetFillColorWithColor(context, [[UIColor lightGrayColor] CGColor]);
    }
    [priceString drawInRect:CGRectMake(86, 35, textSize.width, textSize.height)
                            withFont:font];
    CGContextRestoreGState(context);
}

- (void)observeValueForKeyPath:(NSString *)keyPath
                                    ofObject:(id)object
                                      change:(NSDictionary *)change
                                     context:(void *)context {
    if ([keyPath isEqual:@"productImage"]) {
        [self setNeedsDisplay];
    }
}

- (void)dealloc {
    [super dealloc];
}

@end
```

Before we run the application, an important thing to note on these custom cells is the fact that the highlighted and selected states need to be handled. Since we are drawing our text on the view being displayed, we don't get the benefits of being in a `UILabel`. This is the price we pay for doing our own custom drawing within our view.

Now profile the application with the Core Animation and turn on the blended layers option. No more layered views sending the compositor into overtime. Scroll up and down, and take a look at the frame rate. The frame rate is consistently higher now that we're combining a number of performance updates from basic image caching to reducing the amount of compositing the system has to do for animation. Figure 5–19 shows several runs of the Core Animation instrument with different versions of Super Checkout as these views were being debugged. There's not much of a difference, but notice that the top run performed the best.

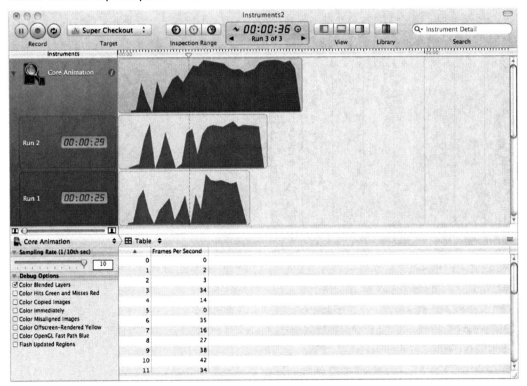

Figure 5–19. *Different runs of Super Checkout through the Core Animation instrument*

NOTE: The table cells we are using should be created by using a built-in cell type. The only thing that would still need to be implemented is the code that loads the image and scales it down to fit within cell's image view. This technique, however, is perfect for any complicated cell that can't be accomplished by using a cell that Apple provides in UIKit.

Learning from Apple

The engineers at Apple have given us clues to how they make their apps perform so well. These engineers have an intimate knowledge of how these frameworks work, so let's use the blended layers debug option to take a look at Springboard and a bundled app to see how Apple designs its applications.

Let's take a look at the Stocks application that ships with iOS (see Figure 5–20). As you learned previously, compositing is expensive, and the most expensive part is drawing transparent views. So how would you implement rounded corners in a custom view? You could have an image that serves as a background image on a view and place transparent views on top of it. That would work out fine if the view didn't have to animate around. If we used the full image and placed transparent views for animations, the compositor combined with Core Animation would make for a poorly performing animation.

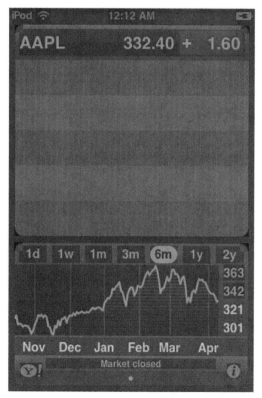

Figure 5–20. *Stocks app with blended layers turned on*

As Figure 5–20 shows, the Stocks app uses rounded corners. To accomplish this effect, the app has small rounded corner images placed on each corner of the app. Because the app does not use one large image, the compositor has to composite the transparency only on each of the corners. This technique gives us rounded corners that are quick to draw and easy to implement. By implementing this idea, keeping views lightweight, and drawing custom views where it makes sense, we can create great-looking applications that animate and scroll like a dream.

The main reason we're looking at the Stocks app is to learn from Apple. The developers know the platform the best and have plenty of tricks up their sleeves on how to make applications appear to be smooth. Users expect this level of polish, and this attention to detail sets the bar pretty high for us as we implement our applications.

Summary

We covered a lot of ground in this chapter. We talked about how important it is to keep the run loop, well, running. We also talked a bit about compositing and how to implement the fancy designs handed to us by designers. Sadly, Super Checkout didn't have a real designer to design it, but we were able to get a blazingly fast table cell thanks to an approach given to us by Loren Brichter.

Now that we have our application rendering quickly, what do we do now? We'll look at the networking stack of iOS and the tools at our disposal to detect strange network-related issues. We're also going to talk about caching and power management. The next chapter is all about the radios inside an iOS device. No amateur radio license is required.

Chapter **6**

Networking, Cache, and Power Management

So far, we've looked at how to remove memory leaks and make our interfaces scroll and animate without much lag. The application is starting to perform and act like a polished app that is ready for prime time. What is the next step in our process? Networking is the next step.

The problem that comes with developing these applications is that we have high-speed Internet connections most of the time while we're developing and debugging our application. We're going to look at tools to help mimic slow and unreliable networks so we can see how our application is going to perform in the field.

Mobile devices communicate via a very unreliable and relatively slow network (when not connected on a Wi-Fi network). This makes our job as software developers very difficult because we need to use some very complicated techniques to hide this complexity from our users. A very common technique to do this is to implement a caching solution.

Balancing live data with caching is a big problem in which Ph.D.s have been granted in the search of finding the perfect technique. Instead of looking at the theory of caching and tracking hits and misses, we're going to look at how you might implement a simple cache and what kind of cache you would want to use in certain situations. We'll also look at some APIs that give you caching to save some time in development.

Finally, we're going to look at how much power our application is using while in the field. Since our users are running their devices off of a battery, we need to be very cognizant of battery life and understand that our application needs to be a good citizen inside of the iOS system.

Fortunately, Apple and other developers have provided us some great tools for accomplishing all of these tasks. This chapter will discuss how to balance live data with caching and how to squeeze the most out of the device's battery. In the end, you'll have a good caching solution for Super Checkout and a clearer understanding on how to determine how an application affects battery life.

Understanding Networking and Cache Control

Most applications written for the iOS platform have some sort of networked communication. Since this is the case, understanding how to design APIs on the server side and how to consume these services is vital. In Super Checkout, the API–consuming code was already developed. Since the API was developed already, we're going to spend some time looking at some of the thoughts behind the design of the API.

Exploring the Client API

The client API of Super Checkout was based heavily on Matt Gemmel's MGTwitterEngine (http://instinctivecode.com/). The idea behind the API design can be best described in Figure 6–1. The basic architecture is to have all of your networking code flowing through one object. This object can live as a property on your controller or as a singleton, though I'd recommend having a discrete instance of the engine for each controller.

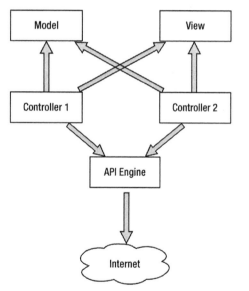

Figure 6–1. *The basic networking architecture for Super Checkout*

Before we dive into what the API engine does, let's consider what the application would look like without this design pattern. Figure 6–2 shows what the application might look like.

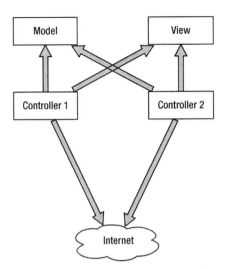

Figure 6–2. *The application without an API engine*

The difference between Figures 6–1 and 6–2 is very subtle, yet it is important enough to spend time discussing.

With the power and ease of use of NSURLConnection and ASIHTTPRequest (more on that one later), it is tempting to use those APIs in your controller logic. This introduces some coupling to a specific web service and your application. This is why the API engine was created and inserted between the controllers and the Internet.

By decoupling the web service and abstracting it into its own class, we are able to react to changes in the services as they are invariably made. If the application's architecture were implemented as in Figure 6–2, each controller that was affected by the service change would have to be updated. Even in a small application like Super Checkout, this can be tedious and time consuming, especially if there was a model change.

This idea is more of a guideline and won't fit every situation. This type of software architecture is the hardest part of application development. The goal is to have a reusable, self-contained component that handles the networked communication, performs well, and can be used throughout the application.

With the simplicity and single-service nature of Super Checkout, the decision to have a single engine that is included in each view controller was made. Your application will have some similarities and some differences. Analyze the problem, and architect based on that.

Delving into Super Checkout's API Engine Design

The API for communicating with Super Checkout's server-side API was designed to have a single interface to the networking component. Figure 6–3 shows the public interface to the API. Since the server has a simple interface, it made sense to have a single class that handled all of the interaction with the server. If the service was more complex, or we had to communicate with more services, the architecture would look completely different.

SuperCheckoutAPIEngine
delegate
connections
getProducts
getImageForProduct:
buyProduct:withQuantity:
removeProductFromCart:withQuantity:
getCart
checkout

SuperCheckoutAPIEngineDelegate
@required
requestSucceeded:
requestFailed:withError:
@optional
productListReceived:forRequest:
cartContentsReceived:forRequest:
imageReceived:forRequest:
connectionStarted:
connectionFinished:

Figure 6–3. *The public interface for the engine*

The basic idea for the SuperCheckoutAPIEngine class is to send the request and get data back. So each request follows the same path as in the sequence diagram found in Figure 6–4.

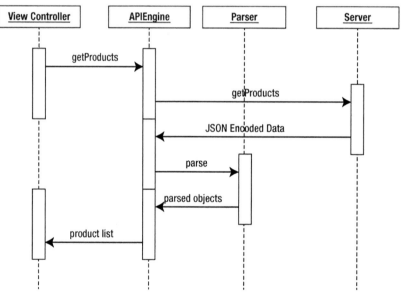

Figure 6–4. *The path of a request retrieving the products list from the server*

Behind the scenes, the engine uses an NSURLConnection subclass (SuperCheckoutHTTPURLConnection) and the classes that go with NSURLConnection. The engine holds on to each connection and associates it with its identifier inside the connections dictionary. By doing this, we can have multiple requests going at the same time and are able to have the delegate callbacks reference the appropriate request.

This is the basic formula for performing asynchronous requests and removes any blocking that might occur. There is a problem, however. NSURLRequest still lives on the main thread. All it does is tie itself into the main thread's run loop and get data back while this run loop is in its default run mode. This means that when a scroll view is scrolling or any other operation takes the run loop out of the default mode, the connection will not receive data.

If your application needs to get data as it comes across and can't wait, you can do this instead:

```
//aRequest was allocated and configured above and someRunLoop can be the main run loop
//or another thread's run loop
NSURLConnection *connection = [[NSURLConnection alloc] initWithRequest:aRequest

delegate:self

startImmediately:NO];
[connection scheduleInRunLoop:someRunLoop forMode:NSRunLoopCommonModes]
[connection start];
```

This approach has quite a few caveats, however. When scheduling a connection on another run loop, the delegate methods are called on the same thread in which the connection is created. This makes using NSURLConnection very complicated, and sometimes that complexity is unnecessary.

There is another popular networking library that uses the CFNetwork layer behind the scenes. This library is called ASIHTTPRequest (http://allseeing-i.com/ASIHTTPRequest/).

Setting up ASIHTTPRequest

Before you start modifying the project, create a new Git branch, and call it Networking_and_cache.

Setting up ASIHTTPRequest is as simple as downloading the source, importing it into the project, and adding some libraries. To download the latest version, visit http://allseeing-i.com/ASIHTTPRequest/ (the URL at the time of this writing is http://github.com/pokeb/asi-http-request/tarball/master).

Once the source is downloaded, extract the tar file, and open the Super Checkout project. Under the External Libraries group, create a new group, and call it ASIHTTPRequest (see Figure 6–5).

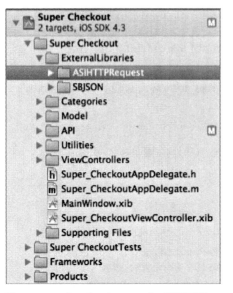

Figure 6–5. *Creating the group for ASIHTTPRequest*

Next, we want to associate that group with a folder. Expand the utility area, and select the newly created group. In the File Inspector tab (**View ➤ Utilities ➤ File Inspector**), there is a button that will associate this group with a new folder (see Figure 6–6).

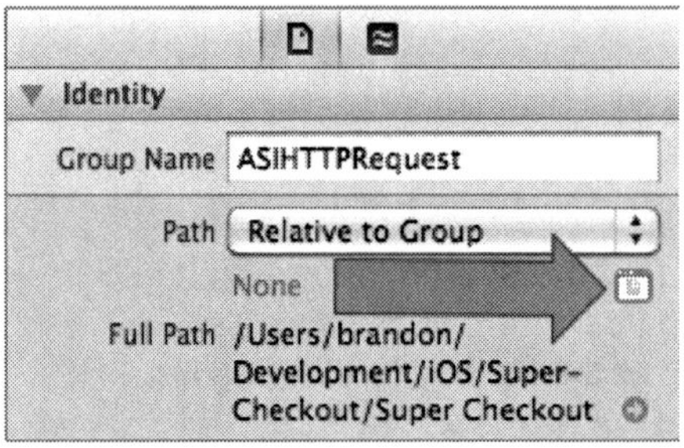

Figure 6–6. *Adjusting the path that the group references*

Click the button, and you will be presented with a dialog box showing the contents of the ExternalLibraries folder. Click the New Folder button to create a new folder for the ASIHTTPRequest code to go in (see Figure 6–7), and after that is created, click Choose to associate the folder with the group.

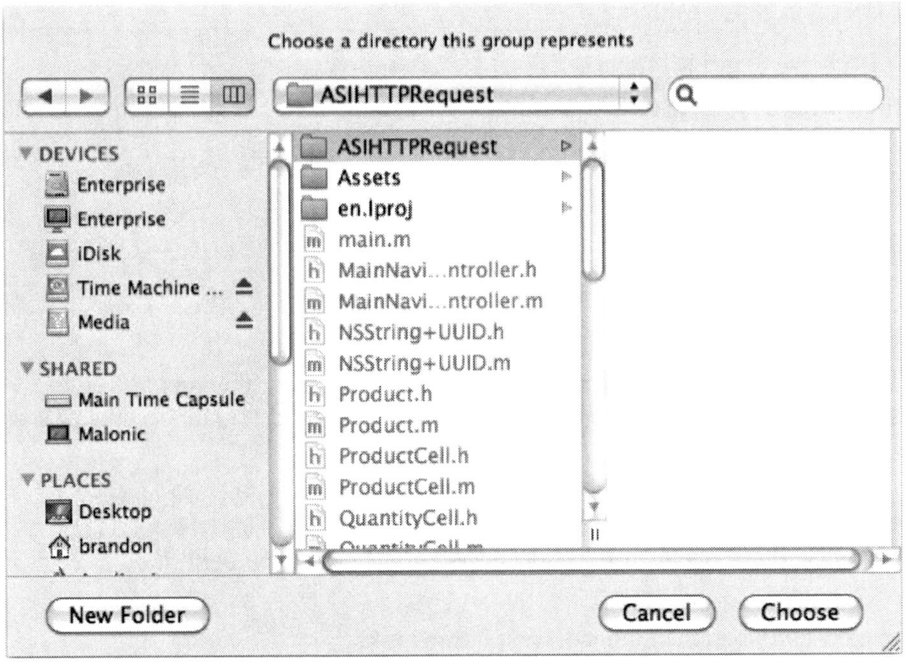

Figure 6–7. *Creating the new folder where the ASIHTTPRequest group points*

Now that we have the group associated with a folder, we can now import the source files in. Right-click the ASIHTTPRequest group, and select "Add Files to Super Checkout". This brings up a file chooser dialog. Navigate to where you downloaded the source to ASIHTTPRequest, and go into the Classes folder. Select all the files (command-click or shift-click the files), but not the folders in the directory. The following files should be selected:

- ASIAuthenticationDialog.h
- ASIAuthenticationDialog.m
- ASICacheDelegate.h
- ASIDataCompressor.h
- ASIDataCompressor.m
- ASIDataDecompressor.h
- ASIDataDecompressor.m
- ASIDownloadCache.h
- ASIDownloadCache.m
- ASIFormDataRequest.h
- ASIFormDataRequest.m
- ASIHTTPRequest.h

- ASIHTTPRequest.m
- ASIHTTPRequestConfig.h
- ASIHTTPRequestDelegate.h
- ASIInputStream.h
- ASIInputStream.m
- ASINetworkQueue.h
- ASINetworkQueue.m
- ASIProgressDelegate.h

Make sure the check boxes to copy the files to the destination location and for adding the files to the application's target are both checked. Click the Add button to finalize the import.

We're not quite done adding files yet. You'll need to include the reachability files (Reachability.h and Reachability.m) that are located in the External/Reachability folder. Import those into the same group using the import steps you performed a moment ago.

Next, link the application against the following frameworks:

- CFNetwork
- SystemConfiguration
- MobileCoreServices
- CoreGraphics
- zlib

To do this, select the project name in the project navigator, and select the application's target in the left-hand pane of the panel that appears. In the Build Phases tab, we will add some libraries to the Link Binaries With Libraries phase. Expand the section, and click the plus sign. A list of available libraries is presented (see Figure 6–8). Select the libraries listed previously (zlib is libz.dylib in the list), and click Add.

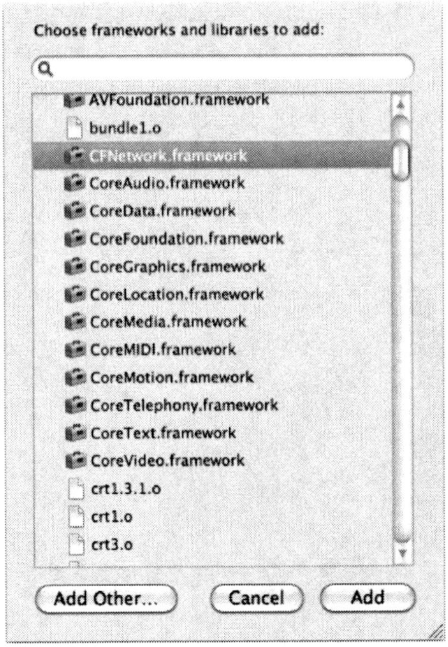

Figure 6–8. *Adding frameworks to Super Checkout*

The linking build phase should look like Figure 6–9.

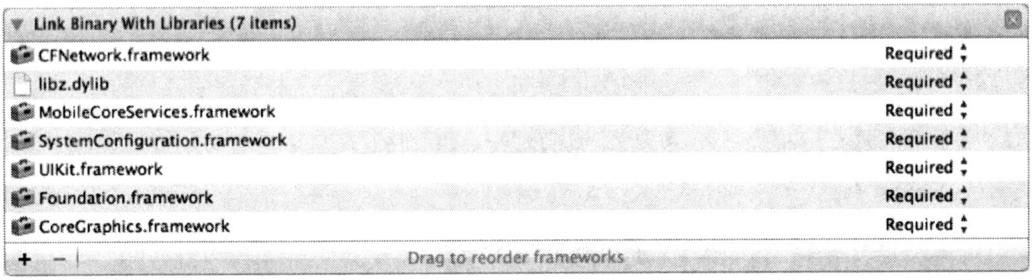

Figure 6–9. *The final list of linked libraries*

Now, build the target, and ensure there are no compilation errors.

Implementing ASI in Super Checkout

A great thing about abstracting the HTTP request code into its own class is being able to change what our request code looks like and not have to make any other changes. We are going to keep the contract between the module starting the requests and the delegates the same, and we're going to completely refactor the behind-the-scenes code.

Ready? Here we go!

Open SuperCheckoutAPIEngine.m, and update the #import section to look like Listing 6–1.

Listing 6–1. *A Few Imports for Our API Engine*

```
#import "SuperCheckoutAPIEngine.h"
#import "SuperCheckoutRequestTypes.h"
#import "SCJSONParser.h"
#import "Product.h"
#import "ASIHTTPRequest.h"
#import "NSString+UUID.h"
```

Next, add the macros in Listing 6–2. Macros are great for centralizing a particular value, and you don't need a constant.

Listing 6–2. *Macros for Our API Engine*

```
#define REQUEST_TYPE          @"requestType"
#define RESPONSE_TYPE         @"responseType"
#define REQUEST_ID            @"requestIdentifier"
```

Now, we're going to modify the class extension. The class extension is a great way to add private methods to a class. Modify it to look like Listing 6–3.

Listing 6–3. *Our Modified Class Extension*

```
@interface SuperCheckoutAPIEngine ()

// Utility methods
- (NSString *)_queryStringWithBase:(NSString *)base parameters:(NSDictionary *)params
prefixed:(BOOL)prefixed;
- (NSString *)_encodeString:(NSString *)string;

// Connection/Request methods
- (NSString *)_sendRequest:(NSURL *)theURL
              withRequestType:(SuperCheckoutRequestType)requestType
                   responseType:(SuperCheckoutResponseType)responseType;
- (NSString *)_sendRequestWithMethod:(NSString *)method
                              path:(NSString *)path
        queryParameters:(NSDictionary *)params
                          body:(NSString *)body
                   requestType:(SuperCheckoutRequestType)requestType
              responseType:(SuperCheckoutResponseType)responseType;

- (NSString *)_sendImageRequestWithURL:(NSString *)imageURL;
- (NSURL *)_baseURLWithMethod:(NSString *)method
                                              path:(NSString *)path

requestType:(SuperCheckoutRequestType)requestType
                          queryParameters:(NSDictionary *)params;


// Parsing methods
- (void)_parseDataForConnection:(ASIHTTPRequest *)connection;

// Delegate methods
- (BOOL) _isValidDelegateForSelector:(SEL)selector;

@end
```

The next line to look out for is `// Connection/Request` methods. Replace the code from that line down to the line that has `#pragma mark - API Methods` with what you find in Listing 6–4.

Listing 6–4. *The Connection/Request Management Implementation*

```
// Connection/Request methods
- (NSString*)_sendRequest:(NSURL *)theURL
                withRequestType:(SuperCheckoutRequestType)requestType
                    responseType:(SuperCheckoutResponseType)responseType
{
        ASIHTTPRequest *request = [ASIHTTPRequest requestWithURL:theURL];
    [request setDelegate:self];
    NSString *requestIdentifier = [NSString stringWithNewUUID];
    [request setUserInfo:[NSDictionary dictionaryWithObjectsAndKeys:
                        [NSNumber numberWithInt:requestType], REQUEST_TYPE,
                        [NSNumber numberWithInt:responseType], RESPONSE_TYPE,
                        requestIdentifier, REQUEST_ID,
                        nil]];


    if (request == nil) {
        return nil;
    }

        if ([self _isValidDelegateForSelector:@selector(connectionStarted:)])
                [delegate connectionStarted:[[request requestID] stringValue]];

    [request startAsynchronous];
    return requestIdentifier;
}
- (NSString *)_sendRequestWithMethod:(NSString *)method
                                path:(NSString *)path
                    queryParameters:(NSDictionary *)params
                                body:(NSString *)body
                        requestType:(SuperCheckoutRequestType)requestType
                        responseType:(SuperCheckoutResponseType)responseType {
        NSURL *theUrl = [self _baseURLWithMethod:method

path:path

requestType:requestType

                                                    queryParameters:params];

    return [self _sendRequest:theUrl
                withRequestType:requestType
                    responseType:responseType];
}

- (NSString *)_sendImageRequestWithURL:(NSString *)imageURL {
        NSURL *theURL = [NSURL URLWithString:imageURL];

        return [self _sendRequest:theURL
                    withRequestType:SuperCheckoutProductImage
                        responseType:SuperCheckoutImage];
}
```

```objc
- (NSURL *)_baseURLWithMethod:(NSString *)method
                         path:(NSString *)path
                  requestType:(SuperCheckoutRequestType)requestType
              queryParameters:(NSDictionary *)params
{
    // Construct appropriate URL string.
    NSString *fullPath = [path
stringByAddingPercentEscapesUsingEncoding:NSNonLossyASCIIStringEncoding];
    if (params && ![method isEqualToString:HTTP_POST_METHOD]) {
        fullPath = [self _queryStringWithBase:fullPath parameters:params prefixed:YES];
    }

    NSString *connectionType = @"http";

    NSString *urlString = nil;
    if(requestType == SuperCheckoutProductImage) {
        urlString = path;
    } else {
        urlString = [NSString stringWithFormat:@"%@://%@/%@",
                    connectionType,
                    BASE_URL, fullPath];
    }

    NSURL *finalURL = [NSURL URLWithString:urlString];
    return finalURL;
}

// Parsing methods
- (void)_parseDataForConnection:(ASIHTTPRequest *)request {
        NSData *jsonData = [[[request responseData] copy] autorelease];
        NSString *identifier = [[[[request requestID] stringValue] copy] autorelease];

        SuperCheckoutRequestType requestType =
                                              [[[request userInfo]
objectForKey:REQUEST_TYPE] intValue];
    SuperCheckoutResponseType responseType =
                                              [[[request userInfo]
objectForKey:RESPONSE_TYPE] intValue];

    switch ([[[request userInfo] objectForKey:RESPONSE_TYPE] intValue]) {
            case SuperCheckoutProductList:
            case SuperCheckoutCartContents:
                [SCJSONParser parserWithJSON:jsonData
                                                    delegate:self
connectionIdentifier:identifier
                                                requestType:requestType
                                                responseType:responseType
URL:nil];
                            break;

            default:
            break;
    }
}

// Delegate methods
- (BOOL) _isValidDelegateForSelector:(SEL)selector
```

```
{
        return ((delegate != nil) && [delegate respondsToSelector:selector]);
}

#pragma mark ASIHTTPRequestDelegate Methods
- (void)requestFinished:(ASIHTTPRequest *)request {
    NSString *requestIdentifier = [[request userInfo] objectForKey:REQUEST_ID];
    if ([request responseStatusCode] >= 400) {
        // Assume failure, and report to delegate.
        NSData *receivedData = [request responseData];
        NSString *body = [receivedData length] ? [NSString
stringWithUTF8String:[receivedData bytes]] : @"";

        NSDictionary *userInfo = [NSDictionary dictionaryWithObjectsAndKeys:
                                    [request responseString], @"response",
                                    body, @"body",
                                    nil];
        NSError *error = [NSError errorWithDomain:@"HTTP" code:[request
responseStatusCode]

userInfo:userInfo];
                if ([self
_isValidDelegateForSelector:@selector(requestFailed:withError:)])
                        [delegate requestFailed:requestIdentifier withError:error];

        // Destroy the connection.

                NSString *connectionIdentifier = requestIdentifier;
                [connections removeObjectForKey:connectionIdentifier];
                if ([self _isValidDelegateForSelector:@selector(connectionFinished:)])
                        [delegate connectionFinished:connectionIdentifier];
        return;
    }

    NSString *connID = nil;
        SuperCheckoutResponseType responseType = 0;
        connID = requestIdentifier;
        responseType = [[[request userInfo] objectForKey:RESPONSE_TYPE] intValue];

    // Inform delegate.
        [delegate requestSucceeded:connID];

    NSData *receivedData = [request responseData];
    if (receivedData) {
        if (responseType == SuperCheckoutImage) {
                        // Create image from data.
            UIImage *image = [[[UIImage alloc] initWithData:receivedData] autorelease];

            // Inform delegate.
                        if ([self
_isValidDelegateForSelector:@selector(imageReceived:forRequest:)])
                                [delegate imageReceived:image

forRequest:requestIdentifier];
        } else {
                // Parse data from the connection (either XML or JSON.)
                [self _parseDataForConnection:request];
```

```
            }
        }

    // Release the connection.
    [connections removeObjectForKey:connID];
        if ([self _isValidDelegateForSelector:@selector(connectionFinished:)])
            [delegate connectionFinished:connID];
}

- (void)requestFailed:(ASIHTTPRequest *)request {
    NSString *requestIdentifier = [[request userInfo] objectForKey:REQUEST_ID];;

    // Inform delegate.
        if ([self _isValidDelegateForSelector:@selector(requestFailed:withError:)]){
            [delegate requestFailed:requestIdentifier
                    withError:[request error]];
        }

    // Release the connection.
    [connections removeObjectForKey:requestIdentifier];
        if ([self _isValidDelegateForSelector:@selector(connectionFinished:)])
            [delegate connectionFinished:requestIdentifier];
}

#pragma mark - SCJSONParserDelegate Methods
-(void)parsingSucceededForRequest:(NSString *)identifier

ofResponseType:(SuperCheckoutResponseType)responseType
                                        parsedObjects:(NSDictionary *)parsedObject {
        switch (responseType) {
            case SuperCheckoutProductList:
                if([self
_isValidDelegateForSelector:@selector(productListReceived:forRequest:)]) {
                    NSArray *result = [parsedObject objectForKey:@"result"];
                    NSMutableArray *newResult =
                                                    [NSMutableArray
arrayWithCapacity:[result count]];

                    for(NSDictionary *obj in result) {
                        Product *prod = [[Product alloc] initWithDictionary:obj];

                        [newResult addObject:prod];

                        [prod release];
                    }

                    [delegate productListReceived:[NSArray arrayWithArray:newResult]
                                                    forRequest:identifier];
                }
                break;
            case SuperCheckoutCartContents:
                if([self
_isValidDelegateForSelector:@selector(cartContentsReceived:forRequest:)]) {
                    id cart = [parsedObject objectForKey:@"result"];
                    if([cart isKindOfClass:[NSNull class]]) {
                        cart = nil;
```

```
        }
        [delegate cartContentsReceived:cart forRequest:identifier];
    }

    default:
        break;
    }
}
```

We have now successfully replaced our networking code with ASIHTTPRequest. Imagine having to go into all of the view controllers to make this update!

Let's look at a little piece of the code we just implemented.

In Listing 6–5, you'll see we're creating an ASIHTTPRequest, setting the delegate, and adding a dictionary that gets passed around with the request. This dictionary holds the request identifier (to hold backward compatibility with the previous API), the request type and response type. ASIHTTPRequest handles cookies automatically, so we don't have to worry about dealing with them.

As far as threading goes, ASIHTTPRequest is a subclass of NSOperation, and the startAsynchronous method adds it to a local NSOperationQueue that spawns new threads and the delegate callbacks occur on the main thread. This also means that, if it was found to be necessary, our SuperCheckoutAPIEngine class could manage its own NSOperationQueue to control how many requests are occurring at once.

Listing 6–5. *The code that creates the actual request*

```
ASIHTTPRequest *request = [ASIHTTPRequest requestWithURL:theURL];
[request setDelegate:self];
NSString *requestIdentifier = [NSString stringWithNewUUID];
[request setUserInfo:[NSDictionary dictionaryWithObjectsAndKeys:
                        [NSNumber numberWithInt:requestType], REQUEST_TYPE,
                        [NSNumber numberWithInt:responseType], RESPONSE_TYPE,
                        requestIdentifier, REQUEST_ID,
                        nil]];

if (request == nil) {
    return nil;
}

if ([self _isValidDelegateForSelector:@selector(connectionStarted:)])
        [delegate connectionStarted:[[request requestID] stringValue]];

[request startAsynchronous];
return requestIdentifier;
```

Commit these changes, and we'll move on to designing and debugging server-side code.

At the time this code was written, ASIHTTPRequest was well supported, and support has since ceased. Since we architected our application to have a clear separation of concerns, we can swap these pieces in and out at will without much change from the consuming code. There are some other popular networking libraries, and the concept that we just implemented is the same for each of these libraries. These libraries are

- AFNetworking (`https://github.com/gowalla/AFNetworking`)

- LRResty (`http://projects.lukeredpath.co.uk/resty/`)

- NSURLConnection (The original approach and is well supported by Apple)

Exploring the Server API

For Super Checkout, we created our own server-side API. This book isn't about developing server APIs. Instead, we'll talk about some good practices when designing server APIs to make life easier when consuming these services. We'll also talk about some techniques for pinpointing where a bug lies.

Designing for Consumption

Designing a server-side API is a completely different beast than designing an application on iOS. Many other considerations need to be made, and thoughtfulness toward the consumer is central. For Super Checkout, we decided on a very simple API that relied on GET requests and query string parameters. The communication medium was JSON due to its lightweight nature. The server manages a session and the current shopping cart.

As far as the data model, the server always returns a wrapper object. Figure 6–10 shows what this wrapper object looks like.

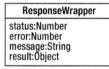

Figure 6–10. *The definition of the response wrapper*

This object gives us everything we need to know about the response. If the call succeeded (i.e., a 200 HTTP status code) and there was a problem with the data, we know what happened. If you'll notice, Super Checkout assumes a successful call every time. This is a problem with the application that could come back to haunt us later.

So how do we handle these errors? Let's get back into the code, and check it out.

Open `SuperCheckoutAPIEngine.m`, and navigate to the implementation of `parsingSucceededForRequest:ofResponseType:parsedObjects:`. This method is the callback from our parser. Since all of our responses have the same wrapper, we'll handle the errors in here.

First, we'll want to add some error constants and an error domain for the `NSError` object we'll be creating. At the top of the file, below the compiler macros, add the following lines:

```
NSString* const APIErrorDomain = @"SuperCheckoutAPIErrorDomain";

typedef enum SuperCheckoutAPIErrorType {
    APIErrorType
} SuperCheckoutAPIErrorType;
```

Now, navigate back to the `parsingSucceededForRequest:ofResponseType:parsedObjects:` method, and add the following code above the `switch` statement:

```
    if([[parsedObject objectForKey:@"status"] intValue] != 0) {
        NSError *error = [NSError errorWithDomain:APIErrorDomain
code:APIErrorType
userInfo:
                                    [NSDictionary dictionaryWithObjectsAndKeys:
[parsedObject objectForKey:@"message"],
NSLocalizedDescriptionKey,nil]];

        if ([self _isValidDelegateForSelector:@selector(requestFailed:withError:)]){
            [delegate requestFailed:identifier withError:error];
        }

        return;
    }
```

Now that we have handled errors, we are sending errors to the view controller with (hopefully) meaningful messages that come back from the server.

Using Debugging Tools

Many times when developing the client engine that consumes the service, data coming back from the server wasn't what I expected. Instead of littering the source with NSLog statements, I used some handy tools to verify what was getting sent to the server and what was being returned. These tools greatly sped up the debugging process when the server-side components were in development and the client code was misbehaving.

Two different tools were used to accomplish each task. The first one was used to test the inputs and outputs from the service to check to see if the services were working. It is called RESTClient and is a plug-in for Firefox. It can be found at `https://addons.mozilla.org/en-US/firefox/addon/restclient/`. Figure 6–11 is a view of what the client looks like after hitting on of the main services in Super Checkout.

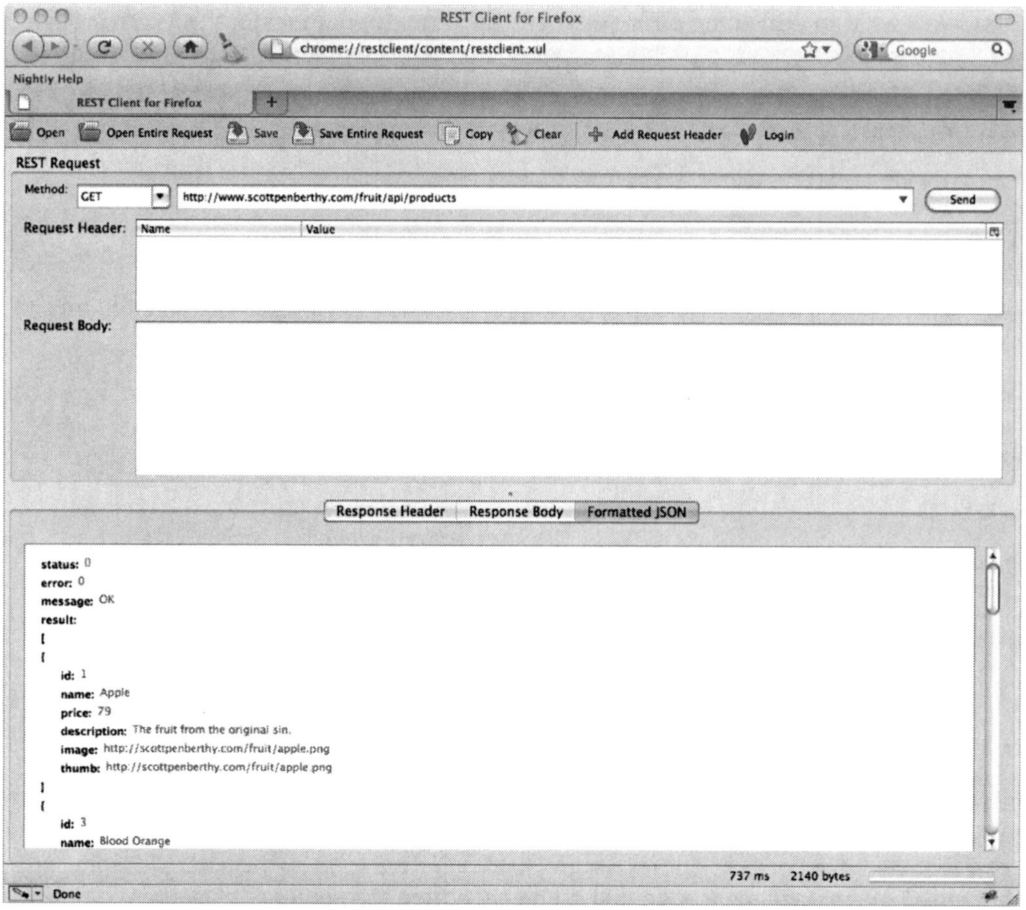

Figure 6–11. *RESTClient for Firefox is a great utility to check service responses*

As Figure 6–11 shows, the interface is pretty simple. It lets you select the request method, enter a base URL, input request headers, and add a request body. Click Send, and the request is made with the response header and body coming back. The tabs to the right of Response Body will be tailored to the request type. In the example in Figure 6–11, RESTClient has formatted the JSON string returned from the service.

This is a great utility when all you need is a quick tool to check the response of a request or debug an issue with the server. Some other great tools that live on the command line are more powerful, but this tool gets the job done. The ultimate point is to find a reliable, quick tool to quickly exercise the end services to make sure the services work as expected as you troubleshoot or test the server component of your application.

The next tool is definitely the more powerful of the two and deserves to be in any developer's toolbox. This application is called Charles, and it is a web proxy. It can be found at http://www.charlesproxy.com/. Charles is a commercial application, but it does have a free trial. This application watches all the web traffic on your machine and logs it (while the recorder is turned on). Figure 6–12 shows Charles logging the traffic from getting products, adding a product to the cart, and checking out.

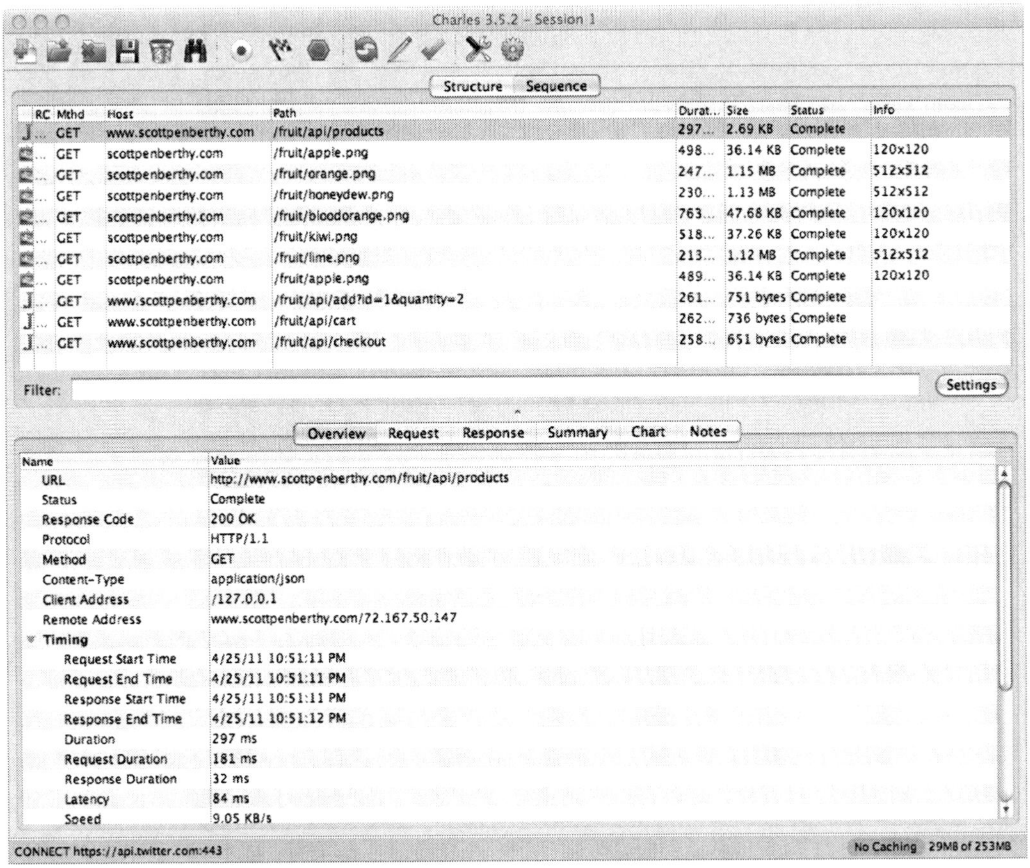

Figure 6–12. *Charles doing its traffic-logging thing*

Charles gives you way more information about the request and response. It gives the same information as RESTClient, but the requests are coming from the app. This information can be used to see what the requests look like coming out of the device to make sure they are formatted properly and to make sure the responses are formatted appropriately too.

> **NOTE:** Charles will not act as a proxy for the device. Any tests that are run need to be run from the iOS Simulator.

Slowing Things Down with the Network Link Conditioner

When testing in the simulator, you are usually testing on a pretty large and mostly reliable Internet connection. The problem with this is that the device communicates over a slower and extremely unreliable network. Replicating real-world scenarios in a sterile development environment is a pretty tricky task to accomplish. Fortunately, developers have solved this problem.

The tool to throttle bandwidth is called the Network Link Conditioner and is bundled with Xcode 4.2 for OS 10.7 (Lion). The preference pane can be found in `/Developer/Applications/Utilities/Network\ Link\ Conditioner`. Open it, and it will install it into System Preferences for you. Network Link Conditioner is a preference pane that lets you enter the ports to throttle, hosts to throttle, latency, and speed to throttle down to. The values for throttling include common speeds for Edge and 3G. Figure 6–13 shows Network Link Conditioner in the process of throttling to our services.

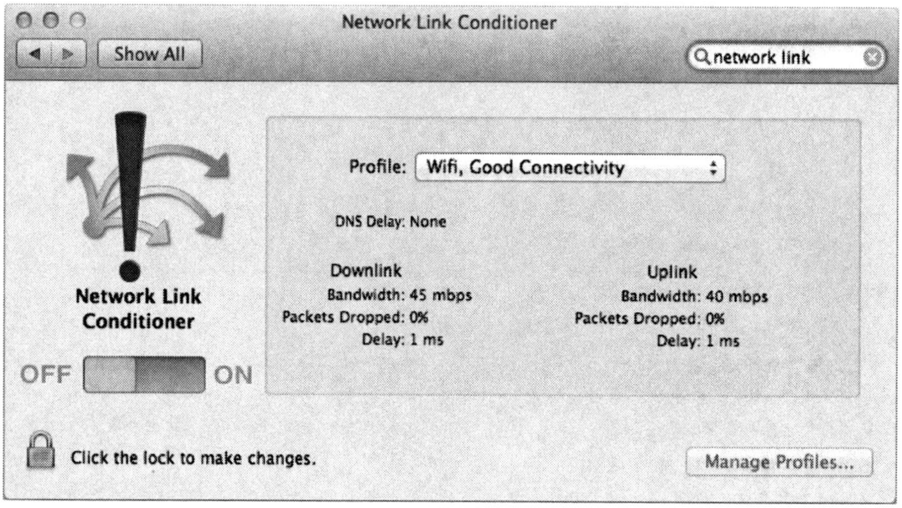

Figure 6–13. *The Network Link in System Preferences needs to be unlocked and enabled.*

Since this chapter is all about networking and most users' data packages for the device are no longer unlimited, testing using the simulator makes a lot of sense. With Speedlimit, we can get a good idea how an application is going to perform in the field. This is vitally important for applications that perform a large number of requests. Understanding how an application will perform on a poorly performing network will help in making decisions on caching approaches.

To turn on the link conditioner, you'll first need to unlock the keychain by clicking on the lock at the bottom of the preference pane. Then you'll select the appropriate profile to mimic and turn the switch to the on position. This will slow down the network for the entire machine, so if you were doing something in another app, you will see a drop in network performance.

Controlling the Cache

What is the best way to give the illusion of a high-performing app that exists on a slow network is through storing responses for a request? Caching. Caching is great because the application gets the requested data quickly, and the user isn't left waiting. If caching is so great, why do we not cache everything? The first reason is because most data on the Internet is real time. If everything was cached, the application would be severely behind on the latest information, and the user would be forced to refresh often.

Given this conflict, you're probably wondering, "What is the best approach for a caching solution?"

Good question! The answer is extremely complicated. As I mentioned earlier, caching approaches have been the focus of dissertations. We're not going to go in depth on how caching algorithms work or which one is the best to use in which situation. That would be an entirely different book altogether. Instead, we're going to see what we can use in Cocoa or other frameworks to achieve the appropriate level of caching for Super Checkout and hopefully get you started on a good path to a caching approach for your app.

Before We Get Started

Before we dive into the code, let's spend some time talking about what cache really is and what kind of data is a good candidate for caching. In the context that we are using cache, cache is a temporary store that greatly improves the speed at which data can be retrieved. The idea is to store as much information locally and retrieve it from the server only when needed.

The basic idea that we are using here is to develop the application without a cache. By avoiding premature optimization, we can ensure the application is feature complete and relatively bug free before we start optimizing the networking layer. This way any bugs that are introduced can be easily tracked down.

Deciding What to Cache

How do we decide on what to cache? The answer to this question can be found by one of two basic methods. The first method is guess and test. This technique might have some positive results, but is not very scientific and could introduce some problems. The second method is basically a statistical analysis of the data that is requested. This involves collecting data from the application and analyzing the data.

To capture the data, we can use Charles to collect the information, and either analyze the data directly in Charles or export the request information to a different format and analyze the data in an application of your choice. For this example, we'll use a relatively small sample size and use a single run through the application from getting products, viewing a product, adding a product to the cart and finally checking out. Figure 6–14 shows the data set we're going to look at.

RC	Mthd	Host	Path	Duration	Size	Status	Info
J 200	GET	www.scottpenberthy.com	/fruit/api/products	297 ms	2.69 KB	Complete	
200	GET	scottpenberthy.com	/fruit/apple.png	498 ms	36.14 KB	Complete	120x120
200	GET	scottpenberthy.com	/fruit/orange.png	2470 ms	1.15 MB	Complete	512x512
200	GET	scottpenberthy.com	/fruit/honeydew.png	2306 ms	1.13 MB	Complete	512x512
200	GET	scottpenberthy.com	/fruit/bloodorange.png	763 ms	47.68 KB	Complete	120x120
200	GET	scottpenberthy.com	/fruit/kiwi.png	518 ms	37.26 KB	Complete	120x120
200	GET	scottpenberthy.com	/fruit/lime.png	2135 ms	1.12 MB	Complete	512x512
200	GET	scottpenberthy.com	/fruit/apple.png	489 ms	36.14 KB	Complete	120x120
J 200	GET	www.scottpenberthy.com	/fruit/api/add?id=1&quantity=2	261 ms	751 bytes	Complete	
J 200	GET	www.scottpenberthy.com	/fruit/api/cart	262 ms	736 bytes	Complete	
J 200	GET	www.scottpenberthy.com	/fruit/api/checkout	258 ms	651 bytes	Complete	

Figure 6–14. *Our data set from Charles*

How did we get that data? Well, fire up Charles, and ensure that the Mac OS X Proxy is enabled by going to **Proxy ➤ Mac OS X Proxy** and making sure it is the selected item. The next thing to do is click the record button in the toolbar and voilà, you are capturing HTTP data. You'll likely notice other entries pop up during the data capture.

Looking at the table, the first item that jumps out is that there are two types of data being requested. The first type of data is the JSON encoded data and the second type is images. The response size is also clearly different. Keeping this information in mind, we also need to look at the usage patterns for the requests.

The products list response contains product information including the price. Since the price can fluctuate, this service call is one that is not a good candidate for caching. We don't want to present the wrong price to the user. If the data set that was returned was much larger, however, we might want to modify the server code to return a paged data set and keep the size as low as possible.

The best candidate for caching data in this case is to cache the images. When we optimized the scrolling performance of the product list, we implemented a very basic in-memory cache. This solution isn't the best because the view controller handles the caching and doesn't take into account memory usage and respond to memory warnings. The `APIEngine` should do the caching. We want to have a two tier approach for caching: in-memory and on disk. The in-memory cache can be cleared out when low memory situations occur and the disk cache will take over and cache the images for about a week or so.

> **NOTE:** These decisions are made based solely on how the application will be used. In a real world scenario, user testing would be performed and would help dictate the appropriate caching strategy.

NSCache

Enough about talking about caching! Let's get into some code and learn what mechanisms exist for caching and how to use them.

The first API we'll work with is NSCache. NSCache is built into Cocoa Touch and was introduced in iOS 4.0. NSCache is simply an in-memory store, similar to what we're using in Super Checkout. NSCache is a key-value store and has mechanisms to remove stale items as the cache fills up and the system needs more memory.

This is going to be the first line of defense for our caching strategy. As a part of this set of refactoring, we'll be taking the caching out of the view controller and let the APIEngine handle the caching. This will allow the APIEngine to cache the data as necessary and each view control using it can clear the cache.

So how do we implement this? Simple! Open SuperCheckoutAPIEngine.m, and make the following changes.

In the class extension, add the method declaration in bold in Listing 6–6.

Listing 6–6. *Adding the Image Cache Method to the Class Extension*

```
- (BOOL) _isValidDelegateForSelector:(SEL)selector;

- (NSCache *) imageCache;

@end
```

And in the implementation, add Listing 6–7 directly above the #pragma mark – API Methods line.

Listing 6–7. *Implementing the Image Cache*

```
- (NSCache *) imageCache {
    static NSCache *imageCache = nil;

    if(imageCache == nil) {
        imageCache = [[NSCache alloc] init];
    }

    return imageCache;
}
```

This adds a static NSCache object to the engine, and we're going to add code to use this cache.

In SuperCheckoutAPIEngine.h, add the following two method declarations:

```
-(void) clearCache;
-(UIImage *) cachedImageForProduct:(NSString *)stringURL;
```

Back in SuperCheckoutAPIEngine.m, add the following implementations for those methods after the checkout method:

```
-(void) clearCache {
    [[self imageCache] removeAllObjects];
}

-(UIImage *) cachedImageForProduct:(NSString *)stringURL {
    return [[self imageCache] objectForKey:stringURL];
}
```

The next step is to use the cache. There are two places to edit to enable its use. The first is when we are getting the response from the request and are preparing to send the image back to the delegate. In requestFinished: find the following line, which decodes the data and creates the UIImage:

```
UIImage *image = [[[UIImage alloc] initWithData:receivedData] autorelease];
```

Underneath this line of code, add the following:

```
[[self imageCache] setObject:image forKey:[[request url] absoluteString]];
```

We now have one more place to edit the engine. In _sendImageRequestWithURL:, replace the implementation with the following block of code:

```
- (NSString *)_sendImageRequestWithURL:(NSString *)imageURL {
        NSURL *theURL = [NSURL URLWithString:imageURL];

    UIImage *image = [[self imageCache] objectForKey:[theURL absoluteString]];

    if(image) {
        NSString *requestIdentifier = [NSString stringWithNewUUID];

        if ([self _isValidDelegateForSelector:@selector(imageReceived:forRequest:)]) {
            dispatch_time_t popTime = dispatch_time(DISPATCH_TIME_NOW, 1ull);
            dispatch_after(popTime, dispatch_get_main_queue(), ^(void){
                [delegate imageReceived:image forRequest:requestIdentifier];
            });
        }

        return requestIdentifier;
    }

        return [self _sendRequest:theURL
                        withRequestType:SuperCheckoutProductImage
                            responseType:SuperCheckoutImage];
}
```

Before we move on to the rest of the changes, let's quickly look over what we just did. The first thing we did was create the cache object. We made the cache static, so all instances of the engine will use the same cache. Since Super Checkout is a small application and we are only caching the product images, this approach is OK. If we were doing more, a more robust system that manages different levels of in-memory cache might be necessary, but for now, we'll just have a master cache that gets cleared when asked.

The next change was to allow a view controller to ask for a cached product image. This method will return nil if the image is not in the cache. It is up to the view controller to handle this case and request an image.

Finally, in _sendImageRequestWithURL:, we are checking the cache for the image and mimicking a full request being made. To do this, the request identifier is created, and then a delayed block is dispatched to Grand Central Dispatch and the method returns. This makes an almost instantaneous delegate callback.

Now, we are ready for the rest of the changes. These changes include updating the ProductCell to have its own image that it manages and the Super_CheckoutViewController to utilize the new APIs in the APIEngine. Open ProductCell.h, and add the following ivar and property:

```
UIImage *productImage;
@property (nonatomic, retain) UIImage *productImage;
```

Since we are handling the images directly in the cell, we can remove the key-value observing code from the productInformation mutator. Open ProductCell.m, and add the new mutator like this:

```
-(void) setProductInformation:(Product *)newProductInformation {
    Product *oldInfo = productInformation;
    productInformation = [newProductInformation retain];
    [oldInfo release];
    [self setNeedsDisplay];
}
```

Next, synthesize the productImage property by adding the following line:

```
@synthesize productImage;
```

Then, add the following code:

```
- (void) setProductImage:(UIImage *)theProductImage {
    UIImage *oldImage = productImage;
    productImage = [theProductImage retain];
    [oldImage release];

    [self setNeedsDisplay];
}

- (void) prepareForReuse {
    [super prepareForReuse];

    [self setProductImage:nil];
}
```

In drawCellView:, modify this line:

```
CGImageRef prodImage = [[productInformation productImage] CGImage];
```

to look like this one:

```
CGImageRef prodImage = [[self productImage] CGImage];
```

Finally, release the productImage ivar in the dealloc method by adding

```
[productImage release];
```

Next, we want to create a category on UIImage that will add a method return a resized version of itself. To do this, go to **File ➤ New ➤ New File**, and under Cocoa Touch, select Objective-C Category. Name the category **Resize**, and make the category on UIImage (see Figure 6–15). Click Next, save the file within the project, and click Create.

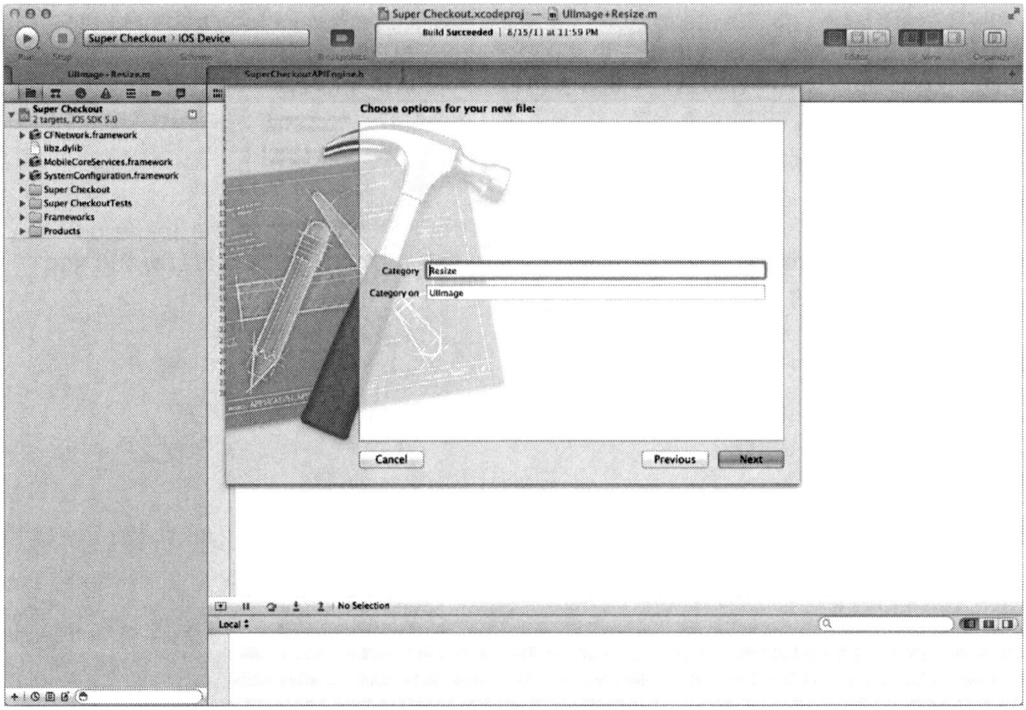

Figure 6–15. *Xcode has added the ability to make categories super easy!*

With the new category created, open the newly created `UIImage+Resize.h` file, and add this method to the header:

```
- (UIImage*) resizedImageWithSize:(CGSize)size;
```

Next, switch to the implementation, and add the implementation in Listing 6–8 to the category. The implementation of creating a resized UIImage is a handy thing to have around.

Listing 6–8. *Creating a Resized UIImage*

```
- (UIImage*) resizedImageWithSize:(CGSize)size {
        UIGraphicsBeginImageContext(size);

        [self drawInRect:CGRectMake(0.0f, 0.0f, size.width, size.height)];

        // An autoreleased image
        UIImage *newImage = UIGraphicsGetImageFromCurrentImageContext();

        UIGraphicsEndImageContext();

        return newImage;
}
```

With the category complete, open `Super_CheckoutViewController.m`. We need to modify only two methods in this file. In `tableView:cellForRowAtIndexPath:`, update it to look like this:

```
- (UITableViewCell *)tableView:(UITableView *)tableView
               cellForRowAtIndexPath:(NSIndexPath *)indexPath {
    ProductCell *cell = (ProductCell *)[tableView dequeueReusableCellWithIdentifier:

[ProductCell  reuseIdentifier]];

    if(cell == nil) {
        cell = [[[ProductCell alloc] initWithStyle:UITableViewCellStyleDefault
                                        reuseIdentifier:[ProductCell
reuseIdentifier]] autorelease];
    }
    Product *item = (Product *)[inventory objectAtIndex:[indexPath row]];

    [cell setProductInformation:item];
    [cell setAccessoryType:UITableViewCellAccessoryDisclosureIndicator];

    //[self setProductCell:nil];

    //Fetch image for the cell
    UIImage *image = [apiEngine cachedImageForProduct:[item thumb]];
    if(image == nil) {
        if (self.tableView.dragging == NO && self.tableView.decelerating == NO) {
            NSString *requestId = [apiEngine getImageForProduct:[item thumb]];

            [imageIndexes setObject:[NSNumber numberWithInt:[indexPath row]]
                                    forKey:requestId];
        }
    } else {
        [cell setProductImage:image];
    }

    return cell;
}
```

Update `imageReceived:forRequest:` to look like this:

```
-(void) imageReceived:(UIImage *)image forRequest:(NSString *)connectionIdentifier {
    NSIndexPath *indexPath =
                [NSIndexPath indexPathForRow:[[imageIndexes
objectForKey:connectionIdentifier] intValue]
                                                    inSection:0];

    ProductCell *prod = (ProductCell *)[[self tableView]
cellForRowAtIndexPath:indexPath];

    [prod setProductImage:[image resizedImageWithSize:CGSizeMake(64.0, 64.0)]];

    [imageIndexes removeObjectForKey:connectionIdentifier];
}
```

Finally, in `didReceiveMemoryWarning`, add this line:

```
[apiEngine clearCache];
```

Now the API engine creates a simple in-memory cache, and the products list view takes full advantage of it. The product details view doesn't need to change anything, however. This is because the API engine checks the cache before making the request. Simple and intelligent caching solutions usually hide the details of the cache from most view controllers.

Since the first level of our two-tier approach is complete, let's take a look at our disk caching solution.

Implementing Our Disk Caching Solution

The ASIHTTPRequest team members have given us the second tier of our caching solution. They have created a class called ASIDownloadCache. This class is the default implementation of the ASICacheDelegate protocol. If you have your own disk caching system, conform to that protocol, and you can tie that implementation into ASIHTTPRequest.

For Super Checkout, we'll be using the default implementation that comes with the project. To implement these changes, we'll be editing only the SuperCheckoutAPIEngine.m source file. Open it, and add #import "ASIDownloadCache.h" to the import statements. Then, modify the class extension interface to look like Listing 6–9.

Listing 6–9. *Modifying the Class Extension to Add Cache Control to It*

```
// Utility methods
- (NSString *)_queryStringWithBase:(NSString *)base
                               parameters:(NSDictionary *)params
                                  prefixed:(BOOL)prefixed;
- (NSString *)_encodeString:(NSString *)string;

// Connection/Request methods

- (NSString *)_sendRequest:(NSURL *)theURL
                withRequestType:(SuperCheckoutRequestType)requestType
                  responseType:(SuperCheckoutResponseType)responseType
                         cache:(BOOL)cache;
- (NSString *)_sendRequestWithMethod:(NSString *)method
                           path:(NSString *)path
                 queryParameters:(NSDictionary *)params
                           body:(NSString *)body
                    requestType:(SuperCheckoutRequestType)requestType
                   responseType:(SuperCheckoutResponseType)responseType;

- (NSString *)_sendImageRequestWithURL:(NSString *)imageURL;
- (NSURL *)_baseURLWithMethod:(NSString *)method
                        path:(NSString *)path
                 requestType:(SuperCheckoutRequestType)requestType
              queryParameters:(NSDictionary *)params;


// Parsing methods
- (void)_parseDataForConnection:(ASIHTTPRequest *)connection;

// Delegate methods
- (BOOL) _isValidDelegateForSelector:(SEL)selector;
```

```
- (NSCache *) imageCache;
```

This way, we can control what requests do or do not get cached.

Now, in the implementation, update the same signature we just modified to match the declaration. Next, add the following block after [request setDelegate:self]:

```
[request setDelegate:self];

if(cache) {
    [request setDownloadCache:[ASIDownloadCache sharedCache]];
    [request setCachePolicy:

        ASIAskServerIfModifiedCachePolicy|ASIFallbackToCacheIfLoadFailsCachePolicy];
    [request setCacheStoragePolicy:ASICachePermanentlyCacheStoragePolicy];
}
NSString *requestIdentifier = [NSString stringWithNewUUID];
```

The next updates are to change the calls to the updated method.

In _sendRequestWithMethod:path:queryParameters:body:requestType:responseType: change the return to pass NO to the method, like this:

```
return [self _sendRequest:theUrl
              withRequestType:requestType
                 responseType:responseType
                        cache:NO];
```

And in _sendImageRequestWithURL: change the return line to look like this:

```
return [self _sendRequest:theURL
              withRequestType:SuperCheckoutProductImage
                 responseType:SuperCheckoutImage
                        cache:YES];
```

The most important updates for this tier of the cache are:

```
[request setDownloadCache:[ASIDownloadCache sharedCache]];
[request setCachePolicy:

ASIAskServerIfModifiedCachePolicy|ASIFallbackToCacheIfLoadFailsCachePolicy];
[request setCacheStoragePolicy:ASICachePermanentlyCacheStoragePolicy];
```

What we're doing here is setting the download cache for the request to the default cache provided by the ASI team. Then, we're setting up the cache policy such that the server is asked if the requested resource has changed. If the resource has not changed, the request will use the cache. If the resource has changed, a new resource will be loaded and cached. If the request fails, the cache will be used (if one exists).

The final line is to tell the cache to store the files permanently. By default, the cache is set to the cache directory on the device. This folder is not synchronized to the computer when the device is plugged in to iTunes and iOS will clear out the folder as necessary.

Now that we have a solid caching scheme in place, we can move on to the final level of testing—Battery Life Management.

Looking at Power Management

"How's the battery life?" is one of the first questions any person asks when talking about a mobile device. As mobile developers, we are responsible for making sure our applications are not only memory efficient but also power efficient. This means we must write efficient code that doesn't leak.

This balance is a difficult, especially with more powerful devices and more types of chips being packed in them. The iPhone 4, for example, has chips for almost every function: A CPU, a GPU, 802.11, GSM/CDMA, accelerometer, compass and a gyroscope round out the main types of chips within that small package powered by a battery. Since we have access to each of the different types of sensors and chips, we have to be extremely careful which ones we use and how long we use them.

The Hardware

Each iOS device has at least one radio of some sort. They all have Wi-Fi radios and iPhone/iPad 3G have GSM/CDMA radios that can communicated over a 3G or 2G network. These radios consume quite a bit of power while powered on. The operating system uses different techniques to turn off each chip when it is not in use, so it is up to the developer to activate those chips when turning them on is absolutely necessary.

Using the 3G chip is the quickest ways to drain the device's battery. This is only exacerbated by the fact that the 3G networks keep the chip on full power for a few seconds after data transmission is complete. Figure 6–16 shows the power usage over time if an application performs short bursts in rapid succession over a 3G network.

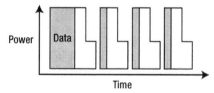

Figure 6–16. *In this power chart for a 3G radio, notice the chip stays on high power for a few seconds.*

The other, non–Wi-Fi radio is the 2G radio. This radio consumes less power than the 3G chip, but the transmission speed is slower, so it might be less efficient for transmitting large payloads across the Internet. The 2G chip is different from the 3G chip in that it will power down to a low power state as soon as the data transmission is complete. Figure 6–17 shows the power usage over time.

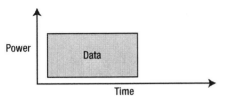

Figure 6–17. *The power chart for a 2G radio*

The last, and most efficient, radio is the Wi-Fi radio. Like the 2G radio, the Wi-Fi radio will enter a low power state when the data transfer is finished. Since the data transfer speed of Wi-Fi is extremely fast, this is the preferred data transfer radio for the device. Since we've shown the power vs. time graphs for the 3G and 2G radios, Figure 6–18 will round out the collection.

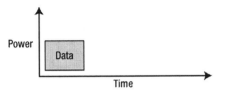

Figure 6–18. *The Wi-Fi chip is the fastest and most efficient chip on the device.*

Managing data communication is very important to maintain good battery life. Keeping transmission session as short as possible and letting the radios idle as much as possible will keep the battery from draining as fast and will make for happier users.

The rest of the chips on the device, the CPU, GPU, GPS and motion chips, all have differing power requirements. The CPU and GPU are responsible for running the code and rendering the on screen content, respectively. This means that writing fast and efficient code keeps the CPU at a lower load and keeping animations/views relatively simple will keep the GPU from taking a large amount of power. These chips are always active, so the only way to keep them idle is to write good code. Frameworks activate the other chips in the device. Core Location controls the GPS and Core Motion controls the accelerometer and gyroscope. As we move on to the more software controllable devices, we will need to discuss how our code affects these chips and ultimately, the battery life.

Coding Techniques

iOS is a very sophisticated operating system. It is built for mobile and is optimized to maximize battery life and still give enough horsepower to power some great applications! For our applications to be good citizens within the iOS environment, there are some techniques for ensuring our applications are performing wonderfully and not draining the battery while doing so.

Networking

As we discussed in the previous section, the radio chips can consume a fair amount of power. However, we can reduce the overhead of keeping those chips powered by being smart with how we request data. Since most network communication is done via HTTP, the only real thing to keep in mind there is content size and content compression. If the data is encoded in JSON and compressed using gzip, the content size will be small and the radios will not be very active.

Another good idea with networked communication is to group requests together. This keeps the radio active for a bit longer, but it is ultimately better than small network pings or keeping a socket open for long periods of time. Polling is also a bad idea. Instead of polling, utilize push notifications. This will keep the radios silent and drawing less power.

As far as finding real performance, use the Activity Monitor instrument to track network usage. Getting to the networking options of the Activity Monitor instrument can be a bit tricky. So fire up instruments with the Activity Monitor instrument and click the information "i" in the instrument area. This brings up what is shown in Figure 6–19.

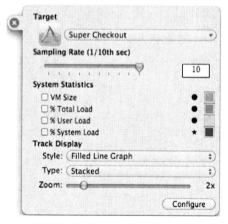

Figure 6–19. *The instrument configuration panel with the default options unchecked*

Notice that the check boxes are unchecked in this example. They come checked by default, but we don't necessarily want to watch the CPU while we are looking at the processor usage. I have them unchecked in this instance. To get the networking options, click the Configure button. The configuration piece flips over, and Figure 6–20 is presented.

Figure 6–20. *The instrument configuration pane that lets you select the visible sensors for the instrument.*

Select the same check boxes that are selected in Figure 6–20. Click Done, and make sure those sensors are checked back in the information pane. Click the "x" where the "i" used to be, and select the Super Checkout target from the Target drop-down. Click the record button to start recording data. The application will launch, and you'll see the network graphs spike as network requests are made. As the application caches more data, you'll see the network requests become less frequent as you navigate the application. Figure 6–21 shows a run after all of the images were cached.

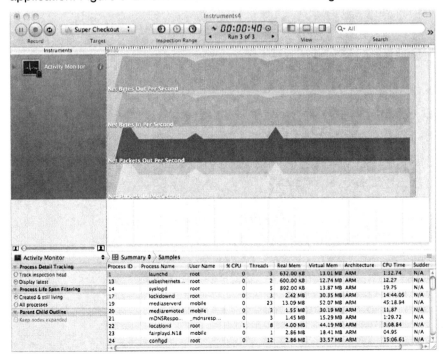

Figure 6–21. *Keeping network spikes to a minimum is a great way to keep the radios silent and leave more battery power.*

Tracking Energy Usage

Modern iOS devices have the ability to log power consumption and Instruments gives you a great way to see how the device consumes power and which chips are consuming the most power. To enable this feature, first the device needs to have development mode activated. This enables the Developer item in the Settings app. Figure 6–22 shows this section.

Figure 6–22. *The Developer settings in the Settings app with the power logging turned off*

Turning power logging on will start a new power logging session. This session will track power consumption by component and by app. After the session is complete, the data can be imported into Instruments to be analyzed.

> **CAUTION:** The power logging diagnostic information is reset every time logging is turned off.
> When the device is power off or runs out of battery, logging is turned off.

To get a good look at how your app behaves within the ecosystem and if it coexists well with other applications, it is a good idea to turn on power logging and use the device normally for an hour or two. Going back and seeing what processes are doing what is very enlightening.

In order to import the collected data, create a new Instruments session, and select Energy Diagnostics (see Figure 6–23).

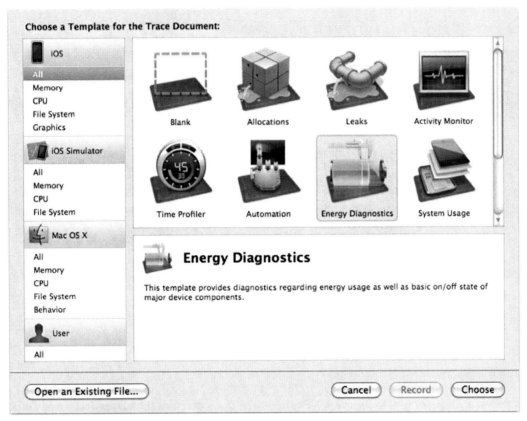

Figure 6–23. *Selecting the Energy Diagnostics instrument template*

Now, plug in the device, and go to **File ➤ Import Energy Diagnostics** from Device. Figure 6–24 shows a session I ran for almost three hours.

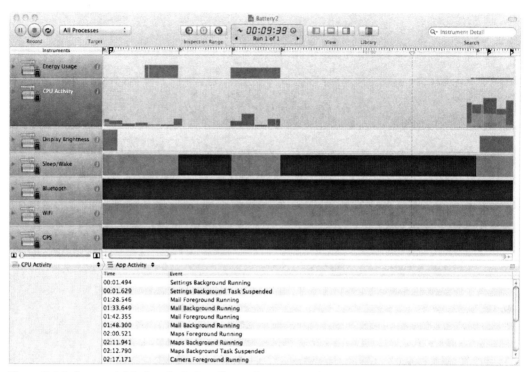

Figure 6–24. *Some real data from the battery diagnostics on the device*

What are we looking at in this view? First, look at the top of the time line. You'll see flags that represent significant events like sleep/wake or an app going to the background or getting suspended. Keeping mental notes, or real notes if you're inclined to do so, while logging power usage will help remember what happened when you start the analysis process.

Each level within the Instruments window gives a different type of information. The Energy Usage bar shows how much power is being used for that particular moment of time. As each component uses more power, the bar will get taller, and vice versa, as chips are turned off.

The CPU activity monitor will show you a good idea of what processes are doing what. In the Jump Bar, you can select App Activity or CPU Activity. In App Activity, you can see what apps are running and when they switch to the background or are suspended. The CPU Activity view lets you see where the processor is spending time doing processing. You can see what part of the processor is processing graphics or audio. Each bar represents a scale. The scale is from 1 to 20. Figure 6–25 gives you an idea as to how this is measured. The numbers really represent a calculation that says, "If the CPU stays like this for a long time, this is how much battery life is left."

Level	Time to Discharge
20	< 1 hour
10	~10 hours
1	20+ hours

Figure 6–25. *CPU Activity reference chart*

Display Brightness tells you what the device's display was doing. The backlight takes power, so knowing how bright the screen is in a situation can be useful. When the chart is 0, the screen is off.

Sleep/Wake shows you, in an on/off view, when the device wakes up. When the brightness is 0 and the device is awake, something is doing some background processing. It is likely that Mail is getting new messages, or you might see some audio processing in the CPU Activity view.

The final three charts show the status of radio instrumentation.

Using the Tricks of the Trade

When doing power consumption testing, there are some good experimental controls to keep in mind. These things can be turned on or off to see how the device behaves in a multitude of situations. These include turning off iOS 4 features like mail fetching, push notifications, and automatic dimming. Another good idea is to test with the various radios on/off. It is also worth noting that colder climates will decrease battery life.

Performance testing and tuning is more like a science when it comes to gathering data. Setting the appropriate experimental controls will help you isolate exactly what is going on when you go to analyze your data. For example, if you notice that your application is spending too much time talking with the server and the battery drain is too much, you can modify how the application is talking to the server. If your application has background tasks, consider changing how the background task is written to potentially shorten the amount of time the task needs to take. This could entail changing how the data is structured when talking to a server or updating the task to run as short as possible. Ultimately, you know your application the best, and each Instrument is going to show you information specific to your application. Sometimes, the data you find can be pretty surprising and eye opening.

Summary

We're all communication experts now, right? We've actually only scratched the surface on what you can do to improve the performance of your networking code and proper caching strategies. The approach we took in this chapter is a pretty common approach, but it is a very blunt approach. If you find your application doesn't fit this scheme, there are plenty of really smart people out there whose entire job is to research caching approaches and squeeze every bit of performance out of the system.

This sums up the performance tuning part of the book. From here on out, we're going to be working on our workflow for distributing builds to beta testers and automating some other pieces of our workflow. Performance tuning is hard work, but seeing the increased performance of the application is worth every bit of tweaking and multiple test runs. I hope you have enjoyed the experience thus far; more fun stuff awaits you in the coming chapters.

Chapter **7**

Prepare the Beta!

So now we have an application that we think is ready to ship. Many a developer has been humbled by an application he or she thought was bulletproof, only to discover a litany of bugs once it was released. Often you, as the developer, will only exercise certain application paths or specific test cases. Sometimes, it takes fresh pair of eyes (and hands!) to truly put your application through its paces.

This is where *beta testing* comes in. Beta testing releases your application to small set of external users, called *testers* or *beta testers*. The goal is to get their feedback on bugs in the application. You'll want to find patient users who are willing to put up with (potentially) erratic, or even buggy, behavior from your application. The last thing you want is an angry tester who trashes your application to people before it's even released.

We'll also want to capture *crash reports* if the application crashes while our beta testers are using it. If you have savvy beta testers, they will be able to access the crash reports when they sync their devices to iTunes. There are several other options where we can have the application send us crash reports via e -mail, to a web server, or to a third-party service that analyzes crash reports for us. We'll briefly touch on those as well.

To distribute your application to your beta testers, you will need to utilize an ad-hoc provisioning profile via the iOS provisioning portal. You access the portal via the iOS Dev Center. It can be a complicated process, but don't worry, we'll walk through the process step-by-step and screen-by-screen. Just a reminder, you'll need to a member of the iOS Developer Program (currently $99 per year) to create an ad-hoc provisioning profile. We'll discuss the program briefly later in the chapter. If you're not a member of the iOS Developer Program, the rest of this chapter will be of limited usefulness.

Managing Beta Testing

So we think our Super Checkout application is ready for testing by outsiders. But we can't just throw our application into the wild and hope that somebody will test it for us. It will require a little bit of preparation on our part. We can break down preparation into five steps. Let's briefly describe all the steps before going into more detail.

First, we need to *define* the beta test. What kind of testers do we want? What kind of devices do we want to test against? Next, we need to *acquire* our beta testers. How are we going to find testers? Once we've gotten our testers on board, we have to *instruct* them. What do we want them to test? How should they submit feedback?

Now that we've explained what we need out testers to do, we can *distribute* the application and *collate* their feedback. Preparing the application for distribution is a difficult task, so we'll discuss that in the section titled "Creating Ad Hoc Builds." Afterward, we'll briefly discuss what do with our testers' feedback.

Defining the Beta

What do we mean by "defining the beta"? It means spending a little bit of time planning what the goals of the beta test are. Normally, if this is the first time you're sending the application out to your testers, your goals may be open ended. You simply want your testers to put the application through its paces, uncovering any bugs, and commenting on general usability. As the testing progresses, you may release application builds that address specific issues. As a result, you may want your users to focus on specific parts of the application.

Once we decide on the goals of the beta test, we can focus on deciding on what kind of testers we want. It is important to remember that you want to find testers who will find your application useful. In our case with Super Checkout, if we have a tester who doesn't like fruit or shopping, they probably won't be a good tester. Simply because they won't find our application useful and won't use it. If they don't use it, we won't get any meaningful feedback about our application, nor will they find any bugs.

Finally, we have to decide what the device requirements are for our application. You may only be targeting the latest and greatest iOS device and operating system. Or you may be targeting many versions of the operating system on a specific device. Typically, you probably decided this before developing your application, but those criteria might have changed as you progressed.

Acquiring Beta Testers

How do we find our beta testers? There are several ways we can go about it, but it all breaks down to one simple step: asking for volunteers. Whatever you think the best way is the find the users your application is targeting. Simply asking your friends and family is one method. Or you can reach out via any number of web sites, forums, or social media to find people who are willing to be guinea pigs.

On the flip side, being a beta tester requires a little bit of commitment. Application developers depend on you to provide meaningful feedback. In addition, providing crash reports and logs are incredibly helpful in finding show-stopping application bugs. We'll show how to find the crash reports later.

Before putting the word out you may want to consider setting up a sign up form. If you intend to have a small testing group, this may be overkill. However, if you are expecting an overwhelming response (don't we all?), a sign up form may have advantages. It may aid you in keeping track of all your volunteers, so you can rotate testers. You may be able to get specific information about your testers if you wish.

Regardless of how you track your testers, you need get one key piece of information from them: their iOS device's Unique Device Identifier (UDID). This information is available when the device is connected to iTunes. Once connected to iTunes, select the device in the navigation pane. iTunes will display the device information (see Figure 7–1).

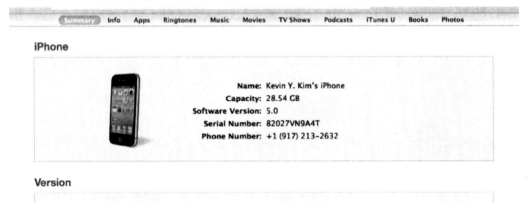

Figure 7–1. *Device information in iTunes*

Click the label Serial Number. The label should change to read Identifier (UDID), followed by a 40-character string (see Figure 7–2). This is the string your testers need to send to you.

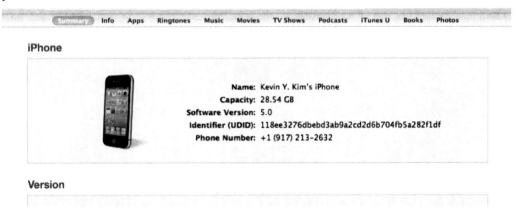

Figure 7–2. *UDID in iTunes*

Giving Instructions

At this point, we've gotten a number people clamoring to beta test our application. Once we select the viable users, we can send them instructions on what we want tested. As mentioned earlier, if this is the first round of testing, we may simply provide users with instructions on how to use the application. As we send out subsequent builds, we provide users with specific instructions on which portions of the application to test and what changes we've made based on their input.

One key task is to instruct our testers how to file bugs. The simplest approach would be to have users send an e-mail every time they encounter a bug in the application. This might work if you have a very small test group. If you do pursue this approach, it's probably a good idea to define a standard bug reporting format. But a better approach would be to install a bug tracking system.

Bug tracking systems are devised to help you keep track of bugs (and other development tasks). We could go on great length about how they work and how they help manage development, but that's outside the scope of this book. In fact, people have written entire books about bug tracking systems. There are several open source options available:

- The Trac Project (`http://trac.edgewall.org`)

- Request Tracker (`http://bestpractical.com/rt/`)

- Bugzilla (`http://www.bugzilla.org/`)

This is by no means a complete list, it just represents some the bug (and issue) tracking systems we've used in the past.

If you do set up a bug tracking system, you can instruct your beta testers to file their reports there. It will make your life and theirs much easier.

Finally, you may want instruct your testers how to submit crash reports. Crash reports are generated when an application crashes on your iOS device. The crash reports are then transferred to your computer whenever you synchronize your device to iTunes. The crash reports is located at `/Users/<USERNAME>/Library/Logs/CrashReporter/MobileDevice/<DEVICE_NAME>`. The crash reports follow a naming convention of `<APP_NAME>_YYYY-MM-DD-HHMMSS_<DEVICE_NAME>.crash`, where YYYY-MM-DD-HHMMSS is the date and time the crash occurred. When submitting an application crash report, ask the users to include the crash report along with a description of what they were doing when the application crashed.

The next step we defined was application distribution. But before we can describe that, we need to know how to build our application for the beta testers.

Creating Ad Hoc Builds

Normally, you would distribute your application via the iTunes App Store. This involves uploading your application via iTunes Connect and waiting for your application to get approved by Apple. But that's not an effective way to distribute an application for beta testing. First, if there are any bugs in your application, Apple will reject it. Additionally, the whole point of beta testing is to gather feedback from a limited set of users before releasing your application. Fortunately, Apple provides ad hoc distribution, which allows us to directly distribute our application to our testers.

Let's get started with creating our beta application.

Certificates, Provisioning, and Distribution, Oh My!

As I mentioned earlier, creating our beta application is a complicated process. First, we need to create a certificate request. Armed with this request, we then create an iOS distribution certificate. Next, we need to enter (or upload) the universal device IDs of our beta testers' devices. Then, we need to create an App ID for our application. Finally, we use all that information to create our ad hoc distribution provisioning profile.

Using with the iOS distribution certificate and the ad-hoc distribution provisioning profile, we build our beta application. We'll package the application, and distribute it to our beta testers with the provisioning profile. From there, our beta testers can install the application via iTunes and start sending us feedback.

Creating a Certificate Request

The certificate request is created on our computer, using the Keychain Access application. Keychain Access can be found in Applications ➤ Utilities. Launch Keychain Access, and you should see a window like the one shown in Figure 7–3.

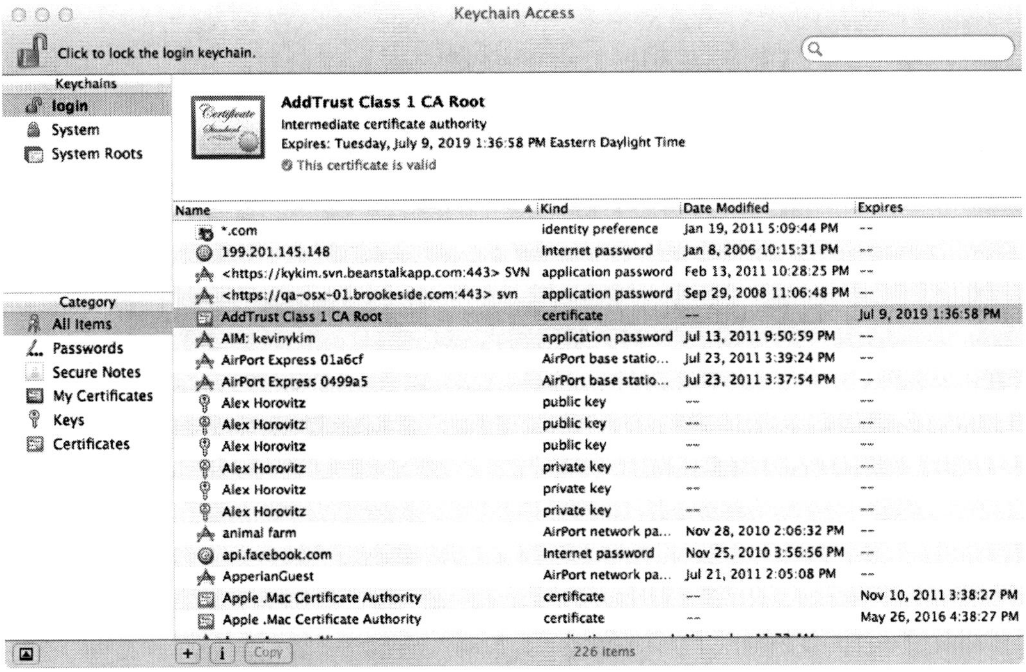

Figure 7–3. *Keychain Access application window*

Open the preferences window via Keychain Access ➤ Preferences, and select the Certificates tab (see Figure 7–4). Set both Online Certificate Status Protocol (OCSP) and Certificate Revocation List (CRL) to Off.

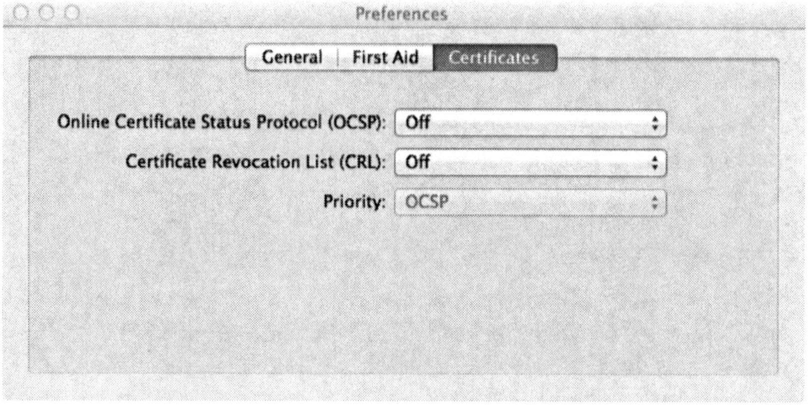

Figure 7–4. *Certificates tab of Keychain Access Preferences window*

Next choose Keychain Access ➤ Certificate Assistant ➤ Request Certificate From a Certificate Authority (see Figure 7–5). The Certificate Assistant window (see Figure 7–6) should appear. Fill in the User Email Address field with the email address used when you registered as an iOS developer. For Common Name, use the Company/Organization/Department name used when you registered as an iOS developer. Leave the CA Email Address field blank. Select "Saved to disk", and check "Let me specify key pair information". Click Continue.

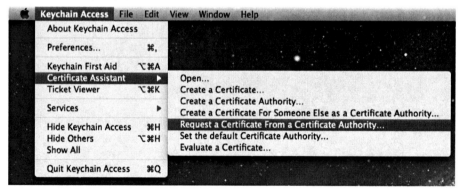

Figure 7–5. *Creating a certificate request*

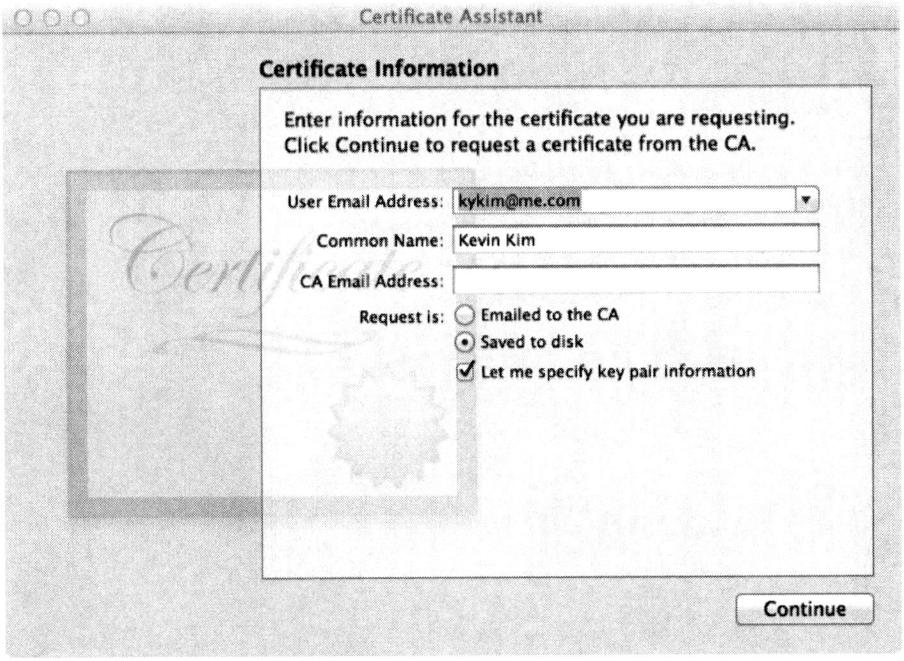

Figure 7–6. *Certificate Assistant window*

You will be prompted to save a file named
CertificateSigningRequest.certSigningRequest. You may change the file location if
you wish, and click Save. The Certificate Assistant window will change to ask for key
pair information (see Figure 7–7). Set Key Size to 2048 bits, and Algorithm to RSA, if it is
not set to that already. Click Continue.

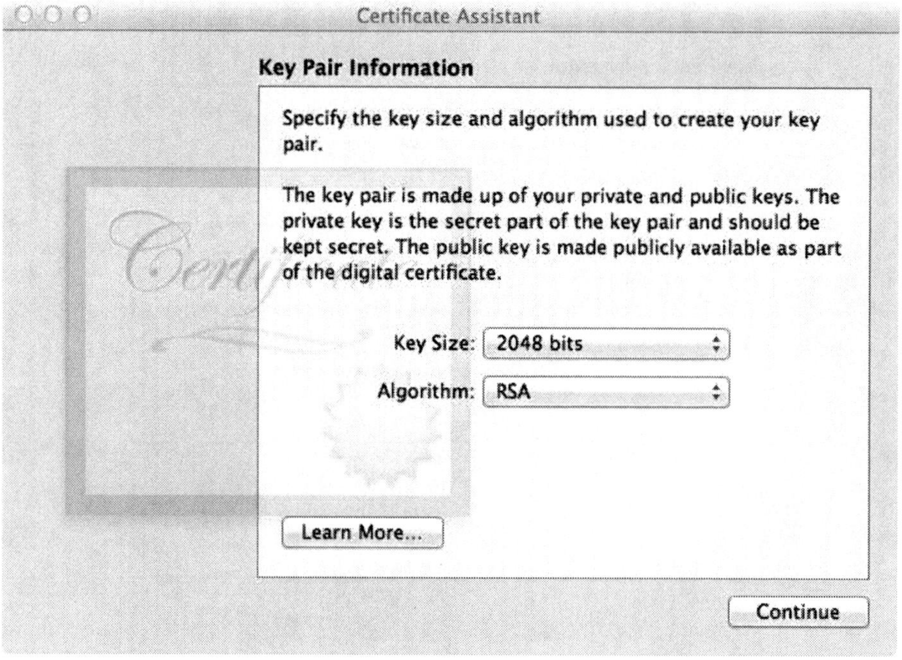

Figure 7–7. *Key pair information*

The Certificate Assistant should create the certificate request and report back (see Figure 7–8). You may view the location of the request by clicking Show In Finder. Click Done to exit the Certificate Assistant.

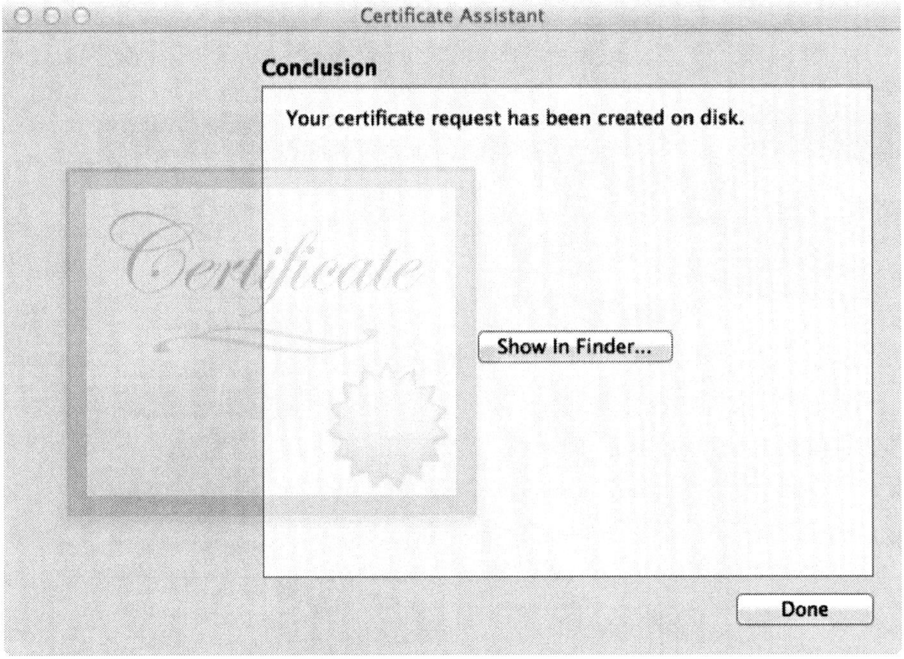

Figure 7–8. *Certificate assistant, the conclusion*

Now that we've created our certificate request, we can create our iOS distribution certificate.

Creating the iOS Distribution Certificate

To create our iOS distribution certificate, we need to enter the iOS provisioning portal. We access the provisioning portal via the iOS Dev Center (see Figure 7–9). You can only access the provisioning portal if you signed in as a register developer. In addition, you'll need to sign up for the iOS Developer Program. The program currently cost $99 per year for individuals. In addition to the benefits of the Registered Developer Program, you receive access to pre-release software and tools, internal developer forums, and technical support from Apple. Additionally, you will be able to test your applications on physical iOS devices (rather than just the simulator). Most importantly, you can distribute your application, either ad hoc or via the App Store. If you're interested, you can find out more about it at http://developer.apple.com/programs/ios/.

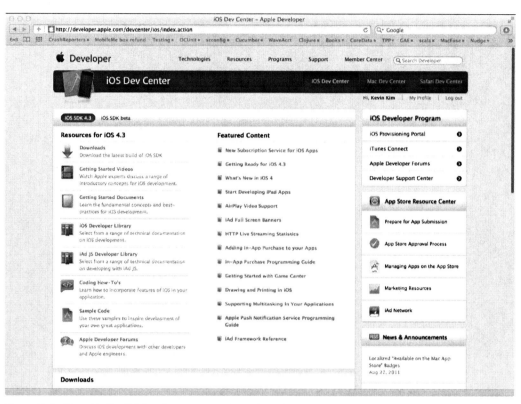

Figure 7–9. *Signed in the iOS Dev Center as a registered developer*

If you signed in properly, you should see iOS Provisioning Portal on the right site of the iOS Dev Center, under the title iOS Developer Program (see Figure 7–10). Click the iOS Provisioning Portal link.

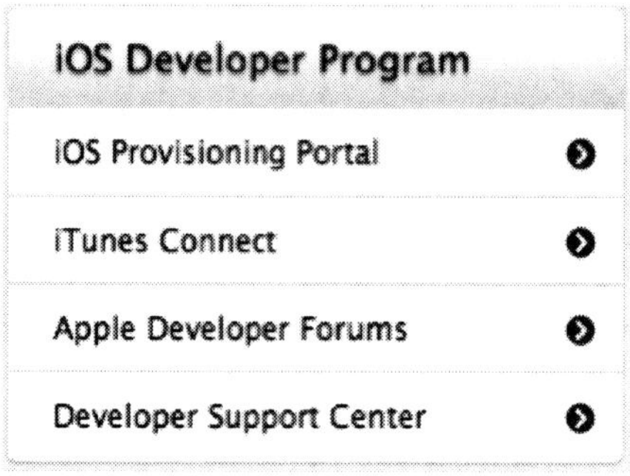

Figure 7–10. *iOS Developer Program links*

Once you enter the iOS Provisioning Portal page (see Figure 7–11), you should see a menu of options on the left side (see Figure 7–12). The first option under Home is Certificates. Click it.

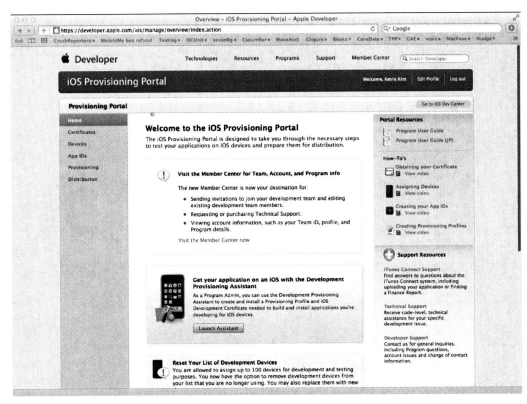

Figure 7–11. *iOS Provisioning Portal page*

Figure 7–12. *Provisioning Portal menu*

Once the Certificates page, click the Distribution tab (make sure not to click the Distribution link shown in Figure 7–12!) at the top to show your distribution certificates. There may a certificate that Xcode would have created for you automatically, or there may be no certificates present (see Figure 7–13). Regardless, we'll create a new one. Find the row of the table that ends with a button labelled Request Certificate. Click this button.

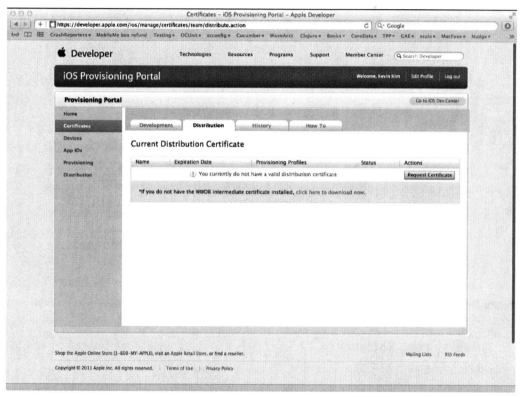

Figure 7–13. *Distribution tab of the Certificates page*

The panel should change to expose a set of instructions. These are instructions to create a certificate request, which we just completed. Click the button labelled Choose File at the end of the instructions. In the file chooser, navigate to the location where you saved CertificateSigningRequest.certSigningRequest, and select that file. Confirm that the file name appears next to the Choose File button (see Figure 7–14), and click Submit.

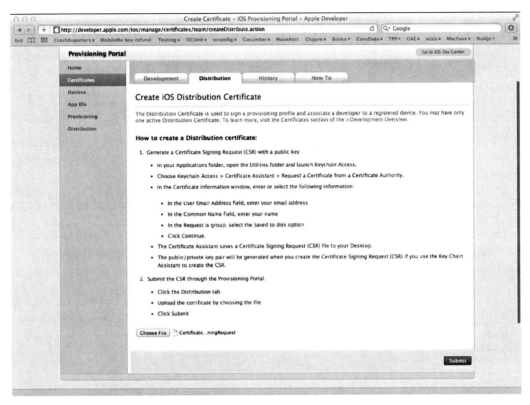

Figure 7–14. *Submitting the Certificate Request*

Once submitted, the Distribution Certificate pane should refresh, listing the certificate with a status of Pending Issuance (see Figure 7–15). Wait a few moments, and refresh the pane by clicking on the Distribution tab. The certificate status should update to Issued (see Figure 7–16) and have an expiration date one year in the future. Click the Download button on the right of the certificate row. This should download a file named distribution_identity.cer. Also download the WWDR intermediate certificate. This file should be named AppleWWDRCA.cer.

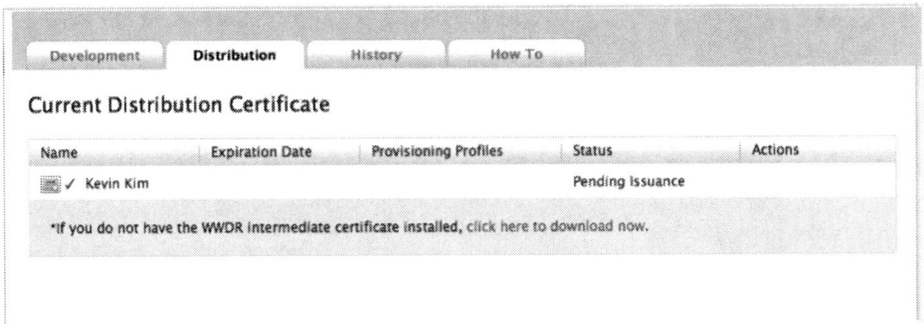

Development	Distribution	History	How To		
Current Distribution Certificate					
Name	Expiration Date	Provisioning Profiles	Status	Actions	
✓ Kevin Kim			Pending Issuance		

*If you do not have the WWDR intermediate certificate installed, click here to download now.

Figure 7–15. *Distribution certificate pending issuance*

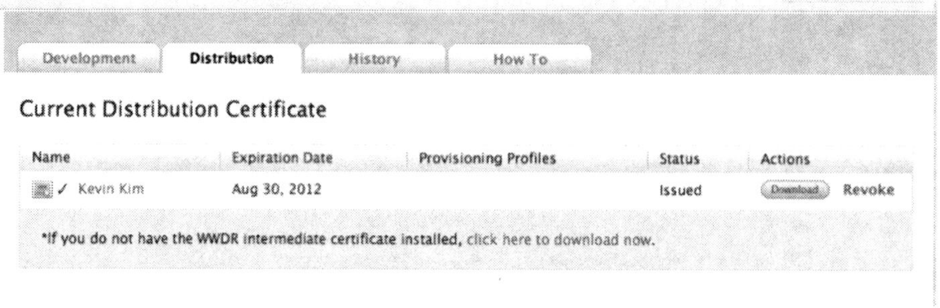

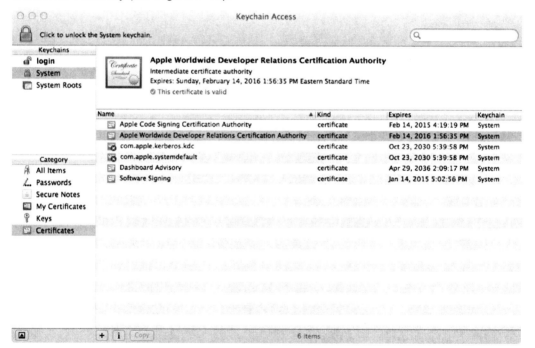

Figure 7–16. *Distribution certificate issued*

Find the `AppleWWDRCA.cer` file in the Finder, and double-click it. This should launch
Keychain Assistant, and install the Apple WWDR Intermediate certificate. You can
confirm this is installed by selecting Certificates on the lower left pane of the Keychain
Assistant window and searching for the name Apple Worldwide Developer Relations
Certificate Authority (see Figure 7–17).

Figure 7–17. *Confirming Apple WWDR Intermediate Certificate installation (highlighted)*

Repeat the installation process for `distribution_identity.cer`.

Uploading UDIDs

Head back to the iOS Provisioning Portal, and click Devices on the left side menu. You should be on the Manage tab of the Devices page (see Figure 7–18).

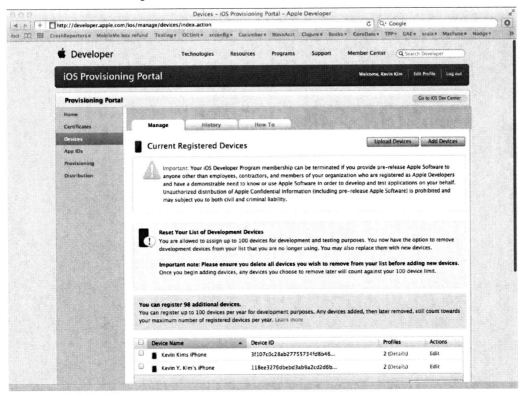

Figure 7–18. *Devices page of the iOS Provisioning Portal page*

You are allowed to add up to 100 devices per year for development and testing purposes. While you can remove devices, those devices, even if removed, count toward your annual allotment of 100. So be careful about adding devices.

There are two ways to add devices: individual and bulk. Individual is exactly what you would expect, you enter the devices one by one via a web form. Bulk on the other hand, allows you to add multiple devices at once. You accomplish this via uploading a file. The file is in a simple tab delimited format.

Let's go over each process.

Individual

From the Devices page, navigate to the Manage tab. On the right side of the Manage page, click the button labelled Add Devices. The Manage pane should refresh to provide a form where you can add the device name and ID (see Figure 7–19).

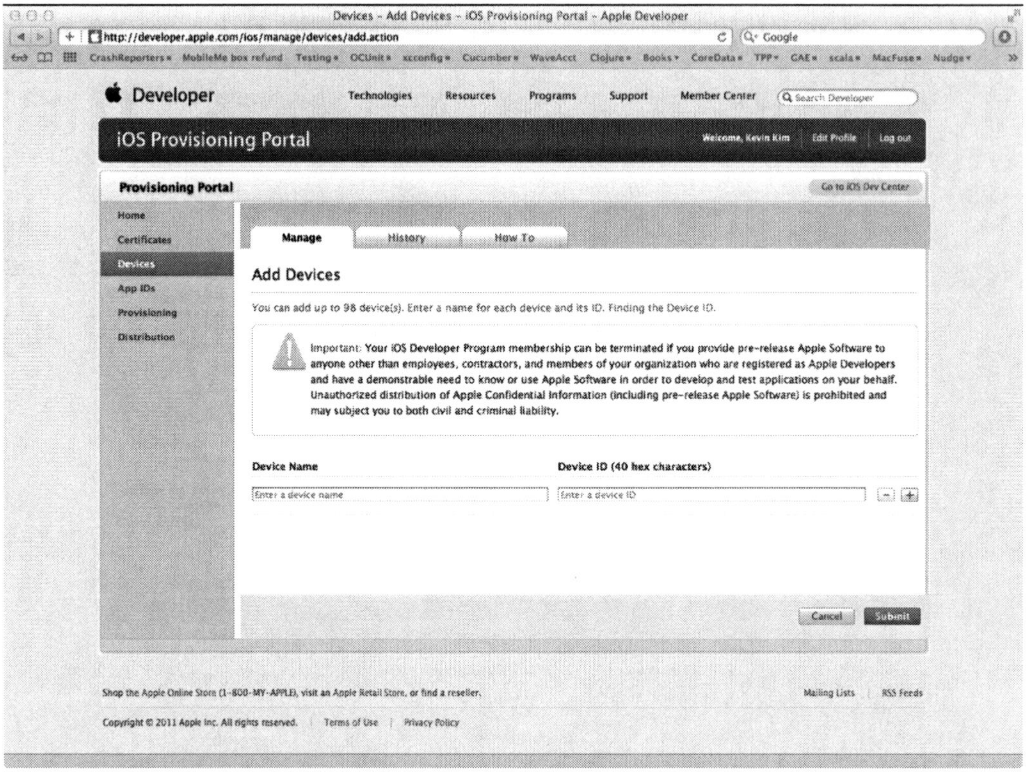

Figure 7–19. *Add Device page*

The Device Name can be a free-form string that you will use to identify the device. It could be your beta tester's name or e-mail address. Or it could be some identifier you assign to your tester. The Device ID is the unique device identifier. You will need to collect this information from your beta testers. You can find the UDID by launching Xcode and opening the Organizer window. Choose the Devices icon at the top of the window. On the left side, select the relevant device. You should see the device information displayed. Next to the label Identifier should be the 40-character UDID of your device (see Figure 7–20). Remember, I showed you how to access the UDID in iTunes earlier in the chapter (see Figures 7–1 and 7–2).

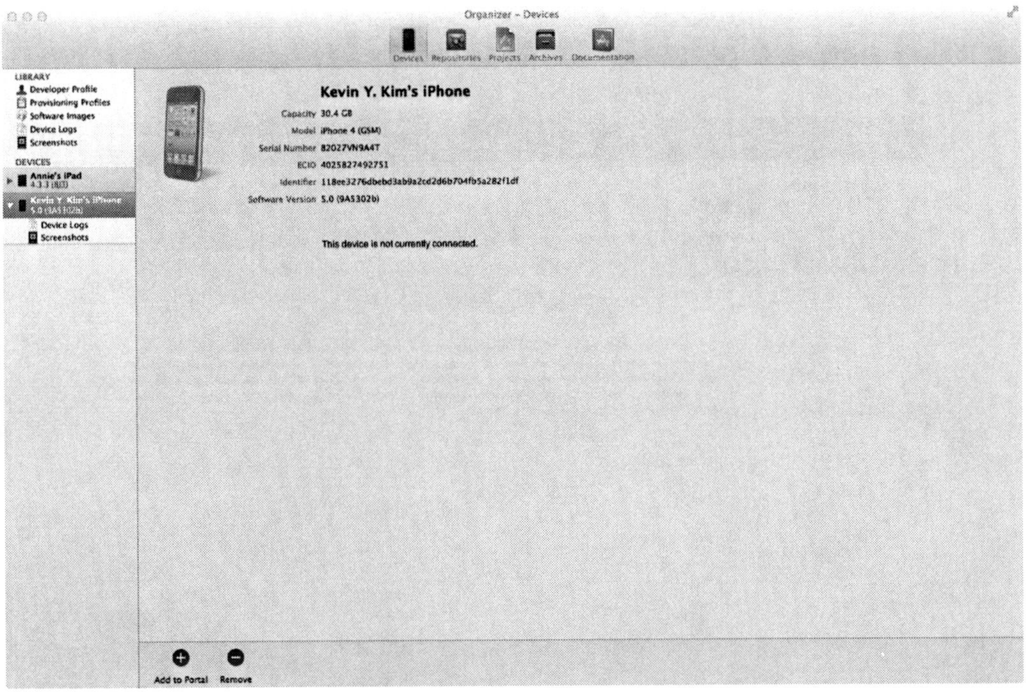

Figure 7–20. *Xcode Organizer window, Device details*

It is possible to enter more than one device name and ID via the web form. Once you have filled in the name and ID, click the plus button to the right. An additional row should appear (see Figure 7–21), allowing you to enter another device name and ID.

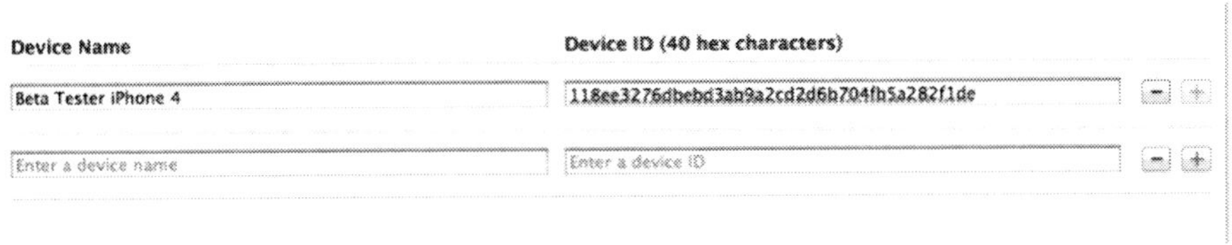

Figure 7–21. *Entering another device via web form*

When you have completed entering the device information, click the *Submit* button.

Bulk

From the Devices page, under the Manage tab, click the Upload Devices button. This will refresh the Manage pane to allow you to upload a file (see Figure 7–22). As we stated earlier, you can upload a tab delimited file.

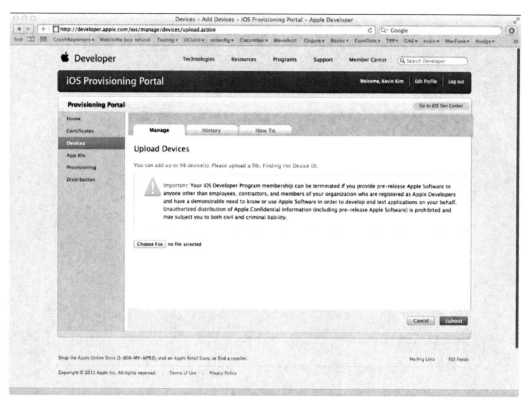

Figure 7–22. *Upload Devices page*

The tab-delimited file follows a simple format. Each line of the file should contain one device ID, followed by the device name, separated by a tab. The first line of the file will be considered a header row and be ignored. The file should end with the extension .txt. Following shows a sample device file:

```
DEVICE UDID                               DEVICE NAME
0aeb4240266f544ef8a4d0bb658a1fc6cf0a559a   iPhone 3GS
1f01c47915477711d8bc700090272ff72528531e   iPhone 4
3b02d9e6d59467382e8f9b9300a64ac3cd6c0e89   iPad 2
```

Click the Choose File button, and select the .txt file containing the list of device names and IDs. Then click Submit to upload the file and add the devices.

Confirmation

Once you have entered or uploaded the information for the device(s), you should be returned to the Devices page, under the Manage tab. To confirm your devices have been added, scroll to the bottom of the page. There you should see a list of all the devices you have information for.

Creating Our App ID

Now, we need to create an entry for our application in the provisioning portal. This information will be used to when we build our application for distribution among our beta testers.

On the iOS Provisioning Portal menu, click App IDs. Like the Devices page, the Manage tab should be selected (see Figure 7–23). Since this is your first application, there should be no App IDs listed at the bottom of the page. If the SuperCheckout application is listed, you can skip ahead to the **Ad Hoc Distribution Provisioning Profile** section. Otherwise, click the button labelled New App ID.

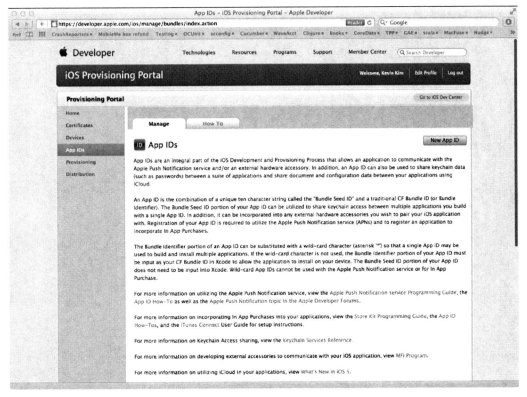

Figure 7–23. *App IDs page of the iOS Provisioning Portal page*

The Manage pane should refresh to display a form to enter your application information (see Figure 7–24). The Description field is a simple name to identify your application. (Note that App IDs never go away! Make sure the name is unique!) Enter **SuperCheckout**. The Bundle Seed ID (App ID Prefix) is a unique ten-character sequence. Leave this selection at Use Team ID. The Bundle Identifier (App ID Suffix) is a unique identifier for your application. The convention is to use reverse-DNS style name. Use the value com.whilethis.SuperCheckout. Click Submit.

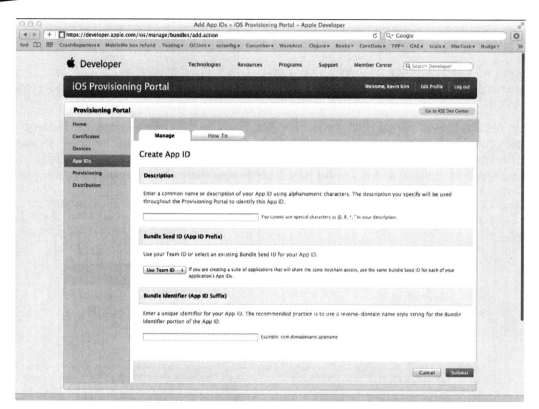

Figure 7–24. *New App ID form*

Once completed, you should be returned to the App IDs page, Manage tab. The new App ID should be present at the bottom of the page (see Figure 7–25).

Figure 7–25. *The new App ID entry*

Almost there. Now, we need to create an ad hoc distribution provisioning profile.

Ad Hoc Distribution Provisioning Profile

From the iOS Provisioning Portal menu, click Provisioning. Once on the Provisioning page, choose the Distribution tab (see Figure 7–26). Click the New Profile button.

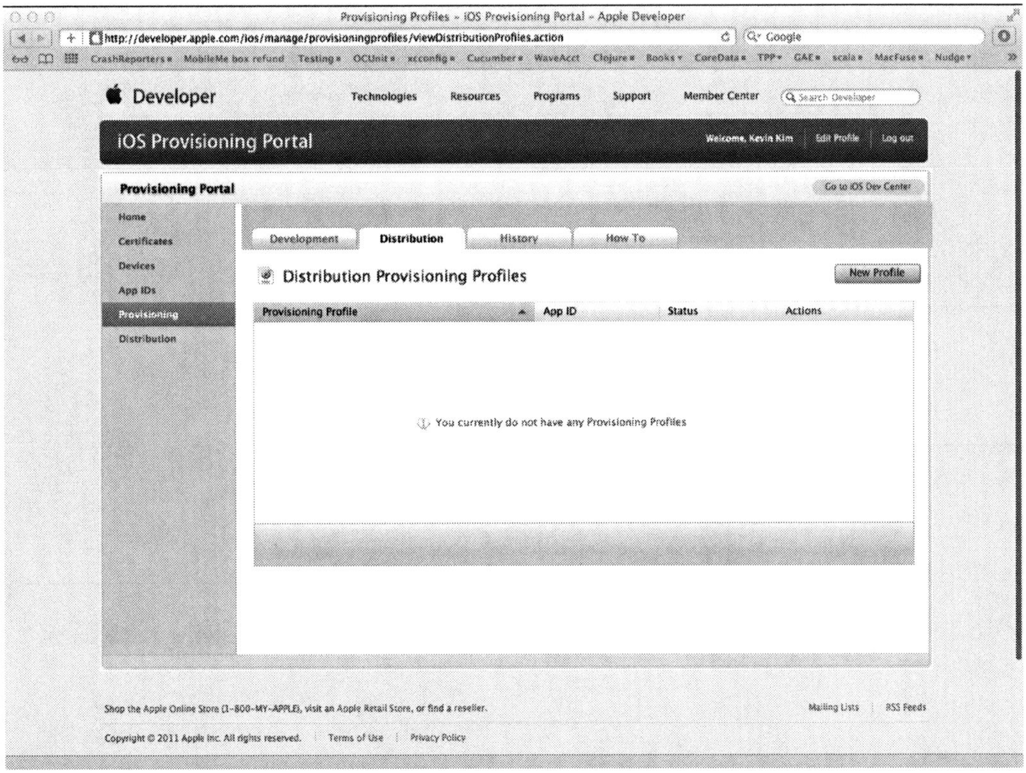

Figure 7–26. *Distribution tab of the Provisioning page*

The Distribution pane should refresh to display a form (see Figure 7–27). First, for the Distribution label, select the Ad Hoc radio button. The Profile Name field is for you to enter descriptive text. We'll use SuperCheckout AdHoc Provisioning Profile. The iOS Provisioning Portal should have automatically selected the Distribution Certificate we created earlier. For the App ID, select the SuperCheckout ID we created previously. Finally, select the devices you want the application to be able to run on. This should be the list of devices of your beta testers. Once you've selected all the devices, click Submit.

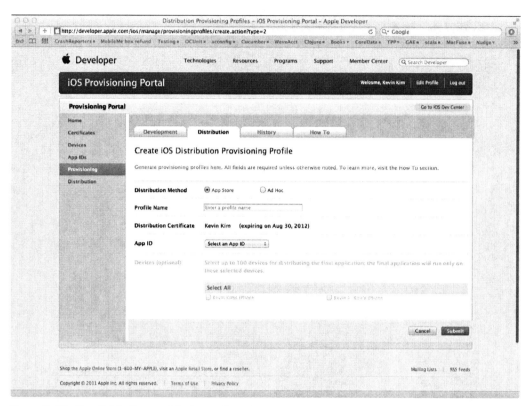

Figure 7–27. *New distribution provisioning profile entry*

Once submitted, the Distribution pane should refresh, listing the new ad hoc distribution provisioning profile. Its status should read Pending (see Figure 7–28). Wait a few moments, and click the Distribution tab to refresh the view. The status should change to Active (see Figure 7–29).

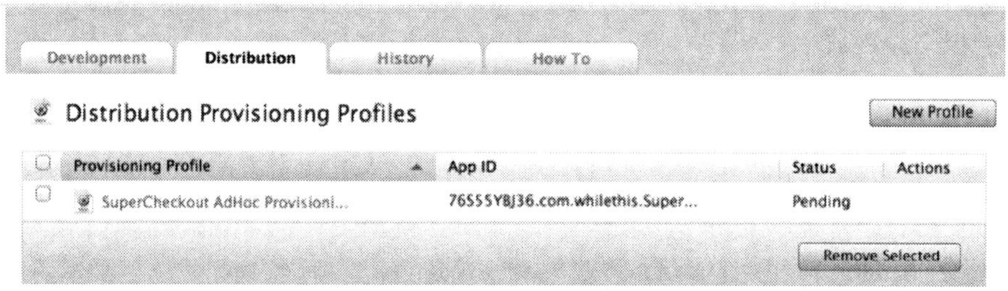

Figure 7–28. *Ad hoc distribution provisioning profile pending activation*

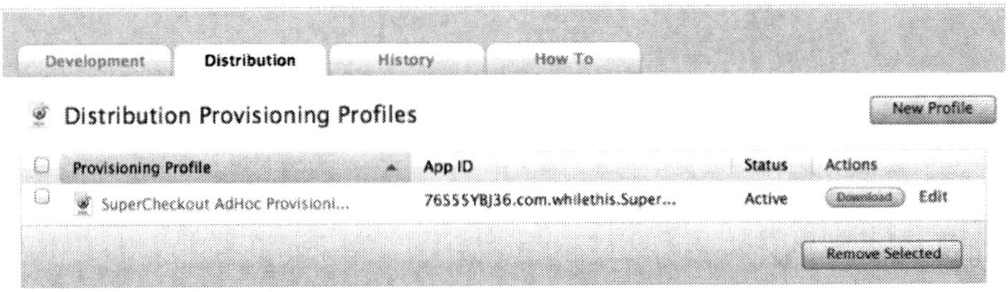

Figure 7–29. *Ad hoc distribution provisioning profile active*

Click the Download button for your new provisioning profile. This should download a file named SuperCheckout_AdHoc_Provisioning_Profile.mobileprovision onto your computer. Make a note of where the file is, as we'll need it soon.

We've gone through quite a few steps to create the ad hoc distribution provisioning profile (the .mobileprofile file we just downloaded). Now, let's build the beta version of Super Checkout, so we can distribute it to our beta testers.

Building the Beta

If it's not already open, open the Super Checkout project in Xcode. The first thing we want to do is install the new provisioning profile we just created. Open the Finder, and navigate to where the file SuperCheckout_AdHoc_Provisioning_Profile.mobileprovision was downloaded. Drag the file to the Xcode icon on the Dock. If you've done it right, the Xcode Organizer window should open, and the provisioning profile should be listed (see Figure 7–30).

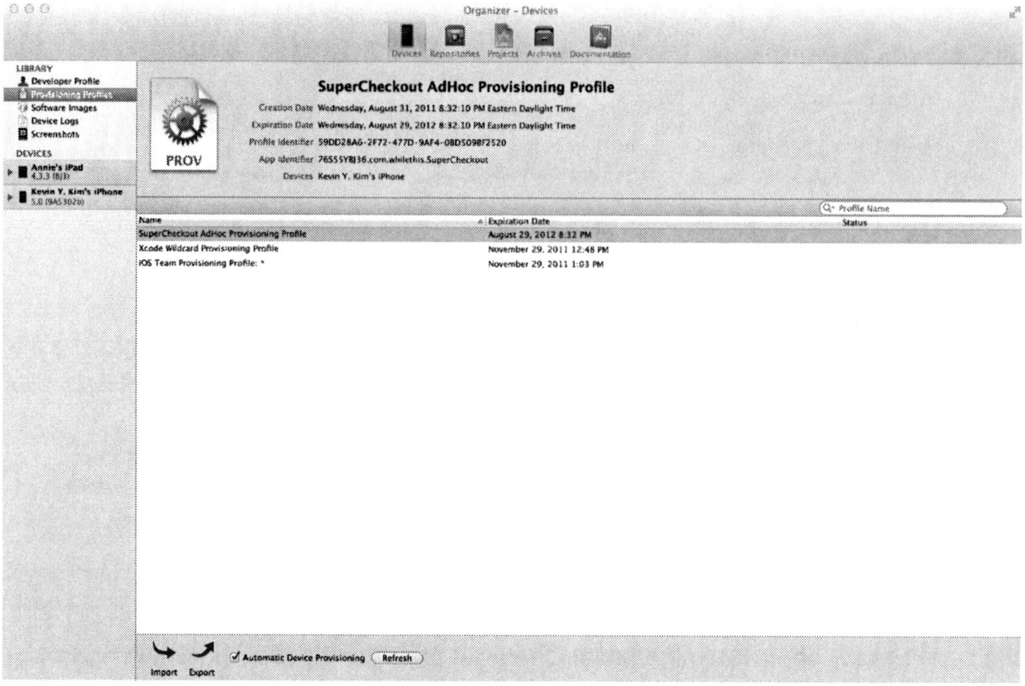

Figure 7–30. *The new provisioning profile, installed*

Return to the Super Checkout project window. Click the project name at the top of the Navigation pane, so that we enter the project editor view. Select the target Super Checkout in the project editor view, and select the Build Settings tab. Make sure you expose all build settings by selecting the All button in the row below the Build Settings tab. Scroll down until you find the Code Signing section. Find the row labelled Code Signing Identity, and expand it. Under the Release field, change the value to be the distribution profile, under the heading SuperCheckout_AdHoc_Provisioning_Profile (see Figure 7–31). Do the same for the row labeled Any iOS SDK, under the Release row.

Setting	SuperCheckout
Debug	build/Super Checkout.build/Debug-iphoneos
Release	build/Super Checkout.build/Release-iphoneos
Precompiled Headers Cache Path	/var/folders/hp/qwgltr3j72n34gm26w89p6tm0000gn/C/com.apple.Xcode.501/SharedPrecompiledHeaders
▼Build Options	
Build Variants	normal
Compiler for C/C++/Objective-C	Apple LLVM compiler 2.1 ‡
Debug Information Format	DWARF with dSYM File ‡
Enable OpenMP Support	No ‡
Generate Profiling Code	No ‡
Precompiled Header Uses Files From B...	Yes ‡
Run Static Analyzer	No ‡
Scan All Source Files for Includes	No ‡

Don't Code Sign

Automatic Profile Selector (Recommended)
 iPhone Developer
 iPhone Distribution

iPad Provisioning Profile (for Application Identifiers '*')
 iPhone Developer: Kevin Kim (AAJBNEQ335)

SuperCheckout AdHoc Provisioning Profile (for Application Identifiers 'com.whilethis.SuperCheckout')
✓ iPhone Distribution: Kevin Kim

iOS Team Provisioning Profile: * (for Application Identifiers '*')
 iPhone Developer: Kevin Kim (AAJBNEQ335)

Xcode Wildcard Provisioning Profile (for Application Identifiers '*')
 iPhone Developer: Kevin Kim (AAJBNEQ335)

Other...

Figure 7–31. *Changing the code signing identity for release*

Now we need to archive our application in order to package it for distribution. First, select iOS Device in the Scheme pop-up menu on the Xcode Toolbar. Then select **Project ➤ Archive**. While the application is building, a window may pop up stating "codesign wants to sign using key "XXX" in your keychain" (see Figure 7–32). Click Allow. This window may appear again. If so, just click Allow. codesign is an application that packages Super Checkout (or any other application) with the distribution certificate and provisioning profile.

Figure 7–32. *codesign asking for permission to access your keychain*

Once your application is compiled, signed and archived, Xcode should open the Organizer window, displaying the Archive view (see Figure 7–33). The new Super Checkout archive should be listed. Select the Super Checkout, and click the Share button on the right side of the upper pane. Xcode will present a pane asking how you want to share the archive (see Figure 7–34).

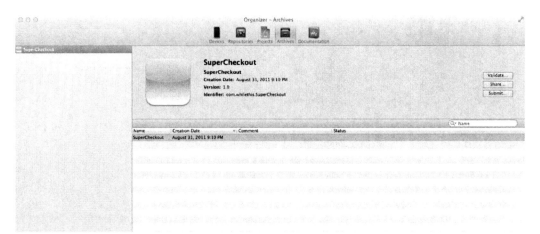

Figure 7–33. *Xcode Organizer window, Archive view*

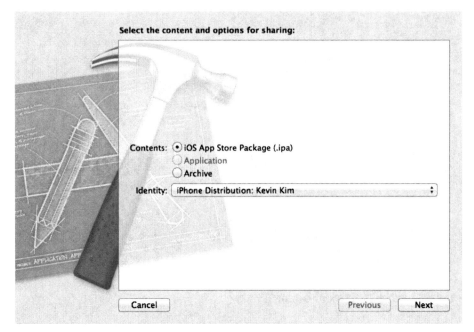

Figure 7–34. *Sharing configuration pane*

Select the iOS App Store Package (.ipa) radio button for the Contents. And select the appropriate distribution profile for Identity. The distribution profile should match the one you configured in Xcode for the Code Signing Identity. You may be asked about allowing codesign access to your keychain. As before, just click Allow. Finally, you will be presented with a file dialog to save the file app.ipa. Choose a location, and save the file as SuperCheckout.ipa.

Distributing the Beta

Whew, that was a lot of work. Now we have two files: the application package, SuperCheckout.ipa; and the provisioning profile, SuperCheckout_AdHoc_Provisioning_Profile.mobileprovision. These are the two files you distribute to your beta testers. How you distribute these files is entirely your decision. With a small group of testers, it may be easier to email them. Remember that many email services limit the size of attachments (generally 10MB). So some users may not receive the larger application package.

Generally, it's a good idea to upload the files to a location where your testers can access them. If you wish to password protect it you may. You don't need to worry extensively about non-testers downloading and running your application. The provisioning profile and codesigning will ensure that the application will only run on the devices you specified.

Once your beta testers have received the files, they simply need to launch iTunes, then drag the two files to the iTunes icon on the dock. At that point, the application is available to install on their iOS device.

Alpha, Beta, Gamma?

Now you've built a beta version of your application and distributed it to your testers. That was the easy part. Beta testing is an iterative process. Soon your testers will be submitting bug and crash reports. You'll have to analyze those reports and determine if a bug is really a bug, if the tester misunderstands the application, or if the application just needs to be redesigned.

As an addendum, there are several tools that aid in the beta testing process. Several developers we know have used them. We mention them here just to make you aware of them.

Several open source crash reporting frameworks have been developed; they aid in the automated delivery and interpretation of application crash reports:

- Plausible Labs' CrashReporter
  (http://code.google.com/p/plcrashreporter/)

- Parveen Kaler's CrashKit (https://github.com/kaler/CrashKit)

- QuincyKit (http://quincykit.net/)

- Steve Streza's CrashReporter
  (https://github.com/amazingsyco/CrashReporter)

There are a number of services out there that aid in the management of beta distribution, bug reporting and crash reporting:

- Hockey App (http://www.hockeyapp.net) built on top of QuincyKit

- BugSense (http://www.bugsense.com/)

- TestFlight (https://testflightapp.com/)

All three of these services offer crash report collection and analysis. They then collate the errors and attempt to assist with tracking down bugs. Hockey App and TestFlight also provide mechanisms for distributing applications to your beta testers.

Evaluate these frameworks and services and see if they fit your needs.

Summary

We've described how you might manage your beta testing process, from determining your beta testing goals to finding developers. Most importantly, we explained how to instruct your beta testers to submit feedback and crash reports. To distribute our beta application, we covered how to create an ad hoc provisioning profile. It's a complicated process that involves registering our application and our beta testers' device IDs. Armed with the beta application and provisioning profile, we are able to send them to our testers for review.

In the next chapter, we'll cover testing our application in an automated fashion. You'll learn how to convert our beta testers' bug reports into a testing bundle. By creating this testing bundle, it will help prevent the same bugs from appearing in our application again and again (developers call this regression).

Chapter 8

Why Are Things Breaking?

Development is over, the beta is out in the wild, and for the first time in weeks, you can sit back and relax. Right? Well, it'd be great if things were that easy, but they aren't, and now you're getting bug reports. Things are crashing, things are slow, and people are finding new and uncharted user journeys, which take them far away from the happy path you so carefully laid out before them.

Don't worry! There are many things you can do to find and fix these problems. The tools provided in the SDK make things much easier. But wouldn't it be great if there was a way to prepare for these problems in advance? If only there were some sort of methodology that focused on finding issues during development, rather than waiting for the bug reports to come rolling in.

> **NOTE:** Before going on, I want to point out that this chapter isn't solely devoted to any one process or methodology. Testing is important, no matter how you write your code. The important thing to learn here is how to test your app well, and how Xcode and the SDK tools make it easy to do so.

Test Driven Development

Test Driven Development (TDD) is a development methodology that places primary focus on (you guessed it) testing. In most development workflows or methodologies, testing is used as a means to measure the quality of code during, but usually after, development (Figure 8–1). TDD (see Figure 8–2) goes a step further than this by using tests to help design and plan your codebase before you start writing code.

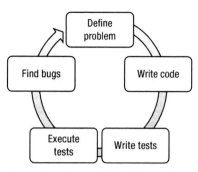

Figure 8–1. *A non-TDD workflow puts emphasis on writing code, rather than testing.*

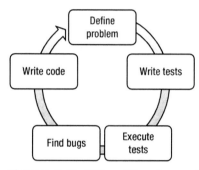

Figure 8–2. *The TDD workflow places writing code at the end of the lifecycle.*

You'll notice that the TDD workflow (Figure 8–2) has the same steps in a very different order. In TDD, you build against your tests, rather than the requirements or specs. Theoretically, when all of your tests pass, you should have a finished product that matches your requirements (and is bug free).

Notice the third and fourth steps in the TDD flow. When you've finished your test suite, you run the tests and catalog bugs. You do this before writing any code. If you find yourself thinking "But then all the tests will fail," you're right. You could argue that the purest form of TDD views the application as a series of defects that need to be fixed. The application isn't finished when it runs; it's finished when all of the tests pass. Since the test suite was designed to ensure the requirements were met, the tests become the measure of completion, rather than simply a measure of quality.

DON'T BE AFRAID OF TDD. (YOU'RE PROBABLY DOING IT ALREADY.)

If you haven't been exposed to it much, TDD (or testing, for that matter) can be a little daunting. The good news is, it's a lot more natural than you might expect. The great news is, you're probably already practicing it in a few ways you didn't realize. For example, before you start building a user interface, you probably plan the user journey, sketch out the possible flows, and write down interaction steps and expected results. Believe it or not, that's TDD. Test scripts, unit tests, automated user interface tests, manual user interface tests; these are all part of TDD.

When Should I Start Testing?

Whether you're doing TDD or just need to test a seemingly irreproducible bug, the only good time to start testing is right now. The sooner you start, the easier it will be to define tests that accurately test against your requirements without being clouded by preconceived notions or but-I've-already-spent-so-much-time-doing-it-this-way-itis.

Building tests definitely takes time. However, it can also save time in the long run. One of the benefits of tests is that they run extremely quickly. It only takes a few moments for Xcode to execute a test suite. This means you can run your tests a lot more often, without sacrificing much time. Running a fully baked test suite will almost always be exceedingly faster than re-creating a bug in an app in order to diagnose it.

Another benefit to testing is that well-written tests only need to be written once. If you write tests that match up to your requirements, then your tests shouldn't need to change unless your requirements do. If you're adding a new feature, you should only need to add new tests. Your previously written tests should all remain valid. The benefit of having a fully baked test suite is that it protects your code from regression bugs.

Xcode Makes It Easy to Test

Xcode does many things that make testing easy, no matter how much you want to do. There are two main categories of testing that Xcode helps with: unit testing and UI testing.

Unit testing is done within Xcode using a framework called OCUnit. Don't worry about needing to learn a new framework. From an interface perspective, OCUnit is one of the simplest frameworks you'll work with. In addition, Xcode does a lot of the setup and heavy lifting for you by providing target and file templates. As you'll see in a moment, starting a new unit testing-enabled project in Xcode is as simple as clicking a single checkbox.

UI testing is handled by running scripts in Instruments using the Automation template. This instrument uses a custom JavaScript framework to traverse a running application's user interface, allowing you to interact with the application without actually touching the screen.

The Target

There are two ways to get a unit test target into your project. The first, simplest way is to tell Xcode to include the target when you set up your project (see Figure 8–3). Before incorporating unit tests in the Super Checkout project, let's get comfortable with the way they work in a new, separate project. For this example, you'll be building a very simple calculator.

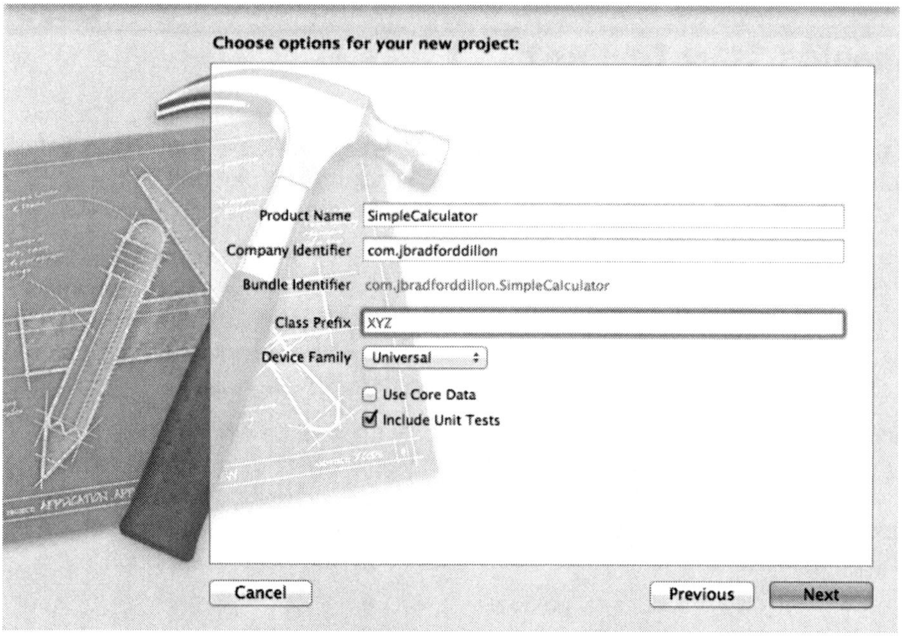

Figure 8–3. *Including a unit test target in your new project is as simple as checking a box.*

If you're adding testing to an existing project, need to add another testing target, or simply forgot to check the box during setup, you can always add a unit testing target to your project by simply adding a new target to your project and choosing the unit test template. From the menu bar, choose **File ➤ New ➤ New Target** (Figure 8–4).

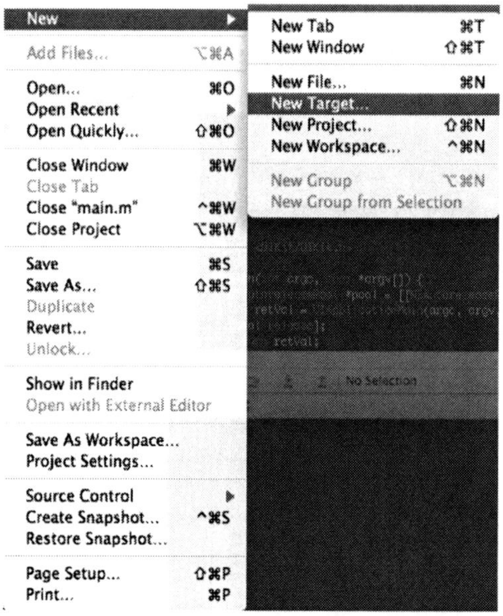

Figure 8–4. *You can also create new targets from the project screen's Add Target button.*

This will present the target template dialog (Figure 8–5). You'll find the Unit Testing Bundle target template in the section labeled Other.

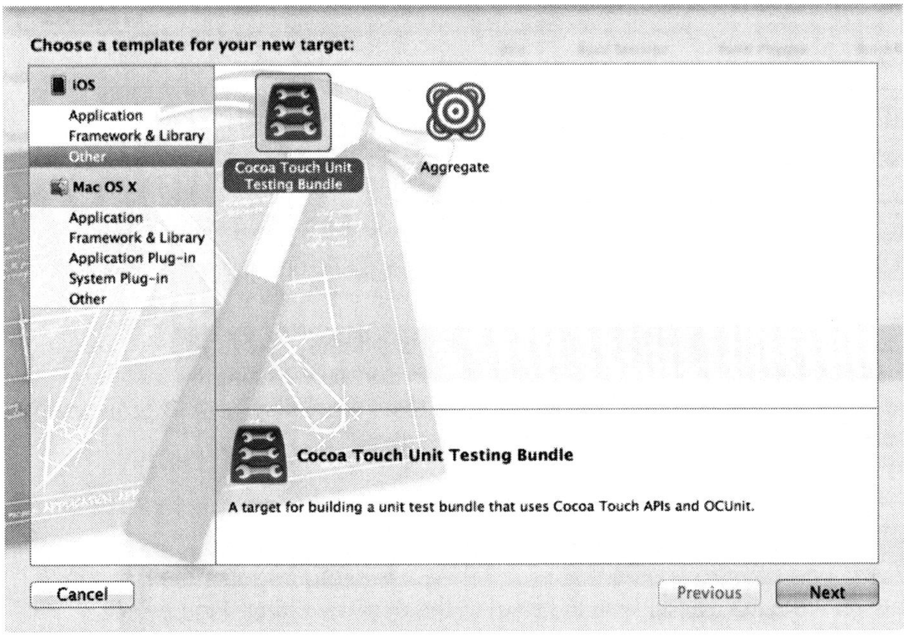

Figure 8–5. *You can add multiple unit testing bundles to your project.*

Once you've got your target created, you can begin writing tests. Before we get to that, let's take a look at the contents of the new testing target. If you created the test target as part of a new project, the target will be named the same as your project, appended with the word "Tests." If you created the target as a part of an existing project, it will be named whatever you chose to name it. It's important to follow a naming convention, so it's wise to name your test target after your project, appended with the word "Tests."

In the Project Navigator, there will be a group for each target. Inside the test target's group, you'll find a class that is named the same as your target, as well as a Supporting Files group, similar to what you would find in any other target group.

In SimpleCalculatorTests.m, you should see the following:

```
@implementation SimpleCalculatorTests

- (void)setUp
{
    [super setUp];

    // Set-up code here.
}

- (void)tearDown
{
```

```
        // Tear-down code here.

        [super tearDown];
    }

    - (void)testExample
    {
        STFail(@"Unit tests are not implemented yet in SimpleCalculatorTests");
    }

    @end
```

We'll get to the details of this in a moment. For now, it's sufficient to understand that this sets up a single, failing test.

Now that you've got a testing target, you need to run the tests. Before you do that, you need to get comfortable with the testing configuration and ensure that the tests are active. Xcode makes it really simple to control what tests are being run and provides the ability to modify some of your testing environment variables as well.

Setting Up the Tests

To run the tests, you need to ensure that your scheme is setup for testing. From the menu bar, select **Product ➤ Edit Scheme** to bring up the scheme editor (Figure 8–6).

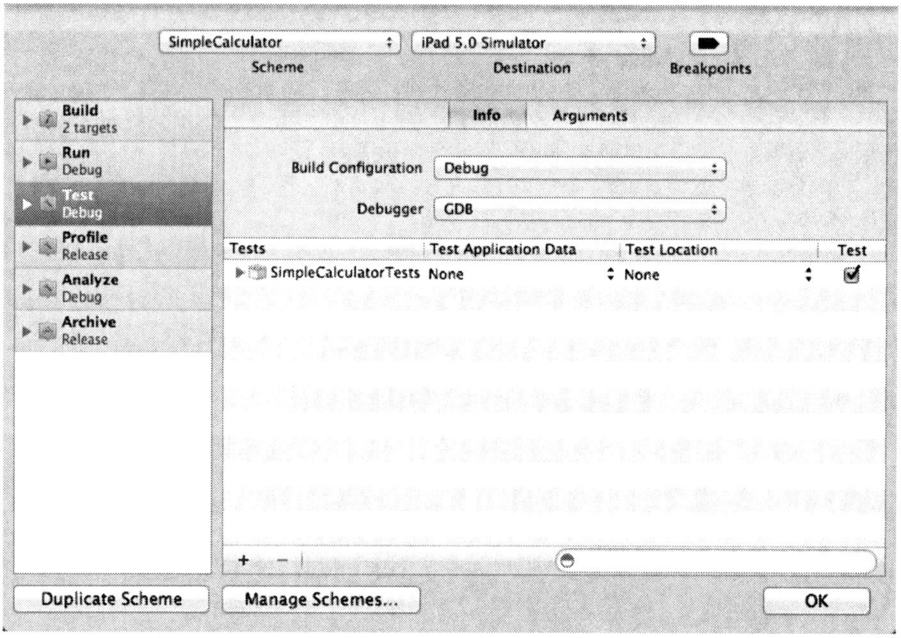

Figure 8–6. *If you don't include a testing target in your scheme, the Test action will be disabled.*

From the sidebar, select Test. If you opted to include a unit testing target during project setup, you should see the test target listed in the Info pane. If you created your unit test target manually, you'll have to add it to the scheme manually. Click the + button to bring up a list of all unit test targets included in your project. Select your target and add it to the Test action of your scheme.

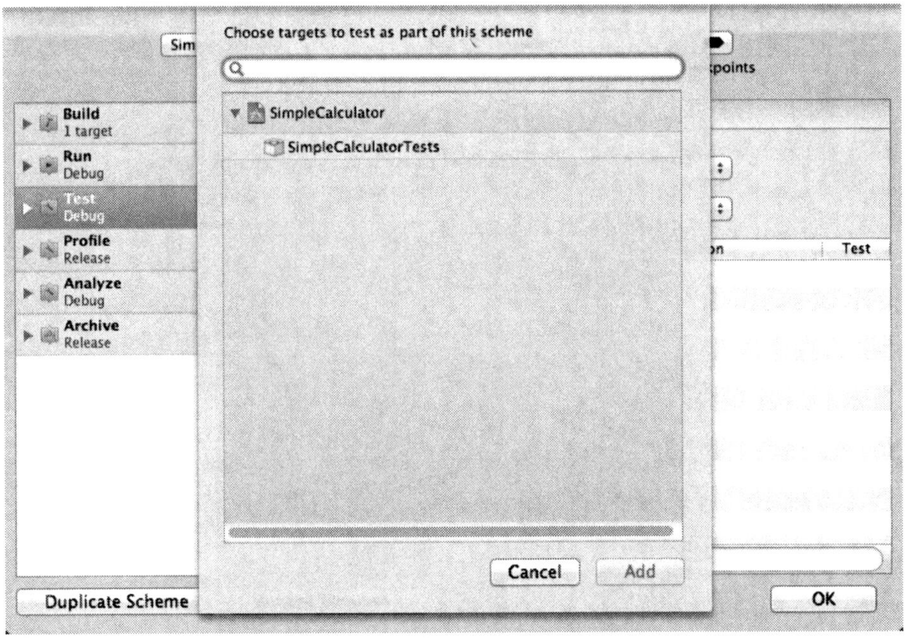

Figure 8–7. *All unit testing targets for all projects in the workspace will be available here.*

Once you have your target included in your scheme, you can do some more advanced configuration. The drop-down menus above the test target list allow you to choose the build configuration and debugger to use for the tests. These settings apply to all test targets in the current scheme. The target list allows you to modify configurations for the individual targets. If you expand a target, you'll see a list of all the SenTestCase subclasses in the target. In your example, you'll see a single list item, SimpleCalculatorTests. Expanding one of these test cases will expose the individual tests, listed by method name (Figure 8–8). Each of these items has a corresponding checkbox on the right, which allows you to toggle them on and off. Prior to Xcode 4, this would be done in code by configuring SenTestSuite objects.

Also of note on this screen is the Test Location column, which allows you to specify the locale from which the test should be run. This allows you to test behaviors that depend on locale, including CoreLocation, NSDate, NSCalendar, etc.

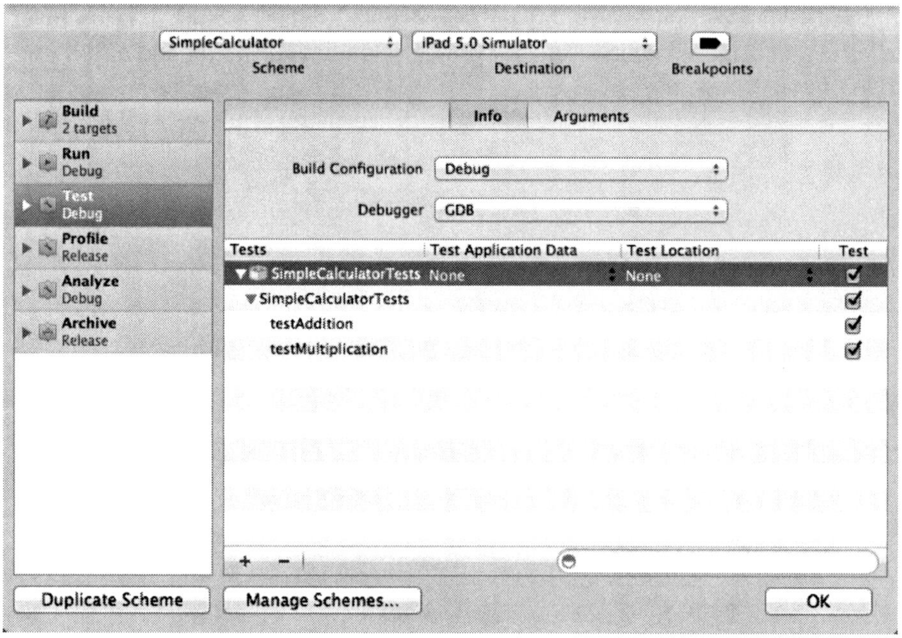

Figure 8–8. *Once you have a fully baked test suite, the ability to select which tests to run will come in handy.*

The Arguments pane (Figure 8–9) allows you to modify the action's environment arguments. By default, the "Use the Run action's options" checkbox is checked, which will be the preferred choice for most cases. As in any testing scenario, it's important to keep the testing environment as similar to the running environment as possible.

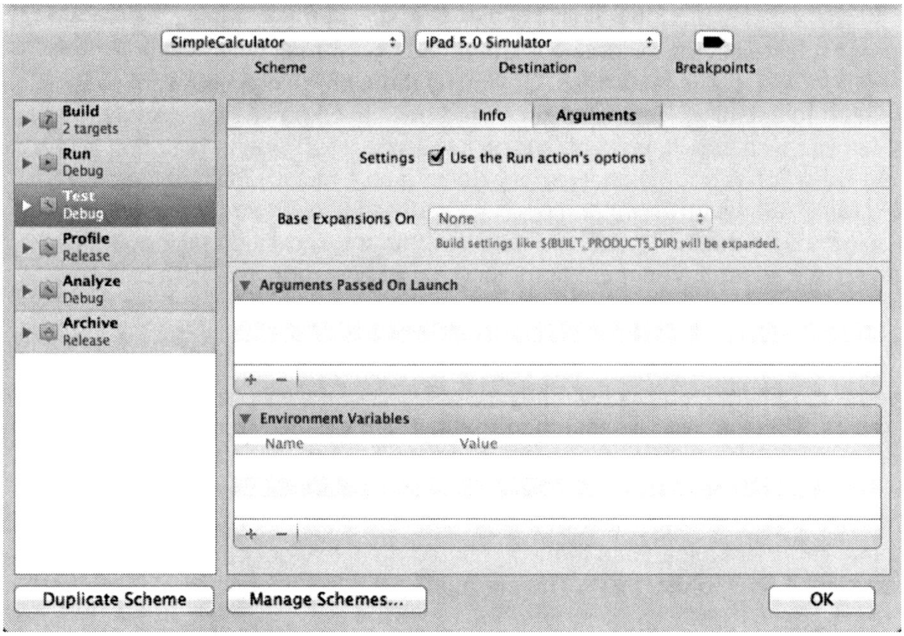

Figure 8–9. *Modifying the arguments of the test action causes a divergence from the running environment.*

Meet OCUnit

OCUnit is an Objective-C unit test framework that is bundled with Xcode and is used to write unit tests. OCUnit has been a part of Xcode since 2005; it's a simple yet elegant interface to unit tests, similar to Smalltalk's SUnit and Java's JUnit. It was previously developed as an open source project by Sente SA under the name SenTestingKit, and as such, many of the classes and macros included in the framework still maintain prefixes like "ST" and "Sen," and the framework linked to in your project is still labeled "SenTestingKit.framework."

To enable testing, you simply need a subclass of SenTestCase in your testing target. SenTestCase is the base class for test cases (also known as fixtures) and is the only class in SenTestingKit that you are concerned with.

SenTestCase follows the Convention over Configuration philosophy. Within a SenTestCase subclass, you provide tests in the form of methods whose selector begins with the word "test." At runtime, OCUnit automatically detects these subclasses, instantiates them, and calls each of the test methods in succession. Each test invocation is preceded by a call to the test class's -setUp method and is followed by the -tearDown method. Overriding these methods allows you to set up and configure the environment that the tests require. It's important to note that the order in which the tests are run is undefined, and there is no means to know which test is about to be run from within -setUp or -tearDown.

A test wouldn't be a test without the ability to fail. In a SenTestCase, raising an exception creates failure. If a test finishes executing without any exceptions being raised or any other crashing conditions, it is a success. Obviously there are things you want to test that are unrelated to crashing. That is where assertions (also known as asserts) come in. If you're not familiar with assertions, you will be once you finish writing your first batch of test cases. An assertion is a function (typically defined as a macro) that evaluates a condition and raises an exception if the condition proves false. Typically, assert functions also provide a means to express details about the exception by logging or producing an error message. The most common type of assertion in Cocoa is the NSAssert, which simply evaluates a Boolean expression and throws if it is false.

```
NSAssert((1+1 == 2), @"This assert will pass, and this message will never be seen");
```

The SenTestingKit framework provides many more types of asserts, which are useful for a variety of things. There is even an assertion that tests to ensure a piece of code *will* raise an exception (which, as you will learn, is much more useful than it sounds). SenTest asserts start with the prefix ST. They are technically macro functions. The benefit of this is that you can see most of their implementation in SenTestCase_Macros.h. Below are a few important assertions that you should definitely get comfortable using, along with a word on how to use them. The complete list can be found in SenTestCase.h.

- STAssertNotNil(a1, description, ...) raises an exception if object a1 is nil. Useful when testing a method that should return an object. Also see STAssertNil(), which does the exact opposite.

- STAssertTrue(expression, description, ...) raises an exception if the expression evaluates to false. This is essentially the same as using NSAssert(), except that it reports as a test failure, where NSAssert() simply halts execution. This function's compliment is STAssertFalse().

- STAssertEquals(a1, a2, description, ...) raises if values a1 and a2 are not equal. It's important to note that if two different objects are passed with the same values (e.g. two different NSStrings with the value "Hello World"), these will not evaluate as equal, as objects are unique. If two pointers to the same object are passed in, this will evaluate as true. To test the equality of different objects, use STAssertEqualObjects().

- STAssertNoThrow(expression, description, ...) raises if an expression (usually a method call on an object) throws an exception. This function, along with its counterpart STAssertThrows(), are possibly the most useful assertions available when building any sort of framework for consumption by third parties. For example, if a method in your framework requires a non-nil parameter, you might check its value using NSAssert(). Two great unit tests would then be to use STAssertNoThrow() with a valid call (with a non-nil parameter) to the method and to use STAssertThrows() with an invalid call (passing a nil parameter). It's important to understand STAssertThrows(), as it may feel backwards at first. Your test passes if the method fails!

- ▨ STFail(description, ...) is not an assertion. It is a catchall function that fails a test, no matter what. It can be used when none of the assertion functions work. If, for example, you were writing a test to check the values of error codes returned by a gracefully failing method, you could use a switch-case block to execute appropriate tests based on the enumerated error codes. In the default case of this block, you would probably want to call STFail() to ensure un-recognized error codes weren't getting introduced into your object.

Buggy Code

To explain exactly how unit testing works, let's start off with a simple example. Below is the SimpleCalculator class. It has two methods. One simply adds two integers and returns the result, and the other subtracts the two integers and returns the remainder. Or at least, that is what is supposed to happen. For the sake of demonstration, I've introduced a relatively obvious bug. Rather than subtracting the two parameters in the second method, I'm adding them. It appears that someone has been doing some copy-and-paste programming.

Here is the header for the SimpleCalculator class:

```
#import <Foundation/Foundation.h>

@interface SimpleCalculator : NSObject

- (int)resultOfAdding:(int)foo to:(int)bar;
- (int)resultOfSubtracting:(int)foo from:(int)bar;

@end
```

And here is the implementation:

```
#import "SimpleCalculator.h"

@implementation SimpleCalculator

- (int)resultOfAdding:(int)foo to:(int)bar {
    return (foo + bar);
}

- (int)resultOfSubtracting:(int)foo by:(int)bar {
    return (foo + bar);
}

@end
```

Writing the Tests

Before writing tests, it's important to consider what actually needs to be tested. For this overly simple class, it would seem that I would have some fairly simple tests, but that's not necessarily the case. I should probably test each of these methods, but with what data? Let's take a look at some sample tests.

> **CAUTION:** It's important to remember that test case targets *are* targets, and any required sources must be included in the target in order to use them. As such, you must remember to include implementation files (`SimpleCalculator.m`, for example) in the Compile Sources phase of your test target.

Here's the interface for my test case class. It's extremely simple, with only one local variable, which will hold an instance of the calculator:

```
#import <SenTestingKit/SenTestingKit.h>
#import "SimpleCalculator.h"

@interface SimpleCalculatorTests : SenTestCase {
        SimpleCalculator *myCalculator;
}

@end
```

The implementation is also simple. In -setUp, I create an instance of the SimpleCalculator class. In -tearDown, I release that instance. There are also two test methods, -testAddition and -testSubtraction, which test their relative methods of SimpleCalculator. Each of these methods uses the STAssertEquals() macro to test their results against the expected outcome.

> **CAUTION:** It's incredibly important that you manage memory correctly when writing tests. Introducing memory leaks in your unit tests can create bugs that are a real headache to diagnose.

```
#import "SimpleCalculatorTests.h"

@implementation SimpleCalculatorTests

- (void)setUp {
        myCalculator = [[SimpleCalculator alloc] init];
}

- (void)tearDown {
        [myCalculator release];
}

- (void)testAddition {
        int result = [myCalculator resultOfAdding:2 to:3];
```

```
        STAssertEquals(result, 5, @"Addition of 2 and 3 failed. Expected 5, received
%i", result);
}

- (void)testSubtraction {
        int result = [myCalculator resultOfSubtracting:2 from:3];
        STAssertEquals(result, 1, @"Subtraction of 3 from 2 failed. Expected 1, received
%i", result);
}

@end
```

> **TIP:** STAssert functions, just like NSAssert, take test condition as the first argument and subsequent arguments make up a formatted string, similar to using NSLog or –stringWithFormat.

Running the Tests

Now that you've got your scheme in order, you can run the test. This part's easy. First, it's important to note that the tests will be executed on the device and using the SDK version selected in the scheme drop-down. Once you've got your device and SDK selected, you're ready to go. From the menu bar, simply select Product ➤ Test.

When you run a test, two things will start to happen in Xcode. First, the simulator or device you have selected will launch and display a black screen. That's all it will display throughout the testing phase. Second, the debug pane will start displaying the output of the tests (Figure 8–10).

```
All Output ⬍                                                    ( Clear ) (□□) (■■) (□□)
Test Suite '/Users/jbradforddillon/Library/Developer/Xcode/DerivedData/SimpleCalculator-
bwlxzmbadtykfsduvqohpzvqekjc/Build/Products/Debug-iphonesimulator/SimpleCalculatorTests.octest(Tests)'
started at 2011-09-18 02:54:40 +0000
Test Suite 'SimpleCalculatorTests' started at 2011-09-18 02:54:40 +0000
Test Case '-[SimpleCalculatorTests testAddition]' started.
Test Case '-[SimpleCalculatorTests testAddition]' passed (0.000 seconds).
Test Case '-[SimpleCalculatorTests testSubtraction]' started.
/Users/jbradforddillon/Projects/Scratch/SimpleCalculator/SimpleCalculatorTests/SimpleCalculatorTests.m:28:
error: -[SimpleCalculatorTests testSubtraction] : '5' should be equal to '1': Subtraction of 3 from 2
failed. Expected 1, received 5
Test Case '-[SimpleCalculatorTests testSubtraction]' failed (0.000 seconds).
Test Suite 'SimpleCalculatorTests' finished at 2011-09-18 02:54:40 +0000.
Executed 2 tests, with 1 failure (0 unexpected) in 0.000 (0.000) seconds
Test Suite '/Users/jbradforddillon/Library/Developer/Xcode/DerivedData/SimpleCalculator-
bwlxzmbadtykfsduvqohpzvqekjc/Build/Products/Debug-iphonesimulator/SimpleCalculatorTests.octest(Tests)'
finished at 2011-09-18 02:54:40 +0000.
Executed 2 tests, with 1 failure (0 unexpected) in 0.000 (0.025) seconds
Program ended with exit code: 1
```

Figure 8–10. *Success by failure!*

That's a lot of data. Let's break it down a little.

```
Test Suite 'SimpleCalculatorTests' started at 2011-09-18 02:54:40 +0000
Test Case '-[SimpleCalculatorTests testAddition]' started.
Test Case '-[SimpleCalculatorTests testAddition]' passed (0.000 seconds).
```

The test suite has started, and the first test has run and passed. It also only took 0 seconds.

```
Test Case '-[SimpleCalculatorTests testSubtraction]' started.
/Users/jbradforddillon/Projects/Scratch/SimpleCalculator/SimpleCalculatorTests/SimpleCal
culatorTests.m:28: error: -[SimpleCalculatorTests testSubtraction] : '5' should be equal
to '1': Subtraction of 3 from 2 failed. Expected 1, received 5
Test Case '-[SimpleCalculatorTests testSubtraction]' failed (0.000 seconds).
```

The second test wasn't quite as lucky as the first. It failed (as you expected), and the message you included in your assertion has been included.

```
Test Suite 'SimpleCalculatorTests' finished at 2011-09-18 02:54:40 +0000.
Executed 2 tests, with 1 failure (0 unexpected) in 0.000 (0.000) seconds
Test Suite '/Users/jbradforddillon/Library/Developer/Xcode/DerivedData/SimpleCalculator-
bwlxzmbadtykfsduvqohpzvqekjc/Build/Products/Debug-
iphonesimulator/SimpleCalculatorTests.octest(Tests)' finished at 2011-09-18 02:54:40
+0000.
Executed 2 tests, with 1 failure (0 unexpected) in 0.000 (0.025) seconds
Program ended with exit code: 1
```

Lastly, you get a summary of the test results. Your SimpleCalculator went 1 for 1, in 0.073 seconds flat. Thankfully, Xcode simplifies this output in the Issue Navigator, showing the failed tests as errors with the description of the test failure intact (Figure 8–11).

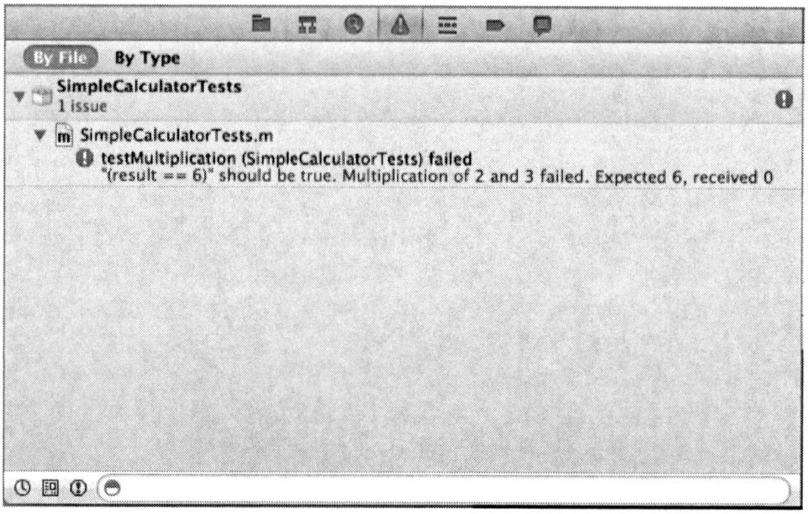

Figure 8–11. *All test failures will be displayed in the Issue Navigator, along with the info that was logged by the assertion.*

Refining the Tests

These tests work as expected. The addition test passes, and the subtraction test fails. The subtraction result would evaluate to 5, rather than 1, and the STAssertEquals() function would throw an exception. These tests successfully uncovered a bug in your code. But is that enough? Not quite. It's important to remember that the goal isn't just to pass tests, but to write good code. Unit tests aren't just obstacles to overcome; they should help clarify your problem and shape your solution so that you can write code effectively and efficiently.

So why are these tests insufficient? Here is an example of one way you might "fix" the bug these tests have uncovered:

```
- (int)resultOfSubtracting:(int)foo by:(int)bar {
      return 1;
}
```

Boom! With a single keystroke, your class now passes all the tests! Mission accomplished! Ship it!

What you've done here is missed the forest for the trees—or the algorithm for the tests, if you will. You need a better test. You need a test that doesn't allow for false positives. When you wrote the test, you had a preconceived notion of how the code worked. Writing tests before you start writing code gives you the advantage of foresight without the encumbrance of a pre-existing algorithm or design. When you're in the middle of trying to solve a problem, you're invested in your solution so you are much more likely to "hack something together" to pass the test. Taking the time to pause and really think about all that could go wrong with a component or piece of code will help you write better tests, which will help you write better code.

So what can you do to improve your test? How can you make it impossible to sidestep the test? Take a look at this:

```
- (void)testSubtraction {
      int foo = arc4random();
      int bar = arc4random();
      int dif = bar - foo;
      int result = [myCalculator resultOfSubtracting:foo from:bar];
      STAssertEquals(result, dif, @"Subtraction failed.");
}
```

By introducing randomization by way of the arc4random() function, you've made it impossible to predict the desired result. The only way to pass the test is to subtract foo from bar, no matter what their values are.

Let's take a look at how you would write a test before writing code. You're going to add a method to the calculator class that will return the quotient of two numbers. First, you'll add it to the interface of your SimpleCalculator class.

```
- (int)resultOfDividing:(int)foo by:(int)bar;
```

Next, you can start on your tests. Since the method is similar, a good starting point would be to follow the same form you have for your addition and subtraction methods.

```
- (void)testDivision {
      int foo = arc4random();
      int bar = arc4random();
      int quot = foo / bar;
      int result = [myCalculator resultOfDividing:foo by:bar];
      STAssertEquals(result, quot, @"Division failed.");
}
```

This test will definitely ensure the accuracy of your math. The random values ensure that you can't predict or cloud the results of this test. But does it test all possible problems you could face when writing this code? What if bar were a zero? What would you like the intended result to be?

These are the types of questions you should be asking while writing tests. Not only do they help to ensure all of your bases are covered, but they help to define the problems you're trying to solve, both implicit and explicit. When the problems are well defined and you've written tests against them, the solutions are simpler and easier to identify.

Let's write a test case for division by zero. For simplicity sake, let's say that this use case should throw an exception using an assertion. You may be asking why you would do this when division by zero already throws an exception. Throwing your own exception gives you control over how the app crashes and allows you to provide more information to the developer about what exactly they've done wrong. This will also give you an opportunity to try out another STAssert macro.

You want your test to pass only if attempting to divide by zero throws an exception. Here's how you can use STAssertThrows() to detect a valid exception:

```
- (void)testDivisionByZero {
      int foo = arc4random();
      int bar = 0;
      STAssertThrows([myCalculator resultOfDividing:foo by:bar],
            @"Divide by zero should have thrown");
}
```

STAssertThrows() detects whether or not an exception is thrown by a given expression. If no exception is thrown, the condition proves false, and STAssertThrows() will throw its own exception, failing the test. In order to pass this test, your code must throw an exception when the divisor is zero.

Now that you have a great (not merely "good") understanding of what your code must do, you can write it.

```
- (int)resultOfDividing:(int)foo by:(int)bar {
      NSAssert((bar != 0), @"Attempt to divide by zero.
            You are likely to be eaten by a grue.");
      return (foo / bar);
}
```

If you run your tests now, they should all pass, and you should feel pretty confident that the new feature is well thought out and well tested.

Putting It to Use with Your App

Now that you're comfortable with OCUnit and have a decent understanding of how to write good tests, you should start applying your new skills to the Super Checkout app. To start off, write a test suite for the project's JSON parser, SCJSONParser.

Testing SCJSONParser

The Super Checkout project already has a test target with the default initial SenTestCase subclass, Super_CheckoutTests. You could go ahead and start writing all of your tests in this class, but that would get unruly and disorganized really quickly. It's a good idea to have a one-to-one relationship between your test classes and test subjects. Since you're going to be testing SCJSONParser, create a new test case class called SCJSONParserTests.

To create a new OCUnit test case class, select the test case group and choose **File ➤ New ➤ New File** from the menu bar. From the file template dialog, choose the Objective-C test case class template, and click Next. Name the file SCJSONParserTests and click Next. Before clicking Create, you need to ensure the file is associated with the right target. Check the test target box (Super CheckoutTests), and uncheck the app target. The new test case class will contain stubbed out -setUp and -tearDown methods, but no tests. Also, if you check your scheme settings, you'll find that the new class has automatically been added to your test list.

Since you're going to be testing the SCJSONParser class, you need to make sure the class is included in your test target. Select the class in the Project Navigator, and check the Super CheckoutTests target in the Target Membership section of the File Inspector Utility. Since the SCJSONParser class depends on the SBJSON library, you'll need to include those classes as well. It's important to remember this step. Xcode manages a lot of the target membership stuff for you, so it's easy to forget when you need to manage it yourself.

Now you're ready to start writing tests for your JSON parser. SCJSONParser has two methods. One is an initializer, and the other is a convenience method that returns an autoreleased instance of the parser. Each of these methods takes in six parameters. There are no public properties. The parser notifies a delegate of completion using a method defined in the SCJSONParserDelegate. You need to test both of the initialization methods as well as some JSON data. Since SCJSONParser is a wrapper around SBJSON, and you're fairly comfortable with the library, you're not going to be testing the parsing capabilities. You're mainly focused on testing to ensure your wrapper is doing what you want it to do: provide a delegated interface to the parser, maintaining context through the provided request type and response type.

This test requires two objects: the parser and a delegate object that conforms to the parser's protocol. One solution would be to make your test case class act as the delegate for the parser. This is a bad idea because it involves your test agent, the test case class, in your test. In order to ensure you're getting accurate results, you need to keep your test class as separate from the test subject as possible. What you need is a simple object that conforms to the required protocol and reports results back to the test case.

Mock Objects

Mock objects are used when test subjects are depended upon by, or were designed to be dependent on, other objects. Composite objects, delegation pattern objects, and responder chain objects are good examples of this. A mock object is an extremely simple object with limited functionality. The purpose of a mock is only to confirm the functionality of the test subject, not to provide any functionality of their own. You want your mocks to be simple enough to avoid introducing any defects into the test.

An example of a good mock object is a simple echo object, also known as a recorder object. An echo object simply waits for the output of your test subject and stores it. You can then test the received output against the expected output in your test case. You need to create a mock echo object to act as the delegate for your JSON parser so that you can test the output.

Creating an object in a test target is the same as creating an object in any other target. You just need to make sure it's associated with the test target and not your app target. Here's the interface for your MockJSONDelegate object:

```
#import <Foundation/Foundation.h>
#import "SCJSONParser.h"
#import "SuperCheckoutRequestTypes.h"

@interface MockJSONDelegate : NSObject <SCJSONParserDelegate>

@property (nonatomic, copy) NSString *identifier;
@property (nonatomic, assign) SuperCheckoutResponseType responseType;
@property (nonatomic, copy) NSDictionary *parsedObject;

@end
```

As you can see, it's an extremely simple interface. The class extends NSObject and conforms to the SCJSONParserDelegate protocol. It has three properties to store the three outputs of the parser's delegate method, -parsingSucceededForRequest:ofResponseType:parsedObjects:. The implementation is equally simple.

```
#import "MockJSONDelegate.h"

@implementation MockJSONDelegate
@synthesize identifier;
@synthesize responseType;
@synthesize parsedObject;

-(void)parsingSucceededForRequest:(NSString *)anIdentifier
                ofResponseType:(SuperCheckoutResponseType)aResponseType
                    parsedObjects:(NSDictionary *)aParsedObject {
    self.identifier = aIdentifier;
    self.responseType = aResponseType;
```

```
        self.parsedObject = aParsedObject;
}

@end
```

The object is as simple as possible. It conforms to the required protocol and simply stores the values it is sent by the parser. In your tests, you can then check these values against your expected output and evaluate the results.

Since `SCJSONParser` receives all required data during initialization, and you are going to want to provide various data sets to see how it behaves, you probably shouldn't use the `-setUp` or `-tearDown` methods. You're going to want to do all of your instantiation within the tests themselves. As a result, your test class interface is pretty vanilla.

```
#import <SenTestingKit/SenTestingKit.h>

@interface SCJSONParserTests : SenTestCase

@end
```

Since you're not going to use the `-setUp` or `-tearDown` methods, you can go ahead and remove them from the class. Your first order of duty should be to test valid JSON input. It should look something like this:

```
- (void)testParseWithValidJSON {

        MockJSONDelegate *mockDelegate = [[MockJSONDelegate alloc] init];

        NSString *testIdentifier = @"testParseWithValidJSON";
        NSURL *testURL = [NSURL URLWithString:@"http://www.test.com"];
        NSString *jsonString = @"{ \"hello\" : \"world\" }";
        NSData *jsonData = [jsonString dataUsingEncoding:NSUTF8StringEncoding];

        SCJSONParser *parser = [[SCJSONParser alloc] initWithJSON:jsonData
                        delegate:mockDelegate
                        connectionIdentifier:testIdentifier
                        requestType:SuperCheckoutCheckout
                        responseType:SuperCheckoutCheckoutResponse
                        URL:testURL];

        STAssertEqualObjects(mockDelegate.identifier, testIdentifier,
                @"Mock delegate didn't receive the identifier that was passed in");

        STAssertEquals(mockDelegate.responseType, SuperCheckoutCheckoutResponse,
                @"Mock delegate didn't receive the responseType that was passed in");

        STAssertEqualObjects([mockDelegate.parsedObject objectForKey:@"hello"],
        @"world",
        @"The JSON was not parsed correctly, or the delegate was given incorrect data");

        [parser release];

}
```

Let's briefly walk through this. First you initialize your mock delegate. It needs no configuration, since you're only going to pass it to the parser during initialization. Next, you set up the test criteria. You need several parameters to pass in to the parser: you need an identifier string, a URL, and JSON data. For simplicity, you're providing a very simple JSON object with a single key-value pair. Finally, you initialize your JSON parser with your inputs. If all has gone well, the parser should have parsed the incoming JSON data using SBJSON and passed the result, along with some reference data, to the mock delegate object.

Your assertions test each of the mock object's properties against the values you passed in. If there is any discrepancy between the input and the output, the test is a failure. For the JSON object, you're making some assumptions around the resulting data. You can do this because you know the behavior of SBJSON and what the result should be. It's important not to complicate this issue, because as stated, you're testing SCJSONParser, not the SBJSON library.

If you run this test, you'll find that it passes with flying colors. This is entirely expected, since you've just written a test case to prove out existing functionality. As the test name indicates, this test only tests valid JSON input. You should definitely include a test against invalid input.

Negative Testing

At the moment, your SCJSONParser is designed to simply pass through the result of the SBJSON library's work. As such, the result of invalid input is to return nil. Your test for invalid input should test for nil from the mock delegate. The other parameters should remain the same. This test will look very similar to the previous one, but with some very important changes.

```
- (void)testParseWithInvalidJSON {

        MockJSONDelegate *mockDelegate = [[MockJSONDelegate alloc] init];

        NSString *testIdentifier = @"testParseWithInvalidJSON";
        NSURL *testURL = [NSURL URLWithString:@"http://www.test.com"];
        NSString *invalidString = @"Hello World";
        NSData *invalidData = [invalidString dataUsingEncoding:NSUTF8StringEncoding];

        SCJSONParser *parser = [[SCJSONParser alloc] initWithJSON:invalidData
                                delegate:mockDelegate
                                connectionIdentifier:testIdentifier
                                requestType:SuperCheckoutCheckout
                                responseType:SuperCheckoutCheckoutResponse
                                URL:testURL];

        STAssertEqualObjects(mockDelegate.identifier, testIdentifier,
                        @"Mock delegate didn't receive the identifier that was passed
    in");

        STAssertEquals(mockDelegate.responseType, SuperCheckoutCheckoutResponse,
                        @"Mock delegate didn't receive the responseType that was passed
    in");
```

```
        STAssertNil(mockDelegate.parsedObject,
                        @"The JSON parser should have returned nil due to invalid
input.");

        [parser release];

}
```

If you run your tests again, you'll find that they continue to pass. That's fantastic! Your code is perfect! Right?

Negative Testing and Useful Failures

There's something bothering me about that last test. There's no indication to the delegate that the JSON was invalid. The input could have been nil to begin with, and you would have gotten the same result. What you need is an error condition. Rather than jumping straight into the code, start by writing some tests to help you think about how you'd like the parser to work.

Right now, SCJSONParser only has one delegate method, which indicates success. Since you're using the delegate pattern, you should use it to indicate an error as well. The error method should pass along information about the error. SBJSON offers a method that populates an instance of NSError if necessary, so for simplicity you'll just plan to pass that through to your delegate. You're getting a little ahead of yourself, so for now you'll just add this method to your delegate protocol in SCJSONParser.h.

```
- (void)parsingFailedForRequest:(NSString *)identifier
        ofResponseType:(SuperCheckoutResponseType)responseType
        error:(NSError *)error;
```

Next, you need to modify your MockJSONDelegate object. First, you'll add a property to store the NSError.

```
// MockJSONDelegate.h
@property (nonatomic, retain) NSError *error;
```

```
// MockJSONDelegate.m
@synthesize error;
```

Next, you'll implement your new delegate method.

```
- (void)parsingFailedForRequest:(NSString *)aIdentifier
        ofResponseType:(SuperCheckoutResponseType)aResponseType
        error:(NSError *)aError {

        self.identifier = aIdentifier;
        self.responseType = aResponseType;
        self.error = aError;

}
```

Now that your mock delegate is set up, you're ready to write your test. Actually, since you've already got a test for invalid input, you just need to modify the test conditions. Let's add a check for the error property of your mock delegate in SCJSONParserTests.m. When invalid input goes in, the error should not be nil. Note that you don't want to remove any of the other assertions. You still want to ensure that the identifier and response type are coming through, and the parsed object property should definitely be nil.

```
STAssertNotNil(mockDelegate.error,  @"JSON parser should have passed through an error");
```

So you've modified your mock object, and you've added a test for the error. The next step is to validate your test by running it and observing a failure. The console should contain something like this:

```
Test Suite 'SCJSONParserTests' started at 2011-07-26 03:52:27 +0000
Test Case '-[SCJSONParserTests testParseWithInvalidJSON]' started.
/Users/jbradforddillon/Projects/whilethis-Super-Checkout-
a05a56c5c6396e8200a0bdf84a279406dc814ef0/Super CheckoutTests/SCJSONParserTests.m:100:
error: -[SCJSONParserTests testParseWithInvalidJSON] : "((mockDelegate.error) != nil)"
should be true. JSON parser should have passed through an error
Test Case '-[SCJSONParserTests testParseWithInvalidJSON]' failed (0.001 seconds).
Test Case '-[SCJSONParserTests testParseWithValidJSON]' started.
Test Case '-[SCJSONParserTests testParseWithValidJSON]' passed (0.000 seconds).
Test Suite 'SCJSONParserTests' finished at 2011-07-26 03:52:27 +0000.
Executed 2 tests, with 1 failure (0 unexpected) in 0.001 (0.001) seconds
```

Now that you have a failing test case, you can write the code to satisfy it. Let's take a look at the current initialization method of SCJSONParser:

```objc
- (id)initWithJSON:(NSData *)jsonData
            delegate:(id<SCJSONParserDelegate>)theDelegate
            connectionIdentifier:(NSString *)requestIdentifier
            requestType:(SuperCheckoutRequestType)reqType
            responseType:(SuperCheckoutResponseType)theResponseType
            URL:(NSURL *)theURL {

    self = [super init];

    if(self) {
        //Initialization stuff
        json = [jsonData retain];
        identifier = [requestIdentifier retain];
        delegate = theDelegate;
        requestType = reqType;
        responseType = theResponseType;
        URL = [theURL retain];

        //Do JSON parsing here
        SBJsonParser *parser = [[SBJsonParser alloc] init];
        NSString *jsonString = [[[NSString alloc] initWithBytes:[json bytes]
                                     length:[json length]
                                     encoding:NSUTF8StringEncoding] autorelease];
        parsedObject = (NSDictionary *)[parser objectWithString:jsonString];
        [parser release];

        [delegate parsingSucceededForRequest:requestIdentifier
                ofResponseType:responseType parsedObjects:parsedObject];
    }
```

```
        return self;
}
```

As alluded to earlier, you'd like to take advantage of the SBJSON library's error conditions, so the first thing to do is to replace the call to line

```
parsedObject = (NSDictionary *)[parser objectWithString:jsonString];
```

with these lines

```
NSError *err = nil;
parsedObject = (NSDictionary *)[parser objectWithString:jsonString error:&err];
```

Now, if the parsing fails within SBJSON, you've captured the error. Next, you need to check the condition of the error and send the right message to the delegate. You'll wrap your delegate callback in an if...else statement, like so:

```
if(err == nil) {
        [delegate parsingSucceededForRequest:requestIdentifier
                ofResponseType:responseType
                parsedObjects:parsedObject];
} else {
        [delegate parsingFailedForRequest:requestIdentifier
                ofResponseType:responseType
                error:err];
}
```

Running your tests again, you'll find that your changes have worked and your test cases pass. Fantastic! You just upgraded your parser object without breaking existing functionality and without needing to test with live data.

There are many more tests that could be written here. For example, what happens when a delegate doesn't fully implement the delegate protocol? Passing SBJSON's NSError through can tie you pretty closely to the library, so you might want to provide your own error data. You could write tests for all of these things to drive development toward a more complete and well designed solution.

Unit tests are incredibly valuable tools, whether used as part of a TDD process or just to help find bugs during your QA cycle. The explicit costs of developing a good test suite are often outweighed by the implicit savings in bug tracking and fixing time.

UI Testing and the Automation Instrument

Unit testing will help you break your application into smaller, independent, testable parts. Automated UI testing allows you to test the application as a whole. By scripting user journeys and testing expected outcomes, you can build a library of tests that will allow you to monitor changes in your application's behavior and performance throughout the development cycle.

In the development tools, automation is done in Instruments, using the Automation Instrument. The Automation Instrument simply allows you to record, edit, and run scripts on the simulator or device. The scripts are written in JavaScript using an API exposed by the UIAutomation framework. UIAutomation is a part of the Core Services Layer and uses UIKit's accessibility features to traverse the hierarchy of visible elements.

In order to get the most of UIAutomation, it's a good idea to become really comfortable with UIAccessibility protocol and put it to use in your code. Interface Builder makes this extremely easy, providing direct access to the `accessibilityLabel` property and some of the `accessibilityTraits` data. If your application's interface contains a lot of custom controls or gesture recognizers, it becomes incredibly important to use UIAccessibility to indicate to the scripting interface what roles your view objects are playing.

> **NOTE:** One of the added benefits of setting up automated testing is that it encourages you to make your interfaces accessible. This is one of the most overlooked, and most important, tasks when developing apps.

The UIAutomation API's root element is `UIAElement`. `UIAElement` provides the common interface for all interface elements. One of the most useful components of this object are its traversal methods. In addition to methods to access a given element's parent or its children, `UIAElement` allows you to get a list of children of one of several different types. For example, if you have an element object that references a given `UIView`, you can get a list of all the buttons contained in that view like so:

```
var buttons = myViewElement.buttons();
```

This would return all subviews of the related view that report as buttons. That is, it would return all subviews that have an accessibilityTrait of `UIAccessibilityTraitButton`. `UIButton` has this set by default, but if you've made a `UIView` tappable using a gesture recognizer or the `UIResponder` methods, you'll need to set this trait in order for UIAutomation to see it as a button.

In addition to traversal, `UIAElement` provides methods to perform gestures and interactions on elements, inspect the element's state, examine the accessibility details, and log the element to the Instrument's logging interface. The gestural functionality of the element is perhaps the most interesting and useful for testing complex interfaces. For example, if your interface includes an element that can be dragged incrementally within a specified bounds, you could test this using the `dragInsideWithOptions` method. It might look something like this:

```
element.dragInsideWithOptions({
        startOffset: { x: 0.0, y: 5.0 },
        endOffset: { x: 24.0, y: 5.0 },
        touchCount: 1,
        duration: 1.5
});
```

Beyond `UIAElement`, UIAutomation offers a library of objects that correspond to UIKit components plus several things that UIKit doesn't give you direct access to, like the keys of the keyboard.

In addition to the interface, UIAutomation offers a few objects to enable your scripts to interact with the device, the app, the instrument, and even the computer running the test.

- UIATarget gives you access to the device with which you're currently interacting. This device could be the simulator or a connected device. With this object you can manipulate the device orientation and accelerometer, simulate pressing of hardware buttons, take screen shots, and many more things.

- UIAApplication exposes information about the running application, like the bundle identifier, version, windows, etc. In addition, it provides access to application-level interface elements. For example, UIAlertViews are not presented within your view hierarchy, but at the application level. You would use UIAApplication to respond to alerts, action sheets, the status bar, etc.

- UIALogger is a basic logging object with the ability to log several different types of messages, including pass/failure, debug, and errors.

- UIAHost allows you to execute commands on the host computer from the context of Instruments.

Being a JavaScript interface, it's extremely easy to traverse through complex hierarchies in only a few lines of code. For example, you could drill down to a specific button of a screen using a single line. Let's assume that the button's accessibility label is set to "Hello World."

```
var button = UIATarget.localTarget().frontMostApp().mainWindow().buttons()["Hello
World"];
```

If the accessibility label were not set, you would not be able to reference it this way. You would instead have to get all of the mainWindow's buttons, and either identify the button by other means or specify the index of the button directly. Either one of these methods would be fragile and undesirable.

As of iOS 5.0, the Automation Instrument includes the ability to record scripts by simply interacting with the target device. The script is recorded in real time, using the same UIAutomation elements we've been discussing. As such, the script is completely human readable and editable. Coupled with a good understanding of the scripting interface, this feature is incredibly powerful and will save you hours of scripting time.

Getting Started

To get started, you need to build your app for profiling. To take advantage of the new script recording features, you'll need to build for iOS 5.0. Set your scheme to iPhone 5.0 Simulator and then go to **Product ➤ Profile** (or just hit ⌘ + I). When Instruments launches, you'll be asked to select an instrument template (Figure 8–12). Choose the Automation template and click Profile.

Figure 8–12. *The Automation tool can be combined with multiple instruments.*

When the instrument has loaded, it will probably automatically start recording and launch the simulator. This is a real time saver if you've got scripts already written, but you haven't gotten that far yet, so for now you can stop the profiling.

Let's take a look at the Automation tool (Figure 8–13). The Detail view contains a sidebar, an editor pane, and an extended detail view. The editor pane's jump bar allows you to switch between the Trace Log, Editor Log, and Script views. The Trace Log displays debugging data you post from your scripts. The Editor Log shows you the script execution process. The Script view is where you will write and record your scripts.

The detail view on the right displays details about specific output from the detail view. It's also where you'll see screenshots of your interface on test failures.

On the left sidebar you'll see the various settings for the tool. These settings are broken into four sections: Status, Scripts, Script Options, and Logging. Let's go through these one at a time.

- *The Status section* simply tells you whether the script is currently running. No more, no less. However, double-clicking on this section of the sidebar will toggle the editor pane between the current view and the Script view.

■ *The Scripts section* allows you to add or remove scripts from the current Instrument. Clicking the Add button will allow you to create a new script or import an existing one.

■ *The Script Options section* lets you choose to run your scripts as soon as the instrument begins recording or to wait for you to start them. There is also a Pause button to halt the current script temporarily.

■ *The Logging section* allows you to choose where logging should occur, export the current log, and take screenshots of the current app state.

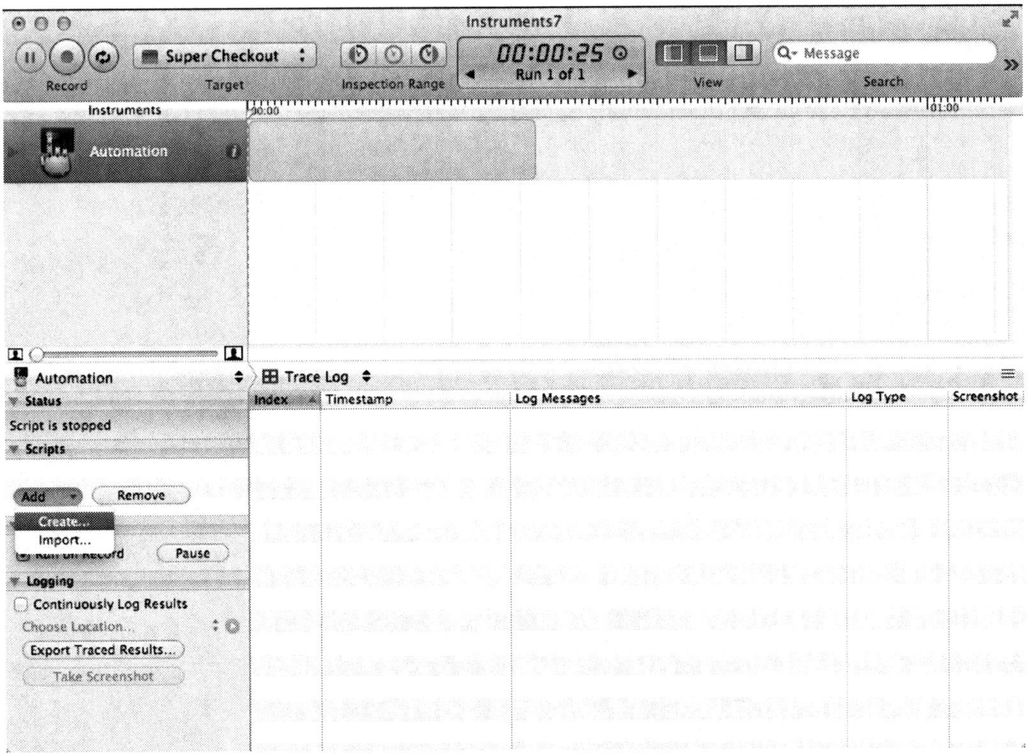

Figure 8–13. *As your script library expands, the script section of the sidebar will help you keep track.*

Go ahead and create a script. From the Scripts section in the sidebar, click the Add button and choose the Create menu item. You'll notice a New Script item has appeared in the Scripts section, and the editor pane has switched to the Script view. To rename your script, simply double-click the script item in the sidebar.

> **NOTE:** If you have a pre-existing script, or if you want to create a library of scripts separate from Instruments, you can create the script on the filesystem and then choose the Import menu option to navigate to the script.

In the editor pane, your script should already have some code in it.

```
var target = UIATarget.localTarget();
```

At the bottom of the editor, you'll see Play, Record, and Stop buttons. These buttons control the script itself and are different from the Instruments app's own control buttons, found at the top-left of the window. In order to get a jumpstart on this script, you want to use the record functionality. Script recording requires a version of the UIAutomation provided in iOS 5.0, so before you can do that, you need to ensure that Instruments is set to run your app under iOS 5.0.

Although you built our app for 5.0, Instruments can still simulate the app under a different OS version, and depending on your settings, may default to a prior version. To ensure you have the right configuration, you need to change the Launch Options. From the target drop-down, go to Options, and choose "iPhone - Simulator - iOS 5.0" under the Simulator Configuration section (Figure 8–14). Note that you'll need to make sure the instrument is stopped before changing this configuration.

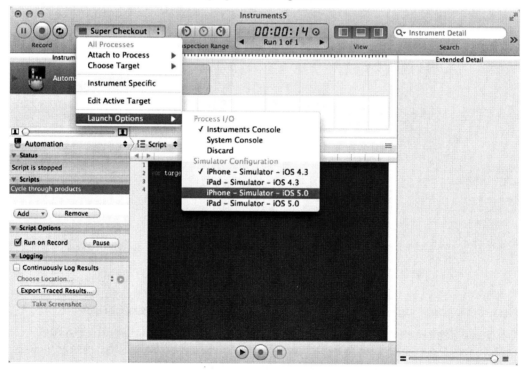

Figure 8–14. *It can be very handy to test your user interface in multiple iOS versions.*

Now that you're set up, you can click the Record button to start the simulator. The app should launch automatically. Once Super Checkout has launched, you can start interacting with it. As you do so, you'll see the script editor start to populate with JavaScript actions. These actions are broken out into tokens. Clicking the disclosure arrow on the right side of these tokens will display other options. This will come in handy in a moment. You can stop the script recording session at any time by clicking the

Record button again. If you then click the Instrument Session Record button (not the Script Record button) at the top-left of the window, your script should begin replaying on the device.

> **NOTE:** If you have any trouble launching the app from the Record button, ensure that the simulator isn't being used by any other processes. If Xcode is currently debugging an app in the simulator, this can prevent Instruments from attaching correctly.

Let's write a useful script using the recorder and learn a little more about the UI Automation JavaScript library. From the sidebar, remove the script you just wrote, and create a new one called "Cycle Through Products." Start recording your new script. First, select a product from the product table. From the product details view, click the Back button. Your script should look something like this:

```
var target = UIATarget.localTarget();

target.frontMostApp().mainWindow().tableViews()["Empty
list"].cells()[0].scrollToVisible();
target.frontMostApp().mainWindow().tableViews()["Empty list"].cells()[0].tap();
target.frontMostApp().mainWindow().navigationBar().leftButton().tap();
```

> **NOTE:** It's important to be aware that because the Automation Instrument is recording every UI event, your results may be slightly different, depending on your interactions with the simulator.

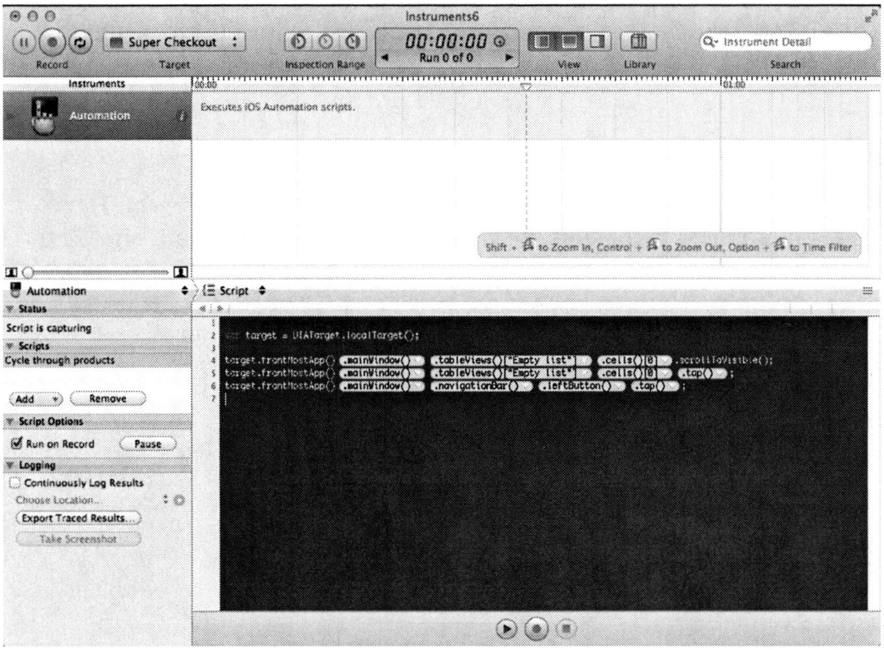

Figure 8–15. *The automation script's tokens are incredibly useful when creating iterative scripts.*

If you play this script back, it will do exactly what you recorded, and nothing more. Not very useful, but this is a great jumpstart on a script. The element tokens (Figure 8–15) in each of those expressions are extremely powerful. Clicking the arrow on the right-hand side of one will display options for that token. Each of these options is another way of pointing to the exact same interface element. For example, 'cells()[0]' might evaluate to the same cell as 'cells()["First Cell"]', and both of these options would be present in the token. If you double-click on a token, it will be converted to plain text, and you can modify it as needed.

What you want to do is loop through all the cells and perform the same action on each of the products in the table. First, you need to get the cells as an array so that you can use its length as the limit of a for loop. Let's take one of the lines of the recording, trim it down to just the cells array, and store it in a variable.

```
var cells = target.frontMostApp().mainWindow().tableViews()["Empty list"].cells();
```

Next, write a simple for loop that will iterate over the cells and execute your recording on each of them. To do this, you'll just double-click the 'cells()[0]' tokens and replace the 0 with your iteration index.

```
for(var i = 0; i < cells.length; i++) {
        target.frontMostApp().mainWindow().tableViews()["Empty
list"].cells()[i].scrollToVisible();
        target.frontMostApp().mainWindow().tableViews()["Empty list"].cells()[i].tap();
        target.frontMostApp().mainWindow().navigationBar().leftButton().tap();
}
```

If you run this script, the app should launch, and the script should cycle through each product in the table. You've got a pretty good iterative script going now, but it doesn't do anything useful. Take what you've learned, step back, and write a useful script that tests a complete user flow.

Scripting User Interface Tests

You've decided to write a series of tests for a handful of connected user flows. The flows include adding products to the cart, moving from the store to the cart, checking out, and returning to the store. These four actions will each be tested using the expected interface state as validation. You also want to be able to gauge the app's performance and automate repetitive actions so that you don't have to test them by hand.

Here's the script to accomplish this:

```
var target = UIATarget.localTarget();

var cells = target.frontMostApp().mainWindow().tableViews()["Empty list"].cells();

for(var i = 0; i < cells.length; i++) {
        UIALogger.logStart("Opening product "+i);
        cells[i].scrollToVisible();
        cells[i].tap();

        var productDetailsTable = target.frontMostApp().mainWindow().tableViews()["Empty
list"].cells()["Add To Basket"];
```

```
        if(productDetailsTable == UIAElementNil) {
                UIALogger.logFail();
        } else {
                UIALogger.logPass();
        }

        UIALogger.logStart("Adding product "+i+" to cart");
        productDetailsTable.tap();

        var cartButton =
target.frontMostApp().mainWindow().navigationBar().rightButton();
        var quantity = i + 1;

        if(cartButton.label().search("("+quantity+")") == -1) {
                UIALogger.logFail("Expected cart button to display "+quantity+" items,
but found "+cartButton.label());
        } else {
                UIALogger.logPass();
        }
}

UIALogger.logStart("Opening the cart");
target.frontMostApp().mainWindow().navigationBar().rightButton().tap();

var storeButton = target.frontMostApp().mainWindow().navigationBar().rightButton();

if(storeButton.label().search("Store") == -1) {
        UIALogger.logFail("Expected to find Store button in navigation item");
} else {
        UIALogger.logPass();
}

UIALogger.logStart("Checkout");
var cartTable = target.frontMostApp().mainWindow().tableViews()["Empty list"];
var checkoutButton = cartTable.groups()["Checkout"].buttons()["Checkout"];
checkoutButton.scrollToVisible();
checkoutButton.tap();

target.delay(2);

if(cartTable.cells().length > 1) {
        UIALogger.logFail("Checkout should have emptied the cart, but cart still holds
"+cartTable.cells().length+" cells");
} else {
        UIALogger.logPass();
}

UIALogger.logStart("Return to catalog");
target.frontMostApp().mainWindow().navigationBar().rightButton().tap();

var cartButton = target.frontMostApp().mainWindow().navigationBar().rightButton();

if(cartButton.label().search("Cart") == -1) {
        UIALogger.logFail("Expected to find Cart button in navigation item");
} else {
        UIALogger.logPass();
}
```

Let's break this script down into its individual parts. First, as in the previous example, you need to set up a for loop to iterate over each cell in the product catalog table. UIAElementArray behaves similarly to a traditional JavaScript array, but with one added benefit: you can use the label attribute of an element to retrieve it from the array. The length property provides access to the number of UIAElements contained in the array.

```
for(var i = 0; i < cells.length; i++) {
```

In the for loop, you're going to perform two test scenarios. The first test is to open a product's details screen, and the second is to add that product to the cart. In order to create a test scenario, you use the UIALogger function logStart(). This function indicates to the instrument that you've begun a scenario and will log out a message passed in as a parameter. To end the test scenario, you call either the logFail() or logPass() function. The scenario will be displayed as passed or failed, based on which of these functions were called. The logFail() function has the added feature of taking a screenshot when it is called. This, along with any information about the failure, will be available in the instrument. All debug logs and element logs that occur within a test scenario (that is, between a logStart() and either a pass or fail call) will be enveloped by the scenario in the log.

> **NOTE:** In addition to logging success and failure, the logStart() and related log functions will break up the feedback visible in the instrument timeline so that you can easily identify passes and failures. In addition, scrubbing the playhead through the timeline will display related log messages in the detail view. This is great for associating actions with data from other instruments.

The first test will simply scroll to the cell in question, tap it, and then look for a cell with the label "Add to Basket." If that cell is found, the product details have successfully displayed, and the test is passed. If that cell is not found, you must fail the test. It's important to point out that when a test fails, the script does not stop. It will continue running, logging pass and fail for subsequent tests.

```
        UIALogger.logStart("Opening product "+i);
        cells[i].scrollToVisible();
        cells[i].tap();

        var addToCartCell = target.frontMostApp().mainWindow().tableViews()["Empty
list"].cells()["Add To Basket"];
        if(addToCartCell == UIAElementNil) {
                UIALogger.logFail();
        } else {
                UIALogger.logPass();
        }
```

Next, you want to test adding the product to the cart. You're going to tap the "Add To Basket" cell. This should result in the details view controller being popped off of the navigation stack, and the cart button being updated to show the new quantity. You should be able to test the cart button's label for the expected quantity to pass or fail this test.

```
        UIALogger.logStart("Adding product "+i+" to cart");
        addToCartCell.tap();

        var cartButton =
target.frontMostApp().mainWindow().navigationBar().rightButton();
        var quantity = i + 1;

        if(cartButton.label().search("("+quantity+")") == -1) {
                UIALogger.logFail("Expected cart button to display "+quantity+" items,
but found "+cartButton.label());
        } else {
                UIALogger.logPass();
        }

}
```

Now that you've added all of the products to the cart, you can open the cart. The cart view's right navigation bar button is labeled Store, so you'll look for that to indicate that you've successfully moved to that view.

```
UIALogger.logStart("Opening the cart");
target.frontMostApp().mainWindow().navigationBar().rightButton().tap();

var storeButton = target.frontMostApp().mainWindow().navigationBar().rightButton();

if(storeButton.label().search("Store") == -1) {
        UIALogger.logFail("Expected to find Store button in navigation item");
} else {
        UIALogger.logPass();
}
```

Finally, you can checkout. You're going to find the button labeled Checkout, scroll to it, and tap it. This will cause the table to empty in an animated fashion. Once it's empty, you can check the number of cells in the table. It should only contain one cell, the one labeled Checkout.

You'll notice that there's a call to UIATarget's delay() function here. This function simply pauses the script for the prescribed number of seconds. Because you want to test the table's cell count, rather than test for the existence or value of an interface element, the traditional timeout methods won't work. You need to give the animation time to complete before you test the table's cell count. If the cell count is not what you expect, you need to log a failure (Figure 8–16). You don't need to log the contents of the table cells, as a screenshot will be taken for you to examine later. This occurs every time a failure is logged (Figure 8–17).

```
UIALogger.logStart("Checkout");
var cartTable = target.frontMostApp().mainWindow().tableViews()["Empty list"];
var checkoutButton = cartTable.groups()["Checkout"].buttons()["Checkout"];
checkoutButton.scrollToVisible();
checkoutButton.tap();

target.delay(2);

if(cartTable.cells().length > 1) {
        UIALogger.logFail("Checkout should have emptied the cart, but cart still holds
"+cartTable.cells().length+" cells");
```

```
} else {
        UIALogger.logPass();
}

UIALogger.logStart("Return to catalog");
target.frontMostApp().mainWindow().navigationBar().rightButton().tap();

var cartButton = target.frontMostApp().mainWindow().navigationBar().rightButton();

if(cartButton.label().search("Cart") == -1) {
        UIALogger.logFail("Expected to find Cart button in navigation item");
} else {
        UIALogger.logPass();
}
```

Index	Timestamp	Log Messages	Log Type	Screenshot
488	12:07:21 AM EDT	▶ Adding product 8 to cart	Pass	
491	12:07:23 AM EDT	▶ Opening the cart	Pass	
494	12:07:24 AM EDT	▼ Checkout	Fail	☐
495	12:07:25 AM EDT	target.frontMostApp().mainWindow().tableViews()["Empty list"].groups()["Checkout"].buttons()["Checkout"].scr...	Debug	
496	12:07:26 AM EDT	target.frontMostApp().mainWindow().tableViews()["Empty list"].groups()["Checkout"].buttons()["Checkout"].tap()	Debug	
497	12:07:27 AM EDT	Checkout should have emptied the cart, but cart still holds 9 cells		■
498	12:07:28 AM EDT	▶ Return to catalog	Pass	
501	12:08:10 AM EDT	▶ Opening product 0	Pass	
505	12:08:12 AM EDT	▶ Adding product 0 to cart	Pass	
508	12:08:14 AM EDT	▶ Opening product 1	Pass	
512	12:08:17 AM EDT	▶ Adding product 1 to cart	Pass	
515	12:08:19 AM EDT	▶ Opening product 2	Pass	
519	12:08:21 AM EDT	▶ Adding product 2 to cart	Pass	
522	12:08:23 AM EDT	▶ Opening product 3	Pass	
526	12:08:26 AM EDT	▶ Adding product 3 to cart	Pass	
529	12:08:27 AM EDT	▶ Opening product 4	Pass	
533	12:08:30 AM EDT	▶ Adding product 4 to cart	Pass	
536	12:08:31 AM EDT	▶ Opening product 5	Pass	
540	12:08:34 AM EDT	▶ Adding product 5 to cart	Pass	
543	12:08:36 AM EDT	▶ Opening product 6	Pass	
547	12:08:39 AM EDT	▶ Adding product 6 to cart	Pass	
550	12:08:40 AM EDT	▶ Opening product 7	Pass	
554	12:08:43 AM EDT	▶ Adding product 7 to cart	Pass	
557	12:08:45 AM EDT	▶ Opening product 8	Pass	
561	12:08:48 AM EDT	▶ Adding product 8 to cart	Pass	
564	12:08:49 AM EDT	▶ Opening the cart	Pass	
567	12:08:50 AM EDT	▶ Checkout	Pass	
571	12:09:00 AM EDT	▶ Return to catalog	Pass	

Figure 8–16. *Remember to add delays to account for custom or non-transitional animations.*

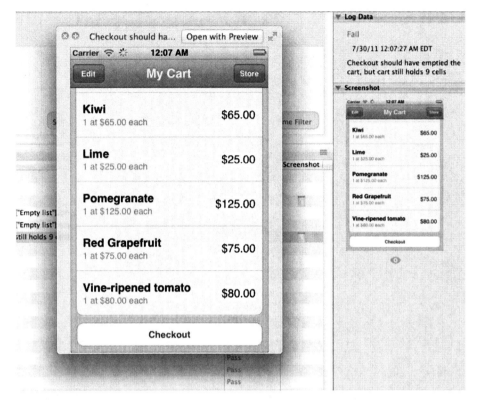

Figure 8–17. *Calling logFail() will automatically take screenshots. This is incredibly useful for debugging failures.*

Introducing a Bug

Now that you have a fully functional Automation test script that tests a given user flow successfully, let's look at how this can be useful. Unlike unit tests, it's extremely difficult, though not at all impossible, to write Automation scripts before you've built your application. You should definitely document and plan out your user journeys and interfaces, and you could absolutely write scripts based on that documentation, but writing scripts by hand can be tedious. The primary use cases for automated interface testing are to maintain the integrity of user journeys, weeding out regression bugs as development proceeds, and performance testing. Let's take a look at how your test can accomplish this in your app.

As an example, imagine you've adopted a new logging format and need to update the NSLog functions used throughout your app. You're working on the ProductDetailsViewController. When the API engine notifies you that it received your request to add a product to the cart, you post a notification and make a log message. This needs to be re-worked, and during the development process, you absent-mindedly make a few minor mistakes.

Before your changes, the method looked like this:

```
-(void) cartContentsReceived:(NSDictionary *)cart forRequest:(NSString
*)connectionIdentifier {
        NSLog(@"Shopping cart contents: %@", cart);
        NSNotification *note = [NSNotification notificationWithName:@"CartUpdated"
object:[NSNumber numberWithInt:[[cart objectForKey:@"items"] count]]];

        [[NSNotificationCenter defaultCenter] postNotification:note];

        [self.navigationController popViewControllerAnimated:YES];
}
```

The new method, which was intended to simply add more logging, looks like this:

```
-(void) cartContentsReceived:(NSDictionary *)cart forRequest:(NSString
*)connectionIdentifier {
        NSLog(@"%s Shopping cart contents: %@", __PRETTY_FUNCTION__, cart);
        NSNotification *note = [NSNotification notificationWithName:@"CartUpdated"
object:[NSNumber numberWithInt:[[cart objectForKey:@"items"] count]]];

        [[NSNotificationCenter defaultCenter] postNotification:note];

        NSLog(@"%s Notification posted: %@", __PRETTY_FUNCTION__, note);
}
```

You may notice that there is one major undesirable difference between the old method and the new. In your overzealous logging efforts, you accidentally removed the last line of the method, which popped the current view controller off of the stack.

This kind of bug is particularly difficult to detect with the naked eye, because it does not present itself as a bug. The application does not crash, the item is still added to the user's cart, and when the user taps the back button, the cart button has been updated to display the new quantity. The only change has been to the user experience.

Now, let's run the script on the app to see if it can help you find this nasty interface/regression bug. Hit Control+I to launch Instruments and set up an Automation tool. Run the script you ran earlier. As soon as you get to the test in which the product is added to the cart, the script looks for a button in the navigation bar with a label that reflects the new number of cart items.

```
var cartButton = target.frontMostApp().mainWindow().navigationBar().rightButton();
var quantity = i + 1;

if(cartButton.label().search("("+quantity+")") == -1) {
        UIALogger.logFail("Expected cart button to display "+quantity+" items, but found
"+cartButton.label());
} else {
        UIALogger.logPass();
}
```

Since you've accidentally modified the flow of the application, this script will fail. Fortunately, you'll get a screenshot recorded of the moment the script failed, along with a message indicating what went wrong. It shouldn't be terribly difficult to isolate the section of code responsible and then examine the revision history to find what changed.

The Power of Automation

In addition to finding bugs and ensuring user experience integrity, automation can help you fine-tune your app's performance. By coupling it with other instruments, you can get a detailed view of how your app is behaving under a variety of circumstances. Writing scripts for all of your user flows and use cases is a great idea. When all of these scripts have been written, you can run them in conjunction with the CoreData instruments to find places where you might want to optimize your fetching. You can add in the Allocations instrument to see how much memory your app is using at any given time to find possible detrimental spikes to smooth out (Figure 8–18).

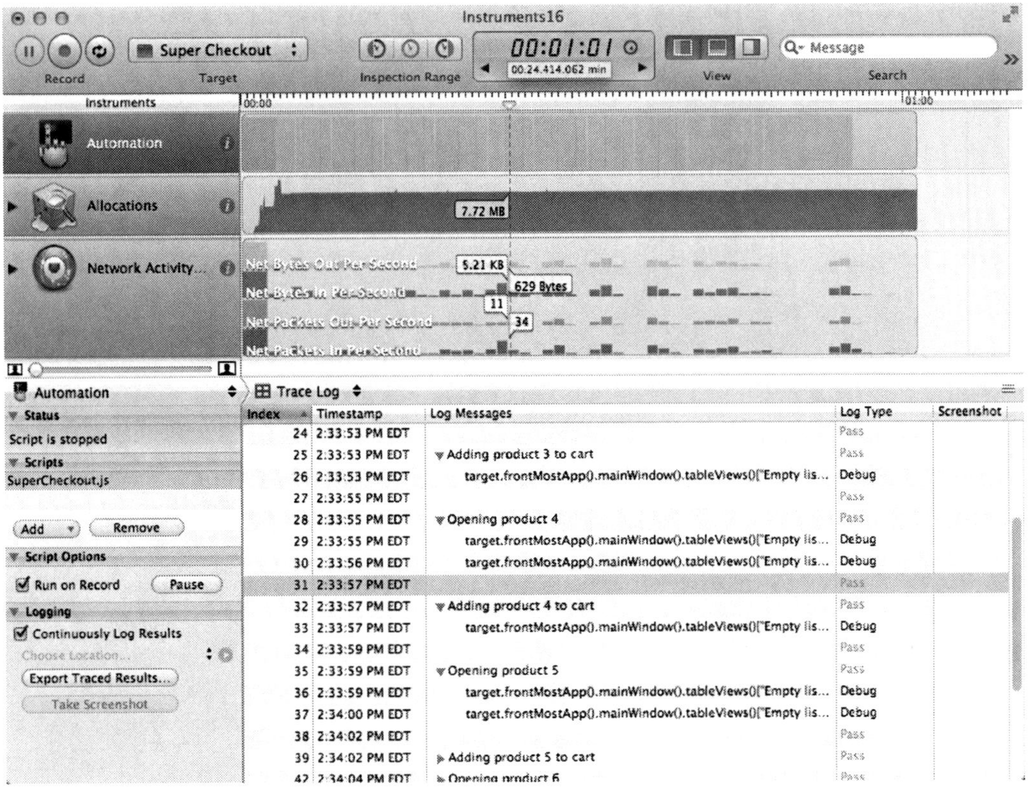

Figure 8–18. *Using other instruments together with Automation lets you to tie data back to user actions.*

Setting up and using automation early in your development cycle and scripting all of your user interactions will pay off greatly in the long run, both in better performance and more sanity.

Test, One Way or Another

That's testing, in a nutshell. You've got the beginnings of a unit test suite, your JSON parser-wrapper is a little better off than when you started, and you've got most of your use cases scripted for the automation instrument. Admittedly, this has all been very ad hoc. What you really need is a testing strategy.

Your testing strategy is what brings method to the madness. As you saw, testing takes time to set up, regardless of how much time it can save. It can do you a lot of good, and save you a lot of time, but if it's always an afterthought, you won't get the most out of it.

Whether you're a TDD stickler or just need to figure out why your app is leaking memory left and right, testing is an important skill to learn, and Xcode and the developer tools well help you do it.

Chapter 9

Can We Automate Some of This?

Now that your app is being thoroughly tested and your beta is underway, you're starting to get requests for some new features. You've decided to bring a couple more people onto the project to help get it over the line. The new developers are good, but they aren't as intimately familiar with the inner workings of your lovely app as you are, so you're concerned that they might get in there and accidentally wreck the place. You're very busy fixing bugs and adding features, so you can't spare the time it takes to run all the tests and static analysis every time one of the new developers pushes an update to the project. Not only that, but adding developers always increases risk in integration bugs, especially on small projects.

Fortunately, you're far from the first person to experience this. In fact, this is such a common problem that there are entire methodologies, processes, and enterprise-level applications in place to help manage development teams. You're not going to implement a new methodology, but you are going to introduce a process and some software that will help the team work better and keep your app on the right path.

Continuous Integration

Continuous Integration, commonly referred to as simply "CI", is a process of performing quality control checks continuously through the life of a project, rather than at intervals. Where a non-CI project team might gather together every week to run tests and evaluate the low-level project health, a CI-oriented team is constantly running tests to stay informed and ensure their integrations are not introducing bugs.

In the past, a Continuous Integration system might have been as simple as having a cron job execute a project's unit tests on an hourly basis. This gives continuous feedback and notifies the developer of integration issues, but it really only works for a team of one developer. Modern CI relies largely on software, which automates the tests and analysis. This software is typically run on a server and is set up to notify developers when their code has broken the build. This server is often responsible for multiple CI jobs; in some cases it's distributed across multiple servers to handle larger build loads.

There are many Continuous Integration software packages on the market. One of the most popular CI applications is Jenkins. In order to keep your new team on the straight and narrow, you're going to set up an instance of Jenkins to automate your building, testing, analysis, and deployment.

Meet Jenkins

Jenkins is a Java-based application with a web interface that allows you to set up build jobs, triggered by a variety of events, using a shell scripting interface or any of a library of plug-ins. Jenkins also offers the ability to manage users and permissions, which is ideal for large teams or teams that include contractors and clients. Jenkins, through the extensive plug-in library, supports multiple version control systems including Subversion, CVS, and Git. Also, Jenkins is open-source and free.

> **NOTE:** While working with Jenkins, you may see reference to a product called Hudson. Prior to 2011, Jenkins was known as the Hudson project, which started at Sun Microsystems. In late 2010, a trademarking issue arose, which caused a fork in the project development, and Jenkins was born. Today, the Hudson project is supported by Oracle, and Jenkins continues to be developed by the community.

Getting Jenkins Up and Running

Jenkins can be downloaded from `http://jenkins-ci.org/`. Being Java-based, it is cross platform and can be installed on a variety of operating systems, including OS X. The minimum requirement for Jenkins at time of writing is the Java Runtime Environment v1.5. In order to install it, you'll need three things: administrator access to the server it'll run on; the ability to create a user for it to run under; and the ability to control the machine, either through remote screen sharing or directly.

When creating a new user, you need to do several things to prepare for Jenkins. First, you need to get new keys made. You're going to need any SSH auth necessary for checking out from your repository, be it Github or anything else. Jenkins is going to be checking out your project regularly, and you need to ensure that it is able to do so. Second, you've got to get certificates and keys from the Apple developer portal. You may already have these keys on your development machine or account, but the Jenkins user needs to have its own keychain with its own keys and certs. You'll also need to get a valid provisioning profile for the certificates and throw it into Xcode's organizer. Once you've got the Jenkins user adequately keyed, certified, and provisioned, you're ready to set up the Jenkins environment.

Jenkins is incredibly easy to install. Simply download the installer package and run it (Figure 9–1). When installation is complete, you'll find a Jenkins folder in your Applications directory.

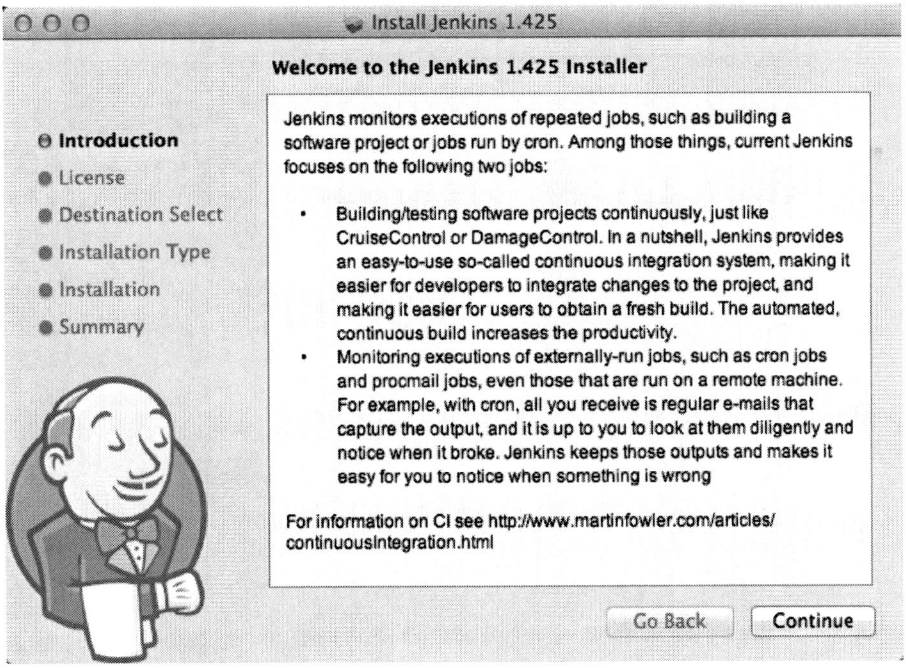

Figure 9–1. *Installation should be a familiar process. No surprises or gotchas.*

Inside the Jenkins folder, you'll find the Jenkins .WAR (Java Web Archive) file. If you're not familiar with Java, this is the executable for the web application. There shouldn't be any need to run the .WAR file, as the installation script should have launched Jenkins for you. To ensure that it's running, simply fire up your browser and go to http://localhost:8080/.

The Jenkins Interface

The Jenkins dashboard (Figure 9–2) will be pretty stark at first. Once you set up a few jobs, it'll give you a status summary of all projects currently being tracked. The sidebar on the left gives you navigation, a list of builds in the queue, and build execution status.

Figure 9–2. *The Jenkins dashboard will be extremely useful, once it's full of data.*

To get more familiar with Jenkins, let's jump into the Management section. From the dashboard's sidebar, click the Manage Jenkins link. The Management page (Figure 9–3) is the hub for configuring and monitoring the various aspects of your Jenkins instance. Lets run down the Management menu.

- *Configure system*: The System Configuration page allows you to change system paths, set the number of concurrent build executions, create environment variables, and perform setup on any plug-ins added to the system. It's important to note that Jenkins was built to be platform and project agnostic, and as such, not all settings will be applicable or interesting to iOS developers.

- *Reload configuration from disk*: The Jenkins configuration files exist on your filesystem and can be modified directly. If you choose to go this route, the reload option will force Jenkins to read these files and apply the new settings to the system.

- *Manage plug-ins*: Jenkins' extensibility is perhaps its most powerful aspect. There are many plug-ins available to add support for various platforms, languages, and version control systems. In addition, there are plug-ins that add new forms of notifications: Jabber, Skype, Twitter, etc. The Plug-in Management page allows you to update, find, install, and remove plug-ins. Make sure to check out the infamous Chuck Norris Plug-in.

▓ *System information*: The System Information page lists basic system info, as well as installed plug-ins and environment variables.

▓ *System Log*: You can configure the types of data that are logged in the System Log page. You can also group and filter log data in individual Loggers.

▓ *Load statistics*: As the number of jobs increases, Jenkins' load will increase as well, and monitoring performance will become more important. The Load Statistics page gives you a nice chart to see your system's peaks and valleys.

▓ *Jenkins CLI*: Yes, Jenkins can be operated from the command line. This is largely unnecessary but can be handy in more complex systems. This interface is also made available through several chat plug-ins (Jabber, Skype, etc).

▓ *Script console*: Jenkins supports a scripting language called Groovy, and this console gives you access to the Groovy interface. You can learn more about Groovy at `http://groovy.codehaus.org`.

▓ *Manage nodes*: Jenkins allows for distributed building through the use of nodes. If you have multiple Jenkins instances on your network, you can link them here.

▓ *About Jenkins*: The About page provides information regarding all of the frameworks (and related licenses) used to build Jenkins.

▓ *Prepare for shutdown*: Job builds can be triggered by a variety of events, so it can be difficult to predict when a job will begin. It's important not to interrupt these jobs, so it's highly recommended that you prepare Jenkins to shutdown before turning off the computer. This will prevent new jobs from beginning and allow you to shut down without risking damage to your project workspaces.

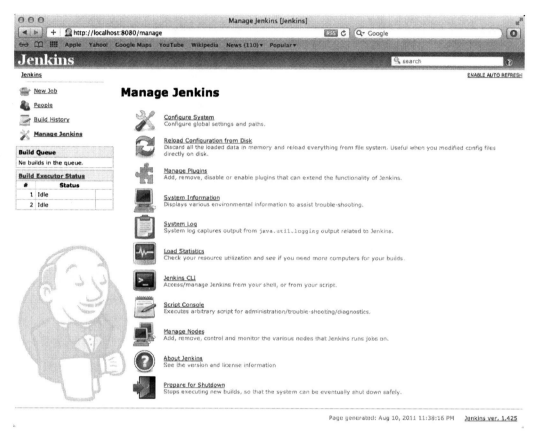

Figure 9–3. *The Management page is the hub for all things Jenkins configuration.*

Before you set up your first job, you need to add a few convenient environment variables and plug-ins. Let's start with the environment variables. Click on the Configure System link on the Management page. On the Configure System page, click the Environment variables checkbox under the Global properties heading (Figure 9–4). This will reveal a key-value pair list, which should be empty. Click the Add button to add a new key-value pair. The environment variables you set here (the keys) will be expanded (into their values) anywhere they're used in your job configuration. This is a great place to put system-wide settings like a final publish directory, web server address, or SDK path. Table 9–1 presents a list of environment variable suggestions.

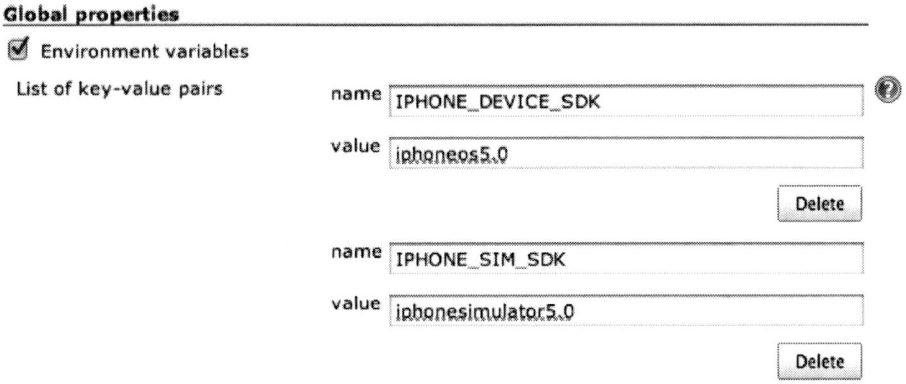

Global properties

☑ Environment variables

List of key-value pairs

name IPHONE_DEVICE_SDK

value iphoneos5.0

[Delete]

name IPHONE_SIM_SDK

value iphonesimulator5.0

[Delete]

Figure 9–4. *It's a good idea to contain any SDK-related arguments in environment variables, so that you can change them all in one place.*

Table 9–1. *Environment Variables*

Environment Variable	le Value
IPHONE_DEVICE_SDK	Iphoneos5.0
IPHONE_SIM_SDK	Iphonesimulator5.0
XCODE_STABLE	/Developer
XCODE_BETA	/Developer_Beta
NIGHTLY_SERVER_FTP	`ftp://nightlies.server.com`

For now, make sure you at least have the SDK variables set. You'll be adding more later when you get to automated deployment. Click the Save button at the bottom of the page when you're done to ensure that the changes stick.

Next, you need to install a few important plug-ins to enable Jenkins to build your project. First, you're going to need the Git plug-in. From the Manage Jenkins page, click on the Manage Plug-ins link. On the Plug-in Management page, jump to the Available tab. The easiest way to find specific plug-ins on this page is to use your browser's Find function (Control+F in most browsers). Once you've found the Git plug-in, check the box on the left to mark it for installation. Note that there are several Git-related plug-ins, including a GitHub plug-in. These may be useful to you but are not required to get your job running. Make sure you've selected the Git plug-in before continuing.

At the bottom of the page is the Install button. When you click this, you'll be presented with the plug-in installation status page (Figure 9–5), which will notify you of the installation progress. You'll need to restart Jenkins in order for the plug-ins to take effect, so check the "Restart Jenkins when installation is complete and no jobs are running" checkbox to ensure Jenkins restarts when they're finished.

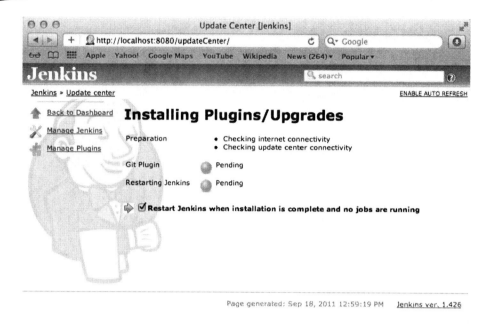

Figure 9–5. *Plug-in installation is easy, but make sure you restart Jenkins before configuring any plug-ins.*

Once your plug-ins are installed and Jenkins is restarted, you're ready to set up your first job. First, however, you need to ensure you have Jenkins running under the right user with the rights to check out from your repository.

Whenever you install a new plug-in, the plug-in's configuration options will be added to the Configure System page. Github requires that users identify themselves before using any repository, so you need to provide a name and e-mail address to the plug-in. From the Dashboard, click Manage Jenkins and then Configure System. Scroll down to the Git Plug-in section and add the name and e-mail address you'd like to be associated with Jenkins. Don't forget to click the Save button at the bottom of the page.

Exorcising Jenkins' Daemon

You're going to set up your Super Checkout job, which is hosted at Github. The Git plug-in adds support for Git as a version control system (VCS) in Jenkins, but since Github requires SSH auth keys, Jenkins isn't going to be able to communicate with it just yet, as it's run by a hidden user named daemon. In order to enable SSH keys, you'll need to replace this user with your own (which you set up prior to installation). Alternatively, you could simply use Git over HTTPS, but that wouldn't be as fast.

Getting Jenkins to use your custom user is fairly easy. First, you need to shut Jenkins down. Even if you haven't gotten any jobs set up, it's a good idea to get in the habit of notifying Jenkins that it's about to go down, so start by going to the Jenkins dashboard in your browser. From the sidebar, click Manage Jenkins, then click Prepare for Shutdown at the bottom of the page.

With Jenkins ready to shutdown, open up the terminal. You need to shut down the Jenkins daemon entirely. The right way to do this is to unload it using launchctl, which can be used to load and unload daemons by specifying their configuration plist. The configuration plist contains information about how launchctl should run the daemon, including what user it should be spawned from. Once the Jenkins daemon is unloaded, you can tweak the plist to use your SSH-authorized-Apple-certified user, then restart the daemon.

First, unload the Jenkins daemon, like so:

```
sudo launchctl unload -w /Library/LaunchDaemons/org.jenkins-ci.plist
```

Before you do anything to the plist itself, you need to save a backup of it.

```
cp /Library/LaunchDaemons/org.jenkins-ci.plist ~/Desktop/org.jenkins-ci_backup.plist
```

Next, open the plist in your terminal editor of choice. It's a plist, so the format should look pretty familiar. This is a simple edit, but if you're not too familiar with the terminal, it might make sense to use something like nano to do the editing.

```
sudo nano /Library/LaunchDaemons/org.jenkins-ci.plist
```

The key you're interested in is UserName, which will be set to daemon by default. Simply change this value to jenkins (or whatever you named your user account). That segment of the plist should now look like this:

```
<key>UserName</key>
<string>jenkins</string>
```

You can also modify the location in which Jenkins will store its files. It's a great idea to put the Jenkins home directory in /Users/Shared (the default location) so that all users have access to it. The key for this setting is JENKINS_HOME. Whether you change it or not, make sure you note the location, as you'll need to make sure your new user has read-write access to it in a moment. When you're done, save your changes, and close the plist. If you're using nano, this is done by pressing ctrl+X, and then Y at the confirmation dialog.

The last step is to give your new user ownership of the Jenkins home directory (you may need modify this code if your user and Jenkins home directory are different):

```
sudo chown -R jenkins /Users/Shared/Jenkins
```

Now that the daemon's configuration plist reflects your user, who has sufficient access to Github, you can re-launch the daemon.

```
sudo launchctl load -w /Library/LaunchDaemons/org.jenkins-ci.plist
```

Jump back to your browser and reload the Jenkins dashboard. Jenkins should be starting up. To confirm that it's running under the right user, open the Activity Monitor utility (Figure 9–6), and search for a java process running under the jenkins user (or whatever name you chose to give Jenkins) under All Processes.

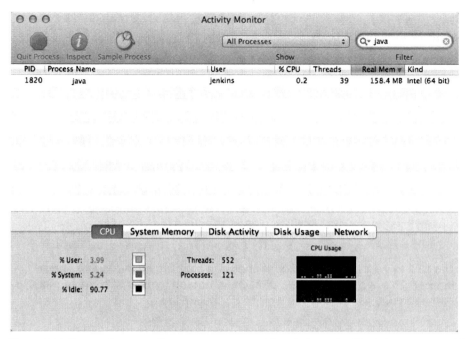

Figure 9–6. *You may have more than one process named java, but you should only have one owned by jenkins.*

Get a Job

In Jenkins, as in many CI systems, a job (also referred to as a project) is a set of build instructions to be executed when a trigger event occurs. This set of instructions commonly includes a fresh checkout or update of the source code from the repository, a fresh build from source, unit testing, static analysis, documentation generation, and deployment. In short, jobs make project builds on triggers.

Triggers are simply events that can be used to start a job. Jenkins supports three types of triggers.

- *Job dependency*: Jobs can be triggered when another job has finished. This is great for cascading a set of jobs when a dependent library is modified.

- *Interval*: Jobs can simply be triggered when a given amount of time has passed. This is great for nightly builds or projects that aren't using source control. But you wouldn't work on a project like that, would you?

- *SCM polling*: This is probably the most useful trigger. Essentially, Jenkins will poll a given repository for updates and trigger a build if any are found. This ensures the build is always made from the bleeding edge codebase and cuts down on the unnecessary builds that can result from using an interval trigger.

So let's get your job set up. First, click the New Job link in the Jenkins sidebar. The job creation page (Figure 9–7) allows you to give your job a name and select the starting point for the project. You're going to focus on the free-style software project option. Once you've got a job in the system, another option will appear at the bottom of this list that will allow you to use an existing job as a template for new jobs.

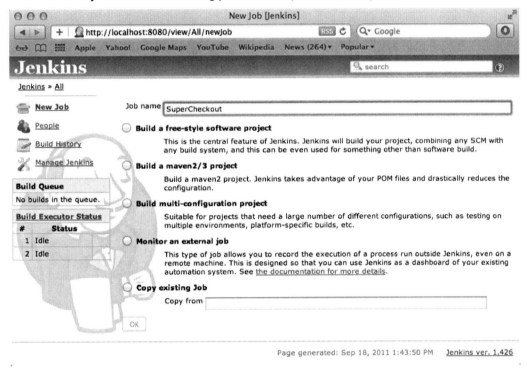

Figure 9–7. *Make sure to give your job a unique and recognizable name, as you may find the dashboard gets cluttered quickly.*

> **CAUTION:** The name of your job will be used to create a directory in the Jenkins home directory, which will house all of the assets and metadata for the project. Due to the way that some plug-ins have been written, it's advisable to avoid spaces or other non-filesystem-friendly characters in your job name.

Once you've named your project, click OK to continue on to the Job Configuration page. The Configuration page lets you manage many aspects of your job, including version control info, triggers, build steps, and build options. Let's go through each of the sections of the Configuration page at a high level.

- *Basic project info*: The topmost section of the page allows you to edit the name and description of the project, as well as some other basic configurations. The Disable Build option allows you to disable the job.

- *Advanced project options*: The advanced options are primarily used in more complex jobs or in jobs for projects that have large teams. The Quiet Period option allows you to prevent Jenkins from building for every VCS commit in a "commit burst," which can often overload the system. It creates a grace period during which it will wait to see if any other commits are processing before building.

- *Source code management*: This is where you select and configure your repository. Out of the box, Jenkins supports a few SCMs, but as you add plug-ins to the system to enable others (Git, for example), they will be added to this list.

- *Build triggers*: As discussed, a job's execution must be triggered by an event. The trigger section allows you to choose which events will execute the job.

- *Build*: This is the meat of the job configuration. It allows you to add build steps to the procedure, which can take many forms. The most common form, at least the form you're going to be most interested in, is the Execute shell build step type (more on that in a moment).

- *Post-build actions*: Once you've got a successful (or unsuccessful) build, you should do something with it. The post-build actions allow you to notify users, publish the build results somewhere, or even kick off another job execution.

Jobs are procedural, so before you start configuring yours, let's think about the steps of execution. First, you're going to want to check out the project from Github. Once Jenkins has a fresh copy of the latest code, you need to build it. Once it's been built, you need to run it through the static analyzer and archive the binary.

Checking out from Github is simple enough to set up, assuming you've got the Git plug-in installed. Simply scroll down to the Source Control Management section (Figure 9–8) of the Configuration page and select the Git radio button. If you've given Jenkins access to SSH keys, you can use the SSH repository URL from Github, which looks something like this:

```
git@github.com:<username>/<ProjectName>.git
```

If you haven't done this or are unable to use SSH, you can use the HTTPS repository URL with basic authentication, which will look something like this:

```
https://<username>:<password>@github.com/<username>/<ProjectName>.git
```

If you're at all familiar with security, you'll see a risk with this situation right away. The username and password for the Github repo will be stored in plain text. This isn't an ideal situation, which is part of the reason you should be going the SSH key route.

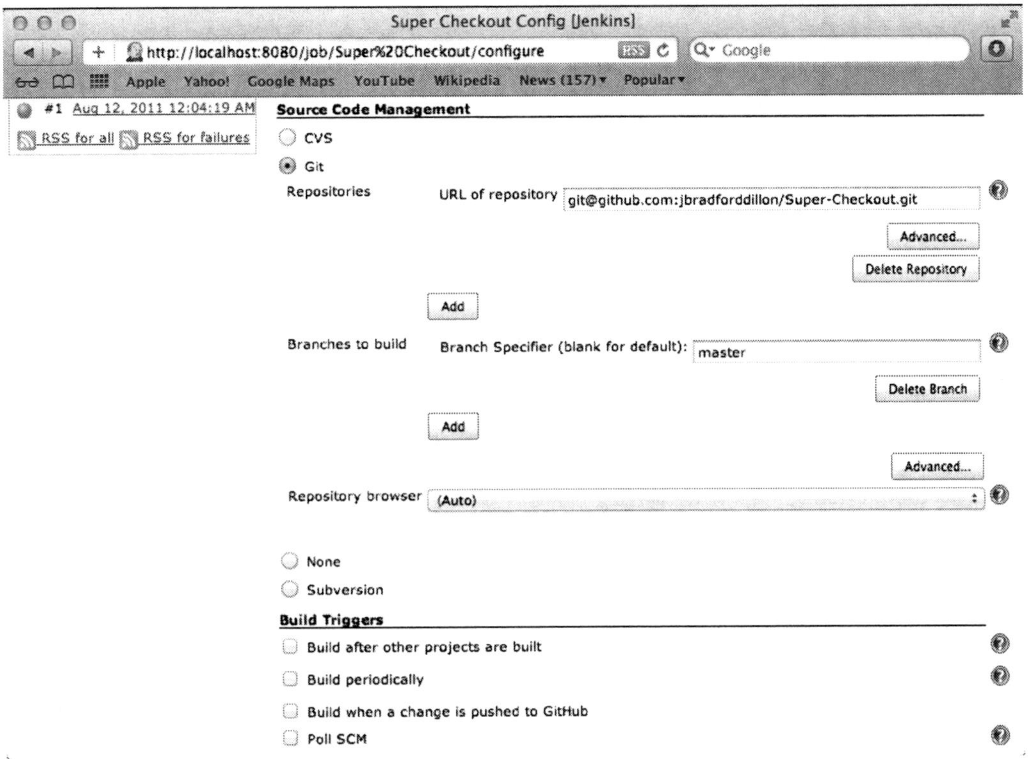

Figure 9–8. *Fortunately, once you've got the Jenkins user sorted out, setting up Git over SSH is easy.*

In addition to the repository URL, the Git plug-in allows you to specify which branch to check out, as well as several other advanced settings.

Once you've got the Git settings plugged in, go ahead and test your job. Scroll to the bottom of the page and click the Save button. This will take you to the Job Details page (Figure 9–9).

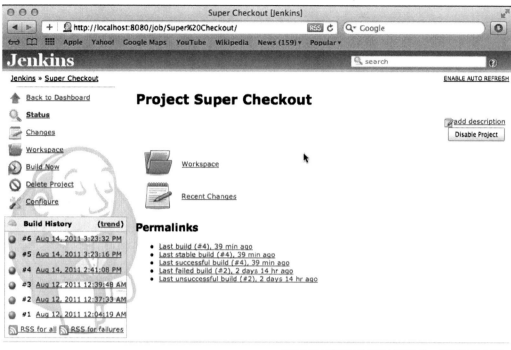

Figure 9–9. *The Job Details page can become an extremely useful tool as your job gets more fleshed out.*

The Job Details page will give you a bird's eye view of the job, its history, and its current products. It has three primary sections: the sidebar, the Build History module, and the Permalinks section. The sidebar offers navigation options similar to what you've seen elsewhere in Jenkins. The Build History module, located below the sidebar, provides links to the most recent job executions. The Permalinks section has some extremely handy links to the most recent successful builds, failed builds, etc.

At the moment, the Details page will probably look pretty stark. In the sidebar, you should see the Build Now link (Figure 9–10), which allows you to manually start a job's execution. Go ahead and click it now to add your job to the build queue. If the queue is clear (which you can assume), the job will build immediately. Of course, "build" is a relative term at the moment, since all your job is set up to do is checkout a working copy of your project.

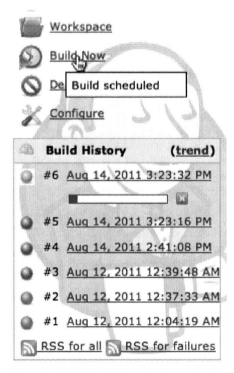

Figure 9–10. *The build status indicators in the build history sidebar module tell you whether previous builds were successful.*

Once your build has finished, click on its link in either the Build History sidebar module or the Permalinks section. This will bring up the Build Details page. Similar to the Job Details page, the Build Details page bubbles up info about a specific build. With the Git plug-in installed, you'll see some data regarding the checkout. If the job was triggered by a SCM poll, the commit message will be printed near the top of the page. In the sidebar, you'll see a few options, including the ability to edit build information. This is useful for indicating a milestone build. There's also a link to the console output for the build. Click on that to review the output for this build. The output should look something like this:

```
Started by user anonymous
Checkout:workspace / /Users/Shared/Jenkins/Home/jobs/Super Checkout/workspace -
hudson.remoting.LocalChannel@56de24c5
Using strategy: Default
Last Built Revision: Revision 6eaa5c595fa51a898434f5d300f4a49712f567b4 (origin/master)
Checkout:workspace / /Users/Shared/Jenkins/Home/jobs/Super Checkout/workspace -
hudson.remoting.LocalChannel@56de24c5
Fetching changes from 1 remote Git repository
Fetching upstream changes from git@github.com:jbradforddillon/Super-Checkout.git
Commencing build of Revision 6eaa5c595fa51a898434f5d300f4a49712f567b4 (origin/master)
Checking out Revision 6eaa5c595fa51a898434f5d300f4a49712f567b4 (origin/master)
Finished: SUCCESS
```

The Console Output page is extremely useful for debugging a job. If you entered the Git repo information incorrectly, for example, the console will display information about the failed checkout, and you can determine the cause.

Now that you've got a working Github checkout, let's finish configuring the job. Head back to the Job Details page and click the Configure link. On the Job Configuration page, scroll down to the Build Triggers section (Figure 9–11).

Being based on your Github project, this job should be built every time a change is made to the master branch. So, an SCM polling trigger is just what the doctor ordered. Clicking the Poll SCM checkbox will display the Schedule textbox where you can tell Jenkins how often to poll the repo for changes. When changes are found during an interval, the build will be triggered.

The polling schedule is essentially a CRON expression. The input consists of five fields: minute, hour, day of the month, month, day of the week. An asterisk is a wildcard, which means all values are valid for that field. There are also several useful directives you can use, including @hourly and @midnight. You want your job to poll Github every five minutes, so your schedule expression will be 5 * * * *

Build Triggers

- [ ] Build after other projects are built
- [ ] Build periodically
- [x] Poll SCM
- Schedule
  ```
  5 * * * *
  ```

Figure 9–11. *The CRON expression format gives you a great deal of control.*

Your trigger is set, so you're ready to set up your build steps. As always, don't forget to save at the bottom of the page.

Scripting Xcode

Xcode comes with a fantastic command line interface: xcodebuild. The xcodebuild tool searches the current path for an Xcode project file, reads the configuration, and compiles the project. It also allows you to override any and all configurations and compiler flags from the command line. Essentially, anything you can do in Xcode related to compiling code, you can do from the command line with xcodebuild. Since Jenkins works well with shell scripting, xcodebuild will manage your compilation during your job execution.

Before going in depth on xcodebuild, let's see it in action. Open up a terminal window and run the following commands:

```
cd <PATH/TO/SUPER/CHECKOUT>
xcodebuild -sdk iphonesimulator5.0 -configuration Debug
```

Next, you should see the raw compiler output as xcodebuild works its magic. It should look something similar to this:

```
Build settings from command line:
    SDKROOT = iphonesimulator5.0

=== BUILD NATIVE TARGET Super Checkout OF PROJECT Super Checkout WITH CONFIGURATION
Debug ===
Check dependencies
<LOTS OF OUTPUT WHILE EACH FILE IS COMPILED AND LINKED>

** BUILD SUCCEEDED **
```

If there were any errors during compilation, you'd see them in the terminal, exactly like you would in Xcode. If your build resulted in any warnings, you could scroll through the compiler output and find them, exactly like you would in Xcode.

xcodebuild has several option flags, which give you control over the build process. Here are a few of the important ones:

- -project: This flag allows you to specify the project to build, relative to the current directory. Specifically, you provide the full name of your xcodeproj file. If this flag is not provided, xcodebuild will look for a project in the current directory. If multiple projects (or workspaces) are found, it will fail and will list them for you.

- -target: This flag allows you to specify which target to build. This is extremely handy when working with complex projects or when publishing milestone builds (like a nightly, for example).

- -workspace: In addition to traditional project files, xcodebuild will look for workspace files and parse their schemes and settings. Use this flag to specify the workspace you want to build.

- -scheme: If building a workspace, this flag specifies a scheme. It's important to note that targets and workspaces don't mix, just as schemes and projects don't. Use the right flag combination.

- -sdk: This flag allows you to choose which SDK to compile against. Typically, you use this to distinguish between a simulator build and a device build.

- -configuration: Most targets have at least two configurations: Debug and Release. The configuration flag lets you choose which configuration you want to build, by name. The default configuration to be used by xcodebuild can be specified in Xcode, under the Info tab of the Project Details view.

- -showsdks: You can find out what SDKs are available, as well as what xcodebuild calls them by using this flag.

- Others: There are several other flags and options. You can learn more about them by viewing the main page for xcodebuild.

In addition to these flags, you can append any additional compiler flags or settings you want. Here's an example of using these basic flags:

```
$ xcodebuild -project MyAppProject -target MyApp -sdk iphone5.0 -configuration Release
```

This example would build the MyApp target of the MyAppProject Xcode project against the iOS 5.0 SDK for device, using the Release configuration. Whatever settings relate to the Release configuration in the Xcode project will be applied to the build during compilation. If you wanted to add a compiler flag, you could simply append it to the command like this:

```
$ xcodebuild -target MyAppTarget -sdk iphone5.0 SOME_COMPILER_FLAG=1 ANOTHER_FLAG=0
```

xcodebuild can do more than simply build your project, though that is the default behavior. It has several functions, including build, clean, and archive. To specify the function, simply include it in the flags. In order to clean your project, you can simply call

```
$ xcodebuild -target MyAppTarget clean
```

They can also be chained together. So, to clean a project and then archive it (which implies building it), you can call

```
$ xcodebuild -target MyAppTarget clean archive
```

Now you've got a good understanding of xcodebuild. It's an extremely powerful tool, and it's unusually easy to use for a command line interface. You're ready to write your Jenkins build step.

Open up your Jenkins build job configuration page and scroll down to the Build section. This is where you customize the build process. You need to add a build step that runs the xcodebuild command from the shell. Simply click the Add build step button and select Execute shell from the drop-down to insert a new shell step.

In the Command text area, enter an xcodebuild command suitable for your project (Figure 9–12). For Super Checkout, the shell command is as simple as the following (note the use of the environment variable you set up earlier):

```
xcodebuild -sdk $IPHONE_DEVICE_SDK
```

Figure 9–12. *You can get a full list of built-in environment variables by clicking the link below the text area.*

This will cause xcodebuild to find the single project in your repository, select the single app target in the project, and use the default command-line configuration (Release) to build. The only thing you're specifying is the SDK to be used. If your project were much more complex, or if your repository contained more than one project, the build command would be a bit more complex.

After you've entered your xcodebuild command, scroll to the bottom of the page and click Save. From the Job Details page, click Build Now to start a build of your project. Jenkins will first checkout or update the working copy of your project from the repository, then run your xcodebuild command. If everything is as it should be, the project should build successfully, and your new build will have a blue indicator icon next to it.

> **NOTE:** Depending on your system's configuration, your first build using xcodebuild against a device SDK may require you to give xcodebuild and codesign permission to use the keychain. If this is the case, your build will stall. Simply log into the build server as the Jenkins user you created during setup and run the build again. You should see a permission dialog with the option to always allow access to the keychain. Once you've done this, you'll be good to go.

This is great! You've automated builds, and it wasn't that painful. But all you're doing is building the source. This is handy for integration with large teams, but it isn't all that powerful. What you really need is to get some hard data about the quality of the code. You need accountability. You need failure notifications and static analysis.

Who Broke the Build?

Notifications are a simple way to ensure everyone is aware of the current state of the code. It's also an effective means to ensure people aren't checking in bad code. If Johnny Sigabort checks in a completed feature, Jenkins will kick off a build. If the build fails, a notification will go out to a predefined list of people (usually the whole development team) to announce that Johnny's commit broke the build, along with a link to the detailed build results. After Johnny is shamed into cleaning up his own negligence, another notification can be sent out to let the team know that the build has been restored.

Setting up notifications is dead simple and highly extensible. There are a variety of plug-ins available to broadcast build failure notifications over a wide range of mediums. You can even tweet build results if you want to be that transparent about your progress (or if you want to step up Johnny's shame).

The standard and built-in notification type is e-mail. To enable e-mail notifications, you first have to configure the mail server information. Head over to the System Configuration page in the Manage Jenkins section and scroll down to the E-mail Notification section (Figure 9–13). In the fields provided, you can specify you mail server's settings.

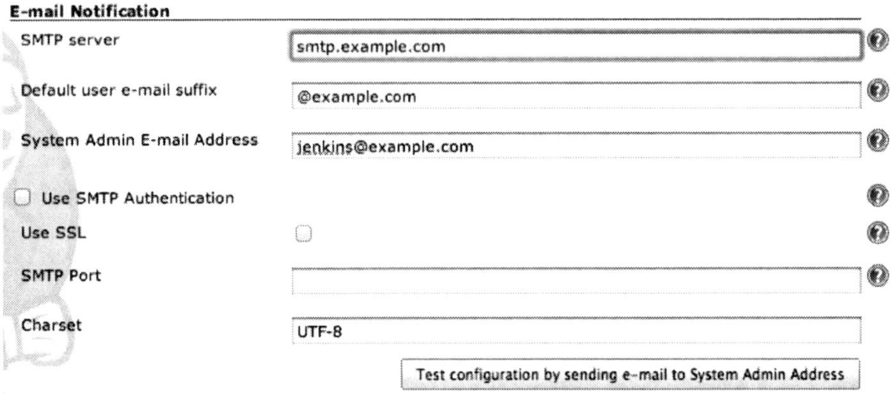

E-mail Notification

SMTP server	`smtp.example.com`
Default user e-mail suffix	`@example.com`
System Admin E-mail Address	`jenkins@example.com`
☐ Use SMTP Authentication	
Use SSL	☐
SMTP Port	
Charset	`UTF-8`

Test configuration by sending e-mail to System Admin Address

Figure 9–13. *Your system may require a real account for Jenkins, lest all notifications go into a spam bin.*

Once you've enabled e-mail, you can set up the notification. Go back to your Job Configuration page and scroll down to the Post-build actions section. Check the E-mail Notification box to reveal the notification settings form (Figure 9–14). Enter your team's e-mail addresses in the Recipients field, and check the unstable build checkbox. Click the Save button, and you're done!

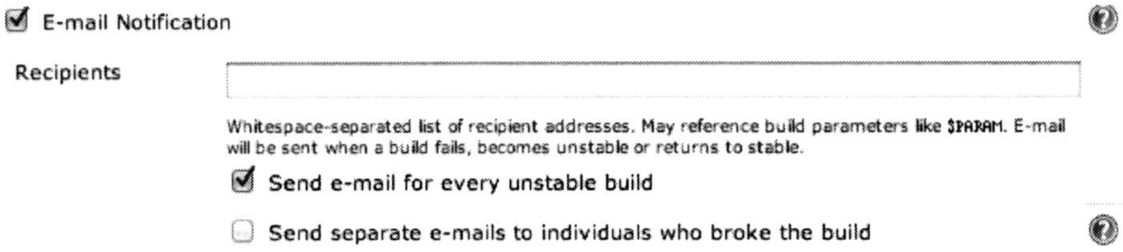

☑ E-mail Notification

Recipients

Whitespace-separated list of recipient addresses. May reference build parameters like $PARAM. E-mail will be sent when a build fails, becomes unstable or returns to stable.

☑ Send e-mail for every unstable build

☐ Send separate e-mails to individuals who broke the build

Figure 9–14. *You can configure e-mail notifications for individuals or mailing lists.*

Quality, Controlled

As any good developer knows, a successful build doesn't mean the code is good. That's why there are tools like the static analyzer to find any gotchas for us. Xcode projects can be configured to run static analysis during compilation, which is fantastic when building within Xcode itself. However, in order to do something meaningful with the analysis findings, you need help from a couple of tools. First, you need to get your own copy of the LLVM foundation's scan-build CLI, so that you can extract the results of the build and present them in a more human-friendly way. Second, you need to install the Clang Scan-Build plug-in in Jenkins, which will add a new type of build step to your jobs and manage the scan-build results for you.

The Clang Static Analyzer tools are available from the LLVM foundation's web site at `http://clang-analyzer.llvm.org` (Figure 9–15). Scan-build is an extremely powerful command line tool that wraps around a call to xcodebuild and extracts static analysis results, generating reports in both plist and (using the included scan-view tool) HTML form. To use the tools, simply download and extract the latest tarball. They can be run from anywhere, but in order to be run within Jenkins, they need to be placed somewhere that your Jenkins user can access. For now, let's place the extracted folder in the Jenkins user's home directory and rename it "static-analyzer."

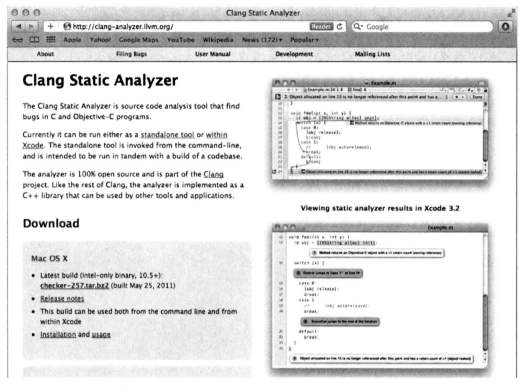

Figure 9–15. *The LLVM site has a wealth of information on the compiler, analyzer, and associated tools.*

The scan-build command itself is an extremely simple tool, similar to xcodebuild. It has a variety of flags to allow for deep customization and configuration, and it also requires an xcodebuild call as its input. To learn more about the flags you can use to customize the results, simply execute the scan-build script from the terminal to see the usage content. For your purposes within Jenkins, you don't need to worry about these flags, as they'll be handled by the build step plug-in.

For now, to see the scan-build script in action, pop open terminal and navigate to directory containing an Xcode project (and an xcodeproj file). From there, simply execute an xcodebuild command, prepended by the path to scan-build, like so:

```
/path/to/static-analyzer/scan-build xcodebuild -sdk iphonesimulator5.0
```

You should see the normal xcodebuild output, followed by the output from scan-build. It should look something like this:

```
scan-build: 2 bugs found.
scan-build: Run 'scan-view /var/folders/pz/k88r03q535g2ztqwgb52bv4c0000gq/T/scan-build-
2011-08-21-1' to examine bug reports.
```

Executing the command in single quotes (starting with 'scan-view') will launch your web browser and point it at 127.0.0.1:8181, which will serve up the static analysis results (Figure 9–16) until you stop scan-view by pressing Ctrl+C in the terminal window.

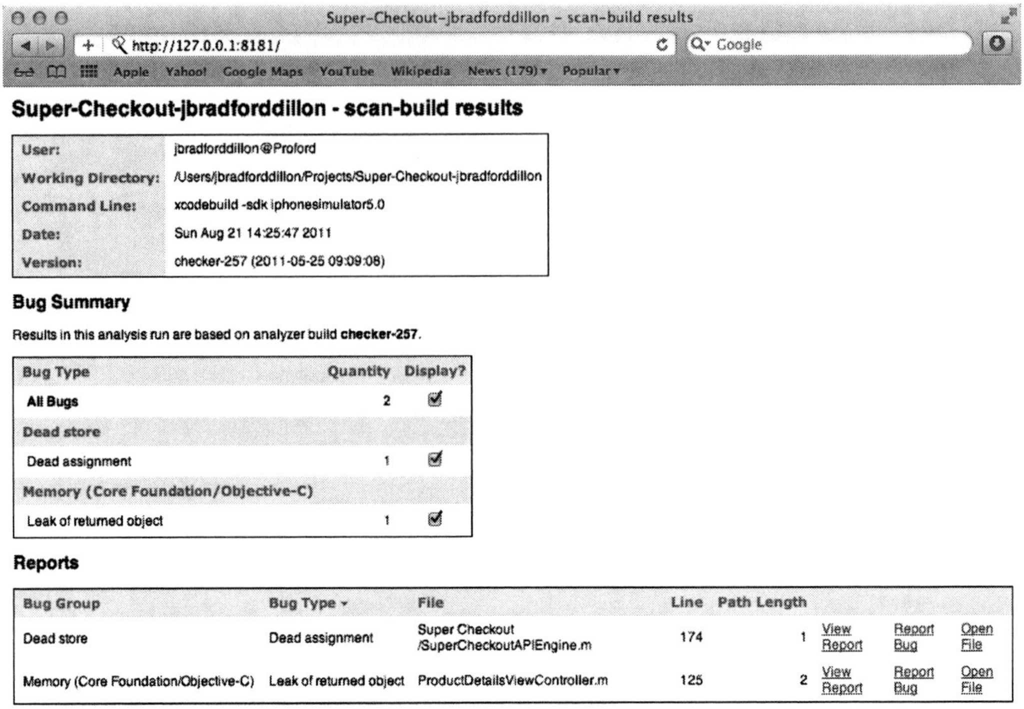

Figure 9–16. *The static analyzer's results page provides a great summary of the findings.*

Now that you've got your own static analyzer, let's get the Jenkins plug-in set up. From the Jenkins Management page, open the Manage Plug-ins page. Open the Available tab, look for the Clang Scan-Build Plug-in. As with the Git plug-in, it'll probably be easiest to hit Command+F and search the page for "Clang." Check the plug-in's checkbox and click the Install button at the bottom of the page. Make sure you remember to restart Jenkins after the plug-in is installed.

With the plug-in installed, head over to the Configure System page and scroll down to the Clang Static Analyzer section to configure the plug-in (Figure 9–17). The Clang plug-in needs to know the location of your copy of the static analyzer tools. Click the Add Clang Static Analyzer button to reveal the form. The plug-in allows you to add multiple versions of the toolset, which comes in handy when working with beta toolsets. We'll talk more about that in a moment, but for now, give the toolset a name and enter the absolute path to the scan-build script, then save your configuration and head over to your build job.

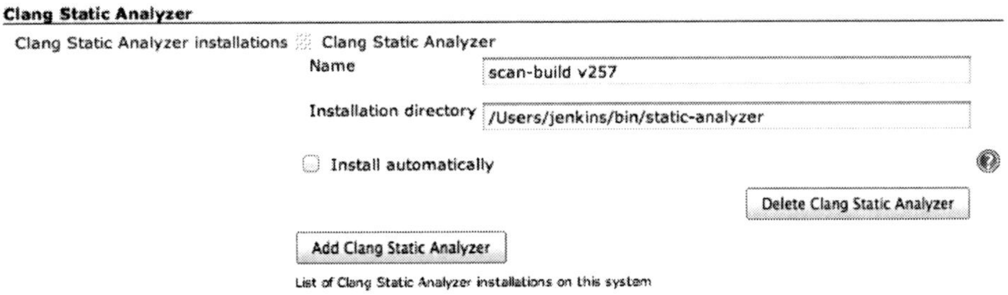

Clang Static Analyzer

Clang Static Analyzer installations   Clang Static Analyzer

Name   scan-build v257

Installation directory   /Users/jenkins/bin/static-analyzer

☐ Install automatically

Delete Clang Static Analyzer

Add Clang Static Analyzer

List of Clang Static Analyzer installations on this system

Figure 9–17. *It's a good idea to give the analyzer a name that reflects its version number*

In the Job Configuration screen, you need to add a new build step. The Clang Scan-Build option has been added to the Add build step drop-down menu, so select that to create a new static analysis step (Figure 9–18). Specify the target (or workspace and scheme) that needs to be built. In the advanced options, you can also choose which analyzer to use, what configuration send to xcodebuild, as well as which SDK to use.

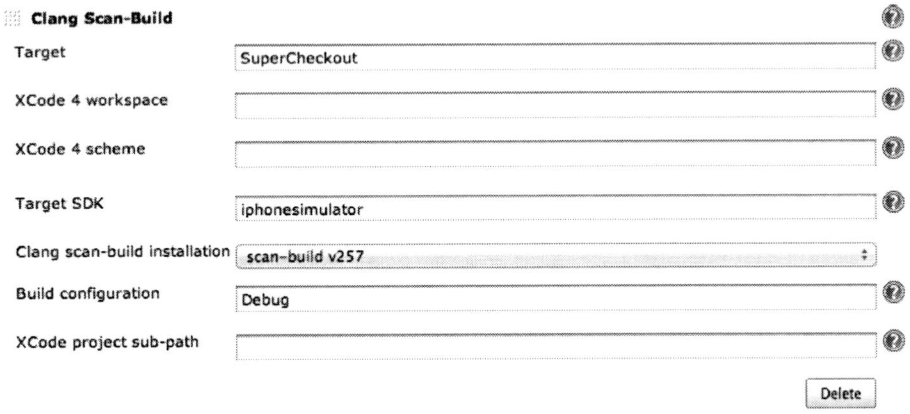

Clang Scan-Build

Target   SuperCheckout

XCode 4 workspace

XCode 4 scheme

Target SDK   iphonesimulator

Clang scan-build installation   scan-build v257

Build configuration   Debug

XCode project sub-path

Delete

Figure 9–18. *Ensure that you are using a debug configuration, as you'll want the debug symbols in tact.*

> **NOTE:** Similar to whitespace in job names, the Clang Scan-Build plug-in doesn't escape whitespace in target names, so you'll need to rename targets like "Super Checkout" to "SuperCheckout," as shown in Figure 9–18.

Once you've got the build step configured, you need to tell the plug-in to publish the results so that you can see the status of your codebase at a glance. In the Post-build Actions section you'll see a checkbox marked "Publish Clang Scan-Build Results." Checking this box will tell the plug-in to publish a nice chart of your project's aggregate analysis results on the Job Details page and will also reveal another checkbox labeled "Mark build as unstable when threshold is exceeded?" This feature, coupled with the e-mail notifications you set up earlier, provides an invaluable means to keep track of code quality. When Johnny Sigabort's build is completed, if the number of bugs reported by the static analyzer is higher than a threshold you specify, the build will be marked as unstable, which will trigger e-mail notification action, and the team will be notified that Friday night's drinks are all on Johnny.

Once the build step is configured and the post-build action is enabled, save the job configuration and fire off a build. When the build is finished, refresh the Job Details page to reveal a chart (Figure 9–19) on the right-hand side, depicting the number of analyzer warnings over time. It will be pretty empty at the moment.

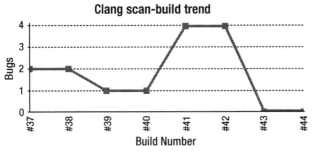

enlarge

Figure 9–19. *This chart shows a project that has (finally) gotten back on track*

Open the results of the build that just finished by either clicking its link in the Build History sidebar or by clicking the right point in the chart. In the Build Results page, you'll see a few new features added by the static analysis plug-in. Note that in order to see these features in their full effect, your project needs to have some bugs. This might be the only time you'll ever benefit from introducing bugs into your project, so just go nuts. In the Summary section, there will be a new data point that lists the number of bugs found by the analysis, with a link to the details. These details are also linked to in the sidebar. Click on one of those links to see the bug report for the build (Figure 9–20).

Clang scan-build bug report for build #42

File	Bug Type	Category	Description	
/Super Checkout/SuperCheckoutAPIEngine.m	Dead assignment	Dead store	Value stored to 'contentType' is never read	Details
/Super Checkout/../ProductDetailsViewController.m	Leak of returned object	Memory (Core Foundation/Objective-C)	Potential leak of an object allocated on line 127	Details
/Super Checkout/../ProductDetailsViewController.m	Leak of returned object	Memory (Core Foundation/Objective-C)	Potential leak of an object allocated on line 127 and stored into 'leak'	Details
/Super Checkout/../ProductDetailsViewController.m	Dead initialization	Dead store	Value stored to 'leak' during its initialization is never read	Details

Figure 9–20. *Something is horribly wrong with line 127 of the ProductDetailsViewController!*

Clicking on the Details link for one of these bugs will open the same HTML view you get when running scan-view (Figure 9–21).

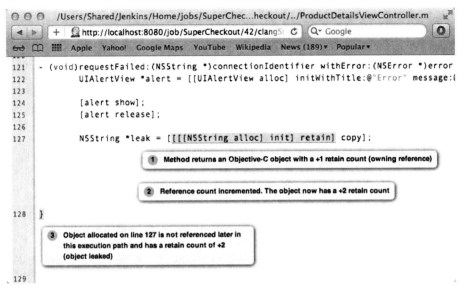

Figure 9–21. *Oh, Johnny, what have you done now?*

So there you have it: automated builds, static analysis, and e-mail notifications to promote good code quality and accountability. In addition, your app is being built for distribution in a central, accessible location, so you can stop playing hot potato with certificates. But wouldn't it be great to be able to distribute builds to your beta testers on a regular basis?

Distribution Made Easier

In order to get your app in the hands of your beta testers, you need to build an archive of your project (an IPA file), with a copy of your provisioning profile included, to allow you to use iOS's OTA distribution method. To do this, you have some options. If you are working with an Xcode 4 workspace, you can simply uses xcodebuild's archive action. However, if you're building a simple project, you're going to have to make the archive yourself. This isn't very hard, and in fact, the developer toolset comes with a very handy interface for doing this: the PackageApplication command. PackageApplication performs all the tasks necessary to convert an application bundle (MyApp.app) into an application archive (MyApp.ipa), with all of the necessary provisioning embedded within.

Before you can do anything to your application bundle, you need access to it. In the dark days before Xcode 4, build products were stored relative to the project in a Build folder. This meant that, from within Jenkins, you simply needed to perform your distribution scripts in $WORKSPACE/Build. When working with an Xcode 4 workspace, however, the Build folder will be placed in the Derived Data folder, and it won't be as easy to find. One way to get to the app bundle in those cases is to use compiler flags to tell xcodebuild where to put the app, such as

```
xcodebuild -sdk iphoneos -configuration Release DSTROOT=/Users/Shared/JenkinsProducts
DEPLOYMENT_LOCATION=YES
```

The DSTROOT compiler flag points to the path containing the Applications folder where the app bundle should be placed after compilation. This is typically used in Mac development, and it points to the root of your filesystem by default, placing built products in /Applications. By pointing to a JenkinsProducts folder, the app bundle will be placed at

```
/Users/Shared/JenkinsProducts/Applications/MyApp.app
```

The DEPLOYMENT_LOCATION flag simply tells xcodebuild to "install" the app bundle in the location specified in DSTROOT, which it wouldn't ordinarily do with an iOS app.

Now that you've got access to your built product, be it in your relative build folder or an installation folder, you're almost ready to package it up. The last ingredient in the app archive is the provisioning profile. You're going to need the absolute path to the profile. Xcode is currently managing your profiles and storing them in the user's Library folder (which means that your Jenkins user has her own set of provisioning profiles, as you may remember from earlier). You could simply use the paths to these profiles, but if you look in the folder, you'll find that they've been renamed to their Profile Identifier, which is unbelievably unmanageable.

```
ls ~/Library/MobileDevice/Provisioning\ Profiles
685FDD6E-5555-4402-BFCC-62F1064EFF2F.mobileprovision
```

What you should do, instead, is export the profiles to an accessible location where you can manage them yourself. From the Organizer in Xcode, select the provisioning profile you want to export and click the Export button at the bottom of the window. Place the profile somewhere that Jenkins can access. Let's use /Users/Shared/JenkinsProvisioning/. Be sure to name the profile something descriptive.

Once you've got the profile in place, you can finally package up your app for distribution. Jump into your Job Configuration in Jenkins, and add a new shell script build step.

Wherefore Art Thou, PackageApplication?

The PackageApplication script is specific to the SDK you're building with. As such, you need to ensure you're using the right one. If you try to use it from the terminal, you'll find that it's not in your path, and it's not in /usr/bin with all the other Xcode command line tools. PackageApplication is stored in the SDK itself. For example, the current iOS device SDK version of PackageApplication will be located here:

```
/Developer/Platforms/iPhoneOS.platform/Developer/usr/bin/PackageApplication
```

However, if you're using a beta SDK with your existing toolset, it might be located elsewhere. Also, it could be moved as the tools are updated. Thus, you need a way to use PackageApplication by simply specifying the SDK. Fortunately, there's a command line interface for that, too!

XCRun

The xcrun command, which is found in /usr/bin and therefore should be in your path, is used to find and execute commands that are part of the Xcode command line toolset. You can use it to find xcodebuild, PackageApplication, and many other tools. The unique thing about xcrun is that it allows you to specify the SDK version of the command you're looking for. Also worth noting, xcrun doesn't just tell you the path to the command (though it can do that as well, with the -find flag), it invokes it as well. Here's an example of a basic xcrun command:

```
xcrun -sdk iphoneos xcodebuild -target MyTarget -configuration Debug
```

This will find the xcodebuild command compatible with iOS5 and invoke it with the specified -target and -configuration flags.

> **NOTE:** In recent versions of the toolset, it's become a standard practice to refer to the latest SDK by simply leaving off the version number, thus "iphoneos" and "iphonesimulator" will default to the latest version available on your system. However, when writing build scripts that will stand the test of time, it's a good idea to be specific, using additional scripts to test against new or beta SDKs.

Just Archive it, Already

Now that you've got an easy way to get to PackageApplication, you need to learn to use it. PackageApplication takes the path to an application bundle (ending in .app), an output path, and an optional provisioning profile path. It can also re-codesign an application by passing an optional codesign identity flag.

So let's get this working in your Jenkins job. Back in the Job Configuration page, in your new, empty build step, execute this shell command. You'll notice that you've taken the additional step of putting your JenkinsProducts path in an environment variable. Also, the output directory is relative to the job workspace (in an Archive directory that you're creating). This makes publishing the finished product a bit easier and keeps all the files related to this job in one place.

```
mkdir -p $WORKSPACE/archive
xcrun -sdk iphoneos5.0 PackageApplication -v $PRODUCTS/Applications/SuperCheckout.app -o
$WORKSPACE/archive/SuperCheckout.ipa --embed /Users/jenkins/Provisioning\
Profiles/SuperCheckout.mobileprovision
```

Now that you've got your archive script in place, you can publish the IPA. This will place a link to the latest stable IPA to your Job Details page. Anyone who needs to grab the latest and greatest can simply open the job and click the link to download it. Scroll down to the Post-Build Actions section and check the box marked "Archive the artifacts." Enter the path to the IPA file, relative to the workspace.

```
archive/SuperCheckout.ipa
```

> **NOTE:** When entering paths to files in a job configurations, Jenkins will try to find the file or folder as you type. You may see warnings about a file or folder not existing. Simply double-check that your paths are correct, and ignore the warnings.

Now save and build! When all is said and done, you should have a link to a successfully archived app in your Job Details page (Figure 9–22), along with the static analysis records. Jenkins is starting to pull its weight in your workflow!

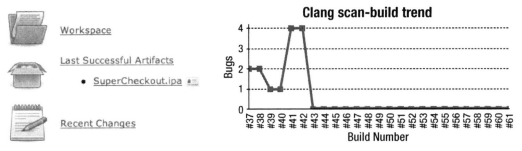

Figure 9–22. *The IPA file here can be downloaded by anyone who has access to Jenkins.*

Exporting Beyond Jenkins

Having the IPA on the Job Details page is useful, but it doesn't exactly solve the problem you set out with. You need to enable over-the-air (OTA) distribution so that your beta testers can quickly and easily get up and running with new updates without the hassle of dealing with provisioning profiles, iTunes, iPhone Configuration Utility, etc.

The ingredients for enabling OTA distribution are fairly simple to whip together. You'll need a manifest property list and a link to the manifest that uses the built in installation URL scheme. This prompts the system to read the manifest and trigger the installation process.

Here's a sample manifest:

```
<?xml version="1.0"?>
<!DOCTYPE plist PUBLIC "-//Apple//DTD PLIST 1.0//EN"
"http://www.apple.com/DTDs/PropertyList-1.0.dtd">
<plist version="1.0">
  <dict>
    <!-- array of downloads. -->
    <key>items</key>
    <array>
      <dict>
        <!-- an array of assets to download -->
        <key>assets</key>
        <array>
          <!-- software-package: the ipa to install. -->
          <dict>
            <!-- required.  the asset kind. -->
            <key>kind</key>
```

```
      <string>software-package</string>
      <!-- optional.  md5 every n bytes.  will restart a chunk if md5 fails. -->
      <key>md5-size</key>
      <integer>10485760</integer>
      <!-- optional.  array of md5 hashes for each "md5-size" sized chunk. -->
      <key>md5s</key>
      <array>
        <string>41fa64bb7a7cae5a46bfb45821ac8bba</string>
        <string>51fa64bb7a7cae5a46bfb45821ac8bba</string>
      </array>
      <!-- required.  the URL of the file to download. -->
      <key>url</key>
      <string>http://www.example.com/apps/foo.ipa</string>
    </dict>
    <!-- display-image: the icon to display during download .-->
    <dict>
      <key>kind</key>
      <string>display-image</string>
      <!-- optional.  indicates if icon needs shine effect applied. -->
      <key>needs-shine</key>
      <true/>
      <key>url</key>
      <string>http://www.example.com/image.57x57.png</string>
    </dict>
    <!-- full-size-image: the large 512x512 icon used by iTunes. -->
    <dict>
      <key>kind</key>
      <string>full-size-image</string>
      <!-- optional.  one md5 hash for the entire file. -->
      <key>md5</key>
      <string>61fa64bb7a7cae5a46bfb45821ac8bba</string>
      <key>needs-shine</key>
      <true/>
      <key>url</key>
      <string>http://www.example.com/image.512x512.jpg</string>
    </dict>
  </array>
  <key>metadata</key>
  <dict>
    <!-- required -->
    <key>bundle-identifier</key>
    <string>com.example.fooapp</string>
    <!-- optional (software only) -->
    <key>bundle-version</key>
    <string>1.0</string>
    <!-- required.  the download kind. -->
    <key>kind</key>
    <string>software</string>
    <!-- optional. displayed during download; typically company name -->
    <key>subtitle</key>
    <string>Apple</string>
    <!-- required.  the title to display during the download. -->
    <key>title</key>
    <string>Example Corporate App</string>
  </dict>
</dict>
</array>
```

```
    </dict>
</plist>
```

You can find this manifest and more details in Apple's Enterprise Distribution guide at `http://developer.apple.com/library/ios/#featuredarticles/FA_Wireless_Enterprise _App_Distribution/Introduction/Introduction.html`.

If you take this property list format and modify it to reflect your app's specifics, you can pass the manifest to the system using the built in URL scheme.

`itms-services://?action=download-manifest&url=http://example.com/manifest.plist`

For example, creating an HTML link that will install your app is as simple as

```
<a href="itms-services://?action=download-
manifest&url=http://example.com/manifest.plist">
  Install App
</a>
```

As you can see, once you've got a properly provisioned archive, setting up OTA deployment is extremely simple. It would be fairly simple to create a shell script (or any type of script) that generates the manifest property list for you and publishes a link to install the app.

Can't Someone Else Handle All This?

While Apple makes OTA deployment pretty easy (once you feng shui the archiving), there's plenty of room for improving the process. There are several great organizations out there providing systems to manage the deployment process from simple beta testing to enterprise level distribution. A great option for your Super Checkout beta is Test Flight (`http://testflightapp.com`, Figure 9–23). Test Flight offers fantastic beta app deployment with a great web-based UI to manage your apps and track its installation.

Figure 9-23. *TestFlight has an extremely simple and straightforward distribution method.*

While Test Flight hangs its hat on a simple and beautiful user experience (and rightly so!), it also offers an extremely useful, and equally simple, API for posting new builds and notifying your testers. Once you've set up an account with Test Flight, a Jenkins build step could be created to execute the following shell script (note the use of Jenkins environment variables to add some useful data to the release notes):

```
curl http://testflightapp.com/api/builds.json
  -F file=@SuperCheckout.ipa
  -F api_token='<your_api_token>'
  -F team_token='<your_team_token>'
  -F notes='$JOB_NAME, build number $BUILD_NUMBER: For release notes, visit $BUILD_URL'
  -F notify=True
  -F distribution_lists='Internal, QA'
```

Creating Nightlies

You want to use your deployment build step, but you don't want to inundate the beta testers with a new version after every commit to your repo. It would be much better to deploy a single, nightly build. You've spent so much time carefully crafting your build job, it would be a shame to have to redo all of that. Fortunately, Jenkins allows you to duplicate jobs. More specifically, it allows you to create new jobs using a previous job as a template.

From the Dashboard, click New Job in the sidebar. Give the job a name like "SuperCheckoutNightly" (remember that some plug-ins don't like white space), and select the Copy existing job radio button. As you start typing the job name, Jenkins should make some suggestions. Select your existing job and click OK.

The Job Configuration page for your new job should look pretty familiar. To make it a nightly, you just need to change the Build Triggers. Check the Build periodically checkbox, and uncheck any others. In the Schedule text area, you can simply enter the keyword @midnight.

Once you've converted your new job to a nightly build, you can add your deployment script as a build step at the bottom. You can probably lighten the load on the system by turning off steps like static analysis and post-build notifications.

Futureproofing Your Build

So your Jenkins job is building your app, Johnny is FINALLY learning to manage memory, your beta testers are receiving your nightlies, and everything is moving along swimmingly. It's a well-oiled machine, right? Well, it is, until Apple releases a beta SDK. Before you start implementing all the awesome new features you thought of during the keynote, you should probably create a new job to build your project against the new beta.

Running Jenkins jobs against multiple SDKs is a great idea. It allows you to ensure backwards compatibility and to focus on the new beta tools, letting Jenkins worry about the previous versions.

However, running two versions of Xcode on your build server is not without complications. For one thing, you're going to be using multiple xcodebuild commands. In addition, you need to ensure the static analyzer uses the right compiler.

The multiple xcodebuild issue is easy to resolve. Xcode comes with a tool called xcode-select, which allows you to specify the location of the Developer tools that xcodebuild should use. For example, to point xcodebuild at the Xcode beta (located at /Developer Beta), use this code:

```
sudo xcode-select -switch /Developer\ Beta/
```

> **NOTE:** It's important to note that xcode-select's changes are system-wide. This means that if job A switches to the beta SDK and doesn't switch back, when job B kicks off, it's going to be using the beta as well, which may be undesirable. Consider one of two strategies: reverse any changes before a job finishes, or set your environment up at the beginning of every job.

The scan-build script makes choosing a specific clang compiler easy. You simply have to specify the path to clang with the --use-cc flag, like so:

```
/path/to/static-analyzer/scan-build --use-cc /path/to/beta/clang xcodebuild -sdk
iphonesimulator
```

So that's fairly easy, but there's a catch. You don't execute the scan-build script yourself; you rely on the Clang Scan-Build plug-in to run the command for you. Unfortunately, at the time of writing, the plug-in doesn't allow you to specify the location of the clang compiler. It does, however, allow you to specify the location of the scan-build script. This allows you to do a little creative shell scripting to produce a scan-build "wrapper" and configure the plug-in to use it in place of the original for betas.

You need your wrapper script to be named scan-build, call the original scan-build, add the custom compiler flag, and then pass along all the original arguments that were passed to the wrapper. Here's the script:

```
#!/bin/bash
/path/to/original/scan-build --use-cc /path/to/beta/clang $@
```

This script puts the custom compiler flag in front of the arguments passed by the caller. Save this script as scan-build in a custom location. You'll need to make it executable.

```
sudo chmod +x scan-build
```

Lastly, go to the Jenkins System Configuration page and add a new scan-build to the Clang Static Analyzer plug-in (Figure 9–24). When you save, you can create a new Beta job, based off of your existing job, add a call to xcode-select to switch to the beta toolset, and change the scan-build selection to use the wrapper. Done!

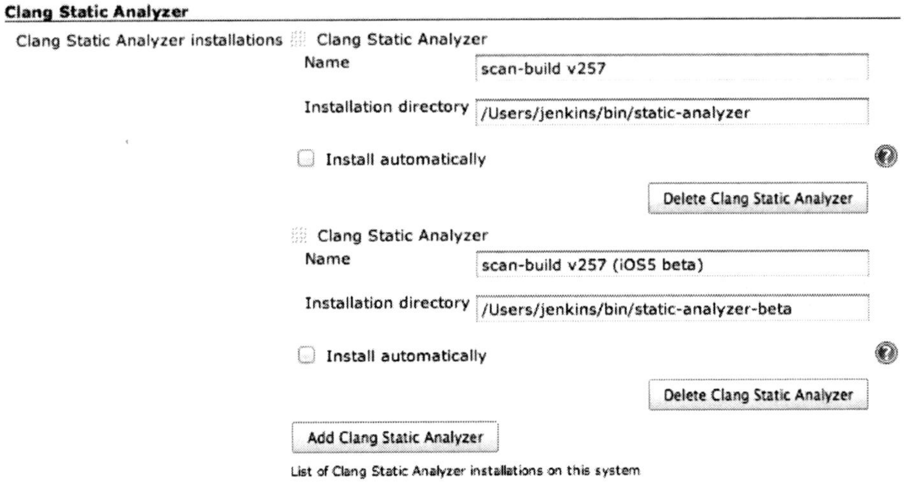

Figure 9–24. *Be sure to give your various analyzers descriptive names.*

What Else Can We Do?

The combination of Jenkins shell build steps and the Xcode command line tools creates some very compelling opportunities for automation. You've already seen that you can build, scan, archive, and deploy your applications. In addition to these very useful actions, recent versions of the toolset have exposed some more useful capabilities to the command line. Unit tests, as an example, can be built as any other target. They can't, however, be built as easily on Xcode Workspaces. The xcodebuild tool does not support them at the time of writing.

Speaking of automated tests, there's even a way to run headless Automation Instrument scripts. Introduced in iOS5, the instruments command line interface offers a way to start UIAutomation tests without a GUI. Here's an example:

```
instruments -t /path/to/template.tracetemplate /path/to/SuperCheckout.app -e UIASCRIPT
/path/to/TestScript.js -e UIARESULTSPATH /path/to/AutomationResults
```

It's a great idea to put your test steps in their own job and to have that job triggered by the completion of your main job. To do this, start by creating a new job based on the original. Customize your build steps to include your testing, then change the Build Trigger to "Build after other projects are built" and enter your original job's name. Don't forget to archive the artifacts so that you can get them from the Job Details page.

So that's it! Jenkins is building and deploying your project for you, and you can finally get down to the business of fixing those bugs and adding new features. Automation is a life saver and an incredible time saver. Also, don't forget to take a look at the plug-in directory in Jenkins from time to time because new features are added all the time.

Chapter 10

Now, They Want an iPad Version

We've taken Super Checkout a long way since the beginning of this book. Testing has gone well, the feedback from the users is coming in, and they overwhelmingly want an iPad version of this application. So what do we do now? Do we separate out some of the common code and build two completely different applications, or do we build a universal binary? That decision depends on your goals for the application; it isn't dictated by technology. It is generally a business decision, because multiple applications can mean more revenue. A universal application, on the other hand, is generally better for the end user, who can purchase one application that will run on the iPhone, iPod Touch, and iPad.

For Super Checkout, we're going to go the universal binary route. The final product will be an application that has an experience that is the same for the iPhone and iPod Touch that we've developed to this point and will also have a native iPad experience. Apple has provided excellent support for detecting the device the application is running on and what features the device has. Before we get started, create and checkout a new branch called Universal_Binary.

Before We Start Coding

Before we start coding, we need to go through a short design phase, so we know how we are going to approach this problem. For this chapter, we're going to look at some wireframes and discuss how we are going to modify the application to support the iPad. These initial steps are crucial, because they can allow you to find mistakes before it is too late. Designing on paper helps to show the big picture. Let's take a look at what the iPad can offer us and see if we can design a solution that is quick to develop and provides value to our users. This isn't a book about user experience, so we're going to gloss over all the user experience details and deal with the creative side of iOS development.

Before we move on, a quick note about design and development. Our first goal is to write the most stable application. But it is also our responsibility to make sure the design is sound. You know the platform well and have hopefully read the *Human Interface Guidelines*. It is up to us to learn a bit about design so we can be better developers. Designing a universal application is a great way to flex your creative muscles.

Designing for the iPad

The iPad SDK introduced some new user interface components that take advantage of the larger screen size. The iPad is also used in multiple orientations as compared to the iPhone. These factors weigh into how we make decisions on what the user interface looks like and how the user will interact with the application on either device. The paradigms used for each device will also need to be similar, so the user will have a similar experience when interacting with the application on each device.

Currently, Super Checkout is designed to have two sides. The main side is the inventory list that drills down into the product details (see Figure 10–1).

Figure 10–1. *The front side of Super Checkout showing the inventory, product details, and one item in the shopping cart.*

Touching the Cart button at the top of the Inventory screen will flip the screen over and show the user's shopping cart (see Figure 10–2).

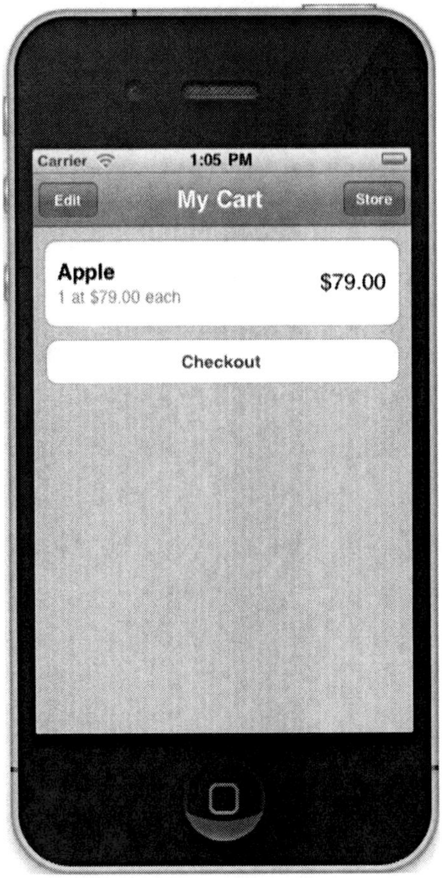

Figure 10–2. *The flipside view of the user's shopping cart*

For Super Checkout, converting the front view of the iPhone/iPod Touch version to split view makes perfect sense. Figures 10–3 through 10–5 show examples of what the application will look like after converting the current user experience to the iPad. The specific table cells and details of the design will follow the iPhone/iPod Touch version. These wireframes are a basic idea of how the application will look after we're done implementing the changes.

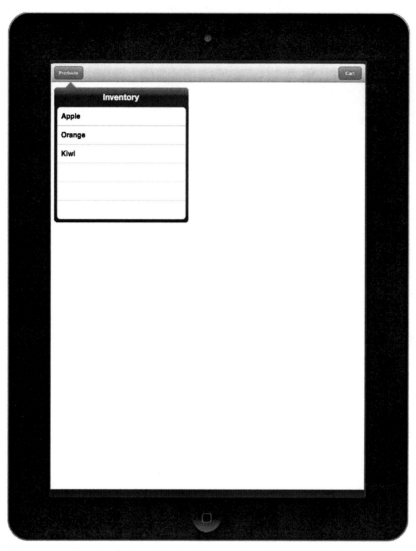

Figure 10–3. *The portrait orientation view of the iPad version of Super Checkout*

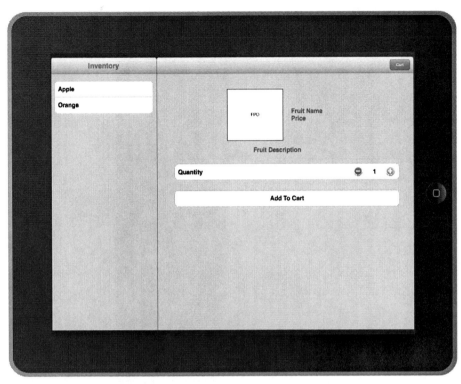

Figure 10–4. *The landscape orientation version of the user interface*

Figure 10–5. *The shopping cart screen shown as a modal view*

These wireframes show two of the iPad-specific interface elements. The first is the split view that has a different view depending on the device's orientation. The inventory view is shown in a popover view in portrait orientation or in the view on the left while the device is in landscape. The shopping cart is still displayed as a modal view, but it is presented over the interface rather than having the entire view flip over like on the iPhone/iPod Touch version.

Implementing the iPad Version

Now, it is time to implement the design. Let's talk about what a universal application is before we start mucking around in the project. A universal binary supports multiple user interfaces based on the device. As a part of the implementation of the universal application, we will have some pieces that are iPad specific and some pieces that will be shared between the devices. From here on out, the word "idiom" will be used to refer to the specific device's form factor. This term is used in the APIs revolving around determining which device the application is running on.

Modifying the Target

The first task in converting an application to a universal application is to update the project's application target. Select the Super Checkout project in the Project navigator panel in Xcode, and select the Super Checkout target. Under the Summary tab, in the iOS Application Target section, there is a drop-down menu for selecting the devices the application supports (see Figure 10–6). Change the Devices configuration from iPhone to Universal.

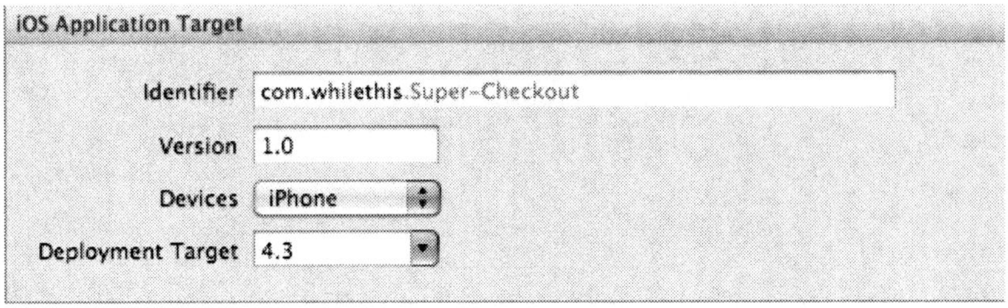

Figure 10–6. *Change the Devices configuration from iPhone to Universal.*

Xcode will then ask if you want a copy of the `MainWindow` nib to be the starting point for the iPad application (see Figure 10–7). Click Yes, and you'll notice a new group under the Super Checkout group called iPad. This contains the `MainWindow-iPad.xib` that was created.

Figure 10–7. *Xcode will create a new MainWindow.xib file when transitioning to a universal application.*

The other file that was touched by Xcode to create the universal target was the
`Super_Checkout-Info.plist` file. The only change made to that file was to tell Cocoa
about the supported orientations and the new nib file.

The App Delegate and Starting UI

Now that we have the entry point to the application complete, we will need to subclass
`Super_CheckoutAppDelegate` and set the new class as the app delegate on the iPad
version of the `MainWindow` nib. To do this, create a new Objective-C class, and call it
`Super_CheckoutAppDelegate_iPad`. Update the header to look like Listing 10–1, in which
our subclass of `Super_CheckoutAppDelegate` sets us up for some custom iPad code.

Listing 10–1. *A Subclass of Super_CheckoutAppDelegate, Ready for Some Custom iPad Code*

```
#import <Foundation/Foundation.h>
#import "Super_CheckoutAppDelegate.h"

@interface Super_CheckoutAppDelegate_iPad : Super_CheckoutAppDelegate {

    UISplitViewController *splitViewController;
}
@property (nonatomic, retain) IBOutlet UISplitViewController *splitViewController;

@end
```

Now, update the implementation to look like Listing 10–2.

Listing 10–2. *The Implementation of Our iPad-specific Subclass*

```
#import "Super_CheckoutAppDelegate_iPad.h"


@implementation Super_CheckoutAppDelegate_iPad
@synthesize splitViewController;

- (void)dealloc {
    [splitViewController release];
    [super dealloc];
}

- (BOOL)application:(UIApplication *)application
    didFinishLaunchingWithOptions:(NSDictionary *)launchOptions {

    self.window.rootViewController = self.splitViewController;
    [self.window makeKeyAndVisible];

    return YES;
}
@end
```

What we're doing here is setting the actual launch point for the iPad version of the
application. The next step is to update the nib for the iPad. Open `MainWindow-iPad.xib`
in the iPad group. From the Object Library, drag Split View Controller into the Objects
list in the editor, and remove Main Navigation Controller from the Objects list (see
Figure 10–8).

Figure 10–8. *The new Objects list in the MainWindow-iPad nib*

> **NOTE:** If the Document Outline is collapsed (it only shows icons, not text), click the arrow button at the bottom of the Document Outline to expand (or collapse) it.

The next part is to configure the split view controller to have the appropriate view controllers. To do this, expand all of children of the Split View Controller object by option-clicking the disclosure triangle. We want the final configuration to look like Figure 10–9.

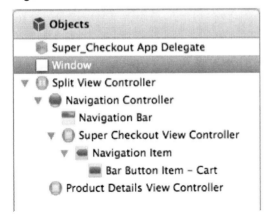

Figure 10–9. *The final configuration of the split view controller in the MainWindow-iPad nib.*

Your view will look slightly different from Figure 10–9. The view controller that is the child of the navigation controller needs to be the Super Checkout view controller. To do this, select the child controller (Table View Controller) of the navigation controller, and open the Identity Inspector by clicking the Show the Identity inspector tab in the right-hand panel. Then, change the Class to Super_CheckoutViewController (see Figure 10–10).

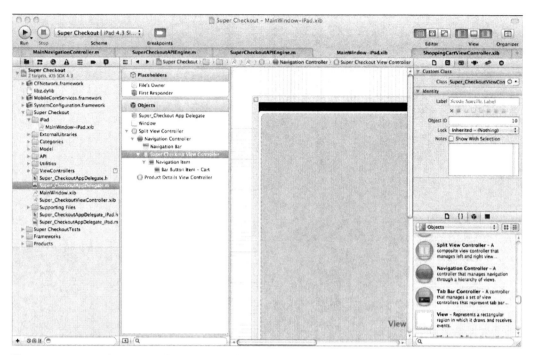

Figure 10–10. *Updating the root view controller of the navigation controller to be the inventory view controller from the iPhone/iPod touch version of Super Checkout*

Do the same thing with the bottom view controller, except make it an instance of `ProductDetailsViewController`.

The final thing to finish up the app delegate and the main nib is to wire up the split view controller to the app delegate. First, select Super_Checkout App Delegate, and in the Identity Inspector of the Utility area, make sure the class type is Super_CheckoutAppDelegate_iPad. Next, control-drag from the Super_Checkout App Delegate proxy to the split view controller, and select splitViewController (see Figure 10–11).

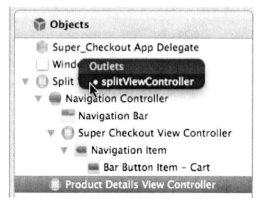

Figure 10–11. *Wiring up the splitViewController property on the app delegate*

Creating and configuring the app delegate and wiring up the nib are now complete. Now, we are off to update some of the user interfaces to support the iPad along with keeping backward compatibility.

Updating Inventory and Product Details

Now that the entry point of the iPad application is set, we can now modify the front side view controllers to support the new idiom. The primary way to detect what device the application is running on is to compare the result of UI_USER_INTERFACE_IDIOM() and see if it is equal to UIUserInterfaceIdiomPhone or UIUserInterfaceIdiomPad.

Revamping the Inventory list

Our first stop for making our edits is the Super_CheckoutViewController class. This class is responsible for showing the inventory list and leading the user to the product details view. Currently, this class pushes the ProductDetailsViewController onto the navigation controller's stack. We need to update it to support the split view controller we added to the main window nib.

In order to do this, open Super_CheckoutViewController.h, and modify it to look like Listing 10–3.

Listing 10–3. *Updating the Main View Controller to Support Both Interface Idioms*

```
#import <UIKit/UIKit.h>
#import "SuperCheckoutAPIEngineDelegate.h"
@class ProductDetailsViewController;
@class SuperCheckoutAPIEngine;
@class ProductCell;

@interface Super_CheckoutViewController : UITableViewController
                                        <SuperCheckoutAPIEngineDelegate,
UIScrollViewDelegate> {
    NSArray *inventory;
    SuperCheckoutAPIEngine *apiEngine;

    UINib *cellNib;
    ProductCell *productCell;

    NSMutableDictionary *imageIndexes;
    NSMutableDictionary *imageDownloadsInProgress;
    ProductDetailsViewController *detailsViewController;
}

@property (nonatomic, retain) IBOutlet ProductCell *productCell;
@property (nonatomic, retain) IBOutlet ProductDetailsViewController
*detailsViewController;

@end
```

The real difference here is that we're adding in the reference to the ProductDetailsViewController. We'll still need to wire it up, but we're not ready for that yet. Open Super_CheckoutViewController.m and hold on tight; we're in for some updates.

First, synthesize the detailsViewController property at the top of the implementation.

Next, in the dealloc method, release the instance variable by adding [detailsViewController release]; before the call to [super dealloc].

For the next update, in tableView:cellForRowAtIndexPath:, remove the following line:

```
[cell setAccessoryType:UITableViewCellAccessoryDisclosureIndicator];
```

and replace it with

```
if(UI_USER_INTERFACE_IDIOM() == UIUserInterfaceIdiomPhone) {
    [cell setAccessoryType:UITableViewCellAccessoryDisclosureIndicator];
} else {
    [cell setAccessoryType:UITableViewCellAccessoryNone];
}
```

What we're doing here is identifying the current idiom by calling UI_USER_INTERFACE_IDIOM(), and if we're on the iPhone/iPod Touch, we're setting the disclosure indicator as the accessory view. For iPads, we don't need an accessory view because the product details screen is already present.

The next update is to replace the entire method for selecting a product. Find the tableView:didSelectRowAtIndexPath: method and replace the entire implementation with this:

```
- (void)tableView:(UITableView *)tableView
                    didSelectRowAtIndexPath:(NSIndexPath *)indexPath {
    ProductDetailsViewController *newVC = [[ProductDetailsViewController alloc]
initWithNibName:@"ProductDetailsViewController" bundle:nil];

    [newVC setSelectedProduct:[inventory objectAtIndex:[indexPath row]]];

    [self.navigationController pushViewController:newVC animated:YES];
    [newVC release];
        if(detailsViewController == nil) {
                ProductDetailsViewController *newVC =
                        [[ProductDetailsViewController alloc]
                            initWithNibName:@"ProductDetailsViewController"
                                                    bundle:nil];

                [newVC setSelectedProduct:[inventory objectAtIndex:[indexPath row]]];

                [self.navigationController pushViewController:newVC animated:YES];
                [newVC release];
        } else {
                [detailsViewController setSelectedProduct:
                        [inventory objectAtIndex:[indexPath row]]];
        }
}
```

In this modification, we're checking to see if the product details view controller is nil. Since we are using the split view controller on the iPad, the details view controller will be set, and we can check to see if it is nil or not to detect which device the application is running on.

The next method to search for is `viewDidLoad:`. In this method, add the following block below [`self setTitle:@"Inventory"`], which sets the view controller's title:

```
if(UI_USER_INTERFACE_IDIOM() == UIUserInterfaceIdiomPad) {
    [[self navigationItem] setRightBarButtonItem:nil];
}
```

Here, we're removing the right button from the navigation bar because we're moving the cart button to the product details screen's toolbar. That update is coming; first we need to finish up the inventory screen updates.

We're almost done in this file, so head on to the `viewDidUnload` method, and add the following line above the call to [`super viewDidUnload`]:

```
[self setDetailsViewController:nil];
```

The final update to make is in `shouldAutorotateToInterfaceOrientation:`. This is the method that tells the application if it should autorotate to adapt to the device's orientation. For the iPad, we want to support both orientations. For the iPhone/iPod Touch, we only want to support portrait. Here is the update to the method to make:

```
if(UI_USER_INTERFACE_IDIOM() == UIUserInterfaceIdiomPad) {
    return YES;
}

return (interfaceOrientation == UIInterfaceOrientationPortrait);
```

For this method, we're checking the device we're on and returning YES for the iPad. The following line is the same as it was in the iPhone/iPod Touch version.

We're done with the inventory list now. The final thing to do is open `MainWindow-iPad.xib` and wire up the `detailsViewController` `IBOutlet` on the Super Checkout view controller to the Product Details view controller (see Figure 10–12).

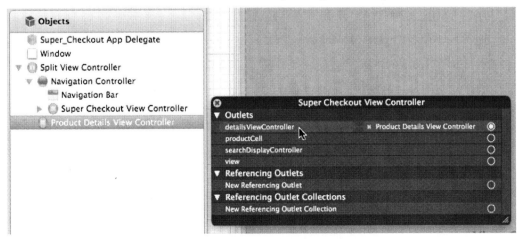

Figure 10–12. *The final set up for the Inventory screen for the split view controller*

Now that the inventory screen is complete, we have quite a bit of work left to update the product details screen.

Updating the Product Details

The `ProductDetailsViewController` class has to undergo a pretty large update. The iPhone/iPod Touch version of Super Checkout had the product details screen being pushed onto a navigation controller, and there is no navigation controller in the split view controller on the iPad. To accomplish this, we will be loading different nibs to the details controller based on the device we are running on. We will need to have the `ProductDetailsViewController` support both idioms, so we are going to change it to be a subclass of `UIViewController` instead of being a subclass of `UITableViewController`.

The first thing we'll do is update the `ProductDetailsViewController.h` file to look like Listing 10–4.

Listing 10–4. *Updating the ProductDetailsViewController Class to Support the iPad Idiom*

```
#import <UIKit/UIKit.h>
#import "SuperCheckoutAPIEngine.h"
#import "SCModalDelegate.h"
@class QuantityCell;
@class Product;

@interface ProductDetailsViewController :
UIViewController<SuperCheckoutAPIEngineDelegate,
 SCModalDelegate, UITableViewDelegate, UITableViewDataSource,
UISplitViewControllerDelegate,
UIPopoverControllerDelegate> {
    Product *selectedProduct;
    UIView *productDetailsHeader;
    UIImageView *productImage;
    UILabel *productNameLabel;
    UILabel *productPriceLabel;
    UITableViewCell *addToBasketCell;
    QuantityCell *quantityCell;

    SuperCheckoutAPIEngine *apiEngine;

    UIToolbar *toolbar;
    UITableView *tableView;
    UIBarButtonItem *shoppingCartButton;
}

@property(retain, nonatomic) Product *selectedProduct;
@property (nonatomic, retain) IBOutlet UIView *productDetailsHeader;
@property (nonatomic, retain) IBOutlet UIImageView *productImage;
@property (nonatomic, retain) IBOutlet UILabel *productNameLabel;
@property (nonatomic, retain) IBOutlet UILabel *productPriceLabel;
@property (nonatomic, retain) IBOutlet UITableViewCell *addToBasketCell;
@property (nonatomic, retain) IBOutlet QuantityCell *quantityCell;
@property (nonatomic, retain) IBOutlet UIToolbar *toolbar;
@property (nonatomic, retain) IBOutlet UITableView *tableView;
@property (nonatomic, retain) IBOutlet UIBarButtonItem *shoppingCartButton;
- (IBAction)cartButtonPressed:(id)sender;
```

@end

Lets walk through what we've changed.

The class declaration before this update was

```
@interface ProductDetailsViewController :
                        UITableViewController<SuperCheckoutAPIEngineDelegate>
```

With the older version, we are subclassing `UITableViewController` and conforming to the `SuperCheckoutAPIEngineDelegate` protocol. This gives us a basic view controller with a `UITableView` as the view and nothing else. Since this class needs to support both idioms, we need to design this class for the lowest common denominator. For this, we updated the class declaration to this:

```
@interface ProductDetailsViewController :
UIViewController<SuperCheckoutAPIEngineDelegate, SCModalDelegate, UITableViewDelegate,
UITableViewDataSource, UISplitViewControllerDelegate, UIPopoverControllerDelegate>
```

So the `ProductDetailsViewController` class now subclasses `UIViewController` and conforms to the `UITableViewDelegate` and `UITableViewDataSource` protocols. To support the `UISplitViewController` and its features, we need to add the protocols it conforms to. These protocols are the `UISplitViewControllerDelegate` and `UIPopoverControllerDelegate` protocols. There is one more protocol in that list—the `SCModalDelegate` protocol. This is to support the modal view controller that will be presented here for the iPad. We're not there yet, so we won't talk about that right now.

The instance variables we added are:

```
UIToolbar *toolbar;
UITableView *tableView;
UIBarButtonItem *shoppingCartButton;
```

The `toolbar` and `shoppingCartButton` objects are to support the iPad version. The `tableView` object is to support the table view that will be displayed in both the iPad and iPhone/iPod Touch versions of Super Checkout.

Now we're ready to update the implementation file. Like the header file, we have a lot of changes and you'll find them in Listing 10–5.

Listing 10–5. *The Full ProductDetailsViewController*

```
#import "ProductDetailsViewController.h"
#import "QuantityCell.h"
#import "SuperCheckoutAPIEngine.h"
#import "Product.h"
#import "ShoppingCartViewController.h"

@interface ProductDetailsViewController()
@property (nonatomic, retain) UIPopoverController *popoverController;
@end

@implementation ProductDetailsViewController
@synthesize selectedProduct;
@synthesize productDetailsHeader;
@synthesize productImage;
```

```objc
@synthesize productNameLabel;
@synthesize productPriceLabel;
@synthesize addToBasketCell;
@synthesize quantityCell;
@synthesize toolbar;
@synthesize tableView;
@synthesize shoppingCartButton;

@synthesize popoverController=_myPopoverController;

- (id)initWithNibName:(NSString *)nibNameOrNil bundle:(NSBundle *)nibBundleOrNil {
    self = [super initWithNibName:nibNameOrNil bundle:nibBundleOrNil];
    if (self) {
        // Custom initialization
        apiEngine = [[SuperCheckoutAPIEngine alloc] initWithDelegate:self];
    }
    return self;
}

- (id) initWithCoder:(NSCoder *)aDecoder {
    self = [super initWithCoder:aDecoder];
    if(self) {
        apiEngine = [[SuperCheckoutAPIEngine alloc] initWithDelegate:self];
    }

    return self;
}

- (void)dealloc {
    apiEngine.delegate = nil;
    [apiEngine release];
    [selectedProduct release];
    [productDetailsHeader release];
    [productImage release];
    [productNameLabel release];
    [productPriceLabel release];
    [addToBasketCell release];
    [quantityCell release];
    [tableView release];
    [_myPopoverController release];

    [[NSNotificationCenter defaultCenter] removeObserver:self];
    [shoppingCartButton release];
    [super dealloc];
}

- (void)didReceiveMemoryWarning {
    // Releases the view if it doesn't have a superview.
    [super didReceiveMemoryWarning];

    // Release any cached data, images, etc that aren't in use.
}

#pragma mark - Accessors/Mutators

- (void) setSelectedProduct:(Product *)aProduct {
    [self willChangeValueForKey:@"selectedProduct"];
```

```
    Product *oldProduct = selectedProduct;
    selectedProduct  = [aProduct retain];
    [oldProduct release];
    [self didChangeValueForKey:@"selectedProduct"];
    [[self tableView] reloadData];
    [apiEngine getImageForProduct:[selectedProduct image]];

    [productNameLabel setText:[selectedProduct name]];
    [productPriceLabel setText:[NSString stringWithFormat:@"$%1.2f",

[[selectedProduct price] floatValue]]];

    [[self popoverController] dismissPopoverAnimated:YES];
}

#pragma mark - UITableViewDataSource Methods

- (NSInteger)numberOfSectionsInTableView:(UITableView *)tableView {
    if(selectedProduct == nil) {
        return 0;
    }
    return 3;
}


- (NSInteger)tableView:(UITableView *)tableView
    numberOfRowsInSection:(NSInteger)section {
    if(section == 0) {
        return 0;
    } else {
        return 1;
    }
}

- (NSString *)tableView:(UITableView *)tableView
titleForFooterInSection:(NSInteger)section {
    if(section == 0) {
        return [selectedProduct description];
    } else {
        return nil;
    }
}

// Customize the appearance of table view cells.
- (UITableViewCell *)tableView:(UITableView *)tableView
            cellForRowAtIndexPath:(NSIndexPath *)indexPath {
    if([indexPath section] == 1) {
        return quantityCell;
    } else {
        return addToBasketCell;
    }
}

#pragma mark - UITableViewDelegate

- (void)tableView:(UITableView *)aTableView
    didSelectRowAtIndexPath:(NSIndexPath *)indexPath {
```

```objc
    [aTableView deselectRowAtIndexPath:indexPath animated:YES];

    //Add item to cart here.....
    [apiEngine buyProduct:[selectedProduct productId] withQuantity:[NSNumber
numberWithInt:[quantityCell quantity]]];
}
- (NSIndexPath *)tableView:(UITableView *)tableview
  willSelectRowAtIndexPath:(NSIndexPath *)indexPath {
    if([indexPath section] == 2) {
        return indexPath;
    } else {
        return nil;
    }
}

- (UIView *) tableView:(UITableView *)tableView
    viewForHeaderInSection:(NSInteger)section {

    if(section == 0) {
        return productDetailsHeader;
    } else {
        return nil;
    }
}

- (CGFloat) tableView:(UITableView *)tableView
    heightForHeaderInSection:(NSInteger)section {

    if(section == 0) {
        return [productDetailsHeader frame].size.height;
    } else {
        return 0.0;
    }
}

#pragma mark - SuperCheckoutAPIEngineDelegate Methods
- (void)requestSucceeded:(NSString *)connectionIdentifier {
}

- (void)requestFailed:(NSString *)connectionIdentifier withError:(NSError *)error {
    UIAlertView *alert = [[UIAlertView alloc] initWithTitle:@"Error"

message:@"An error occurred adding this item"

delegate:nil

cancelButtonTitle:@"Dismiss"

otherButtonTitles:nil];

    [alert show];
    [alert release];
}

-(void) cartContentsReceived:(NSDictionary *)cart
```

```objc
                                              forRequest:(NSString *)connectionIdentifier {
    NSLog(@"Shopping cart contents: %@", cart);
    NSNotification *note =
            [NSNotification notificationWithName:@"CartUpdated"

object:[NSNumber numberWithInt:[[cart

objectForKey:@"items"] count]]];

    [[NSNotificationCenter defaultCenter] postNotification:note];

    [self.navigationController popViewControllerAnimated:YES];
}

-(void) imageReceived:(UIImage *)image forRequest:(NSString *)connectionIdentifier {
    [productImage setImage:image];
}

#pragma mark - Split view support

- (void)splitViewController:(UISplitViewController *)svc
        willHideViewController:(UIViewController *)aViewController
             withBarButtonItem:(UIBarButtonItem *)barButtonItem
          forPopoverController: (UIPopoverController *)pc {
    barButtonItem.title = @"Products";
    NSMutableArray *items = [[self.toolbar items] mutableCopy];
    [items insertObject:barButtonItem atIndex:0];
    [self.toolbar setItems:items animated:YES];
    [items release];
    self.popoverController = pc;
}

// Called when the view is shown again in the split view, invalidating the button and
popover controller.
- (void)splitViewController:(UISplitViewController *)svc
     willShowViewController:(UIViewController *)aViewController
invalidatingBarButtonItem:(UIBarButtonItem *)barButtonItem {
    NSMutableArray *items = [[self.toolbar items] mutableCopy];
    [items removeObjectAtIndex:0];
    [self.toolbar setItems:items animated:YES];
    [items release];
    self.popoverController = nil;
}

#pragma mark - Notifications
- (void) cartUpdateNotification:(NSNotification *)note {
    //Udpate cart button
    NSNumber *cartCount = [note object];

    [shoppingCartButton setTitle:
            [NSString stringWithFormat:@"Cart (%i)", [cartCount intValue]]];
}

#pragma mark - View lifecycle

- (void)viewDidLoad {
    [super viewDidLoad];
```

```
    // Do any additional setup after loading the view from its nib.
    [self setTitle:[selectedProduct name]];

    if(selectedProduct != nil) {
        [productNameLabel setText:[selectedProduct name]];
        [productPriceLabel setText:
                [NSString stringWithFormat:@"$%1.2f", [[selectedProduct price]
floatValue]]];

        [apiEngine getImageForProduct:[selectedProduct image]];
    }

    [[NSNotificationCenter defaultCenter] addObserver:self

selector:@selector(cartUpdateNotification:)

name:@"CartUpdated"

object:nil];
}

- (void)viewDidUnload {
    [self setProductDetailsHeader:nil];
    [self setProductImage:nil];
    [self setProductNameLabel:nil];
    [self setProductPriceLabel:nil];
    [self setAddToBasketCell:nil];
    [self setQuantityCell:nil];
    [self setTableView:nil];

    [[NSNotificationCenter defaultCenter] removeObserver:self];
    [self setShoppingCartButton:nil];
    [super viewDidUnload];
    // Release any retained subviews of the main view.
    // e.g. self.myOutlet = nil;
}

- (BOOL)shouldAutorotateToInterfaceOrientation:

(UIInterfaceOrientation)interfaceOrientation {
    if(UI_USER_INTERFACE_IDIOM() == UIUserInterfaceIdiomPad) {
        return YES;
    }
    // Return YES for supported orientations
    return (interfaceOrientation == UIInterfaceOrientationPortrait);
}

- (IBAction)cartButtonPressed:(id)sender {
    ShoppingCartViewController *cartVC =
        [[ShoppingCartViewController alloc]
initWithNibName:@"ShoppingCartViewController"

bundle:nil];
    [cartVC setDelegate:self];
    UINavigationController *navController =
        [[UINavigationController alloc] initWithRootViewController:cartVC];
```

```
    [navController setModalPresentationStyle:UIModalPresentationFormSheet];
    [self presentModalViewController:navController animated:YES];

    [cartVC release];
    [navController release];
}

#pragma mark - SCModalDelegate Methods
-(void) viewController:(UIViewController *)vc didFinishWithData:(id) data {
    [self dismissModalViewControllerAnimated:YES];
}

-(void) viewControllerDidCancel:(UIViewController *)vc {
    [self dismissModalViewControllerAnimated:YES];
}
@end
```

This is quite a bit of code, but we'll step through and talk about each update from the original version.

The first change is creating a class extension. The class extension is

```
@interface ProductDetailsViewController()
@property (nonatomic, retain) UIPopoverController *popoverController;
@end
```

All we're doing here is creating a local property for the UIPopoverController from the UISplitViewController. We're synthesizing it with @synthesize popoverController=_myPopoverController; later with the rest of the synthesized properties. We're also synthesizing the new properties, but that isn't very interesting, so all I'm doing here is mentioning it.

The next interesting change is

```
- (id) initWithCoder:(NSCoder *)aDecoder {
        self = [super initWithCoder:aDecoder];
        if(self) {
                apiEngine = [[SuperCheckoutAPIEngine alloc] initWithDelegate:self];
        }

        return self;
}
```

Here, we're implementing initWithCoder: because in the MainWindow-iPad nib, the ProductDetailsViewController is loaded as a part of the nib. Since we're at the mercy of the nib loader, we have to implement the initWithCoder: method. The rest of the method is basically the same as the other initializer.

The next set of changes is in the dealloc method (see Listing 10–6). We're cleaning up after ourselves and removing the object as an observer for notifications from NSNotificationCenter. This is because we start listening for cart updates on the NSNotificationCenter later in the file. Nothing too terribly interesting, but it is still worth mentioning these updates.

Listing 10–6. *The All-Important dealloc Method for Non-ARC Projects.*

```
- (void)dealloc {
    apiEngine.delegate = nil;
    [apiEngine release];
    [selectedProduct release];
    [productDetailsHeader release];
    [productImage release];
    [productNameLabel release];
    [productPriceLabel release];
    [addToBasketCell release];
    [quantityCell release];
    [tableView release];
    [_myPopoverController release];

    [[NSNotificationCenter defaultCenter] removeObserver:self];
    [shoppingCartButton release];
    [super dealloc];
}
```

Next up is a mutator for the selected product (see Listing 10–7). Since we now handle the iPad version and the controller is always around, we had to update the mutator to set the appropriate view properties and tell the popover controller to dismiss.

Listing 10–7. *The Mutator for a Selected Product and the Updates View*

```
- (void) setSelectedProduct:(Product *)aProduct {
    [self willChangeValueForKey:@"selectedProduct"];
    Product *oldProduct = selectedProduct;
    selectedProduct  = [aProduct retain];
    [oldProduct release];
    [self didChangeValueForKey:@"selectedProduct"];
    [[self tableView] reloadData];
    [apiEngine getImageForProduct:[selectedProduct image]];

    [productNameLabel setText:[selectedProduct name]];
    [productPriceLabel setText:
        [NSString stringWithFormat:@"$%1.2f", [[selectedProduct price] floatValue]]];

    [[self popoverController] dismissPopoverAnimated:YES];
}
```

In numberOfSectionsInTableView: (see Listing 10–8), we are returning zero when the selected product is nil. This is because the view controller will be created with a nil selected product, and we don't want to show any UI here because we don't have anything to show.

Listing 10–8. *Changing How the Table Is Built Based on a Selected Product's Existence*

```
- (NSInteger)numberOfSectionsInTableView:(UITableView *)tableView {
    if(selectedProduct == nil) {
        return 0;
    }
    return 3;
}
```

The next significant update is in Listing 10–9; we're adding a split view to the class to make sure our app keeps working on the iPhone/iPod Touch as well.

Listing 10–9. *Adding Split View Support to a Class*

```
#pragma mark - Split view support

- (void)splitViewController:(UISplitViewController *)svc
      willHideViewController:(UIViewController *)aViewController
            withBarButtonItem:(UIBarButtonItem *)barButtonItem
         forPopoverController: (UIPopoverController *)pc {
    barButtonItem.title = @"Products";
    NSMutableArray *items = [[self.toolbar items] mutableCopy];
    [items insertObject:barButtonItem atIndex:0];
    [self.toolbar setItems:items animated:YES];
    [items release];
    self.popoverController = pc;
}

// Called when the view is shown again in the split view, invalidating the button and
popover controller.
- (void)splitViewController:(UISplitViewController *)svc
      willShowViewController:(UIViewController *)aViewController
invalidatingBarButtonItem:(UIBarButtonItem *)barButtonItem {
    NSMutableArray *items = [[self.toolbar items] mutableCopy];
    [items removeObjectAtIndex:0];
    [self.toolbar setItems:items animated:YES];
    [items release];
    self.popoverController = nil;
}
```

This chunk adds support for the split view controller delegate protocol. The first method is called when the device is rotated to portrait mode. This sets up the toolbar that is going to be put in the iPad nib and prepares the popover view controller that will be displayed in portrait orientation. The second method is called when the device is rotated to the landscape orientation and is about to show the full split view controller. It removes the button bar item and disables the popover view controller.

The next significant update was made in the viewDidLoad method. In this method, we are checking to see if the selected product is not nil and updating the user interface with the product details and loading the product's image. The last piece of the method is to begin listening to the notification center for cart updates.

The next updates are in the viewDidUnload method, which is pretty standard. Giving the outlets loaded from the nib nil values and removing itself as an observer of the notification center undoes what occurs in the viewDidLoad method. The next method that was updated was shouldAutorotateToInterfaceOrientation:, and it was updated to return YES when the device running the application is an iPad.

The previous section was pretty simple stuff, the next (and final) set of changes for this file are

```
- (IBAction)cartButtonPressed:(id)sender {
      ShoppingCartViewController *cartVC =
            [[ShoppingCartViewController alloc]
initWithNibName:@"ShoppingCartViewController"

bundle:nil];
      [cartVC setDelegate:self];
```

```
            UINavigationController *navController =
                [[UINavigationController alloc] initWithRootViewController:cartVC];


            [navController setModalPresentationStyle:UIModalPresentationFormSheet];
            [self presentModalViewController:navController animated:YES];

            [cartVC release];
            [navController release];
}

#pragma mark - SCModalDelegate Methods
-(void) viewController:(UIViewController *)vc didFinishWithData:(id) data {
            [self dismissModalViewControllerAnimated:YES];
}

-(void) viewControllerDidCancel:(UIViewController *)vc {
            [self dismissModalViewControllerAnimated:YES];
}
```

The first piece is the action for the cart button that will be placed on the iPad version's nib. Since it is iPad only, we can cater the implementation to the iPad. The final two methods are implementing the delegate methods for the modal view controller. This is a great example of a device-specific implementation where a different nib will be loaded for one view controller. These are the types of design decisions that need to be made when transitioning to or developing universal applications.

The ultimate design is to have the same view controller for details that have different nib files that set the appropriate IBOutlets. This outlines on of the strengths of the MVC design pattern. Maintaining this view controller will stay relatively simple and updating the user interface will be easy and won't require controller changes.

Creating the Product Details Nib for the iPad Version

The nib for the product details screen is iPad specific. It shares the same components as the iPhone/iPod Touch screen except it has a few minor modifications. Figure 10–13 shows the final nib that will be loaded by Super Checkout when it is launched on an iPad. Notice that it shares the same exact cells and other elements as the iPhone/iPod Touch nib with one slight difference—the header view. For the iPad, we need to wrap the image and labels into a view and wrap that with another view. This way, we can get each view centered to the table.

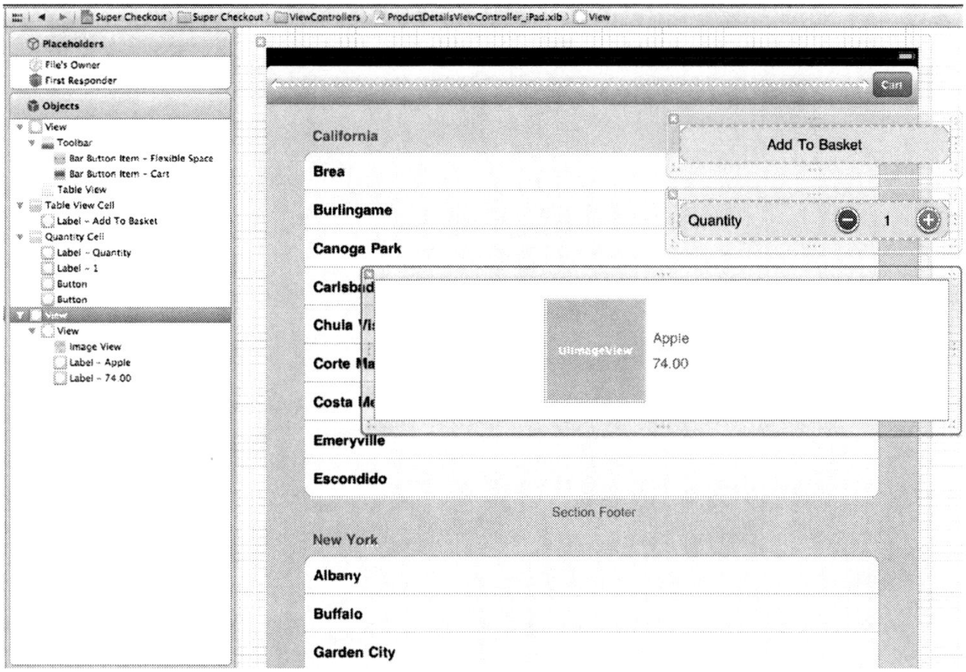

Figure 10–13. *The final Product Details nib for the iPad*

The first thing we need to do to get the nib going is to create it. Go to File ➤ New ➤ New File, and in the sheet that is displayed, select User Interface under the iOS section, and select the Empty nib icon (see Figure 10–14).

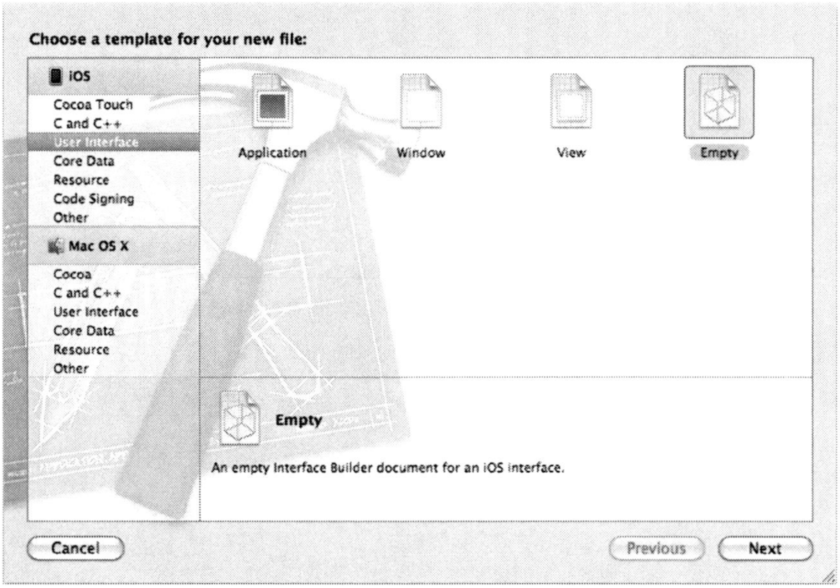

Figure 10–14. *Selecting the type of nib to create*

Click Next, and in the next screen, choose iPad for the Device Family (see Figure 10–15).

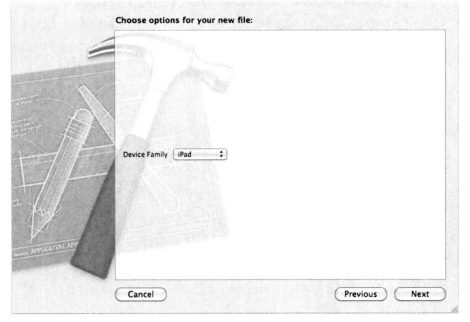

Figure 10–15. *Selecting the Device Family for the nib*

Click Next. Name the nib **ProductDetailsViewController_iPad.xib**, and make sure it is saved to the ViewControllers group. (see Figure 10–16).

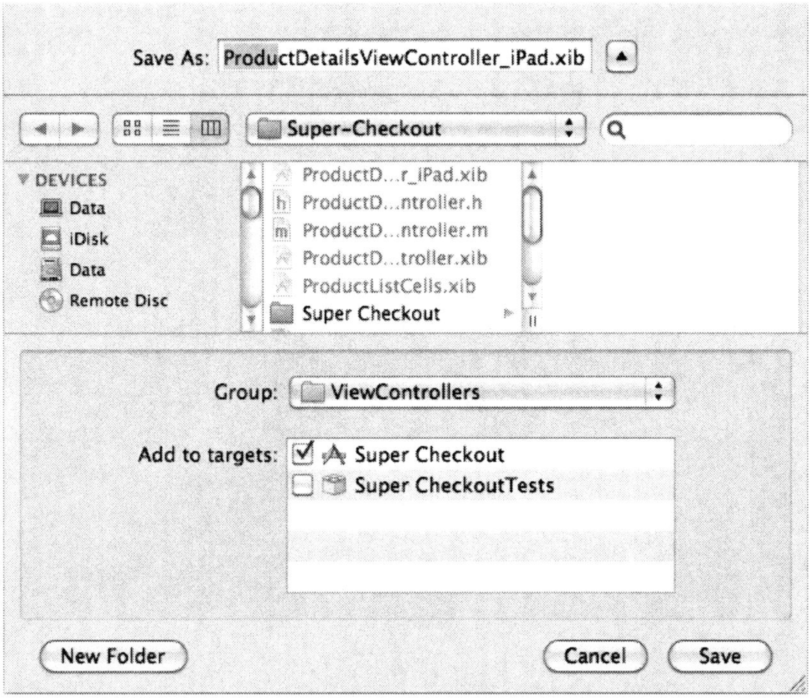

Figure 10–16. *Saving the nib to the right group is important to keep your project organized.*

The first thing we want to do for the new nib is to set the File's Owner proxy. After selecting the nib, select File's Owner so the Custom Class section is visible in the Identity Inspector of the Utility area (expand it if it isn't visible). Change the class from NSObject to ProductDetailsViewController.

Now, we want to set up the view for the view controller. In the Object Library section of the Utility area, select View (UIView), and drag an instance onto the nib's preview area. Now, drag in a Toolbar (UIToolbar), and place it at the top of the view. Inside the toolbar, select and delete the button in the upper-left corner. Next, drag in a Flexible Space Button Bar Item, and to the right of that, drag in a Bar Button Item and set its title to **Cart** (edit it by double-clicking the Item text). The final piece of the view configuration is to drag in a Table View (UITableView) under the toolbar. In the attributes inspector for the table view, set the Style drop-down to Grouped to make it a grouped table. Last, resize the table view to fit the area under the toolbar. The final product should look like Figure 10–17.

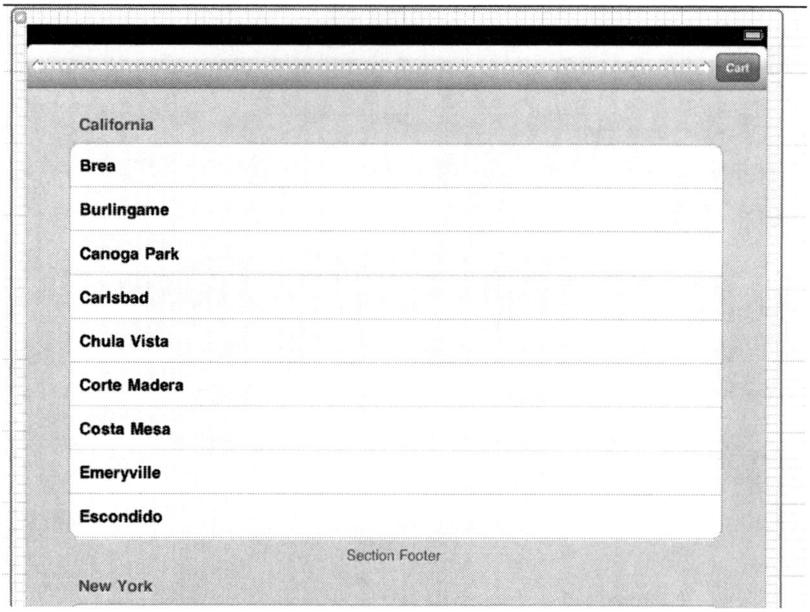

California

Brea

Burlingame

Canoga Park

Carlsbad

Chula Vista

Corte Madera

Costa Mesa

Emeryville

Escondido

Section Footer

New York

Figure 10–17. *The configured main view for the iPad*

Since we are using the same interface elements from the iPhone/iPod Touch version, we can copy the elements we're going to use from the iPhone/iPod Touch nib. The easiest way to do this is to use "Assistant editor" mode to open both nibs. With the `ProductDetailsViewController_iPad` nib editor open, click "Assistant editor" on the right side of the toolbar. Depending on your settings, the assistant editor will be to the right of the main editor or underneath the main editor. Either way, using the Jump Bar of the assistant editor you will be able to choose the appropriate file to view in the assistant editor (see Figure 10–18).

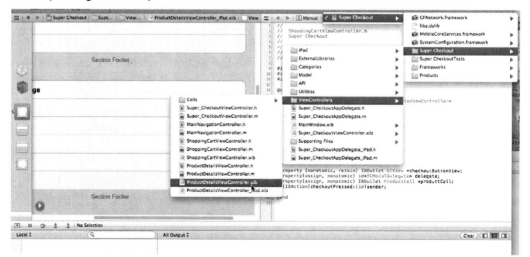

Figure 10–18. *Using the Jump Bar to select a different file in the assistant editor*

Use the Jump Bar to open `ProductDetailsViewController.xib` and select all of the views except the table view. Drag those items over to the iPad version of the nib, and go back to the standard editor view. We're pretty much done except for one piece.

Drag a `UIView` object from the Object library (expand the Utility area if it is not visible). Select the new `UIView` instance, and in the Attributes Inspector, make the background color the clear color and uncheck the opaque check box. In the size inspector, make the width 676 points and the height 160 points. Now, make the view that wraps the image, product name, and price a subview of the new view and center it in the view. Use the automatic snapping to guide you. Once the view is centered, use the springs and struts to make the view centered relative to its parent view (see Figure 10–19).

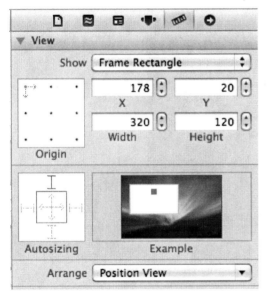

Figure 10–19. *Using springs and struts is a huge help to create views that autoresize.*

> **TIP:** The springs and struts configuration in Interface Builder simply sets the bitmask property
> `autoresizingMask` on `UIView`. The default configuration is to have the top left of the view
> pinned to its frame's origin. By having only the top margin selected (or set in code) and centered
> in its parent's frame, we effectively make it centered no matter the width.

Now that we have the interface elements in the nib, we still have some configuration to do to the other views. The Quantity Cell needs to have the quantity adjustment buttons and label pinned to the right. Use the springs and struts to accomplish this by selecting only the top margin and right margin options. The remaining cell, the one with the Add to Basket label, needs to have its label centered and the top margin option selected.

Now that the interface elements are configured, we can wire them up to the view controller. Figure 10–20 shows the final configuration of File's Owner in terms of outlets and actions. Not every interface element will be wired up.

Figure 10–20. *The final configuration of File's Owner*

Ready to wire up the views? OK, here goes. First, let's connect all of the outlets on File's Owner, starting at the top:

- addToBasketCell is the generic table view cell.

- productDetailsHeader is the large view that wraps the product details.

- productImage is the UIImageView in the productDetailsHeader.

- productNameLabel is the name label in the productDetailsHeader.

- productPriceLabel is the price label in the productDetailsHeader.

- quantityCell is the entire quantity cell.

- shoppingCartButton is the button at the right of the toolbar that says "Cart."

- tableView is the main (and only) table view in the nib.

- toolbar is the toolbar at the top of the main view.

- view is the UIView that wraps the table view and toolbar.

Next, wire up the dataSource and delegate outlets on the table view to File's Owner. The last part is to wire up the sent action from the shoppingCartButton to the cartButtonPressed: selector on File's Owner. Everything is now wired up and ready to go.

Modifying the Shopping Cart View Controller

The final view controller to modify is the ShoppingCartViewController. The changes we need to make here are to update the "I'm done looking at this" button and make it idiom-aware and to update the checkout button and make sure it is centered in its view.

The first thing we need to do is get a reference to the checkout button. We're going to create an outlet in the source files and wire them up to the nib. To do this, open ShoppingCartViewController.xib, and enable the assistant view. If the editor is still showing the Manual selection, go to View ➤ Editor ➤ Reset Editor to reset the assistant editor to the Automatic selection. This will bring up the ShoppingCartViewController.h file in the assistant editor.

The next step is to control-drag the checkout button into the source file (see Figure 10–21). Place the new property in the appropriate place, and make it an outlet called checkoutButton.

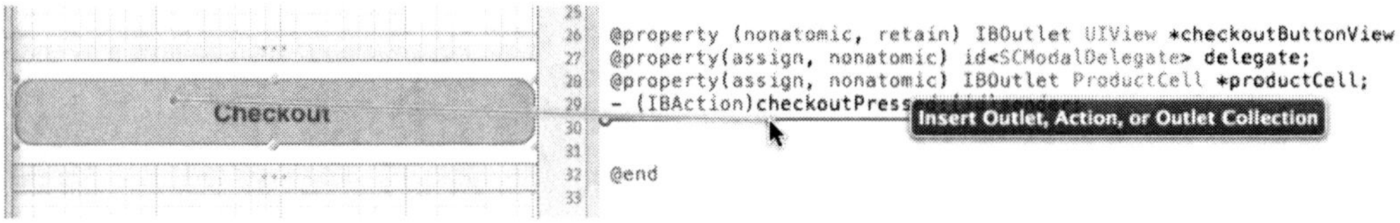

Figure 10–21. *Interface Builder's integration with Xcode makes creating outlets easy.*

Because you're using this integration, Xcode will automatically insert the instance variable, synthesize the property, and place the appropriate code in dealloc and viewDidUnload.

Save all of the modified files by pressing command+option+S. Next, open ShoppingCartViewController.m, and look for the following line in viewDidLoad:

```
UIBarButtonItem *storeButton =
    [[UIBarButtonItem alloc] initWithTitle:@"Store"

style:UIBarButtonItemStyleBordered
                                                            target:self

action:@selector(backToStorePressed:)];
```

Remove that line and replace it with these:

```
UIBarButtonItem *storeButton = nil;
if(UI_USER_INTERFACE_IDIOM() == UIUserInterfaceIdiomPad) {
    storeButton = [[UIBarButtonItem alloc] initWithTitle:@"Done"

style:UIBarButtonItemStyleDone

target:self

action:@selector(backToStorePressed:)];
} else {
    storeButton = [[UIBarButtonItem alloc] initWithTitle:@"Store"
```

```
style:UIBarButtonItemStyleBordered

target:self

action:@selector(backToStorePressed:)];
}
```

This section updates the type of button that is placed as the right button of the toolbar of the modal window that is displayed to present the user's shopping cart.

The next update to make is in shouldAutorotateToInterfaceOrientation:. Add the following code above the existing return statement:

```
if(UI_USER_INTERFACE_IDIOM() == UIUserInterfaceIdiomPad) {
    return YES;
}
```

The last update to make is in tableView:viewForFooterInSection:. Before the return statement, add the following code:

```
if(UI_USER_INTERFACE_IDIOM() == UIUserInterfaceIdiomPad) {
    [checkoutButton setAutoresizingMask:UIViewAutoresizingNone];
    [checkoutButton setFrame:CGRectMake(30, checkoutButton.frame.origin.y,
        self.view.frame.size.width - 60, checkoutButton.frame.size.height)];
}
```

What we're doing here is setting the autoresizing mask to none and resetting the frame of the button so it matches the surrounding cells.

Finishing Up

That's it! We've successfully updated Super Checkout to be a universal binary. We were able to reuse almost all of the application and only had to create one iPad specific nib. The process we just went through is a great start with converting any other existing apps to run on both the iPad and iPhone/iPod Touch.

The key step, as with any new project, was the first step. Designing the application and formulating the plan to convert the existing application to a universal binary was the most important phase; the rest was simply implementation and follow through of the design.

Ideally, the application would be designed and developed as a universal application. This would reduce the number of workarounds that are implemented. A good thing to keep in the back of your mind while working on an application is to design with universal in mind. While the application you are working might run only on the iPhone/iPod Touch, a request to bring the application to the iPad might come later.

The best way to accomplish a design that is ready for a univesal transition is to reduce the number of views that are created in code. If views must be created in code, avoid hard-coding sizes. Using an idiom-detecting APIs is also a key to specializing certain blocks of code to the iPad or the iPhone/iPod Touch. When using nibs, using the springs and struts to have automatically resizing views is also a good thing for nibs that will be used across all devices.

Now that the application is a universal one, we can move on to bigger and better things as we deploy it to our beta testers. Commit the changes, and merge the branch back into the master branch and send out a beta version to your testers. Since they were asking for an iPad version, I'm sure they'll be happy you listened and developed a solution fairly quickly.

Summary

We now have a universal application that runs on both iPhone and iPad. Supporting both families of devices can be difficult, but with enough thought up front, the development of the application will be done quicker than if two separate applications were developed.

So what's next? We've covered almost all of the topics we need to in this book so far, but we have more surprises for you. In Chapter 11, we'll explore how to share your masterpiece with the world. In Chapter 12, we'll talk about navigating Xcode with your keyboard and the all-important developer workflow. Keyboard shortcuts and other ways to improve your workflow are included. I don't know about you, but I'm a keyboard shortcut person. I love being able to hit a few keys and watch the application perform many tasks. I hope you'll find the tips in Chapter 12 useful and will be able to incorporate these items in your workflow. But first, let's share our app.

Chapter 11

How Do I Share Some of This?

Now we've built a universal version of Super Checkout. We can package our application for submission to the App Store and watch the money and accolades roll in. Of course, we'll have to deal with bug reports and adding new features, but we've covered how to handle that. What we really want to do is move on and create the next great iOS application.

We could start from scratch, but that would probably entail duplicating a lot of work we've done for Super Checkout. A simple solution would be to copy the code we want to use from Super Checkout into our new project. As you're probably aware, this approach has many problems.

For example, suppose we receive a bug report from a Super Checkout user that involves some of the code we've duplicated into our new application. We have to fix two sets of identical code (and their associated tests). Of course, we could cut and paste the fixes. But while cutting and pasting, we could make a mistake.

We need to figure out how to maximize our code reuse while minimizing the amount of redundant work. The iOS way of achieving this is with a static library. In this chapter, we'll break out some of the Super Checkout code into a separate static library project in Xcode. Then, we'll integrate the new static library project into Super Checkout.

Selling lots of copies of Super Checkout may be great for our wallets, but it may not boost our programmer ego. One way to boost our geek credibility would be to release some of code as an open source project. Other programmers would then see how great our programming skills are. The real bonus is sharing our work and improving the quality of our code. In his essay, "The Cathedral and the Bazaar" (http://www.catb.org/~esr/writings/homesteading/cathedral-bazaar/), Eric Raymond stated "given enough eyeballs, all bugs are shallow," which alludes to Linus's Law, named after Linus Torvalds of the Linux project. He meant that the broader the source code distribution, the more rapidly bugs will be discovered and fixed. To distribute our new static library, we'll share with the world via GitHub (http://www.github.com/), a source code repository focused on simplifying code sharing.

Finally, we'll briefly cover a few open source software licenses that you may adopt for your new static library, including the pros and cons of each. There is no right or wrong choice. The license you choose is highly dependent on your goals and wishes.

Breaking Out Code into a Static Library

At its simplest, a static library is an archive of compiled files. These files are then linked to an application, making it appear as if the library source is part of your application. As I said before, its main goal is to break out application code into a reusable package that may be shared across many applications.

Let's take a look at our Super Checkout application. What code should be pulled out into a static library? Looking at the groups we've set up, it's pretty clear that the files in the ExternalLibraries folder make good candidates: ASIHTTPRequest and SBJSON (see Figure 11–1).

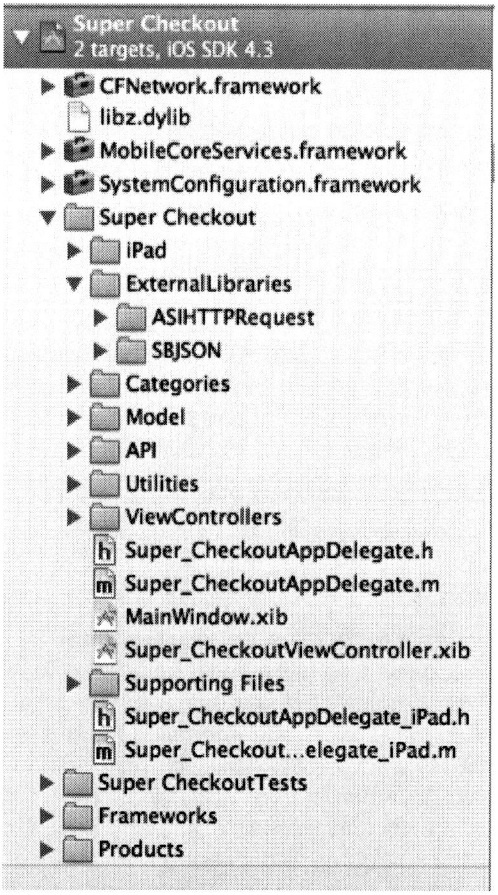

Figure 11–1. *Super Checkout project groups*

> **NOTE:** OUR EXTERNAL LIBRARY codes bases already exist as static libraries and open source
> projects. You can read more about them at their corresponding home pages:
> http://allseeing-i.com/ASIHTTPRequest/ (ASIHTTPRequest) and
> http://stig.github.com/json-framework/ (SBJSON).

Creating a Static Library

If its not already running, launch Xcode. Create a new project (File ➤ New ➤ New
Project). When the new project pane appears, choose Framework & Library under the
iOS group, and choose the Cocoa Touch Static Library template (see Figure 11–2). Click
Next.

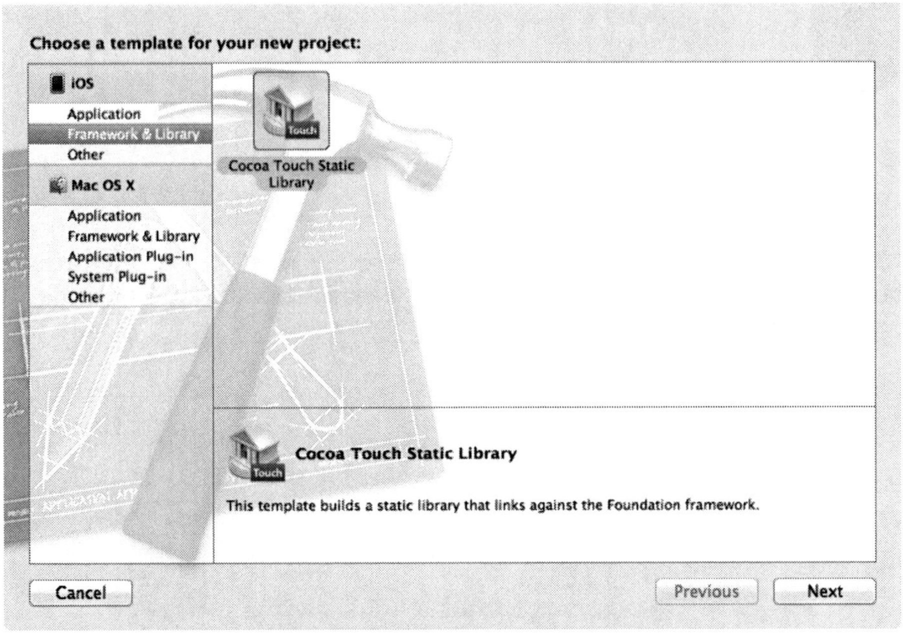

Figure 11–2. *Choose the Cocoa Touch Static Library template*

When prompted for a Product Name, enter **SBJSON** (see Figure 11–3). Make sure the
Include Unit Tests check box is checked, and the Use Automatic Reference Counting
box is unchecked. Click Next.

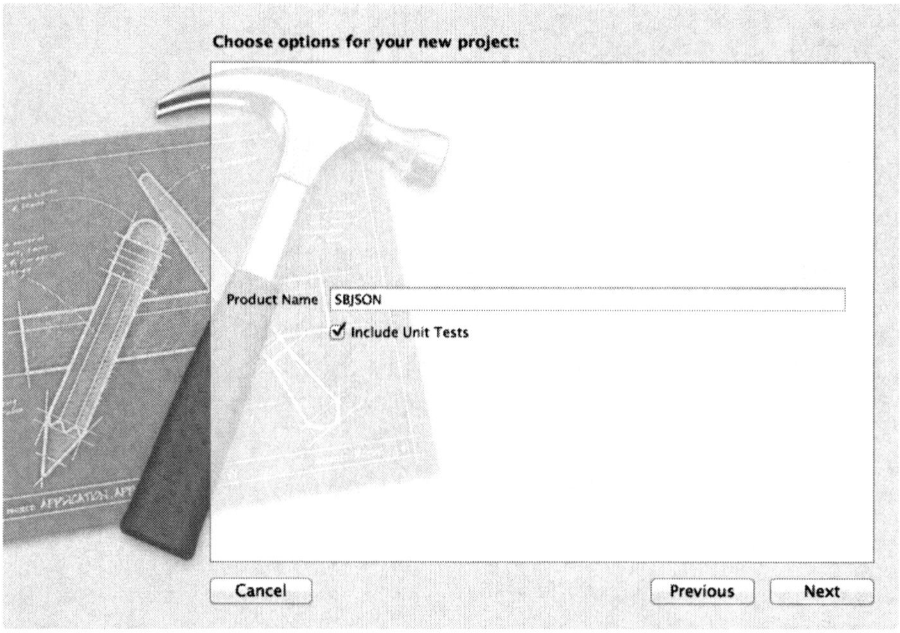

Figure 11–3. *Name the static library*

Save the project next to the Super-Checkout directory (see Figure 11–4). Check "Create local git repository for this project" (we will cover why we want this later). Click Create.

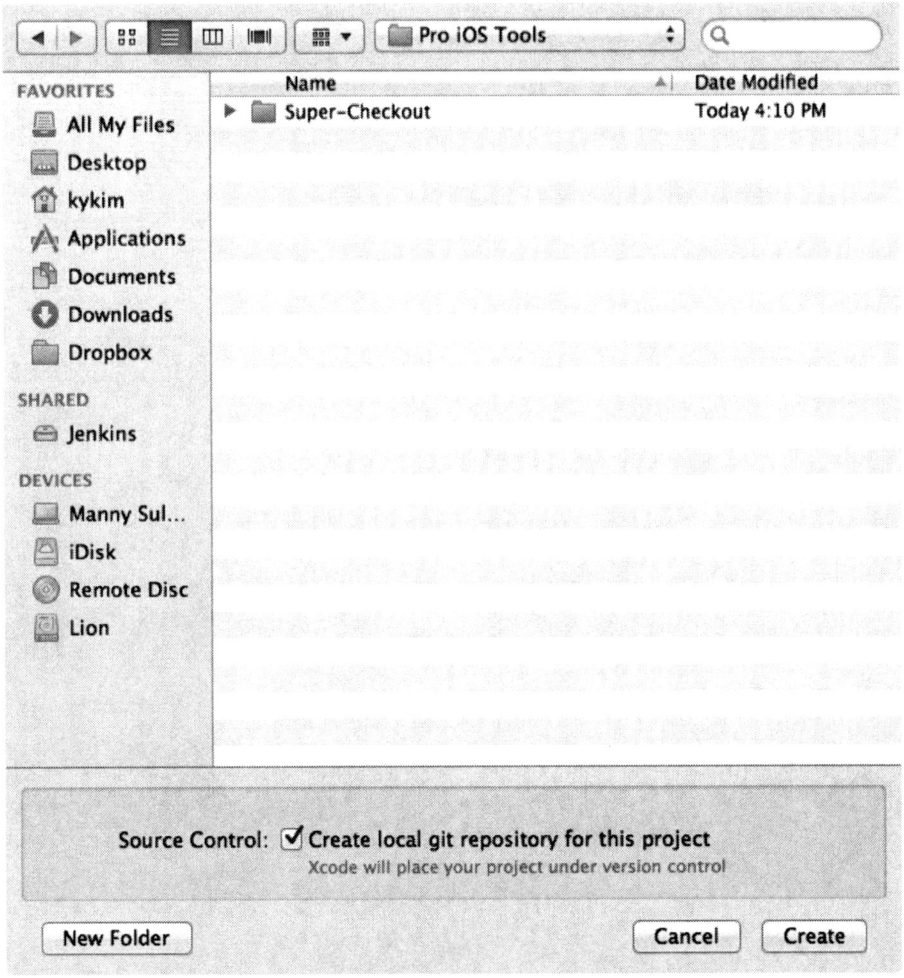

Figure 11–4. *Creating the static library project folder with a local Git repository*

Now our new static library project window for SBJSON should appear (see Figure 11–5).
You should be in the SBJSON target Build Settings pane. If not, navigate to it. Make
sure the All option is selected. Scroll down until you see the section with the heading
Deployment. Look for the row titled Targeted Device Family, and change the value to
iPhone/iPad (see Figure 11–6).

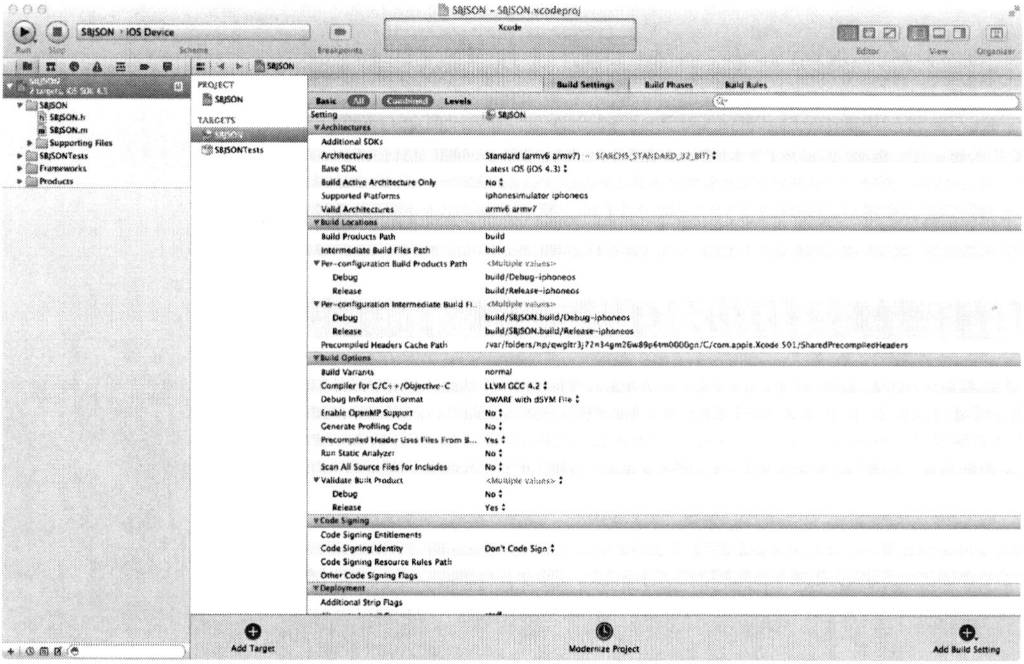

Figure 11–5. *Our SBJSON static library project window*

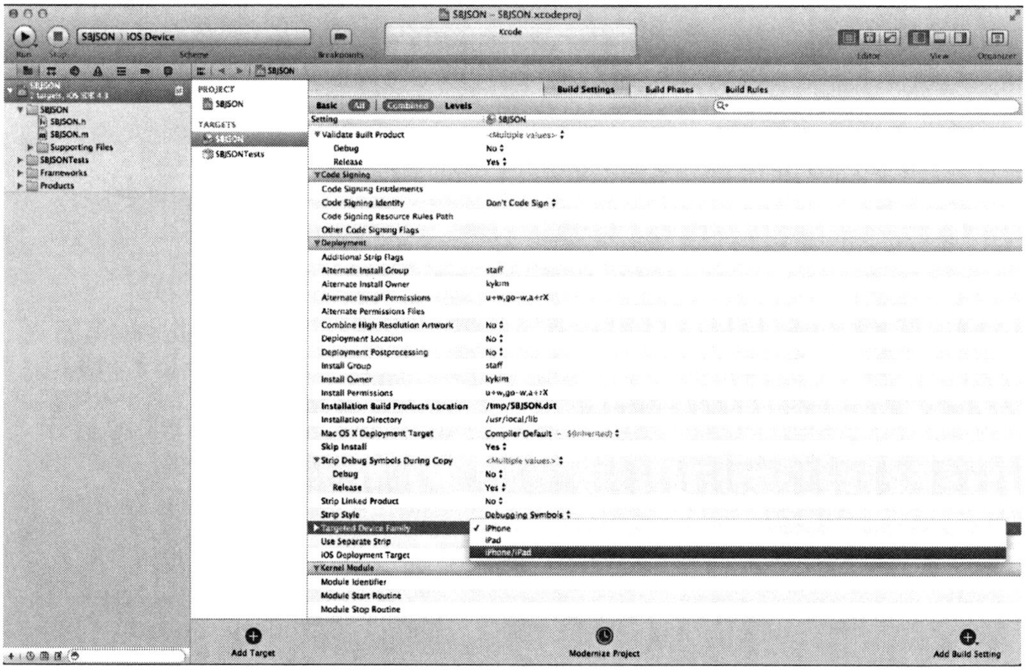

Figure 11–6. *Changing the target device of our library*

In the Navigation pane, hold down the shift key, and select the two files SBJSON.h and SBJSON.m. We don't need these two files, so delete them. A dialog should appear asking if you want remove the file references or really delete them (see Figure 11–7). We really want to delete them, so click Delete.

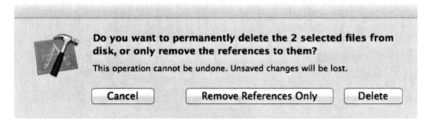

Do you want to permanently delete the 2 selected files from disk, or only remove the references to them?

This operation cannot be undone. Unsaved changes will be lost.

[Cancel]   [Remove References Only]   [Delete]

Figure 11–7. *Yes, we really want to delete the files.*

Now, let's copy the relevant files from Super Checkout. In the Navigation pane, select the SBJSON group. Either click the File menu or right-click the Navigation pane, and choose Add Files to SBJSON. When the file selection dialog opens, navigate to the SBJSON folder inside the Super Checkout project's folder. Select all the files in this folder (see Figure 11–8). Next to the Destination label, check "Copy items into destination group's folder (if needed)". For the Folders option, select the "Create groups for any added folders" option. Finally, make sure only SBJSON is checked in the "Add to targets" list. Click Add. Now, the files should appear in the SBJSON group in the Navigation pane (see Figure 11–9).

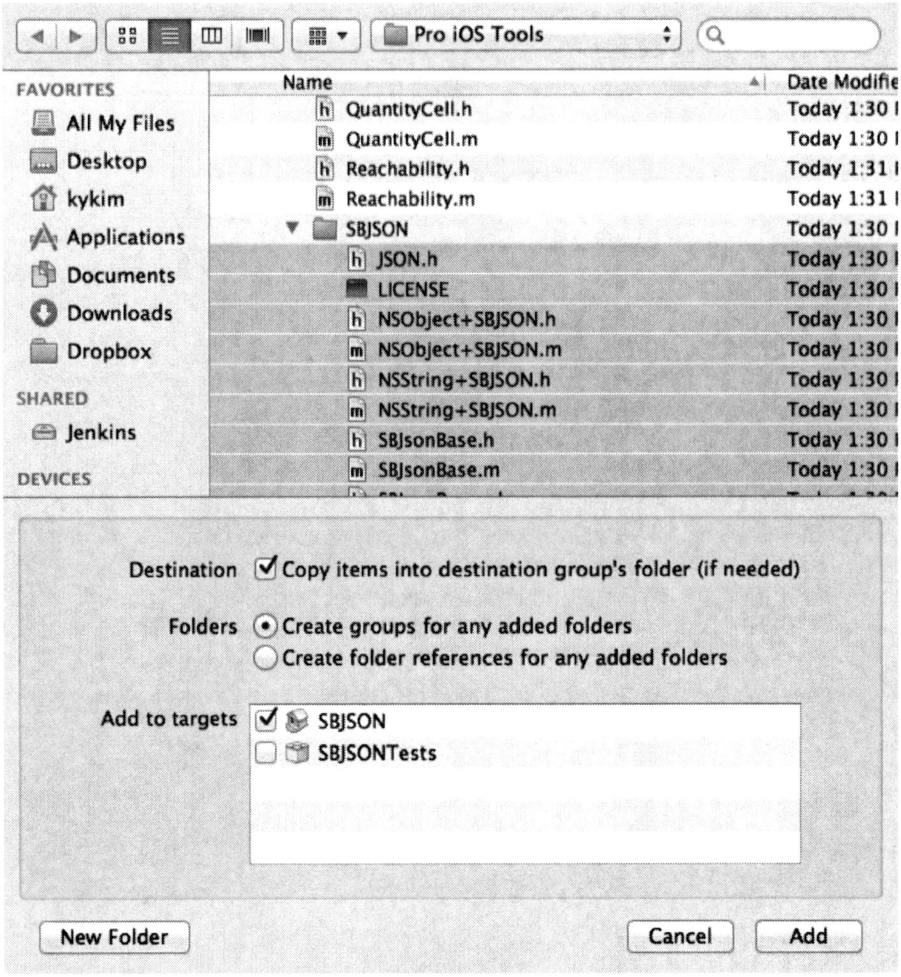

Figure 11–8. *Copying the SBJSON files from Super Checkout*

Figure 11–9. *Source files in SBJSON*

If you try to build the SBJSON static library, it will succeed. But we're not finished yet. When you use a static library, you *link* it to your application. Remember, a static library is an archive of compiled object files. When you link it to your application, it's the same as if you had compiled the code directly in your application (just like how we built Super Checkout to start). The problem is that we don't really know what classes, methods, or functions live inside the static library. Generally, to tell one class how another class works, we include the header file, the file with the .h extension. To do this with a static library, we need to publish our header files.

In the Navigation pane, select the SBJSON project to enter the project editor. Select the SBJSON target, and open the Build Phases view. Expand the build phase named "Copy Headers (6 items)" (see Figure 11–10). Drag the file JSON.h from Project to Public. Drag the remaining header files in Project to Private. Your screen should look like the one shown in Figure 11–11.

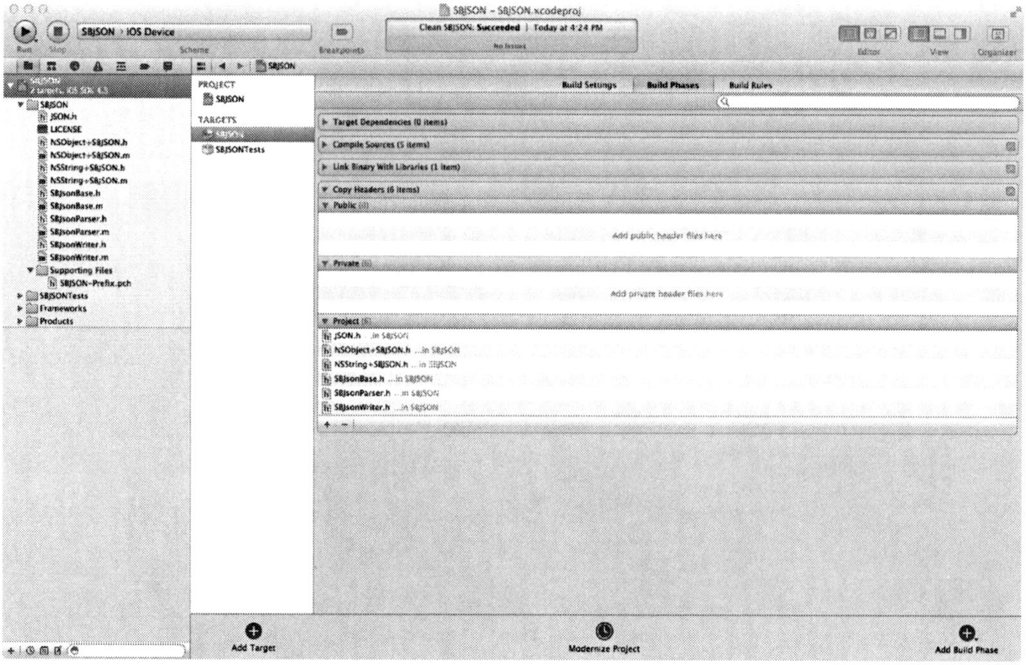

Figure 11–10. *Copying the headers*

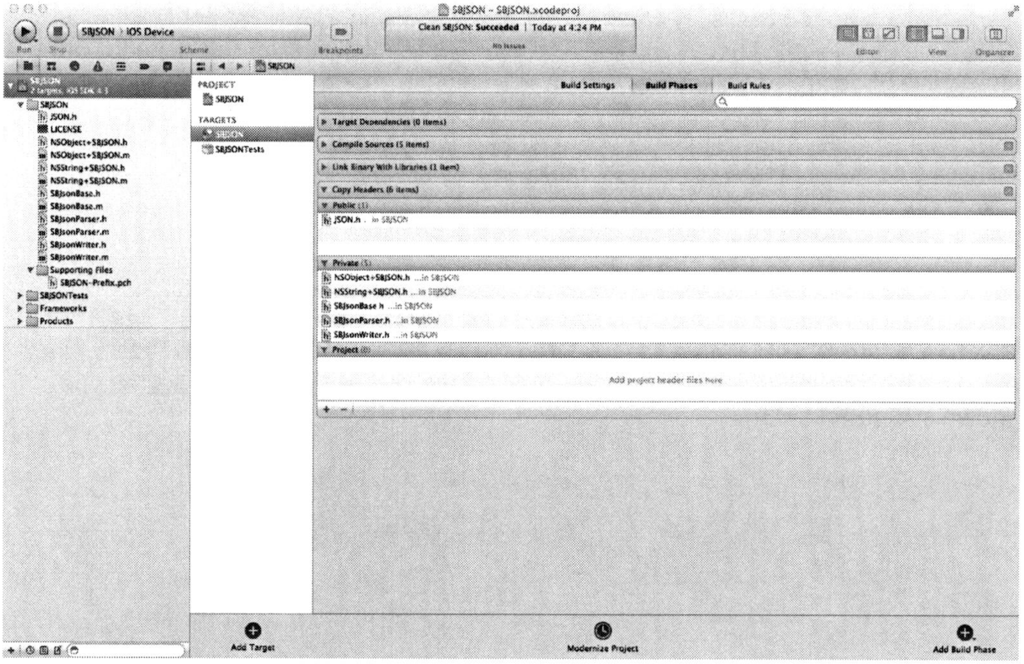

Figure 11–11. *Moving the header files from Public to Private*

Why did we move only the `JSON.h` header file to Public and not the others? Don't we need to know about all the classes and categories? Well, yes, we do, but if you look at `JSON.h`, you will notice that it imports (`#imports`) all the other header files. So by importing `JSON.h`, we will import all the other header files.

Save your work, and build. It should succeed.

> **NOTE:** At this point, I suggest you add the unit tests for the SBJSON code. Testing a static library is very similar to testing an application, and adding these tests is optional. So I'll leave this as an exercise in writing tests.

Let's repeat this process to create a static library for `ASIHTTPRequest`. There are a few differences, which I'll highlight.

Again, create a new Cocoa Touch static library. This time, we'll name it **ASIHTTPRequest**. Make sure you included unit tests and disabled automatic reference counting. Save the project in the same location you saved the SBJSON project.

Once the ASIHTTPRequest project is created and the project window opens, select Target ASIHTTPRequest. Navigate to Build Settings (making sure the All view option is selected), and change the Targeted Device Family in the Deployment section to iPhone/iPad.

Delete the files `ASIHTTPRequest.h` and `ASIHTTPRequest.m`. When asked, make sure you really delete the files. Select the `ASIHTTPRequest` group in the Navigation pane, and either click the File menu or right-click the Navigation pane, and choose Add Files to "ASIHTTPRequest". When the file selection dialog opens, navigate to the `ASIHTTPRequest` folder inside the Super Checkout project, select all the files in this folder, and copy the files into the ASIHTTPRequest project.

Unlike when we built the SBJSON static library, we're not finished adding files. Again, select Add Files to "ASIHTTPRequest", and navigate to the Super Checkout project. Add the files `Reachability.h` and `Reachability.m` to the ASIHTTPRequest project. Remember to make sure you copy the files by checking the "Copy items into destination's folder (if needed)" check box.

Enter the project editor for ASIHTTPRequest, and select the ASIHTTPRequest target. Choose the Build Phases tab, and expand the "Copy Headers (13 items)" build phase. Drag `ASIHTTPRequest.h` and `ASIDownloadCache.h` to the Public section. Drag the remaining header files to the Private section. Build the library.

At this point, we should have two static library projects: SBJSON and ASIHTTPRequest. Next, we'll integrate those two projects into Super Checkout.

Using Static Libraries

One purpose of breaking out some of the Super Checkout code into these two static libraries, SBJSON and ASIHTTPRequest, was to foster code reuse. What better place to start reusing than in the Super Checkout project. Before we get started, we should talk about how we can use these static libraries in Super Checkout.

There are two different methods by which we can use the static library projects in the Super Checkout project: subprojects and workspaces.

A subproject is one project embedded within another. This is accomplished fairly easily with Xcode. Logically, this approach makes sense: the Super Checkout project will depend on the SBJSON and ASIHTTPRequest projects. Embedding the two as subprojects of Super Checkout structurally creates some visual clarity. However, there are some configuration issues that need to be addressed when pursuing this method. We'll address these issues when discussing the subproject approach.

With the release of Xcode 4, Apple introduced the concept of workspaces. A workspace is a logical container for multiple projects. All the projects share the same build directory. By using a workspace, all the projects can use their products when building.

Each approach, subprojects and workspaces, has its pros and cons. You should use the method that best suits your style. I'll discuss both for completeness. Before we start, make a backup copy of all three projects (Super Checkout, SBJSON, and ASIHTTPRequest), so you can try both methods if you wish.

Static Libraries As a Subproject

Open the Super Checkout project in Xcode. Choose File ➤ Add Files to "Super Checkout". When the file dialog appears, navigate to the SBJSON folder, and select the file SBJSON.xcodeproj (see Figure 11–12). Make sure "Copy items into destination group's folder (if needed)" is unchecked. Add it only to the Super Checkout target. Click Add.

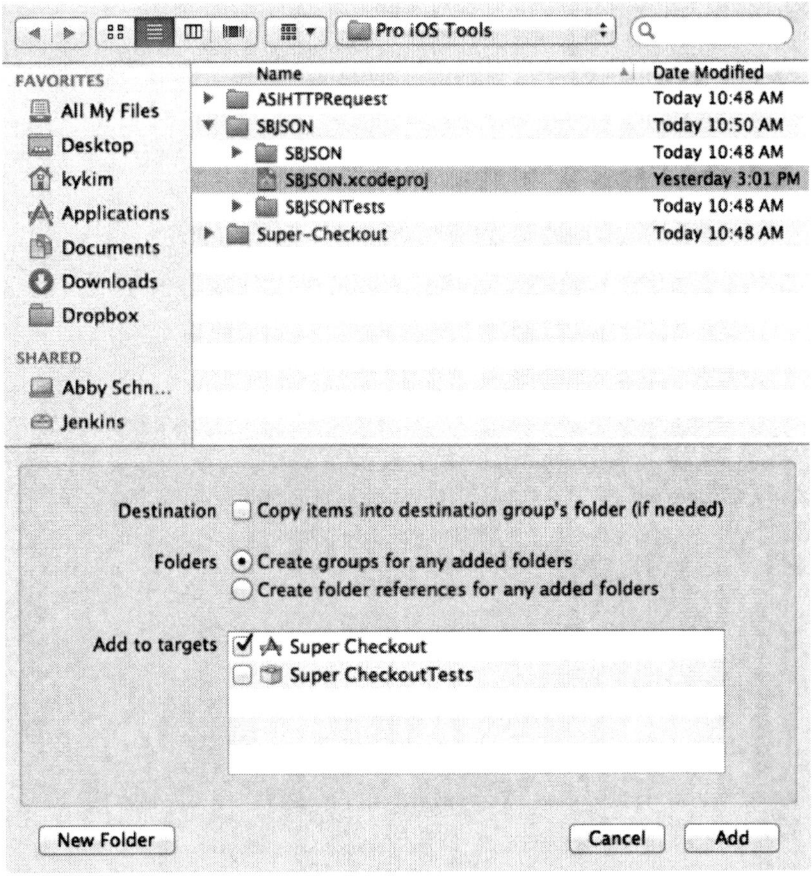

Figure 11-12. *Adding the SBJSON project to Super Checkout*

The SBJSON project should appear in the navigation pane, inside the Super Checkout project (see Figure 11–13).

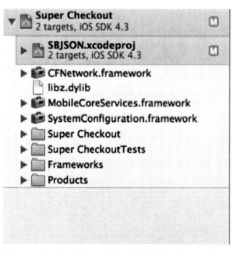

Figure 11–13. *After adding SBJSON to Super Checkout*

When we build Super Checkout, we want the SBJSON project to be built first. We'll accomplish this by adding a Target Dependency to the Super Checkout Build Phases.

In the navigation pane, click the Super Checkout project to open the Project Editor view. Under Targets, select Super Checkout and then the Build Phases tab. The first build phase should be "Target Dependencies (0 items)". Click the disclosure triangle to the right to expand it (see Figure 11–14).

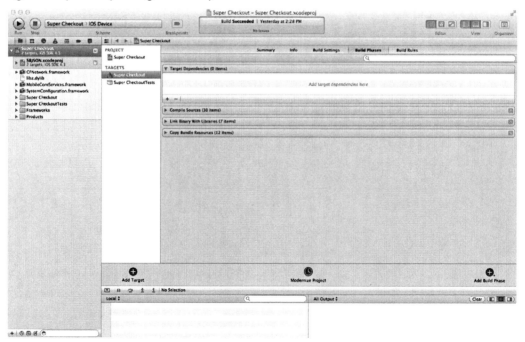

Figure 11–14. *Super Checkout with the Target Dependencies expanded*

Click the plus sign at the bottom of the Target Dependencies build phase. A target selector pane should appear (see Figure 11–15). Select the SBJSON target under the SBJSON project, and click Add. The SBJSON target should appear in the dependency list (see Figure 11–16).

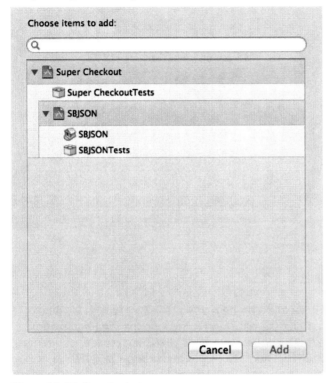

Figure 11–15. *Target selector pane*

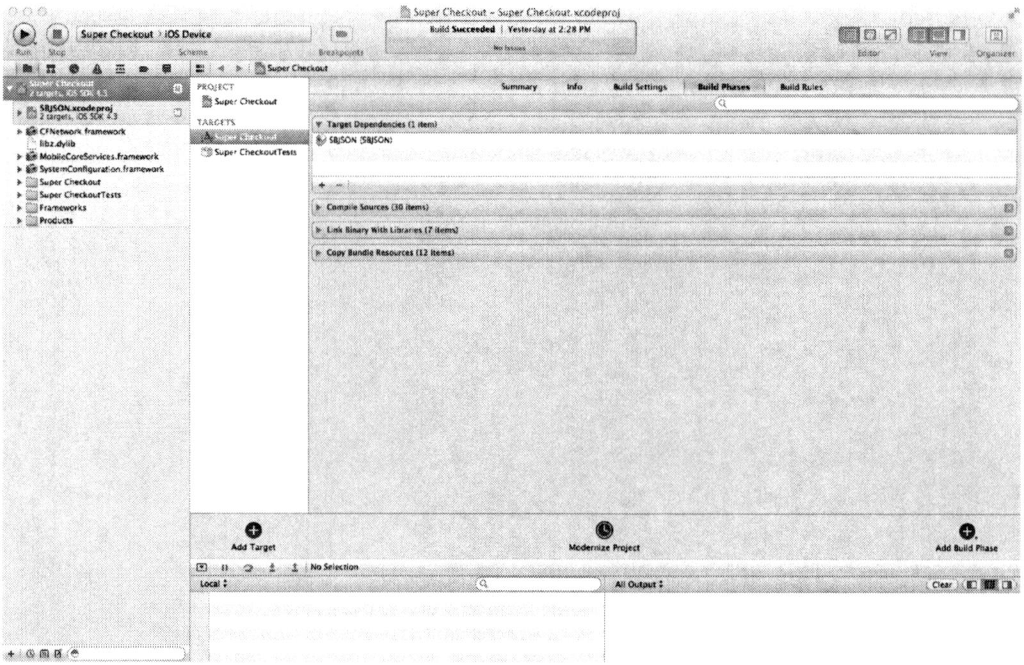

Figure 11–16. *SBJSON in the Target Dependencies*

Lower in the build phases list, there should be an item titled Link Binary with Libraries (7 items). Expand it (see Figure 11–17). Click the plus sign to expose the library selection pane (see Figure 11–18). At the top, there should be a folder titled `Workspace`, containing the item `libSBJSON.a`. Select `libSBJSON.a`, and click Add. The library, `libSBJSON.a`, should appear in red at the top of the Link Binary with Libraries list (see Figure 11–19). Don't worry, the red color just means the library hasn't been built for this project yet.

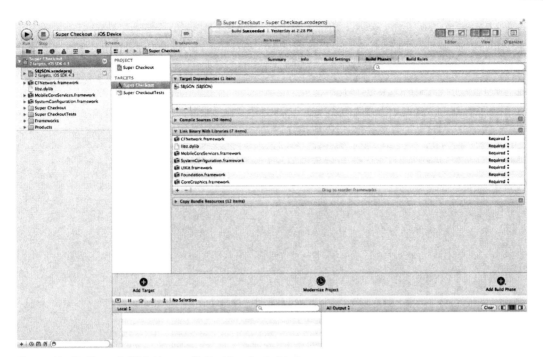

Figure 11–17. *Expanded link binary with the Libraries build phase*

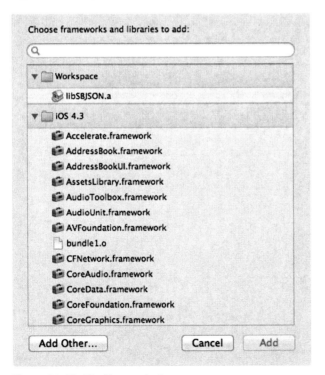

Figure 11–18. *The library selection pane*

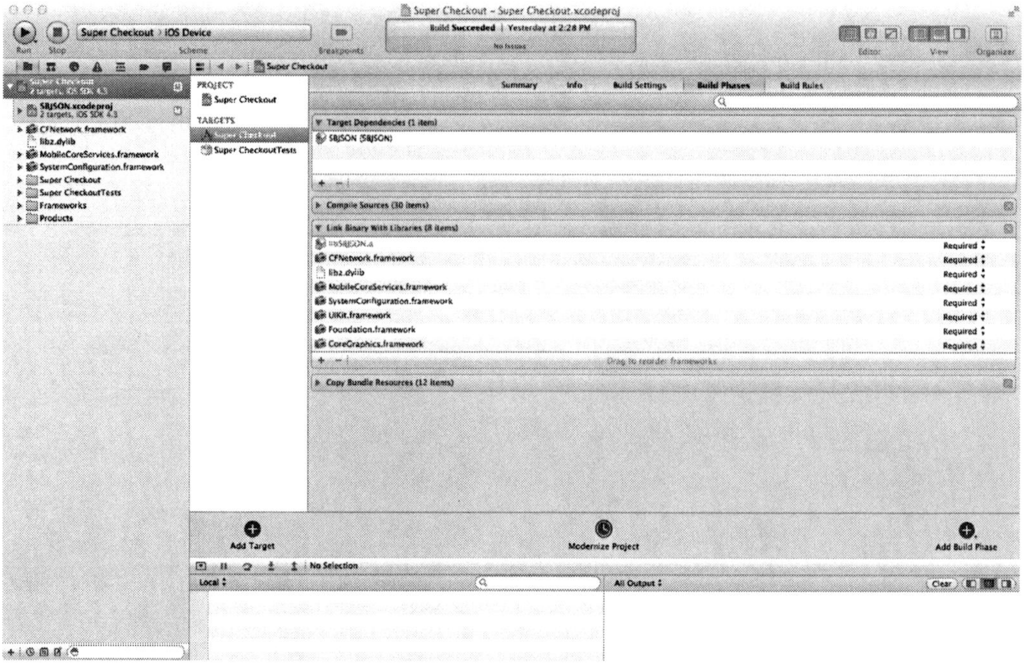

Figure 11–19. *libSBJSON.a added the link binary with libraries build phase.*

Now, we've added the SBJSON static library to our project. However, we still have the original SBJSON code that was embedded in the Super Checkout project. Let's delete those files.

Expand the Super Checkout group in the navigation pane, and then expand the ExternalLibraries folder. Right-click the SBJSON group, and select Delete (see Figure 11–20). A dialog should appear asking if you wish to delete the files or simply remove the references to them (see Figure 11–21). We don't need these files anymore, so click Delete.

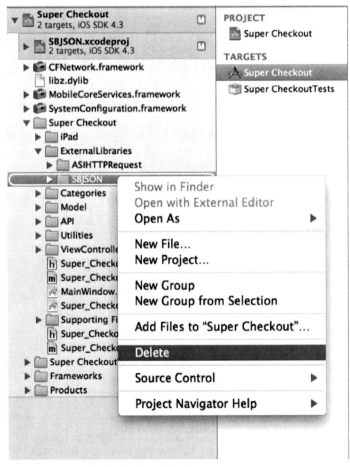

Figure 11–20. *Deleting the Super Checkout group*

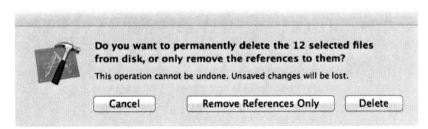

Figure 11–21. *Deletion dialog*

Build the project. Whoa! What happened? The build failed.

Click the Issue Navigator tab in the Navigation pane. The error is in SCJSONParser.m. The error says "Lexical or Preprocessor Issue 'SBJSON/JSON.h' not found." If you click the error explanation, the Issue Navigator will show the offending line in the source code viewer (see Figure 11–22).

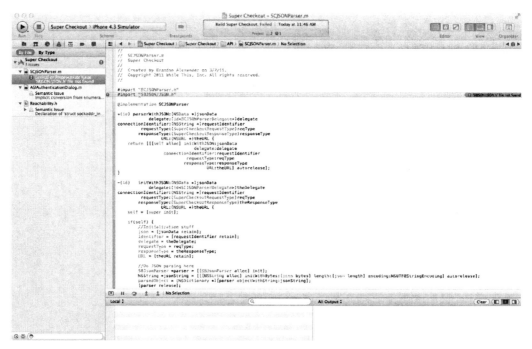

Figure 11–22. *The build error*

When we first built Super Checkout, we put all the SBJSON code in a folder named SBJSON. Among the files in the SBJSON folder was the header file, JSON.h. If you recall, we deleted that folder and all its files. So how do we fix this?

First, where is the header file JSON.h? It's in the SBJSON static library project (see Figure 11–23). JSON.h still lives in a folder named SBJSON. So the #import "SBJSON/JSON.h" line in SCJSONParser.m is technically correct. But Xcode doesn't seem to know how to find it. Notice that the SBJSON and Super-Checkout folders are next to each other. Recall that, as far as Xcode is concerned, all the project files should be located in the Super-Checkout folder, so we need to tell Xcode to look inside the SBJSON folder as well.

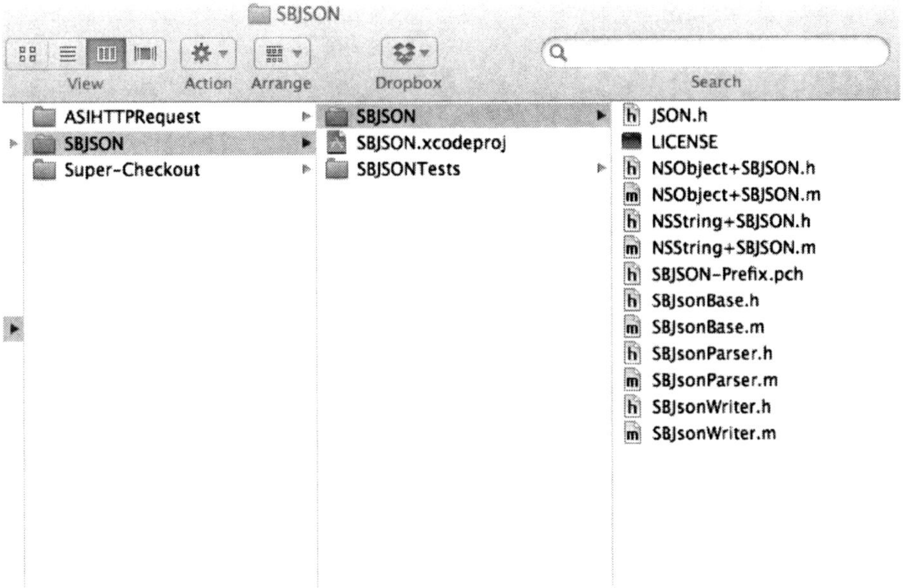

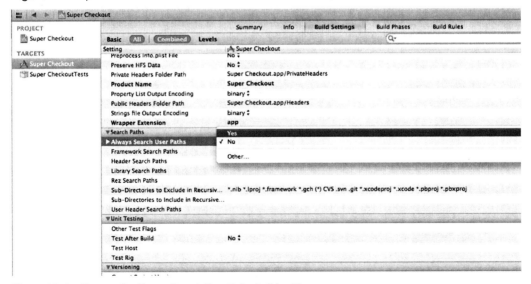

Figure 11–23. *The current location of JSON.h*

Head back to the Project Navigator in the Navigation pane. Click the Super Checkout project to open the Project Editor view, and select the Super Checkout target. Select the Build Settings tab, and make sure the All view setting is selected. Next, scroll down and search for the build setting group with the Search Paths header. The first row of this group should be titled Always Search User Paths. Change this value from No to Yes (see Figure 11–24).

Figure 11–24. *Turn on the Always Search User Paths build setting*

The last row of the Search Paths build setting group should read User Header Search Paths. Double-click this row, to the right of the text "User Header Search Paths". A pane should appear. Click the plus sign button on the bottom-left corner, and enter **../SBJSON** on the row that appears (see Figure 11–25). Click Done. The string, ../SBJSON, should appear on the User Header Search Paths row.

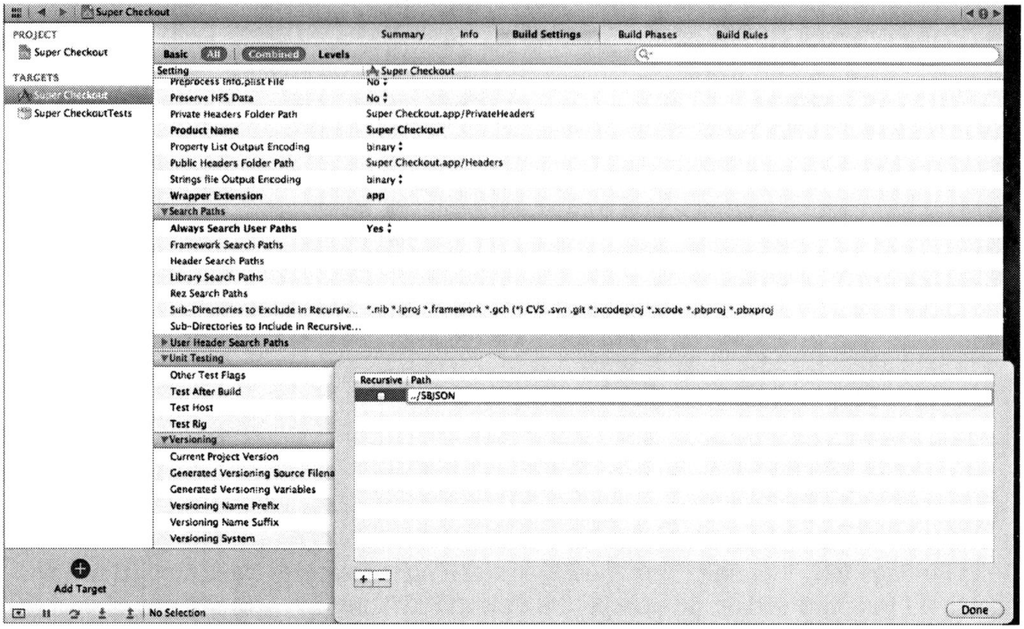

Figure 11–25. *Adding a user-defined search path*

Save your work, and try building again. Success!

Repeat the process for the ASIHTTPRequest library. After you add the library, you can delete the ASIHTTPRequest group in the Navigation pane (if you want, you can delete the ExternalLibraries group as well, just to tidy up the project). Inside the User Header Search Paths build setting, type **../ASIHTTPRequest**.

Build the project. What happened this time?

The Issue Navigator says the problem is in SuperCheckoutAPIEngine.m. The error is "Lexical or Preprocessor Issue 'ASIHTTPRequest.h' not found." Hmm, the fix worked for SBJSON/JSON.h, why is it not working for ASIHTTPRequest.h?

The reason is pretty straightforward. We just need to prefix the imported ASIHTTPRequest.h with its parent directory. So edit SuperCheckoutAPIEngine.m to read as follows:

```
#import "SuperCheckoutAPIEngine.h"
#import "SuperCheckoutRequestTypes.h"
#import "SCJSONParser.h"
#import "Product.h"
#import "ASIHTTPRequest/ASIHTTPRequest.h"
```

```
#import "ASIHTTPRequest/ASIDownloadCache.h"
#import "NSString+UUID.h"
```

Why did we need to add `ASIHTTPRequest/`? We told Xcode to look in the directories `SBJSON` and `ASIHTTPRequest` that are next to the Super-Checkout directory. But when we import (#import) the headers, we are doing two different things. `#import "SBJSON/JSON.h"` says import the file `JSON.h` that lives inside the directory `SBJSON`. If you look inside the `SBJSON` project folder, you'll see another `SBJSON` folder. The file `JSON.h` lives there. `#import "ASIHTTPRequest.h"` says to import the `ASIHTTPRequest.h` file that lives somewhere. If you look inside the `ASIHTTPRequest` folder, there's another `ASIHTTPRequest` folder where `ASIHTTPRequest.h` lives.

Super Checkout should now build.

Using a Workspace

As stated earlier, Apple introduced the concept of a workspace in Xcode 4. A workspace is a common logical container for several related projects. By using a workspace, you let Xcode manage the explicit and implicit relationships between the workspace projects. In our case, Xcode will build the static libraries when we build the Super Checkout application.

> **NOTE:** Remember that you'll need to work from the copy you made before we created the subprojects. If your Super Checkout application project has the static libraries as subprojects, you're working with the wrong project.

If it's not already open, open Super Checkout in Xcode.

Select File ➤ New ➤ New Workspace. When the Save As dialog appears, navigate to the directory containing the Super Checkout project. You should also see the ASIHTTPRequest and SBJSON static library projects we created earlier. Type **Super-Checkout.xcworkspace** for the name of the workspace, and click Save (see Figure 11–26).

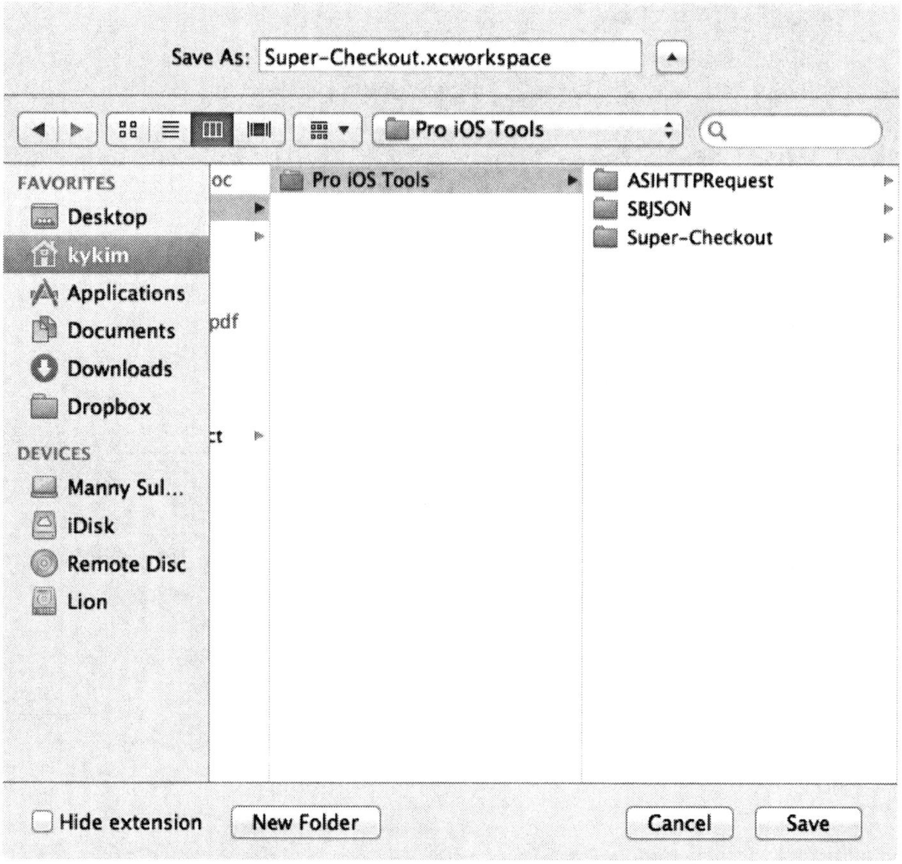

Figure 11–26. *Creating our new workspace*

Now, we need to add our projects to the workspace.

If the Navigation pane is not exposed, open it by clicking on the Navigator area selector (⬚) on the Toolbar. Also, if the Standard Editor (▤) is not selected in the Toolbar Editor Selector, select it.

In the workspace Navigation pane, control-click to expose the context menu. Select "Add Files to 'Super-Checkout'" (see Figure 11–27). When the file selection dialog opens, navigate to the Super-Checkout project's folder. Select Super-Checkout.xcodeproj. Make sure the check box next "Copy items into destination group's folder (if needed)" is unchecked. Select the "Create groups for any added folders" radio button. Make sure your dialog looks like Figure 11–28. Click Add.

> **NOTE:** Don't use the "Add File to 'Super-Checkout'" option from the File menu. This won't add the projects to the workspace in the manner we want.

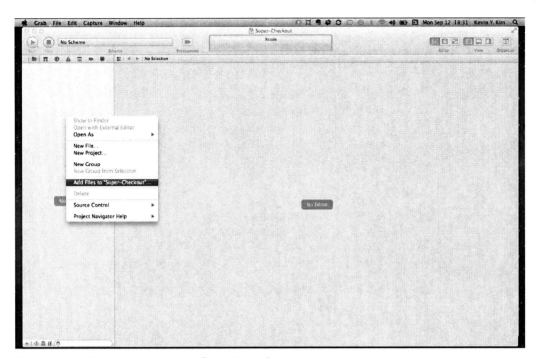

Figure 11–27. *The context menu to add files to the workspace*

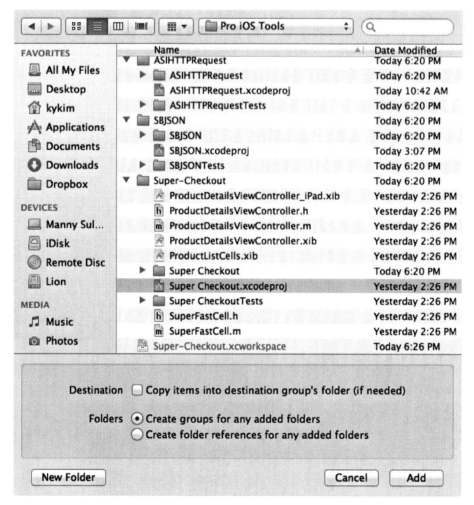

Figure 11–28. *Adding the Super Checkout application to the workspace*

Your workspace should now have one project, Super Checkout (see Figure 11–29). Repeat this process to add the ASIHTTPRequest and SBJSON projects. Again, use the context menu from the Navigation pane, not the File menu. When complete, your workspace window should look like Figure 11–30.

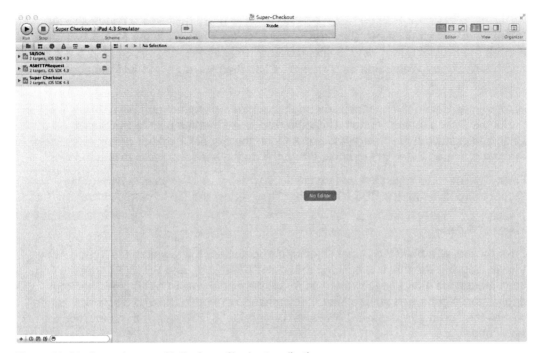

Figure 11–29. *Our workspace with the Super Checkout application*

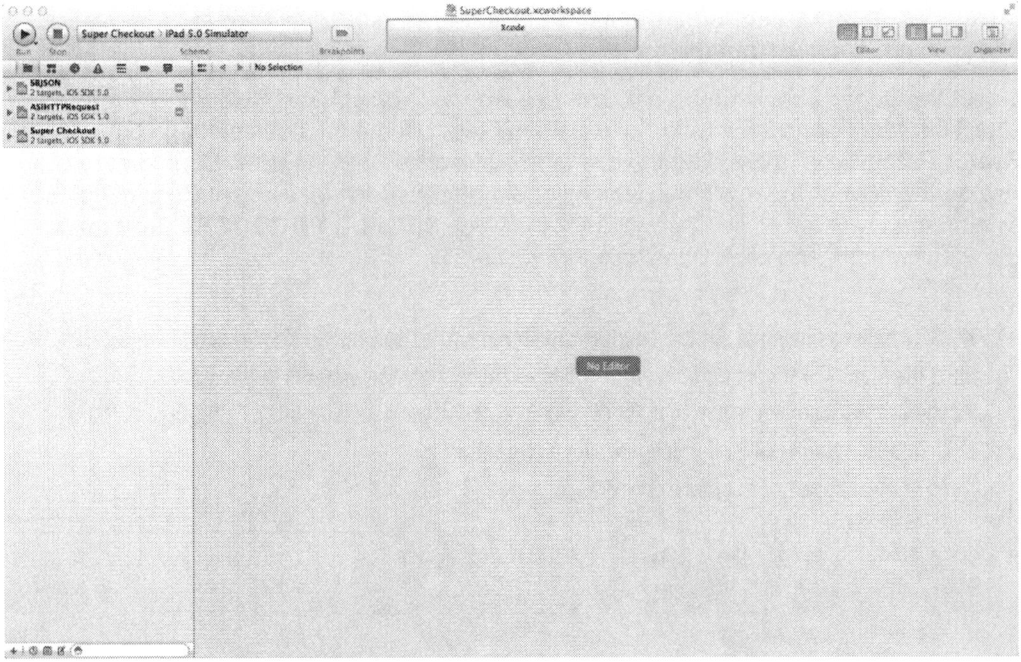

Figure 11–30. *Our workspace with all the projects*

As we did previously, add the libASIHTTPRequest.a and libSBJSON.a libraries to the Super Checkout application. Click the Super Checkout project in the Navigation pane to expose the Project Editor view. Select the Build Phases tab, and expose the build phase titled "Link Binary With Libraries (7 Items)". Click the plus sign, and add the two static libraries.

Also, we can delete the unnecessary original ASIHTTPRequest and SBJSON files within the Super Checkout application. Click the disclosure triangle next to the Super Checkout project in the Navigation pane. Open the Super Checkout group, and delete the group named External Libraries. When the dialog appears, really delete the files.

Finally, we need to adjust the source file SCJSONParser.m. We need to correct the #import directives for the SBJSON header files. Adjust the file to read like this:

```
#import "SCJSONParser.h"
#import "JSON.h"
```

Save the file, and build the Super Checkout application. If you watch the Xcode Activity Viewer, you will see that it is building the ASIHTTPRequest and SBJSON projects first, even though we didn't specify them as target dependencies of the Super Checkout application. Xcode was able to infer that we needed to build those projects first, since we link their products, libASIHTTPRequest.a and libSBJSON.a, to the Super Checkout application.

However, it looks like the build fails with a lexical or preprocessor issue. You may see that Xcode is unable to find one of three files: ASIHTTPRequest.h, ASIDownloadCache.h, or JSON.h. We saw this error before when we included the static libraries as subprojects. The problem is similar, but the solution this time is different.

Select the Super Checkout project, and expose the Project View. Select the Super Checkout target, and select the Build Settings tab. Locate the build settings group titled Search Paths. From there, find the row labeled Header Search Paths. Double-click the row, to the right of the row label, which should open a pop-up window. Click the plus sign on the lower left to add a row. Enter the value **$(BUILT_PRODUCTS_DIR)** under the Path column, and click Done (see Figure 11–31).

> **NOTE:** I believe having to set the Search Paths build setting is a bug in Xcode. Xcode knows to build the static library projects first and builds all the workspace projects in the same build location. It would make sense that Xcode should automatically include BUILT_PRODUCTS_DIR in its header search paths. If you agree, file a bug report at http://bugreporter.apple.com/.

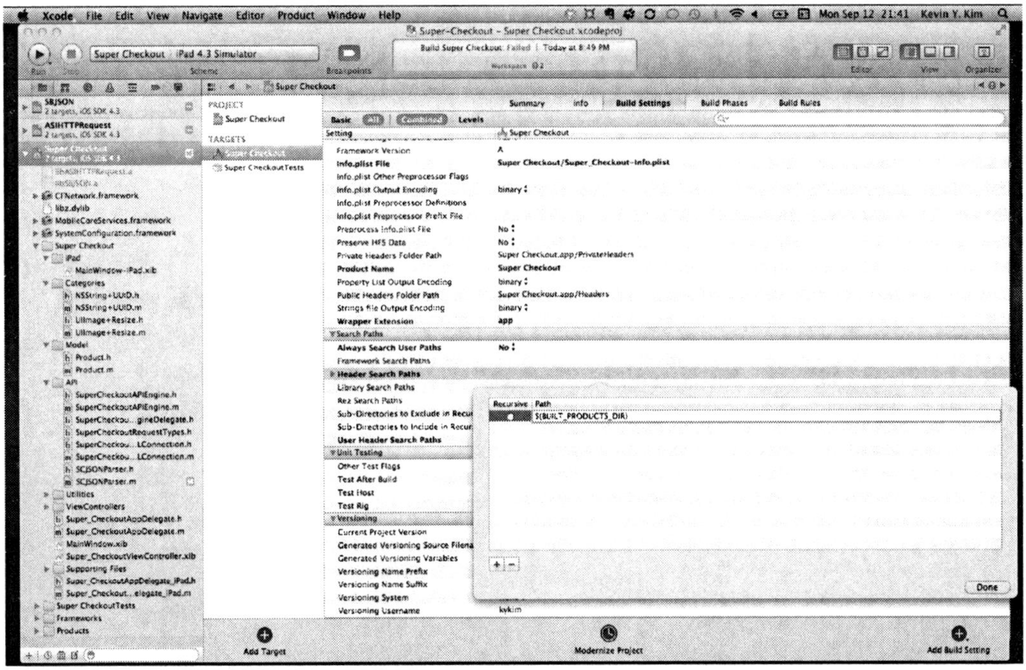

Figure 11–31. *Setting the header search paths*

> **NOTE:** BUILD_PRODUCTS_DIR is an Xcode environment variable. The actual value depends on the build environment. In this case, BUILT_PRODUCTS_DIR depends on the build configuration. If you expose the Header Search Paths row, you will see it resolves into two different values, for the Debug and Release configurations.

Build the project and run it. Success again!

I've shown you two ways to add static libraries to your application. Either method is acceptable, so choose the one that works best for you. However, since the introduction of workspace in Xcode 4, it is clear that Apple will probably make this its preferred method of integrating several projects together.

Sharing on GitHub

Let's take a step away from our application and think about sharing our code. There are many ways we can share the project. We could post a package of the source code on our blog or web site, but a better solution would be to use a public source code repository (repo). A good repository should allow us to limit who can check in the code, while allowing anyone to view or download the code. Other beneficial features should include an integrated bug/issues tracker and wiki system.

There are many choices out there that fulfill this criteria. One popular choice is GitHub (http://www.github.com); see Figure 11–32. GitHub is a web site built on top of the Git distributed revision control system, which emphasizes on speed and was originally developed by Linus Torvalds (him again!) to aid in the development of the Linux kernel. One feature of Git is that every working directory is a full-fledged repository with a complete history and complete revision-tracking capabilities. Each Git repository does not depend on network access or a central server.

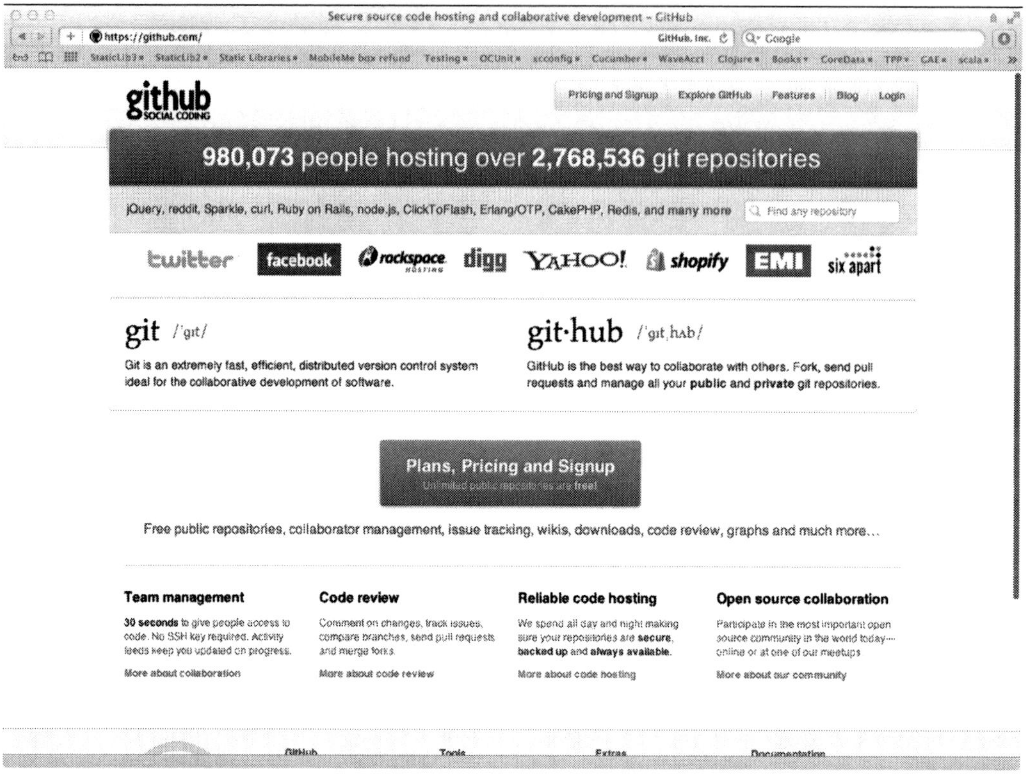

Figure 11–32. *GitHub home page*

If you recall, when we created our projects, we checked the box labeled "Create local git repository for this project." That created a local git repository in our project directory. Normally, this repository is hidden, but using Terminal.app, we're able to see it from the command line using ls -aCF (see Figure 11–33).

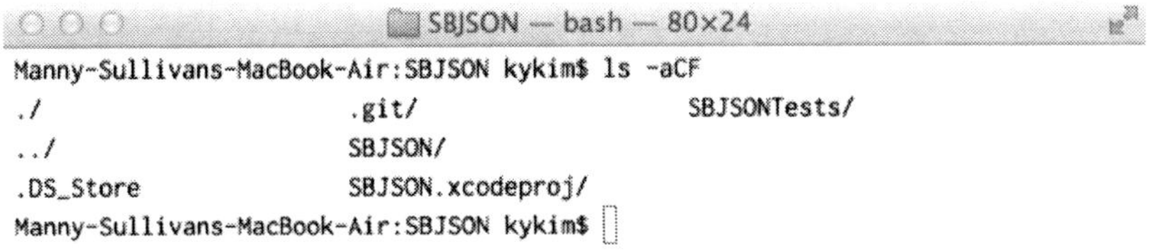

```
○ ○ ○              📁 SBJSON — bash — 80×24                    ⬏
Manny-Sullivans-MacBook-Air:SBJSON kykim$ ls -aCF
./                      .git/                  SBJSONTests/
../                     SBJSON/
.DS_Store               SBJSON.xcodeproj/
Manny-Sullivans-MacBook-Air:SBJSON kykim$ ▯
```

Figure 11–33. *The Git repository, named .git, in the SBJSON project directory*

Signing In to GitHub

The first thing is to log in to your GitHub account. If you haven't created an account yet, do so now. See Chapter 3 for information on setting up an account.

In your GitHub dashboard (see Figure 11–34), on the left side are status updates about the repositories you may be watching. On the right are your repositories. Below your repositories are the repositories you are watching.

When you watch a repository, you are telling GitHub you are interested in following a project but that you probably don't want to contribute to it. This is a fairly convenient feature that lets you easily track a project. You might want to explore the GitHub site, if you're not already familiar with it, to learn more about features like this one.

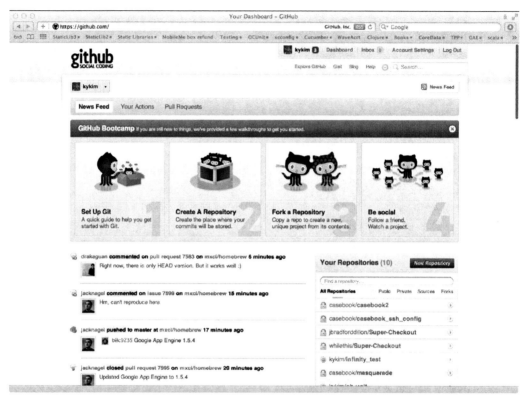

Figure 11–34. *A sample GitHub dashboard*

Create a Shared Repository

From your GitHub dashboard, click the New Repository button next to the Your
Repositories label. This will take you to the new repository page
(https://github.com/repositories/new) ; see Figure 11–35.

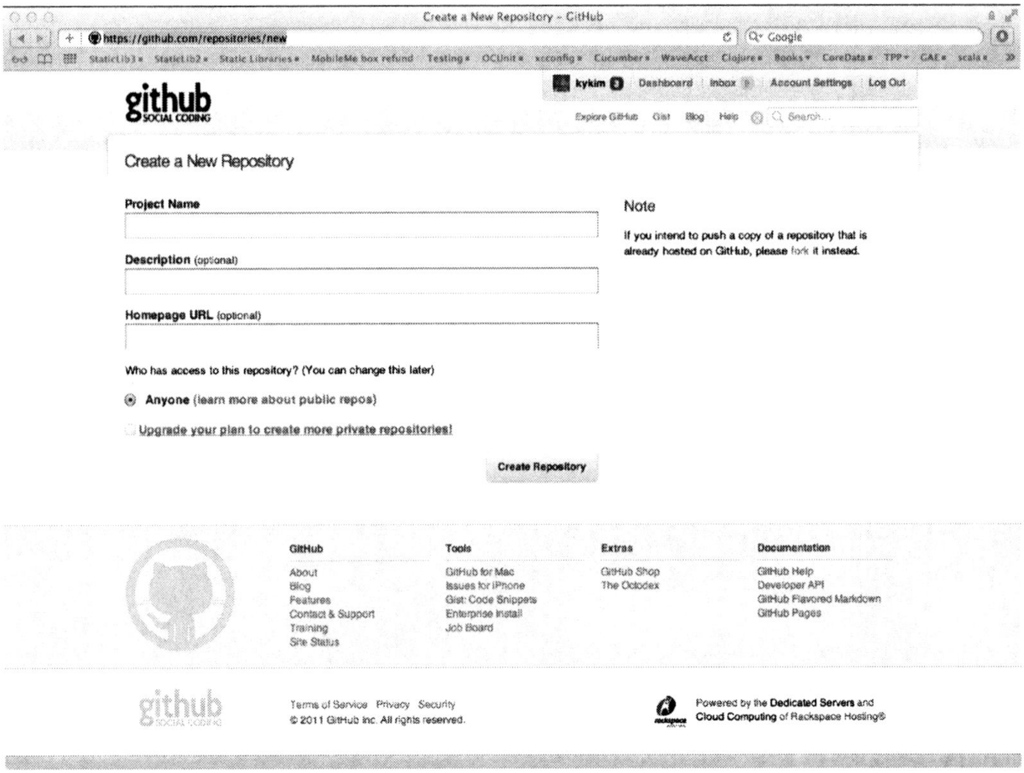

Figure 11–35. *The GitHub new repository page*

Enter **SBJSON** for the Project Name field. The remaining fields are optional, but enter **SBJSON static library for Super Checkout** as the Description. This project doesn't have a home page, so leave that field blank. Since we're using the free account, and we plan on sharing this code with everyone, leave the radio button next to the label "Anyone (learn more about public repos)" selected. Click the Create Repository button.

We should be redirected to our new GitHub repository (see Figure 11–36). Since this is an empty repository, GitHub has helpfully given us the commands we need to execute on our computer to set up our project.

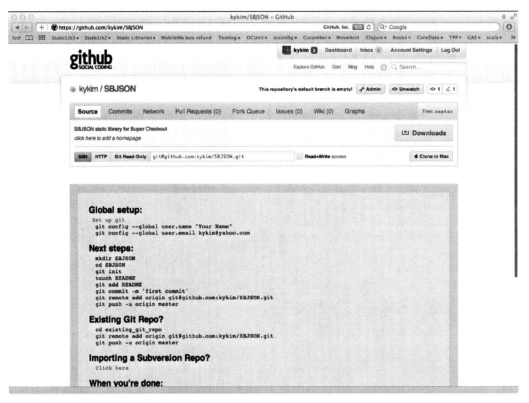

Figure 11–36. *Our GitHub repository's home page*

Back on your computer, open `Terminal.app`. Navigate down to the project directory for the SBJSON static library project. At the command line, enter the global setup commands from the GitHub project page:

```
> git config -global user.name "Your Name"
> git config -global user.email your@email.com
```

Replace `"Your Name"` with the name you wish to use with GitHub. `your@email.com` should be the e-mail address you used to sign up on GitHub.

Next, we're going to tell our local Git repository about the repository on GitHub. We should still be in the SBJSON directory. This directory should have the `.git` directory we saw earlier. Enter this command:

```
> git remote add origin git@github.com:username/SBJSON.git
```

Replace username with your GitHub username. In this command, `git@github.com:username/SBJSON.git` is the URL for the repository on GitHub. This command says we want to add a remote repository and give it the local alias of `origin`.

Committing Our Changes

Before we can put our code into GitHub, we need to commit our changes locally. Remember, each Git repository is a full-fledged, independent repository. From Git's perspective, the canonical copy of your code resides on your computer, and the repository on GitHub is a remote copy. Let's save our work in the local repository.

Open the SBJSON static library project in Xcode. Select File ➤ Source Control ➤ Commit. Xcode should expose the source control pane (see Figure 11–37). On the left side is a list of the SBJSON project files. Most of the file will be checked; some will not. You won't need to change anything. The unchecked files represent files the Xcode has determined don't need to be committed to the repository. Select the file JSON.h. In the file viewer pane, the contents of JSON.h should appear on the left. The right file viewer will read "File has no revisions". Since this is the first commit, there is nothing to display. In a commit of an existing file, the left file viewer will display the current state of JSON.h, while the right file viewer will display the last version in the repository. Xcode will highlight the differences between the file versions, so you can see what you've changed.

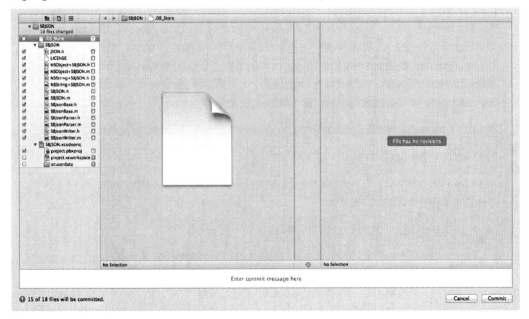

Figure 11–37. *Xcode's source control pane*

Near the bottom, there is a text area with the words "Enter commit message here". This area is for you to enter a comment about the changes going into the repository. You can be as descriptive or terse as you want. In this case, enter **Initial commit**. Click Commit.

Once the changes are committed, the source control pane will disappear, revealing the project window. Now, we're ready to push the changes to GitHub.

This time, select File ➤ Source Control ➤ Push. A dialog should appear (see Figure 11–38). It may take a few moments for the Remote drop-down to populate itself. Give it time; Xcode is checking the existence and accessibility of the remote repository. Eventually, the drop-down should read "origin/master (Create)". This is saying that GitHub is going to create the repository on origin (our alias for the remote GitHub repository) by sending it a copy of master (our local repository). Click Push.

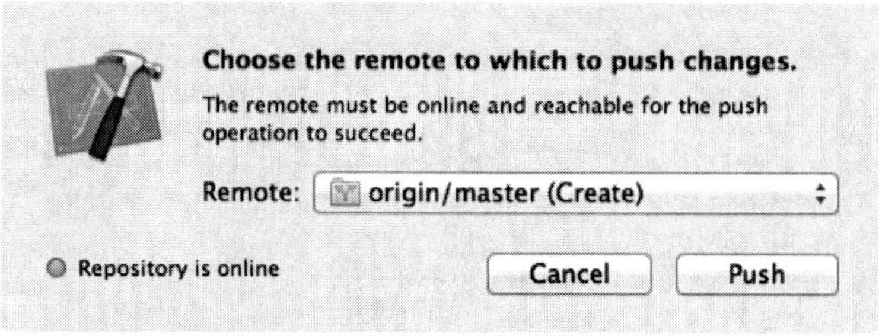

Choose the remote to which to push changes.

The remote must be online and reachable for the push operation to succeed.

Remote: 🔲 origin/master (Create)

⊙ Repository is online   Cancel   Push

Figure 11–38. *Xcode's remote repository dialog*

> **NOTE:** If Xcode is unable to connect to the remote repository, the drop-down will continue to read "Loading Remotes." Additionally, the green dot and "Repository is online" text will not appear. Click Cancel, and check your network connection. If the connection is good, check to make sure you successfully created the repository on GitHub. Finally, check that you correctly entered the GitHub URL when adding the remote repository as follows:
>
> Open a Terminal.app window and navigate to our project directory. Enter the command
>
> ```
> > git config --get remote.origin.url
> ```
>
> Make sure the returned URL matches the URL from GitHub. If the URL is wrong, you can fix it by unsetting it then reentering the URL:
>
> ```
> > git config --unset remote.origin.url
> > git remote add origin git@github.com:username/SBJSON.git
> ```

Once the push is successful, the dialog should disappear. You can confirm the push was successful by logging into GitHub and checking the repository page (see Figure 11–39).

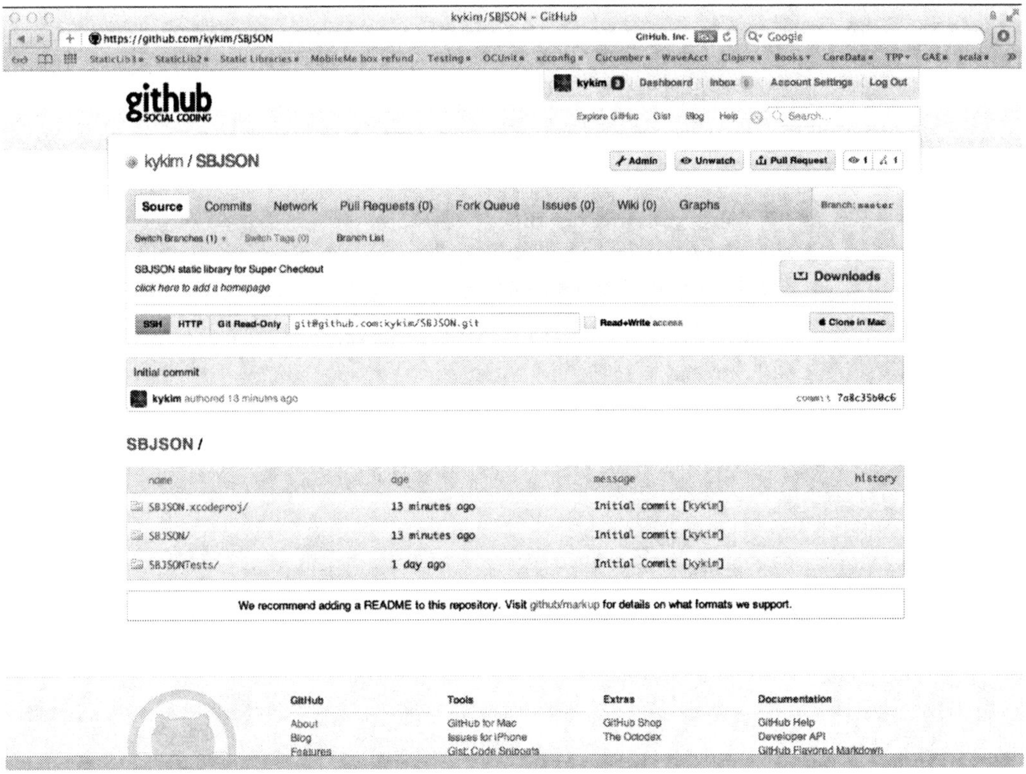

Figure 11-39. *The GitHub repository after the push*

Using GitHub Features

Before we move on, I want to briefly cover some of the features Git and GitHub offer: tagging, pull requests, and issue tracking.

Tagging

The concept of tagging is common to revision control systems. The idea is that once the source code has reached a stable state or achieved a development milestone, we want to mark the source code in some way. Essentially, you're creating a snapshot of the source code at a specific moment in time. This is achieved by tagging the release. With Git, tagging is very simple command line procedure. Once you have committed the changes to Git, simply enter this command:

```
> git tag "tag-name"
```

You can replace `tag-name` with any value you wish. It's commonplace to tag with numbers separated by dots, signifying major and minor versions (e.g., 1.0). To push the tags to GitHub, simply add the `--tags` flag to the push command:

```
> git push --tags origin remote
```

Pull Requests

GitHub offers its users the ability to fork a repository on GitHub. When you fork a project, you make a copy of the repository for yourself, which allows you to make changes to code if you want to fix a bug or add a new feature.

Once you've made some changes to your fork of a repository, you can offer those changes back to the original repository's owner and the world at large. You accomplish this on GitHub via a pull request. A pull request is simply a message to the original repository's maintainer that you have some changes you are offering to them. Creating a pull request is simple: simply click the pull request on your fork of the repository. You will be asked to comment on your pull request and then send it to the original repository's maintainer.

The converse is managing pull requests that have been sent to you by people who have forked your repository. You can review the pull requests, comment on them, reject them or merge them into your project.

GitHub has done an excellent job detailing the pull request process. You can read more at http://help.github.com/send-pull-requests/.

Issue Tracking

Issue tracking is a useful tool in gathering bug reports. It also allows people to comment on what new features they would like to see in an application or library. GitHub uses its issue tracker for every repository. It's fairly straightforward to use. Just click the Issues link at the top of any repository.

> **NOTE:** If your project doesn't show an Issues link in your repository, it's been disabled. This happens when you fork a repository. You can reenable in the administration section of your repository. Click the Admin button of your repository. You should be in the Options administration page. Under Features, click the check box next to Issues. When you return to your repositiory page, the Issues link should be present.

Choosing Your License Wisely

Now that you've got a project up on GitHub, you'll want to pick a license for your code. Since you've made the repository public, you probably want to use an open source license. Depending on whom in the open source community you ask, you'll get different answers as to what makes a project "open source." Generally speaking, open source software is software that is distributed as source code with a license that allows the user to use the software, freely modify it, and distribute it in either the original or modified form. The intent of an open source license is to allow any users of the software the ability to modify the code to suit their needs and assist the community with bug fixes and improvements.

There are a plethora of open source licenses to choose from. A fairly comprehensive list can be found at the Open Source Initiative (OSI) web site (http://opensource.org/). The site offers a simple, ten-point checklist of what constitutes an open source license, and a comprehensive list of licenses that meet these criteria.

Summary

We've covered a lot of ground in this chapter. We've pulled out the reusable components of our Super Checkout application and put them into static libraries. Then, we reintegrated the code into the project, using the subproject and workspace methods. Finally, we shared our project with the rest of the world via GitHub, improving the lives of iOS developers all over the world. This way, if Super Checkout doesn't become a bestseller in the App Store (no way!), we'll still get the love and respect of our fellow iOS hackers.

Before you close this book and move on, I have just "one more thing" to share with you. What is it? Turn the page and find out.

Chapter 12

One More Thing

What a ride! We have a stable application with a good automated testing setup and static libraries too. We've used Instruments to help find bottlenecks in our application. Throughout this process, we've covered some nice features of Xcode and explored how to navigate through the tool set. Xcode has a lot of features that we haven't covered though. That's what this chapter is about. While the chapter is titled "One More Thing," we're going to cover more than that.

In this chapter, we'll cover customizing Xcode as well as common keyboard shortcuts to improve your workflow as you start your own projects. You'll also find a handy quick reference guide to some common keyboard shortcuts for Xcode 4.2. In time, you'll adapt the things you've learned in this book and the contents of this chapter to your own workflow.

Customizing Xcode

Throughout this book, we've simply used the default configurations of Xcode. Now, it is time to start customizing it to your liking. You've seen what Xcode can do, so make it yours. The first place to look is Xcode's preferences (if you haven't poked around already). As with any Mac OS X application, the way to open Xcode's preferences is to go to **Xcode ➤ Preferences** or press ⌘ , (comma). When you do this, the dialog in Figure 12–1 will come up.

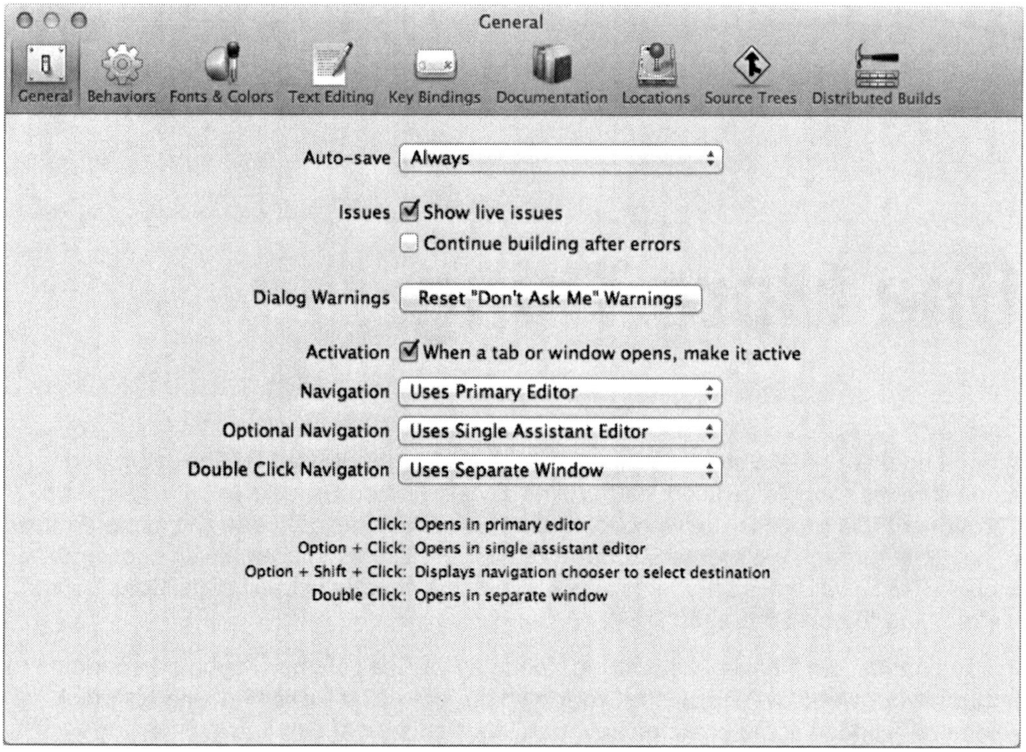

Figure 12–1. *This is Xcode's preferences window. We'll go through each tab in the window to talk about how to customize each piece.*

The General tab (see Figure 12–1) is the starting point for Xcode's preferences. Here, we can set some of the basic options for Xcode like autosave (if you are running on Mac OS X Lion) and control how files are opened from a navigator. The legend at the bottom of the screen gives you a reference for how to use the keyboard to modify clicks when you are editing code.

Behaviors

Behaviors in Xcode 4.2 are a huge lifesaver. Figure 12–2 shows the Behaviors tab open.

Figure 12–2. *The Behaviors tab helps you configure how Xcode behaves and notifies you on certain events.*

With the Behaviors tab, you can configure Xcode to change its appearance when you start a run on your application and play a sound when a build fails.

Clicking the plus button at the bottom lets you add a new behavior and bind it to a keyboard shortcut. Do you want to quickly switch to full screen and have only code open? You can configure it to do that with any keyboard shortcut you wish to map it to.

Fonts & Colors

Figure 12–3 shows the Fonts & Colors tab. This tab lets you configure the appearance of the source editor. This is great for those times when you need to project your code up on a projector because you'll be presenting on some great topics to your local user group, right?

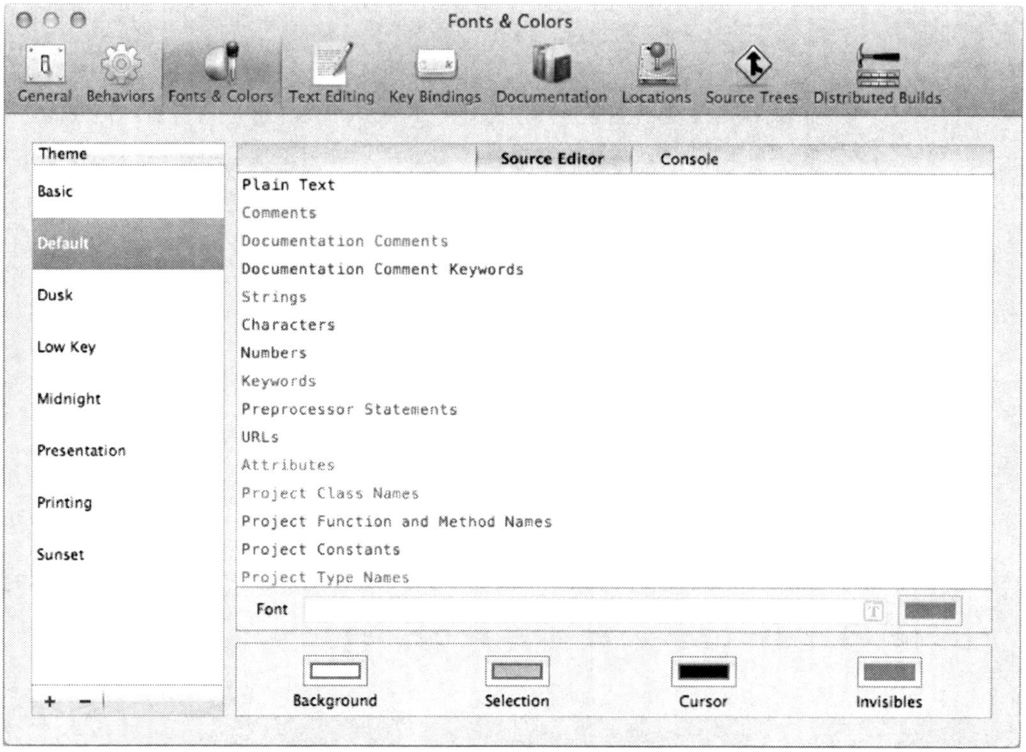

Figure 12–3. *The Fonts & Colors tab lets you configure the appearance of your editor.*

Click the Console button to configure what the console looks like.

If the provided themes aren't your cup of tea and you have a theme you wish to use that is for Xcode 4.2, you can take the dvtcolortheme file and place it in the ~/Library/Developer/Xcode/UserData/FontAndColorThemesfolder.

If you just want to tweak an existing theme, clicking the add button under the list will let you duplicate a theme. A duplicated theme will be placed in the folder mentioned previously.

Text Editing

The next tab is Text Editing (see Figure 12–4). This is where you configure how Xcode handles the features of the code editor. This is where you configure how the editor behaves and how things like code folding and code completion are handled.

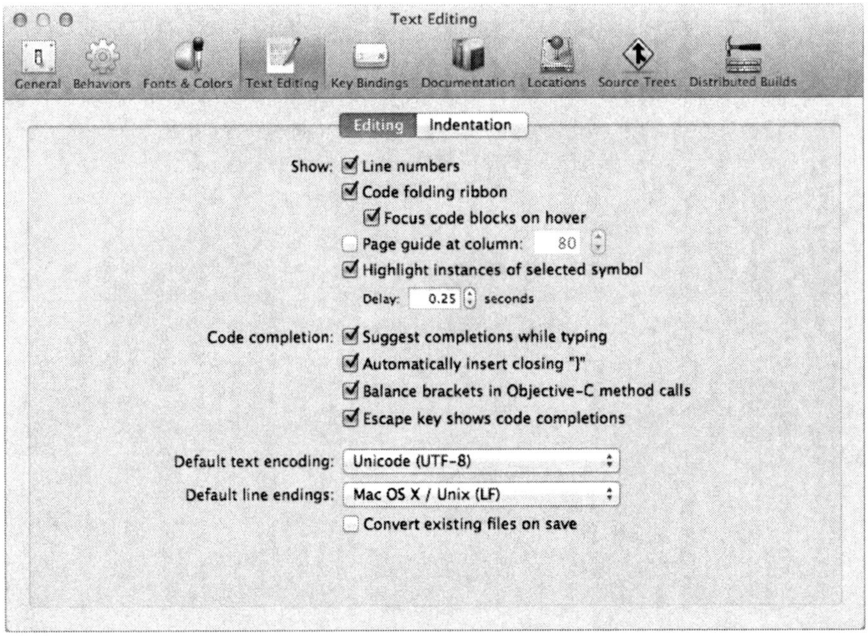

Figure 12–4. *The Text Editing tab allows you to configure how the text editor behaves and controls how the code is automatically structured.*

Figure 12–5 shows the Indentation section for this tab. The famous battle between spaces and tabs is waged in this tab in this section.

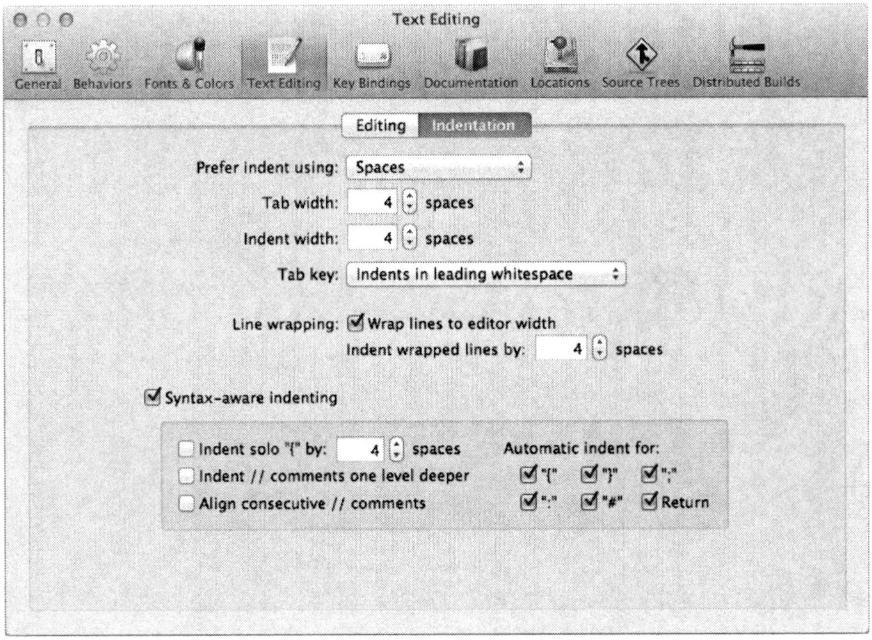

Figure 12–5. *The eternal battle between spaces and tabs! Which will you choose?*

Key Bindings

Need to see what keyboard shortcuts are set or want to modify them? The Key Bindings tab is for you! Figure 12–6 shows the default configuration. This tab behaves similarly to the Fonts & Colors tab. To create your own custom configuration, duplicate the default configuration. As soon as you make a modification, a new configuration file is placed in `~/Library/Developer/Xcode/UserData/KeyBindings`.

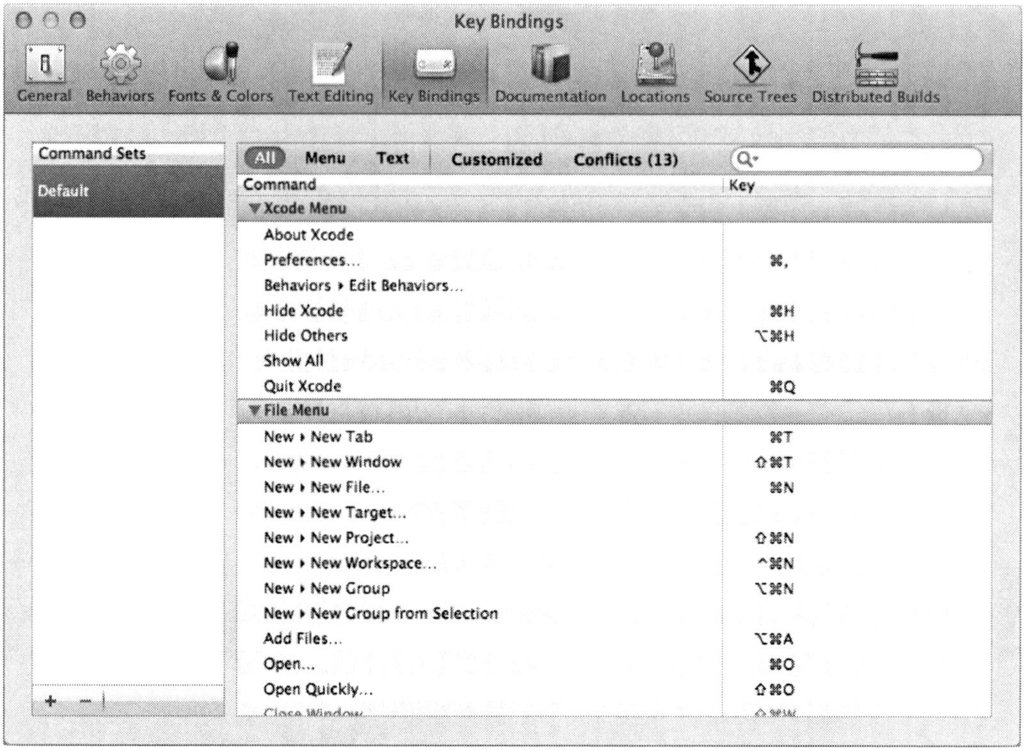

Figure 12–6. *Configuring your keyboard shortcuts is as simple as opening this tab.*

If you are trying to figure out why a certain keyboard shortcut isn't working, check out the Conflicts section. Take a look at Figure 12–7. Currently, there are 10 conflicts on the computer Xcode is installed on.

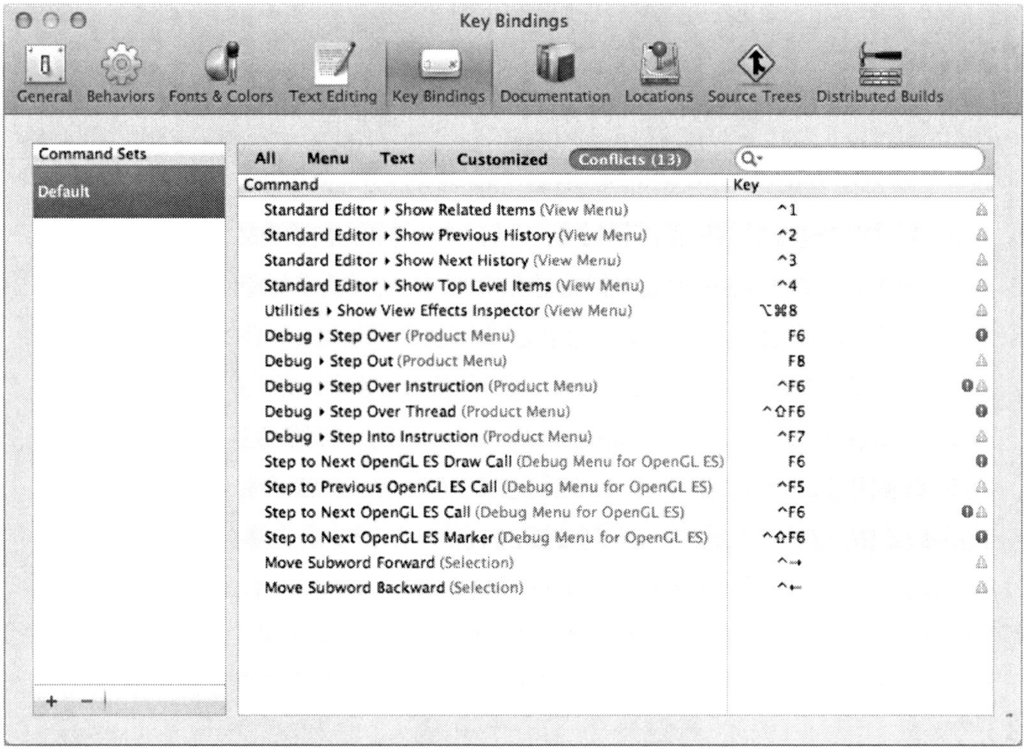

Figure 12–7. *Key binding conflicts prevent your favorite bindings from working.*

The yellow warning triangle indicates a conflict with the system. Since the system handles shortcuts before the application, Xcode is just telling you that the shortcut won't work. The red error indicates a conflict within Xcode. The binding will not trigger as long as there is an internal conflict in Xcode.

Downloads

Moving down the line, we find ourselves in the Downloads tab. In this tab we see two different areas to visit. The first is the Components tab. This tab, found in Figure 12–8, allows you to download extra components into Xcode. These components include older devices support and even older versions of iOS to run in the simulator.

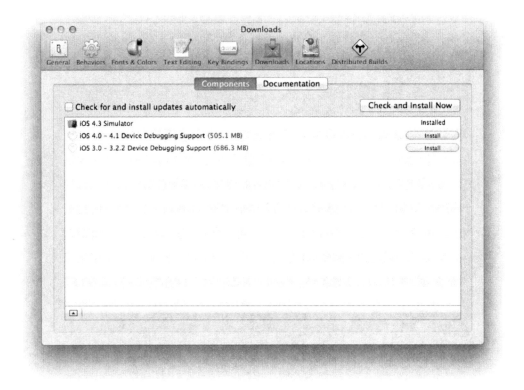

Figure 12–8 *Xcode ships with the latest and greatest of iOS. If you need "legacy" support, go to the downloads preference and download the support here.*

Documentation

The second section in this table is the Documentation section. You can see it in Figure 12–9. In this section Xcode allows you to update your documentation for iOS, Mac, and Xcode as well as third-party docsets that support the appropriate format.

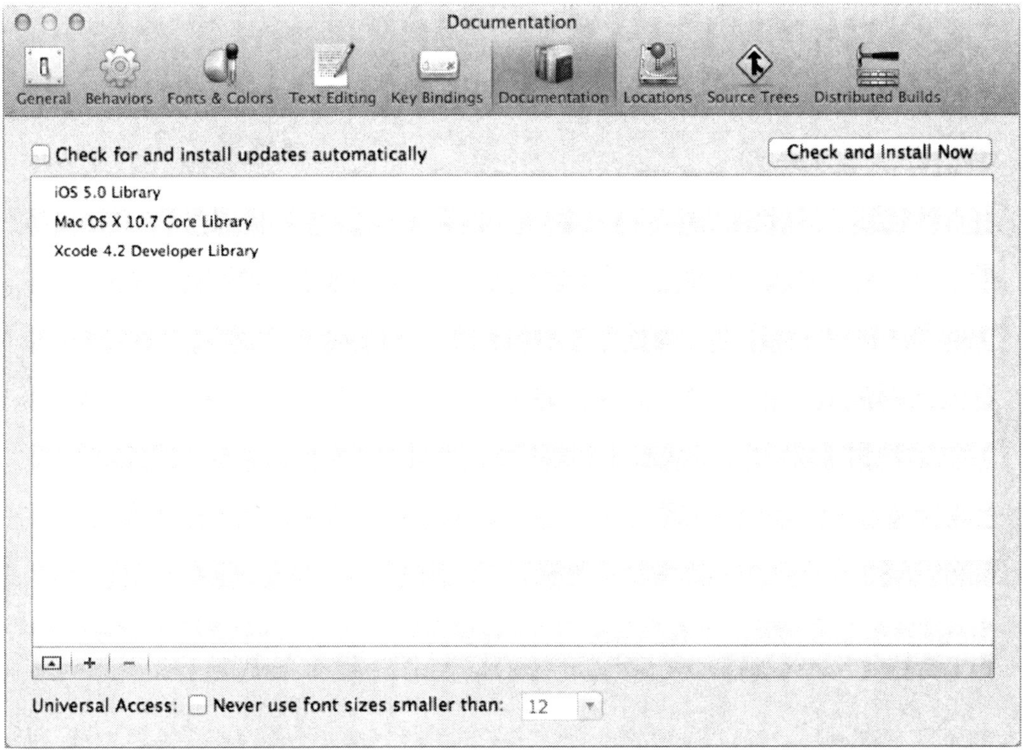

Figure 12–9. *The Documentation tab not only manages iOS/Mac/Xcode documentation, it manages third-party library documentation from any atom feed.*

The documentation sets are downloaded from an Atom feed. Select an entry in the list, and click the triangle button to the left of the Add Feed button, and you'll see the properties of the feed selected (Figure 12–9 again). Since the documentation sets are configured via an Atom feed, Xcode can be configured to automatically check for updates.

Locations

We're almost finished with Xcode preferences. The next tab is Locations (see Figure 12–10). In this tab, you can define custom locations for items such as derived data, snapshots, and archived applications as well as your source trees. Derived data are the actual build artifacts, intermediate build files, logs, and project indexes used by Xcode.

Be careful not to place these files into source control, since they are changed a lot and can be regenerated from the project files.

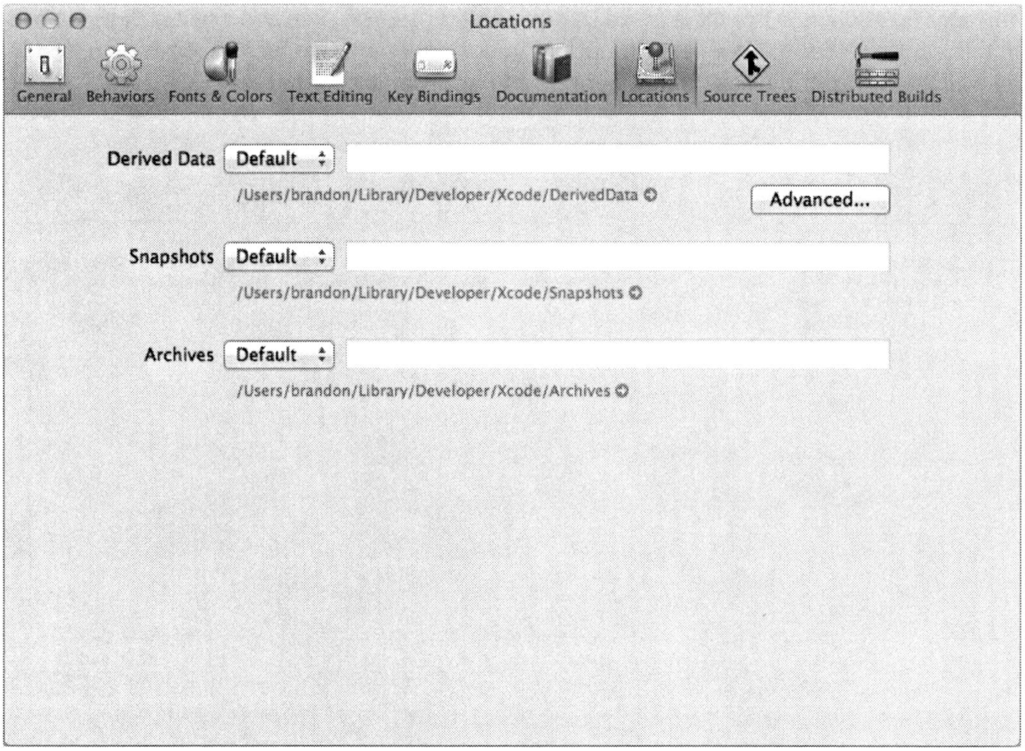

Figure 12–10. *The Locations tab lets you configure the default locations for build artifacts.*

Nine times out of ten, you'll not touch this preference. It is always good to know it exists though.

Source Trees

The next section in the Location tab is the Source Trees section (see Figure 12–11). This tab lets you define common locations for source that can be located outside of your project. The Setting Name is the name that identifies the source tree; it must be the same for every developer who is using the same Xcode project. The Display Name is the name that Xcode uses to display the source tree in the file inspector; it can be any name. The Path is the full path to the source tree on the file system; it will differ from computer to computer and user to user.

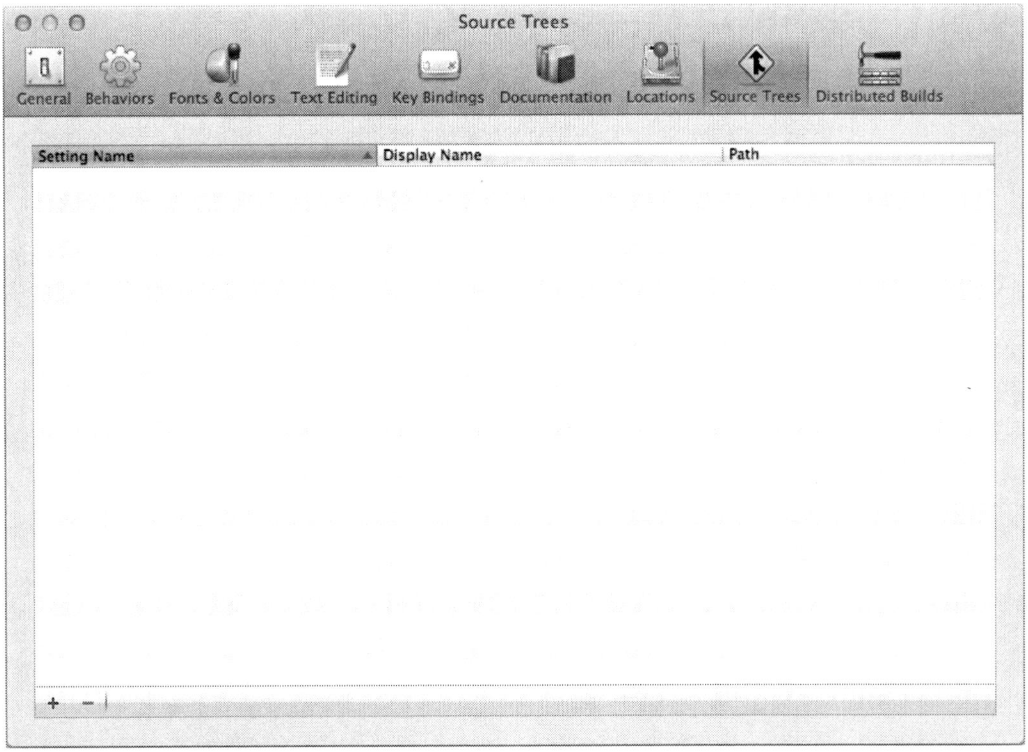

Figure 12–11. *This Source Trees tab displays an empty list. Put paths to common source files in this list to reference them in multiple projects.*

Source Trees preferences are very useful because they let each developer have his or her own development configurations, and they make sharing code between projects super easy.

Distributed Builds

The final tab in the Xcode's preferences is Distributed Builds (see Figure 12–12). Distributed builds are useful when a project takes minutes to compile. When distributed builds are configured, you can either serve out or be served compilations units. For the former, shared resources on the network accessible via Bonjour will be used. You can also define multiple sets for sharing compilation units with.

When you turn on the setting to share your machine, your machine will be available at any time for a distributed build. Xcode does not have to be running, and you do not have to be logged in to share your machine with the build cluster.

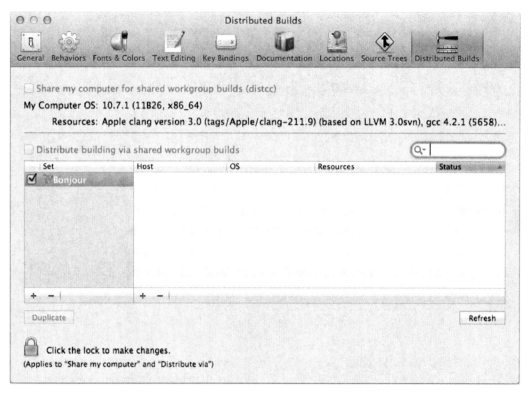

Figure 12–12. *Using distributed builds can speed up projects with a large number of source files.*

Keyboard Shortcuts and More

If you're like me, you don't use a mouse or a trackpad that often. I always keep one hand on the keyboard ready to hit some keyboard shortcut to perform a task. The common ones like cut (⌘+X), copy (⌘ +C), and paste (⌘ +V) are the easiest to call out because they are used in virtually every application.

I remember when I stopped using the context menu and started using the keyboard for those operations. I felt more productive and was able to do even more with the saved time. That was the point where I started learning more shortcuts to streamline my workflow and become more efficient.

In this section, we're going to cover Xcode 4's keyboard shortcuts and how they can improve your workflow.

Migrating from Xcode 3 to Xcode 4

When I started programming for iOS, Xcode 3 was the IDE. Xcode 3 was great, and its integration with Interface Builder was done fairly well. The fact that you had to open two separate applications was a bit annoying, but when you have an app to ship, you get over that pretty quickly. Getting used to navigating through Xcode 3 and learning those keyboard shortcuts didn't take long, and I was able to move rapidly through all of my code.

Then Apple announced static analysis and clang. I didn't think things could get any better. I had a compiler that told me when I would have memory leaks and other things that could cause strange behavior in my application. There was even a new compiler that generated faster code! Xcode 3 started to look a bit outdated.

Fast forward a bit, and we see Xcode 4 come out in a developer preview at WWDC. Interface Builder is integrated, and Xcode is just one big window. I dove in and started looking around and quickly missed Xcode 3. I went back and didn't touch the new tools for a while.

A few beta releases later, Apple had fixed some of the bugs, and I wanted to see what was new. As soon as I saw that I was able to have Interface Builder generate and wire up my actions and outlets directly in my source files, I was sold. There was no turning back, so I started really learning how to navigate such a foreign IDE.

When I first started learning how to navigate through Xcode with the keyboard, I started noticing some patterns. For example, holding down option while interacting with files would open the selected file in an assistant editor. Adding shift to the mix would bring up a nice Open In dialog (see Figure 12–13).

Figure 12–13. *The Open In dialog is a lifesaver when you want to open something in a new tab, editor, or window.*

Consistency like this has helped me find some really nice features in Xcode 4. I love knowing that holding option+shift while clicking something in the navigator area or command+option+shift when clicking a symbol in your editor (command adds the "click me" piece to the symbol) opens the ability to create a new tab or a new window. I can even use the same technique with the Open Quickly (command+shift+o) command and have a file open in a new tab in no time.

Give Me the Shortcuts Already!

I've teased you enough with the shortcuts, so let's go through them by function. Table 12–1 is all about navigating through Xcode. For example, opening and closing some of the areas interacting with Xcode's different editor modes can all be done from the keyboard. Table 12–2 is all about file/symbol manipulation and what you can do while editing a file and jumping around to make editing smooth and painless. Table 12–3 is about schemes and performing scheme actions from the keyboard.

Table 12–1. *Navigating through Xcode*

Command	Shortcut
Show/Hide Navigator Area	⌘0
Show Project Navigator	⌘1
Show Symbol Navigator	⌘2
Show Search Navigator	⌘3
Show Issue Navigator	⌘4
Show Debug Navigator	⌘5
Show Breakpoint Navigator	⌘6
Show Log Navigator	⌘7
Show/Hide Utility Area	⌥⌘0
Show/Hide Debugger	⇧⌘Y
Activate Console	⇧⌘C
Activate Standard Editor	⌘↩
Activate Assistant Editor	⌥⌘↩
Activate Version Editor	⇧⌥⌘↩
Open Quickly	⌥⌘O

Table 12–2. *Manipulating symbols and navigating through files.*

Command	Shortcut
Show Completions	^Space
Edit All in Scope	^⌘E
Fix All in Scope	^⌘F
Show All Issues	^⌘M
Re-Indent	^I
Shift left (by indention level)	⌘[
Shift right (by indention level)	⌘]
Move line up	⌥⌘[
Move line down	⌥⌘]

Table 12–3. *Scheme editing and performing actions.*

Command	Shortcut
Run	⌘R
Run…(opens scheme editor)	⌥⌘R
Test	⌘U
Test…(opens scheme editor)	⌥⌘U
Profile	⌘I
Profile…(opens scheme editor)	⌥⌘I
Analyze	⇧⌘B
Analyze…(opens scheme editor)	⇧⌥⌘B
Build for Running	⇧⌘R
Build for Testing	⇧⌘U
Build for Profiling	⇧⌘I
Run without Building	^⌘R

Command	Shortcut
Test without Building	^⌘U
Profile without Building	^⌘I
Build	⌘B
Clean	⇧⌘K
Clean Build Folder	⇧⌥⌘K
Add Breakpoint at Current Line	⌘\
Activate/Deactivate Breakpoints	⌘Y
Clear Console	⌘K
Edit Scheme	⌘<

This is only a portion of all of the shortcuts available in Xcode 4. The rest can be found in Xcode's preferences and in the menu bar. There is also an exhaustive list put together by Colin Wheeler at https://github.com/Machx/Xcode-Keyboard-Shortcuts.

Viewing Documentation

Now that you are a master at using Xcode directly from the keyboard, we can move on to one final item: viewing documentation. Reading documentation is at least half of our job as developers. Earlier in this chapter, you saw where we can configure custom documentation sets from atom feeds. That is only half of the story.

Once the feed is downloaded (in the case of Apple's provided documentation) or added, you will need to search the documentation and have a quick reference guide to the documentation. The first place we will look is in the main Xcode window.

Open the Super Checkout project (if you don't have it open already), and navigate to Super_CheckoutAppDelegate.h. Next, option-click the UIApplicationDelegate protocol symbol (notice the cursor will change styles, and the symbol will be underlined on hover). The resulting popover (shown in Figure 12–14) shows a brief abstract for the selected symbol.

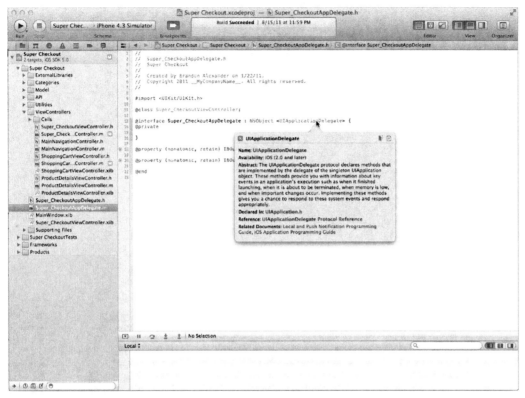

Figure 12–14. *The documentation popover gives you a brief abstract for the selected symbol.*

From here, you can do many different things. Clicking the book at the upper right of the popover will bring up the Organizer with the appropriate documentation for the symbol. Clicking the file with the "h" in the middle of it will bring up the public header provided by the framework author (if one is provided). The rest of the links in the popover will open the Organizer or the header file. You can also see where other, related documents are available for viewing, which can be handy when you need to see sample code or a programming guide for a particular class.

The second way to view documentation is to open the Utility area. Most things have a quick help lookup, and you don't need to option-click the item. Figure 12–15 shows the same instance as Figure 12–14 with the Utility pane open with the Quick Help Inspector selected.

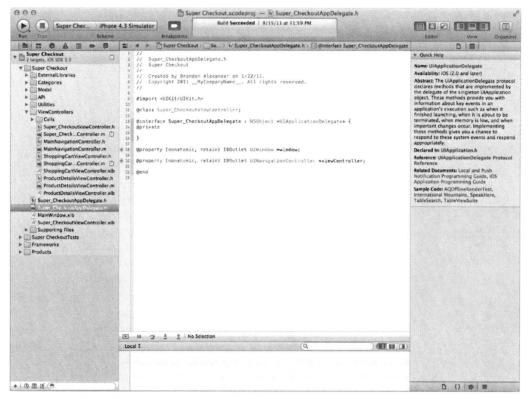

Figure 12–15. *The Quick Help Inspector shows the same information as the help popover, but it will show help for more than just code.*

Something nice about the Quick Help Inspector is its ability to show quick help for more than just code. In the Build Settings for a target, you can select any setting, and the Quick Help Inspector will show you which compiler flag that the setting will set and what that flag does.

The final way to view documentation is through the Organizer. Open the Organizer by clicking the Organizer button at the top-right corner of the Xcode 4 window. This will bring up the Organizer window. Click the Documentation tab, and type **NSObject** (see Figure 12–16).

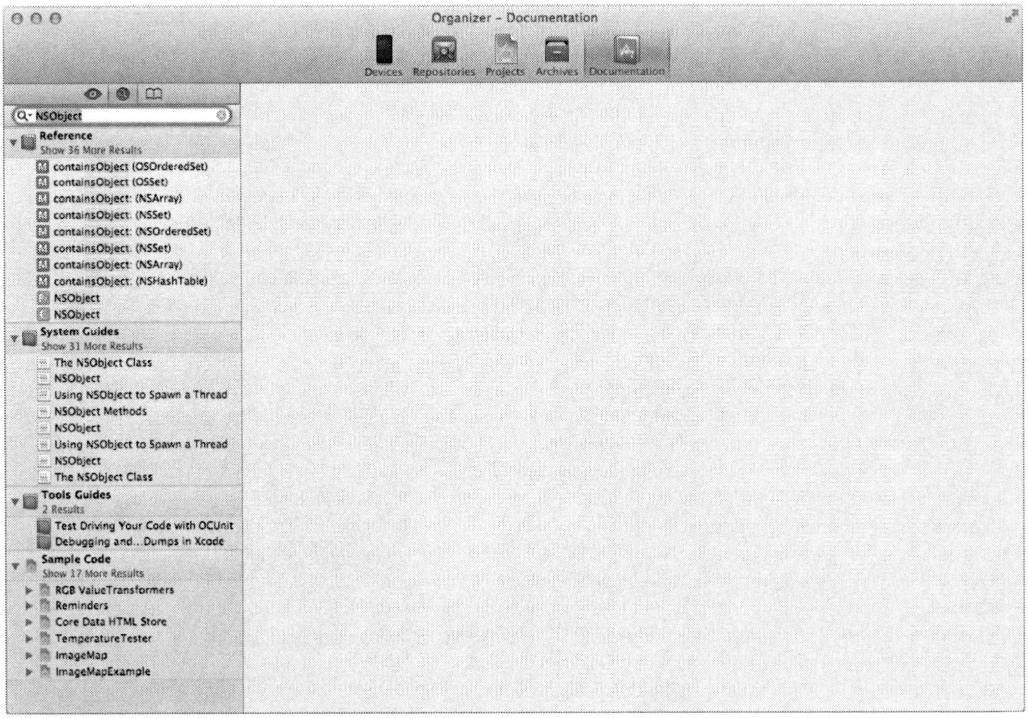

Figure 12–16. *The Organizer's documentation window is extremely useful when you need to search the body of documentation for your project.*

By default, the Organizer will limit your results to the top results, and you can click the "Show . . . More Results" text under each section to see all of the results. It is also likely that you'll see duplicated entries. To fix this, click the magnifying glass, and select Show Find Options to expand some options and narrow your search. It isn't very often that you'll be developing a Mac app and an iOS app at the same time.

That's about all there is for reading documentation. Being able to read the documentation and knowing exactly where to go to get the level of detail you need is important to stay as efficient as possible when developing your applications.

Summary

That's it. We're done here! I hope you have learned as much as I did when writing this book. There are many things that I didn't get a chance to cover in this book, and my hope is that you now have enough background with the developer tools to venture out on your own and learn some of these things on your own. I've given you the knowledge of how to use the tools; it is up to you to use them for good. Now, go write some amazing apps!

Index

CPSIA information can be obtained at www.ICGtesting.com
Printed in the USA
LVOW110205020112

261956LV00003B/42/P